ON ARCHITECTURE

McGill-Queen's/Beaverbrook Canadian
Foundation Studies in Art History

Martha Langford and Sandra Paikowsky, series editors

Recognizing the need for a better understanding of Canada's
artistic culture both at home and abroad, the Beaverbrook
Canadian Foundation, through its generous support, makes
possible the publication of innovative books that advance
our understanding of Canadian art and Canada's visual and
material culture. This series supports and stimulates such
scholarship through the publication of original and rigorous
peer-reviewed books that make significant contributions
to the subject. We welcome submissions from Canadian
and international scholars for book-length projects on
historical and contemporary Canadian art and visual and
material culture, including Native and Inuit art, architecture,
photography, craft, design, and museum studies. Studies
by Canadian scholars on non-Canadian themes will also
be considered.

On Architecture

MELVIN CHARNEY: A CRITICAL ANTHOLOGY

Edited by Louis Martin

McGill-Queen's University Press
Montreal & Kingston | London | Ithaca

© McGill-Queen's University Press 2013
ISBN 978-0-7735-4182-5 (paper)
ISBN 978-0-7735-8973-5 (ePDF)

Legal deposit third quarter 2013
Bibliothèque nationale du Québec

Printed in Canada on acid-free paper

This book has been published with the help of a grant from the Canadian Federation for the Humanities and Social Sciences, through the Awards to Scholarly Publications Program, using funds provided by the Social Sciences and Humanities Research Council of Canada. Funding has also been provided by the Visual Arts Section of the Canada Council for the Arts (Assistance for the Promotion of Architecture Program).

McGill-Queen's University Press acknowledges the support of the Canada Council for the Arts for our publishing program. We also acknowledge the financial support of the Government of Canada through the Canada Book Fund for our publishing activities.

Library and Archives Canada Cataloguing in Publication

On architecture : Melvin Charney : a critical anthology / edited by Louis Martin.

(McGill-Queen's/Beaverbrook Canadian Foundation studies in art history ; 11)
Includes bibliographical references and index.
Issued in print and electronic formats.
ISBN 978-0-7735-4182-5 (pbk.).
ISBN 978-0-7735-8973-5 (ePDF)

1. Charney, Melvin – Criticism and interpretation.
2. Architecture, Modern – 20th century.
3. Architecture, Modern – 20th century – Pictorial works.   4. Architecture – Philosophy.   I. Martin, Louis, 1960–, editor of compilation, writer of added commentary   II. Charney, Melvin. Essays. Selections.
III. Title: Melvin Charney : a critical anthology.
IV. Series: McGill-Queen's/Beaverbrook Canadian Foundation studies in art history ; 11

NA749.C53O53 2013   720.92   C2013-903218-5
C2013-903219-3

Set in 10/13.5 Warnock Pro and 10.2/13.5 Chaparral Pro with Gotham, Museo Sans, and Museo Sans Condensed
Book design + typesetting by Garet Markvoort, zijn digital

CONTENTS

ACKNOWLEDGMENTS

This anthology could not have been possible without the constant collaboration of Melvin Charney, who gracefully gave me access to his personal archive at all times over several years. I also benefited from countless discussions with him about the contents of this compilation.

I am especially grateful to Réjean Legault, who was involved in the initiation of the project and guided its realization with judicious insights. I thank him, as well as George Baird and Georges Adamczyk, for writing original essays for this book.

Basic research, transcription, and image processing were accomplished by graduate students Jonathan Lachance, Yanek Lauzière-Filion, and Christian Semaan with the financial support of the Programme d'aide financière à la recherche et à la création (PAFARC) of the Université du Québec à Montréal (UQAM).

Additional support for Nancy Dunton's translations from French to English as well as for Alessandra Mariani's search for copyrights was provided by the Laboratoire d'étude de l'architecture potentielle (LEAP) of the University of Montreal whose research activities are made possible by a grant from Fonds québécois de recherche sur la société et la culture (FQRSC). Special thanks to Jean-Pierre Chupin, director of LEAP, for believing in this project.

Supplementary research was conducted at the Canadian Centre for Architecture (CCA), where I was granted the privilege of visiting scholars during the 2010–11 academic year. I am particularly grateful to Alexis Sornin, director of the CCA Study Centre, for his generosity. For their valuable collaboration, I thank Paul Chénier, Marie-France Daigneault-Bouchard, Robert Desaulniers, Louise Désy, Renata Guttman, David Rose, and Howard Schubert. I am also thankful to Mirko Zardini and Phyllis Lambert for graciously allowing the reproduction of numerous artifacts from the CCA collection.

At McGill-Queen's University Press, Jonathan Crago was an inspiration for both his patience and guidance. His contribution was essential for obtaining support from the Canada Council for the Arts.

I thank the Art History Department and the Faculty of Arts at UQAM for providing additional funds to cover the cost of the copyrights for the reproduction of the artworks included in the book. I am greatly indebted to Alessandra Mariani, who patiently assembled the final manuscript and accomplished the colossal task of obtaining reproduction rights for the images.

I am also grateful to Ann Charney and Wendy Owens for their help in the completion of this project.

Louis Martin
March 2013

ON ARCHITECTURE

Introduction

LOUIS MARTIN

Montreal artist and architect Melvin Charney is renowned in Canada and abroad for his accomplishments in contemporary art. Montrealers remember that his name first appeared in the international mass media during the 1976 Montreal Olympic Games when, following an order from Mayor Jean Drapeau, his installation *Les maisons de la rue Sherbrooke* was destroyed with the rest of Corridart, the street exhibition he organized as part of the Games' arts and cultural component.

Thereafter, Charney's career took a remarkable course. Admired and extensively studied, his oeuvre has become an integral feature of museums and collections throughout the world and has been the subject of several essays and monographs. He has represented Canada in a number of international art events and has designed public monuments for several cities.

While one of the most significant artists of his generation, Melvin Charney has also been an influential educator. As professor of architecture at the School of Architecture of the Université de Montréal from 1964 to 1989, he inspired several generations of young architects to develop more critical attitudes towards contemporary architectural practice. His teaching and his writings on Montreal were so influential that he was considered, in the early 1990s, the instigator of a genuine "Montreal School."

Yet few people, even those who are familiar with Charney's art and architecture, realize the breadth and originality of his written production. In effect, Charney is one of the rare architects to belong to the select club of architectural critics rooted in the 1960s who have written regularly and lucidly over a long period about the pressing problems of contemporary architecture. In many ways, his essays act like a thermometer, recording the changing temperature of an architectural culture in constant flux during a most turbulent period in architectural history. When read as a whole, his critical writings reveal the movements of his inquisitive mind on a remarkable intellectual itinerary which both recorded and participated in the radical transformations of architectural thinking since the 1960s.

This anthology's extensive collection of Charney's essays is meant to reveal the ideas that nourished his architecture, art, and criticism. It includes most of the essays he published in various books and journals between 1962 and 1989.[1] The essays, previously published only in edited versions, appear here in their original form. In addition, key texts only available in French appear here in English translation for the first time.

A chronological grouping of the various essays was considered the most favourable. Chronology has the distinct advantages of conveying how Charney worked concurrently on several different problems and tracking the transformation of his thoughts over time. The book is consequently divided into four parts highlighting his preoccupations across distinct periods of his professional life. A fifth section presents two interviews with Melvin Charney. Through their directness and personal perspective, they act as both postscript and interpretive key to the collection.

Because the table of contents of this book constitutes a bibliography of Charney's essential texts on architecture, it seemed unnecessary to include a complete bibliography of the writings about his work: not only would it have been incomplete, but such an extensive bibliography is already available in print and online. A short list of further readings identifies the monographs on Charney's art which constitute the natural extension to this book.

The editorial intention was to reproduce, whenever possible, the images published in the original version of the selected essays. Charney picked a large part of his illustrations in contemporaneous publications such as monthly journals, trade magazines, and daily newspapers. He used to make photographs of these ephemeral documents which he used for his lectures and essays. Most of this visual material survives in his personal archive in the form of photographic prints, slides, or black and white negatives. This reproduction technique is responsible for the

high contrast and blurred resolution of many of the images which illustrated his essays until the 1980s. My students and I looked in various collections for original prints of those images to ensure the best possible resolution quality for this new publication, but our search was not always fruitful. In effect, we have not been able to identify the origins of the visual material of some essays. In the case of daily newspapers, we found microfilms, which allowed only poor reproductions. In many instances, Charney's material provided the best documentation. Consequently, we have used extensively Charney's reproductions not only because they were the only documents we had at hand, but also because, for him, their coarse aesthetic poignantly represents the fleeting essence of mass-media images.

Two essays, one about the *Memo Series* and the other about the *Dictionnaire d'architecture*, receive a special treatment. These chapters demanded exceptions because Charney created several versions of these works over the years. As a result, "On the Liberation of Architecture: *Memo Series* on an Airforce Memorial" is illustrated with the images of the original essay published in *Artforum* in 1971 because the texts of the last version of the series, kept at the National Gallery of Canada, are different from the first iteration reproduced here. In contrast, "Learning from the Wire Services," the essay which discussed the ideas that motivated the subsequent creation of the *Dictionnaire*, is illustrated with the final version of this work, which is kept at the Canadian Centre for Architecture. The images of the original essay constitute the core of the successive versions of the *Dictionnaire*; they are reproduced here, isolated from the 232 plates of this cumulative work assembled over three decades.

This anthology focuses on Charney's writings rather than on the entirety of his artistic and architectural projects. Nevertheless, each section of the anthology incorporates visual documentation, in the form of a series of plates, about a "project" that is emblematic of the ideas developed in that section.

Critical Framing

The introductory texts to this anthology intend to provide fresh insights which will hopefully stimulate further investigation.

The first two essays are written by established architectural critics who participated in the debates of the period covered by the anthology, a period marked by an acute critique of functionalism and utopia and a search for new theories capable of both revealing and undermining the traditional ideological structure of the discipline. At the outset, these introductory texts set up a general critical framework.

The first essay is provided by George Baird, architect and educator from Toronto, who has written major critiques of the architecture of the period under study.[2] Baird identifies the shift that occurred in Charney's work at the turn of the 1970s and shows how Charney's critical probing of architectural figuration in the mid-1970s resulted from a mutation of previous belief in the liberatory potential of technology. On his side, Montreal architectural critic Georges Adamczyk develops a sophisticated reading of Charney's architectural installations of the 1970s and 1980s which reveals how these constructions operated, analogous to the act of dreaming, by displacing and condensing figures found on the various sites on which they were erected.

The other texts were written by two former students of Charney: Réjean Legault and myself. Legault is the first scholar to have published a substantial review of the essays Charney wrote during the 1960s.[3] His groundbreaking interpretation suggested that a shift, which was marked by a distancing from the ideals of the modern movement in architecture and the inauguration of an original postmodern critique, occurred in Charney's thinking at the beginning of the

1970s. For this anthology, Legault has written a new essay on the construction and reception of Charney's concept of Montrealness.

My own texts introduce the four main parts of the book, probe in depth the primary material of the anthology, and trace the evolution of Charney's thought. Taken together, my texts constitute the four chapters of a single essay which examines the emergence of an original conception of the "image" in Charney's critical assessment of the architecture of his time.

While the "image" as a critical and dialectical notion was already present in his early texts, Charney's obsessive tracking of architectural images in the anonymous archive of mass media gradually became not only a central characteristic of his work but the site for the conceptualization of a term that has played an important role in recent architectural theory. In effect, the "image" in architecture remained apparently a peripheral concern during the period under study, while more popular catchwords like brutalism, megastructure, prefabrication, flexibility, sign, language, meaning, memory, history, or tectonics, for instance, were successively promoted as means of surpassing functionalism. Yet a closer look at the debates of the period shows that the notion of "architecture as image" triggered developments which, beyond the search for a look, questioned the very essence of architectural representation. I suggest that Charney's originality was to surpass both the semiotic paradigm symbolized by the manifestos of Robert Venturi and Denise Scott Brown, which considered architecture a system of communication, and Aldo Rossi's analogous architecture. In contrast, Charney probed a collective unconscious in architectural images. In manipulating anonymous images, Charney introduced an original psychoanalytical stance which aimed at revealing the mythical content of daily life and suggested a possible grounding for contemporary architectural criticism.

NOTES

1 Among the few texts which are not part of this selection are two substantial reports of great importance for the practice of architecture in Quebec and Canada which could not be included in a book of this size. The first is *The Adequacy and Production of Low-Income Housing,* A Report prepared by Melvin Charney, M.R.A.I.C. in collaboration with Serge Carreau and Colin Davidson for the Task Force on Low-Income Housing. Central Mortgage and Housing Corporation, Ottawa, October 1971. The other is *Le Faubourg St-Laurent: d'un savoir urbain à une vision éclairée du développement du Faubourg: étude préparée pour le Service de l'habitation et du développement urbain de la Ville de Montréal: rapport final.* Un rapport préparé par Melvin Charney, Catherine Blain et le Service d'habitation du développement urbain de Montréal, Montreal, 1991.

2 Among them, C. Jencks and G. Baird, *Meaning in Architecture* (New York: George Braziller, 1970), and George Baird, *The Space of Appearance* (Cambridge, MA: MIT Press, 1995).

3 Réjean Legault, "'Pour une définition de l'architecture ...': Melvin Charney et la modernité architecturale dans les années 1960," in *Architecture et modernité, Trames* no. 15 (Montreal: Éditions Trames, Université de Montréal, 2004): 25–52.

PART ONE

Critical Context

1

From Liberatory Technology to Critical Figuration

GEORGE BAIRD

Melvin Charney has been publishing texts about art, architecture, and urbanism for nearly half a century now. The body of these texts, over that remarkably long time period, includes a number of the most insightful commentaries that have ever been framed by an architect of his generation.

It has been most informative for me recently to read all the texts that appear here in the order in which they were written. Some of them were already familiar to me, but some others – especially the very earliest ones – were not.

It is clear to me that from the very beginning of his writing career Charney was preoccupied with the idea of a popular, non-elitist architecture. One indication of this is his interest in the vernacular. Two of the earliest texts included in the section titled "Beginnings" focus on vernacular forms of ancient dwellings in Turkey and in southern Italy. Both of these articles eschew discussion of major architectural monuments – either historical ones or modern ones – one of the two even arguing for the cultural primacy of vernacular forms over monumental ones. Another one has him question the lack of

public interest at that time in the preservation of vernacular buildings as opposed to monuments – indeed of the vernacular urban fabric as a whole – in that area of downtown Montreal that was situated between the old port to the south and the more modern downtown precinct to the north.

Yet Charney also showed keen interest in the potential of technology in the creation of an "other" architecture. In his assessment of a recent design by the American architect John Johansen for a new library building for Clark University in Massachusetts, Charney expressed admiration for the design's "environmental" quality, that is to say the way in which the design of the building's systems were articulated and expressed. In fact, it is possible to see in Charney's interest in the Johansen project signs of the wariness of conventional architectural monumentality that would grow stronger in the evolution of his critical position in subsequent years. As he said of Johansen's design: "The parts of this building are uncoupled, separated, moved out into the campus and re-engaged so that the building becomes a free assembly and a 'place' where something happens as well as an object."[1] Similarly, Charney's more or less contemporary commentary on Moretti and Nervi's new Place Victoria in Montreal focused much more strongly on the building's "systemic" design features than on its status as an architectural object.

The set of texts grouped in the second section, "Beyond Architecture," consider the capacity of technology to elaborate systems and processes more than to produce "objects" – especially "monumental" ones – even perhaps, to go further still, to facilitate the creation of an architecture that would be liberatory rather than elitist or repressive. Here, Charney speculates on the possibility of an architecture that would be popular in the sense that it could be modified by people themselves. In this connection, he developed a keen interest in the work of such European avant-gardists as Yona Friedman, Cedric Price, and the British group Archigram.

We might say that if one edge of Charney's personal territory of theoretical interest in the second half of the 1960s lay in large-scale urban systems, such as those that were then bringing downtown Montreal's new underground pedestrian network into being, another edge of that same territory lay in his almost anarchist avant-garde interest in liberatory urban possibility. Powerful evidence of Charney's oscillation between these two distinct but related approaches to technology can be seen in his remarkable competition entry for the Canadian Pavilion at Expo 70 in Osaka, Japan.[2] Here, he can be seen to be significantly invested in the kind of utopian hope for technology that typified the approaches of Friedman and Archigram at the same time that he was proposing a design for a phenomenon as institutionalized as an international world's fair!

To be sure, we have to regard Charney's participation in the competition for the pavilion for the world's fair, like his earlier admiration for the recently created urban megastructures in downtown Montreal (Place Ville-Marie, Place Victoria, and Place Bonaventure), as an individual manifestation of the excitement many Montrealers felt about the dramatic urban transformation that was taking place in their city – at least up until 1967 and its epochal climax: Expo 67.

Then, too, it is clear that during the same period Charney was pursuing the liberatory potential of technology he was simultaneously growing increasingly wary of the impact of corporate technologies on the form of the city – especially of his own city of Montreal. Thus his early concern for the fate of vernacular neighbourhoods that were not "historically important enough" to merit heritage preservation was an indicator of sentiments that later made him increasingly critical of urban renewal, of expressway construction, and of corporate redevelopment in his home city.

As the 1960s came to a close, and the decade of the 1970s commenced, one can see that Charney's view of architecture – especially mainstream architecture – and of the urban politics of Montreal started to shift profoundly. To be sure, his commitment to the liberatory potential of architecture and his interest in popular urban and architectural phenomena persisted. However, his view of technology in architecture, and of the international architectural avant-garde's fascination with it, began to darken considerably.

A methodologically fascinating proposition from this transitional phase in Charney's career – both as a designer and as a cultural commentator – is the essay with images that he prepared for *Artforum* magazine in response to an architectural design competition announced in 1969 for the creation of a new air force memorial for Canada. His by then well-established aversion to monuments, and his corresponding interest in systems and processes, led him to write a series of "memos" that focused on historical phenomena having to do with flight, with networks of air routes, and with various significant historical sites in the history of air travel and military activity in

Canada. For him, this series of memos pointed to an entirely new, non-monumental form of "memorial." The text was titled – significantly – "On the Liberation of Architecture."[3] It begins with a quotation from Walter Benjamin's essay "The Author as Producer," which underscores the importance of "the tiniest fragment of everyday life."[4] True to his long-standing aversion to monuments, Charney continues throughout the text to eschew the term "monument," even though the subtitle of his article refers to the "Air Force Memorial." But, of course, Charney's assumption that the idea of "memorial" could accrue to these varied sets of buildings, and of pieces of equipment relating to air flight, was elusive and uncertain. In my view, Charney's mere identification of these heterogeneous phenomena as memorials in no way imbued them with sufficient social symbolic status to actually become such. In fact, I believe we have to declare Charney's air force proposition a conceptual failure on account of his inability at this stage in the development of his distinctive design methodology to enable his putative "memorials" to attain adequate social legibility in the world at large. Still, even as a failure, the Air Force Memorial proposition was methodologically and conceptually intriguing. The 1971 proposal remains important for our understanding of the evolution of his thinking. As I will attempt to show, this development turned out to be propitious for an important project he would later undertake.

During this same transitional period, like many other thoughtful observers of politics and culture in the late 1960s and early 1970s, Charney was becoming increasingly engaged by community activism – especially in regard to contemporary proposals for urban renewal (for example, the contemporary controversy surrounding redevelopment of parts of the Milton-Park neighbourhood east of the campus of McGill University). As well, like other anglophone – and even Jewish – observers of politics in his home province, he was becoming increasingly engaged by newly emergent nationalist political aspirations there (for example, the 1968 decision of René Lévesque to leave the Quebec Liberal Party and form the Parti Québécois). Charney's sensitivity to this complex matrix of issues led to another of his bold interventions in the history and theory of architecture in Canada. This is his very polemical – yet also quite ambitious – text from 1972: "Toward a Definition of Architecture in Quebec."[5]

I call the text polemical, since it would seem to have been written quite hastily by Charney, in response to a pamphlet that had been issued by the Ministère des affaires culturelles of that time focusing on "Contemporary Architecture in French Canada."[6] At the same time that the pamphlet provoked him, it also provided Charney with an opportunity to link together a series of issues he had been thinking about for some time. He found the overview that Claude Beaulieu had provided in the pamphlet both superficial and condescending. Thus his text was in the first instance a rebuttal to Beaulieu. But Charney's indignation did not stop there; he also took it upon himself to challenge the more established interpretation of Quebec architecture that had been promulgated a few years earlier by the historian Alan Gowans in his *Building Canada: An Architectural History of Canadian Life.*[7] If he found Beaulieu's text unsatisfactory, he found Gowans's patronizing and offensive.

Having attacked these two accounts of Quebec architecture, Charney then took on the bold challenge that had been implicit in his critique and proposed a sketch of an alternative history. As he put it, it would be a history which would seek to describe "an authentic architecture born of real things and rooted in people's lives."[8]

The text concluded with a speculative account of what Charney saw as the confusions and the great potential of the emergent Quebec architecture of his own time. Relying in considerable

Trois-Rivières Centre-Ville

Projet urbain

par Hélène Gosselin Geoffrion

Architecture Concept

1.1 A page of *Architecture Concept* used by Charney in the creation of *The Treasure of Trois-Rivières*.

measure on then-topical cultural arguments propounded by Frantz Fanon, he concluded his provocative and indignant polemic with two claims: first that "in Quebec, as elsewhere, all relevant architecture questions the state of architecture itself" and second that "in Quebec, this means that [architecture] depends also on the assertion of a renewed and original Quebec identity."[9] With this bold intervention, Charney placed himself in the vanguard of national-ist cultural aspirations in Quebec, at the very

moment when those aspirations were growing to the point of crisis throughout many sectors of Quebec society.

Given this bold move, it is not surprising that Charney began to ponder more closely many varied vernacular forms of architecture that interested him, both in Montreal and elsewhere in Quebec. This activity led him to what I see as a key methodological breakthrough in his own thinking and creative production. This was his discovery of a newspaper image of a very modest – but seminal – vernacular building he eventually named the "Treasure of Trois-Rivières." In this key building, he was able to identify an artifact that was indisputably ver-nacular and popular but which could also stand as a "monument." Thus, his identification of this image enabled him to transcend the difficulty he had had in 1971 when he was attempting to treat the ephemeral built phenomena of the air force and of air flight in varied locations as capable of memorialization through design. His design strategy at that point had not been sufficient to render those phenomena "memorials," but his discovery of the photograph of the "Treasure of Trois-Rivières" would turn out to be very differ-ent and much more successful. The illustrated building's modest pediment already gave it a tec-tonic dignity. This was reinforced in Charney's reconstructions of its facade in installations in museums, where its putative "monumentality" grew ever more substantial. (See Figs. 30.2, 30.3, 30.4.) The image of the "Treasure" thus became a leitmotif of Charney's thinking and design over the next few years. I don't think it is too much to claim that it came to stand as the hallmark of his growing interest in the history and future potential of the architecture of his native Quebec as well as a new design method that he would be able to use in his own creative work.

An opportunity to do so arose in 1976 when he was awarded the commission to prepare an urban artwork in conjunction with the Olympic Games in Montreal.[10] Thus was conceived the now famous – not to say notorious – project "Corridart," a major public art installation that stretched along Sherbrooke Street in Montreal, from the city's commercial heart in the west to the site of the Olympic Stadium in the east. With Corridart, Charney succeeded for the first time in bringing all the preoccupations that had engaged him in the preceding years into a triumphantly synthetic cultural and political creation. It was the project that made him famous, even if it also eventually caused him acute personal psychological distress. The reason for both the fame and the distress was that just after the installation of the project was completed, and just before the Olympics were to open, the imperious mayor of Montreal, Jean Drapeau, took offence at it and ordered the entire installation dismantled and scrapped during the night. It was an act of political vandalism that gravely compromised Drapeau's historical reputation and continues to echo down the years of modern Canadian cultural history.

What, one might ask, made Charney's Corridart such a successful synthesis of his manifold range of historical, political, and design interests? One might further ask: what made it so controversial as to trigger its precipitous demolition? Let us first deal with the conditions of its conceptual and formal success. I cannot improve on Charney's own description of it in his explanatory text of 1977:

> At varying intervals along the street a series of documentations were mounted. The documents unearthed images of buildings and scenes that have disappeared; evidence of events that affected or were affected by the street were displayed; portraits of some of its residents were shown, along with details of their lives; processions were depicted, and monuments were explained. These documents were mounted on a system of pipe scaffolding and set in a disposition similar to the local idiom of

billboard-like stone facades that are supported by ordinary brick walls. Moreover, the pipe-frame system was of a type used in Italian film sets, a play on baroque staging. The pipe-frames were anchored by concrete counterweights that were cast in the form of ruined Doric columns, as if they were the remains of some under-layer of history and a reminder of the destructive hubris of autocratic rulers. Colours were borrowed from municipal departments such as the city parks, whose budgets had been illegally channelled into Olympic spending.

1.2 A typical Corridart assembly conceived by Melvin Charney and erected in front of the Mount Royal Club by McKim, Mead, and White, 1175 Sherbrooke W, Montreal.

Finally, the common image of a hand with a pointing finger that indicates directions was cast in red plastic and mounted on the pipe supports to guide people along this museum-in-the-street.[11]

In this remarkable installation Charney succeeded in linking his interests in the vernacular and the popular with his growing preoccupation with the history of built form in his home province, as well as with the interpretation of major public events along Sherbrooke Street that had formed part of it. The pipe scaffolding he used for the installations constituted the quintessence of a vernacular technology, as did the plywood, out of which were constructed the simulacra of the facades of *Les maisons de la rue Sherbrooke*, replacing facades which had already been destroyed, and mirroring ones that remained on the other side of the street. Archival and contemporary photography were employed to generate liberatory historical revelation. And the large red plastic pointing fingers could not have been more populist. Whereas his 1971 *Memo Series* in regard to the Air Force Memorial had not been able to synthesize this heterogeneous range of interests, Corridart triumphantly did so.

Historical accounts vary about why this installation was so controversial. But there is no doubt in my mind that it was precisely Charney's success in devising a popular, and perhaps even potentially revolutionary, street installation that so provoked Mayor Drapeau. Corridart successfully mounted a powerful urban historical critique of a whole decade of problematic overdevelopment in some parts of Montreal and equally problematic underdevelopment in others, and it did so in startlingly populist ways. The installation's creation and destruction remain to this day among the most memorable of all the constituent episodes of that controversial period in the urban history of Montreal.

In the wake of the fame – and in some circles the notoriety – that Corridart brought him, Charney was asked to develop installations at art galleries in many parts of North America. And thus, as a result of the searing personal trauma that the destruction of Corridart had been for him, Charney retreated to some degree from the front lines of political engagement in the streets of Montreal to the greater security of the art gallery, within the walls of which he could be certain his works would not be destroyed by municipal authorities. Still, even in his gallery installations he did not leave engagement completely behind. For example, his construction at the Museum of Contemporary Art in Chicago made reference not only to the urban history of Chicago's high-rise modern buildings but also to vernacular motifs in workers' housing in that city. As Charney put it in his descriptive text, "shades of inference which cannot be forgotten are gathered up in the construction."[12] By the early 1980s, the architect/polemicist who had sought so long to devise an architecture that was not monumental, had become one of art and architecture's most definitive and poignant orchestrators of collective memory. And of course, it is one of the greatest powers of successful monuments to evoke precisely such memory.

This late, orchestral capability of Charney was given its most definitive expression in the last of his works on which I will comment in this text. This is the garden for the Canadian Centre for Architecture that he was commissioned to design in 1989 by his friend of long standing, and founding director of the Centre, Phyllis Lambert.[13] The CCA was conceived as a museum, as a space for architectural exhibitions, and as a study centre. It was to be located on a prominent site in the west part of the commercial heart of the city on René-Lévesque Boulevard. It was to be housed partly in a rescued and restored heritage structure – the Shaughnessy house of 1874 – and partly in a new building that both backed onto and framed the existing one. The site was also significantly marked by the presence of two access ramps to the Ville-Marie Expressway to the south – one of those modern "improvements" to the urban infrastructure of the city of Montreal in the 1960s that were eventually seen to have been so destructive to the character of the city.

If the Centre itself was to be located on the north side of the boulevard, the garden was proposed to be located on the south side, in between the two ramps to the expressway. It was here that Charney created his garden, a permanent installation that has become a major contemporary memory device in Montreal. The garden gathers up and structures views of the city. To the south, from its belvedere, one looks out over the plain towards the St Lawrence River, which houses a substantial portion of the tenement housing that was threatened in the 1960s. To the north, it discloses an axial view to the historic seminary of the Collège de Montréal that was degraded by the implementation of a one-way traffic system on the street that forms that axis. The garden also partly reveals and partly fictionalizes a whole archaeology of the city's foundations, presenting a pattern of foundation walls that might have been those of the party walls dividing the row houses that once sat on the site, and that were so typical of much of the historical built fabric of Montreal. It evokes the historical structure of the city's urban morphology at the same time that it civilizes the harsh forms of the transportation infrastructure that frames its site, showing the residual impact of the historic cadastral form of land subdivision that affected even the precise form of the modernizing urban infrastructure itself. And then, there are the columns that Charney ranged along the garden's belvedere. With these, our creator posited a mock-didactic history of world architecture from ancient times to the present and

situated the architecture of Montreal precisely within it.

The garden for the CCA is not exactly populist, but the columns that support its architectural icons poignantly reprise – at least in part – the mock-Doric column bases that were a key component of Corridart. Even though it is not itself "vernacular," it does powerfully honour the vernacular building traditions of the history of Montreal. It is not very "technological" either, even if it both draws pictorial attention to and memorializes the famous grain elevators and other industrial structures that are located on the plain its belvedere overlooks.

It seems to me that the garden for the CCA can be seen as a kind of retrospective summa of the manifold thoughts, conceptions, and polemical battles that Charney mounted throughout his long career as an architect, artist, and author, even if it also constitutes an elegy for his earlier phase of activist political engagement. His youthful conviction in regard to the liberatory potential of technology may have turned out to be largely chimerical, but the history of that technology, he eventually discovered, did turn out to be capable of memorialization. The destruction of many of Montreal's neighbourhoods did take place, but due to the efforts of Charney and others, many other neighbourhoods were saved and now flourish. Indeed, at the present time, Montreal is admired for its innovative planning and urban design initiatives and for its careful consideration of the opinions of residents about the future of their neighbourhoods. Indeed, the design of the CCA complex and its garden comprise an outstanding example of the capacity of art and architecture to mend damage such as that done to the urban fabric by those infrastructure improvements of four decades ago. Again, the largely francophone social entity that is contemporary Quebec did not take on the precise form foreseen by some of its most militant advocates in the 1960s and

1970s, but it is nonetheless today a robust, thriving one, and the history of its historic, linguistic, and cultural transformation in the second half of the twentieth century is also embodied in the symbolic matrix of memory the CCA garden represents.

It seems to me, after all these years, that the CCA garden definitively reflects the long career struggle of the ambitious, restless, cantankerous, and courageous artist, architect, author, and teacher who was Melvin Charney.

NOTES

1   Chapter 11, 120.
2   See "A Self-Erecting Exhibition System," 194–201.
3   Chapter 24, 236–45.
4   Walter Benjamin, "The Author as Producer," *Reflections: Essays, Aphorisms, Autobiographical Writings* (New York: Schocken 1986): 220–38.
5   Chapter 25, 246–64.
6   Claude Beaulieu, *L'architecture contemporaine au Canada français* (Quebec: Ministère des Affaires Culturelles, 1969).
7   Alan Gowans, *Building Canada: An Architectural History of Canadian Life* (Toronto: Oxford University Press, 1966).
8   Chapter 25, 247.
9   Chapter 25, 264.
10 See *Les maisons de la rue Sherbrooke*, 305–13, and chapter 31, 303–4.
11 Chapter 31, 316–17.
12 Chapter 36, 378.
13 See "A Garden for the Canadian Centre for Architecture," 396–416.

2

Displacements and Fragments in the Work of Melvin Charney[1]

GEORGES ADAMCZYK

Architecture: it's the world demanding to become a city.

Paul Claudel, *L'architecte*

I live in a city, hardly an island, less and less river and sea, more and more alley and street, more and more haughty, less and less memorable. I live in a city ignoring herself, more and more new, less and less old, well secured from the names she adopts in order to better forget those who do not forget.

Pierre Perrault, *J'habite une ville**

Architect, artist, analyst and critic of architecture, organizer of events, professor, researcher, and formidable polemicist – Melvin Charney has significantly influenced both the thinking about and the realization of an "urban architecture," an architecture that translates the consciousness of history and the sense of belonging that people have for the places they inhabit every day. Charney touched a whole generation of architects and artists who owe to him the pug-

nacity and the generosity that characterize their practices. His work is a vigorous expression of this fundamental engagement made evident in the multiplicity of different genres he employed. Whether it is architecture, landscape architecture, installation, sculpture, public art, photography, painting, drawing, or writing – all his means of expression come together to produce a body of work whose continuity and coherence are exemplary.

These parallel activities weave together to produce an intertextual strategy that is extremely fertile and entirely his own. But, to restate Catherine Millet's first question to Charney in her interview for the magazine *Art Press*,[2] how do the drawings, the constructions, and the texts relate to one another in his work? Or to put it another way, what does the work of Melvin Charney – whether photographed or drawn or painted or built – tell us about his theoretical and critical vision of architecture? How is this work indivisible from his writing, his commentary on his own work, or his essays on contemporary architecture? If Charney responds to this question with the idea of "superimposition"

* Editor's translation of quotes: Paul Claudel, "L'architecte," *Feuilles de Saints* (Paris: NRF, 1925), and Pierre Perrault, *J'habite une ville* (Montreal: Hexagone, 2009).

(referring to his earlier comments on the difficulty of classifying and categorizing his work when trying to determine his status as architect or artist),[3] it is the idea of "displacement"[4] as proposed by Millet that offers us the most productive means for situating the writing within the work of art.

The "beginnings" – sketches and photographs, observations on the ordinary dwelling architectures around us and on the social liturgies that make a city – set up an intellectual detachment from the scene of the city. From the start, Melvin Charney initiated a sort of archaeological questioning akin to that of Michel Foucault when he proposed to reverse the historical relation between *document* and *monument*.[5] Looking exclusively at the monumental foundation of architecture as a discipline and power is to miss the real meaning of architecture. His approach was unquestionably very much in the spirit of the times and thus anticipated that scattered being called postmodern thinking, which eventually knocked on the doors of art and architecture. The idea of "building one's own architecture" as originated by Le Corbusier or even that of building a "personal vision" of the history of architecture in the manner of Reyner Banham were not new. Expressing his doubts about the heroic nature of the modern movement, Reyner Banham wrote in 1962: "The gravest of all doubts (about the profession) was whether – or how – architects could continue to sustain their traditional role as form-givers, creators and controllers of human environments."[6] But if these ideas were not new, few have had, like Charney, the courage to forgo the professional aspect of architectural practice – uncertain as it may be – to commit themselves to such an intellectually demanding undertaking, to such a lonely way to autonomy. The "beginnings" can thus be seen as an *epistemological displacement*, questioning the relation between the discipline and the profession and the status of high architecture and everyday architecture.

These first displacements, outside of the discipline, away from the "grand narrative," constructed a platform for reflection. From that platform, form and function were challenged to make way for a symbolic recognition of both architecture in society and of a "stock of knowledge"[7] proper to architecture.

In the late 1960s, Melvin Charney was perhaps the only Canadian artist/architect who represented the radical anti-architectural trend that was then becoming evident worldwide, particularly in Great Britain, Italy, and Austria. But one may also say, as Catherine Millet did, that the displacement between art, architecture, and writing takes a more Freudian turn. Charney seems to confirm this analogy when he responds: "The fear of someone in analysis is not having the right words to express his or her fears."[8]

More precisely, the displacement is not movement but rather substitution and transformation. Displacement means looking for something to put in place of something else, like a mask that makes the first thing more acceptable to look at. Because, as Claude Lévi-Strauss emphasized, "a mask is not primarily what it represents but what it transforms, that is to say, what it chooses *not* to represent."[9] So behind the machinery "image" of the project for the Canadian pavilion for the 1970 Osaka World Fair – a plan for a Cedric Price–like "action architecture" – there was also an affirmation of the absence of any monumental or even ephemeral attempt to represent Canada with an architectural gesture that would be both conventional and vainglorious. This is what led Charney, after several years devoted to laying the foundations of his work – already attracting attention from the artistic and architectural milieux – to create the *Memo Series* in 1970. This inaugural work, intended as an alternative to the construction of a military aviation museum, positioned his practice. From that point on, the relationships between art, architecture, and writing would be the symbolic material of his work.

In the conclusion of his lecture of 1971, "Towards a Definition of Architecture in Quebec," Melvin Charney said: "In Quebec, as elsewhere, all relevant architecture questions the state of architecture itself. And the answers can't be found in any of the usual places. Inevitably, the social condition of the architect as individual in relation to other people is evident. This means that the liberation of the architect depends on the political and social liberation of both the individual and the community. And in Quebec, this means that it depends also on the assertion of a renewed and original Quebec identity. Unfortunately, the cultural hegemony of traditional architecture still persists. But now, at least, it is more and more of an anachronism than a viable reality."[10] While the layout of the published text of the conference does not catch the play on words and images of the lecture (a critical relationship that is more clearly articulated in the layout of the 1982 article "To Whom It May Concern: On Contemporary Architecture in Quebec"),[11] this text finally marked out the territory of these displacements away from monumental architecture, in which visual documents become substitutes for buildings. Between "the age of suspicion," which refers to "the little true facts" that Nathalie Sarraute[12] talked about in the 1950s, and the schizophrenic search for autonomy expressed by Giorgio Grassi in 1974 ("Architecture is an experience which, from its beginning until its end, is responsible to itself before anything else"),[13] the search for "significant fragments" in ordinary architecture took on a fundamental critical value in the subsequent architectural and artistic work of Melvin Charney. These fragments are figures in the sense that Alan Colquhoun addresses in his criticism of the modern couple of form and function replacing the creative and rhetoric potential of the classic couple of form and figure. Colquhoun writes: "We must, therefore, see the return of the architectural figure as subject to the same laws of fragmentation which we see operating in all the

2.1 Photo of *Memo 20*, now lost, from Melvin Charney's original *Memo Series*, 1969–70.

other 'modern' arts – fragmentation in the works themselves, and also in terms of their social context."[14] However, fragments for Charney are not quotations, put together in an ill-assorted and anachronistic way, or some other kind of postmodern game of language. A fragment is also a *totality*, as if the fragment acts as the whole architecture, a kind of architectural allegory. It translates the profound meaning of building and

2.2 Melvin Charney, *Wall Piece No. 3*, 1977.

dwelling, the meaning behind the apparent order of the text.

   "Displacements" and "fragments" make it possible to break with all the preconceptions of linear connections between theory and practice, drawings and construction, or even ordinary architecture and erudite architecture. As Johanne Lamoureux makes clear when considering the question of translation, Charney's works are not translating, for example, a drawing into construction, but rather are rethinking the act of translation. She further clarifies this idea by stating, "Those who will say that Charney creates theoretical architecture or sculpture derived from architecture have not understood his work:

he materializes or *actualizes* an architecture indexing his own theory, so that it can inform and deform not only the already built world that surrounds us but also the representations, shifted into other fields, that we maintain of it."[15] Consequently the works of Melvin Charney are curiously transparent and opaque at the same time, and as such they seek to displace the spectator's view. But once again, in his definition of a possible architecture for Quebec, which is effectively also a definition of architecture itself, one might also understand the text as being a rejection of all definitions of architecture. The text becomes a non-definition of architecture, or more precisely an "infinition" of architecture, in the sense intended by Georges Braque when he said that in art "to define a thing is to substitute the definition for the thing itself."[16] Following his critique of Quebec's architecture, Charney began to construct the architectural fragments as analogical extractions of the city.

These works, *The Treasure of Trois-Rivières* (1975) and most of all *Les maisons de la rue Sherbrooke* (1976), while cultivating Alberti's analogy between the city and architecture, anticipated the collective explorations of the famous *Strada Novissima*, composed of nineteen facades built in the roman studio of Cinecittà for the Venice Biennale inside the Corderie of the Arsenal in 1980. From this point on, Charney's international career was established and his influence in the United States, Europe, and Japan was, if anything, stronger than it was at home – local critics no doubt being troubled by the provocative and paradoxical nature of his work. The canonical text, "The Montrealness of Montreal" published in 1980 in *Architectural Review,*which described the architecture of Montreal as "the *knowledge* of its inhabitants to appropriate the

city in an empirical way of collective life,"[17] makes the question of epistemological displacement and of fragment as *totality* much clearer. "The city is a memory for itself," and it is in a constant struggle against oblivion according to Jean Duvignaud.[18] The title of Catherine Millet's article is well chosen: "Melvin Charney, Explorer of Collective Memory."[19] It is not so much the city as a work of art, as a collection of objects or rituals or as representations that Charney is passionate about, but rather the city as destiny and as world. These forms and figures of urban architecture discovered by the architect and transmitted by the teacher are also those fragments which recur in his built work and his photographic work and paintings of the 1980s – works that were produced and reproduced, just as the city produces and reproduces itself.

From then on, it is clear that for Charney the making of installations was the construction of a site within a site. In the time between the

2.3 Melvin Charney, *The Square in a Square*, 1979.

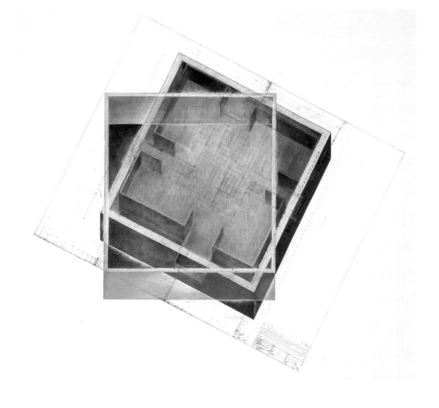

2.4 Melvin Charney, *A Kingston Construction*, 1983.

Dictionnaire (1970–2000) project and the in situ works, Charney's creation reconstituted itself progressively to form an epitome of the meanings of all urban constructions, their semiotic and aesthetic states, and their representations – whether descriptive, contemplative, or projective, concrete or abstract, figurative or allusive. The 1980s Toronto, Montreal, New York, Chicago, and Kingston *Constructions* placed Charney in the company of artists such as Buren, Graham, Smithson, and Matta-Clark. These artists – and others – confronted the question of places in contemporary society, their social production, and their cultural significance and make these questions the central subject of their creations, interventions in urban or natural space. The built figures, worked in superimposition, rotation, and spatial disjunction, anticipated the fiction and the deconstructivist manoeuvres of Peter Eisenman. But they didn't seek to proclaim their autonomy. They were of the site. Can we say that these *Constructions* emerged from the occupation of the expanded field of architec-

ture instead of the field of sculpture (landscape, non-landscape, architecture, non-architecture) as proposed by Rosalind Krauss?[20]

Looked at in these terms, these installations, as displacements and fragments, constitute non-architecture returning into architecture, just as there is a return of the non-site in the site. Charney does not build a site by installing a sculpture, but he constructs a site inside a site, inside a city. One could say that he constructs a text. Installation remains an uncertain genre of artistic or architectural intervention. If the essence of the art of installation is the participation of the spectator – according to a definition of participation that varies considerably from one creator to another as Julie H. Reiss reminds us[21] – it is precisely this highly variable, subjective, and contextual character which distances installation from the status of work of art. More recently, architects have used installation as a means of experimenting in conception and construction.[22] But these different approaches cannot totally encompass the retroactive content of these *Constructions*, which echo the imagination of the avant-garde in a kind of counter-utopian movement. Better to ask the question posed by Hans Ulrich Obrist: "Installations are the answer, what is the question?"[23] One could respond mischievously to this question with the words of Reyner Banham: "Modern architecture is dead: long live modern architecture!"[24]

In the 1983 exhibition, The Villas of Pliny and Classical Architecture in Montreal, the source of Charney's installations *Pliny on My Mind No. 1 and No. 2* (see Figs. 3.7 and 3.8) was the encounter between the classical language of the villa and the more familiar language of the Montreal "plex," revealing by this very fact the similarities between the "ordinary heroism" of the "plex" and the scholarly vanities of architecture. As he points out, from the time of the Romans onwards, the city has been a continuous construction site.[25] In the early 1980s, Charney was not alone in the critical debate on representation in architecture and about the relationship of architecture to artistic practice. The exhibition on the villas of Pliny brought together a group of architects/artists who had all, in their own fashion, invested a lot of thought into the problem of interpretation of classical figures. But Charney had no nostalgia for classical architecture, no pretension to expertise, but rather an archaeological and fragmentary approach to figures and meanings and the concern to connect together the imaginary of the grand city and the imaginary of everyday architecture. The 1983 exhibition at the Montreal Museum of Fine Arts, more than ten years after the exhibition Montreal Plus or Minus? in the same museum, showed clearly the route followed by Melvin Charney and his fidelity to the "real people of Montreal."

The installations for the exhibition/event at the Centre international d'art contemporain de Montréal in 1985, for the Venice Biennale in 1986, at the Musée du Québec in 1989, the Galerie René Blouin in 1990, the Canadian Centre for Architecture in 1991, and the Musée d'art contemporain de Montréal in 1992 were entirely accomplished works that afforded a lot of place to narrative and that multiplied the layers of significance under a familiar appearance. Fragments of architecture and of our popular history that are part of our destiny were here transfigured into shared built "parables" or teachings about the human condition. The work and the word were intertwined, still full of hope.

Melvin Charney's critical force and artistic maturity allowed him to clearly distinguish himself from the attitude that dominated in the 1980s, an attitude bogged down in backward-looking historicism and more concerned about promoting the new-found autonomy of works and assigning it an improvised artistic value. His position was clearly expressed in the stand he took with respect to images. By bringing into museums and contemporary art galleries great architecture, French revolution–era architecture,

Russian avant-garde architecture, and the vernacular architecture of Montreal as if it were all one and the same history, he set aside the question of *transdisciplinarity* to make architecture not only the subject but the mediated subject, like sensitive material. He made very evident the great value of looking at the world in two ways: one as an architect who decodes and looks at the built figures and one as an artist who allows himself to be looked at by these constructions that speak to him. From that time on, Charney put aside the essay but continued to write the commentary that accompanies his work.

The German Series (1981–86), allowed him to address his most serious subject, the oblivion of architecture, the other side of the memory and imaginary dimensions of the city. The tragic elevation of his work affirmed itself. Architecture had lost its innocence forever; it revealed itself as evidence of our most noble acts as well as our most destructive ones. Drawings became more important, more present, and increasingly red. The anxiety of the artist was translated into a rougher form of representation. The movement from one level of representation to another superseded the relative consonance of the modes of representation, resulting in a dissonance created by the profound anxiety of the subject.

Architecture became the body, the flesh. Its representation mirrored a state of crisis. From this point on, the anthropomorphic character of architecture asserted itself as the node of an unseen connection that links us to all constructions. These constructions not only were intended to shelter us but also to represent us, as we inhabit our bodies, as we inhabit architecture. The work of Charney found its universal measure between drama and emotion. The works overwhelmed the text. The city, the primitive hut, gave way to another mythical horizon, which appears to us as the "*Remontages du temps subi*," to use Georges Didi-Huberman's phrase.[26] Or have we perhaps arrived at the stage where the city is us?

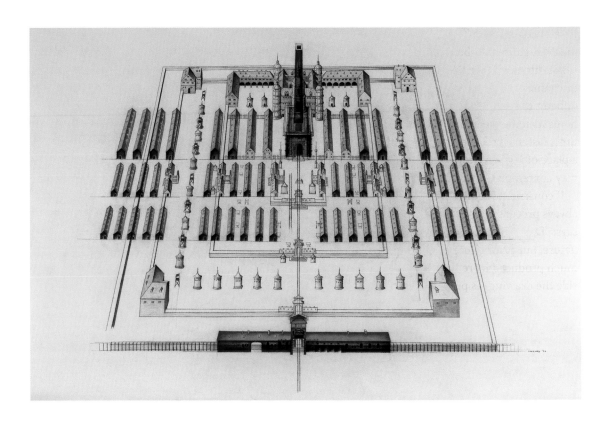

2.5 Melvin Charney, *Visions of the Temple (after Matthias Hafenreffer's Reconstruction of the Temple of Jerusalem, 1631)*, 1986.

In parallel, Melvin Charney inaugurated a new period during which his involvement in a series of works of public art became a concrete contribution to the *longue durée* of the city. These realizations brought him to the attention of the general public and revealed both his deep attachment to local realities and his work's links to the built culture of a city. Projects such as the *Canadian Tribute to Human Rights* in Ottawa (1988–90), the Garden of the Canadian Centre for Architecture (1987–90), *Gratte-ciel, cascade d'eau/ruisseaux … une construction* in Place Émilie-Gamelin (1990–92) establish with authority Charney's role as the forerunner in a new conception of civic space. The Garden of

the Canadian Centre for Architecture was the consequence of a critical opportunity unequalled in its time and can be seen as a great lesson in art and architecture, a paradigm that generates a new direction in the research and creation of the architecture of landscape.

In the garden, column eleven is itself an allegory, a fragment of the whole. It stands tall, on axis with the Grand Séminaire, over-looking the city below the escarpment. Charney describes it thus: "A tubular steel structure that usually supports the directional signs for the expressway now supports a facade, another 'sign,' similar to the pediment of the seminary. One facade is posited as the representation of the other, as elsewhere in the garden. A steel strut extends above the column to hold up a straight-back chair high above the expressway. And on the chair sits a house, the final house in the sequence of 'dwellings' which began at the base of column one."[27] In his shamanic reading of the CCA garden, Robert-Jan Van Pelt writes: "It is not difficult to see the column as an opening or channel to other realms of being; nor is it difficult to see it as some kind of cosmic axle that holds its universe in balance and, at the same time, fastens it to a centre … Column Eleven is a place of regeneration, a point where a person may contemplate a new beginning."[28]

If construction follows the drawing, drawing always precedes construction. As Robin Evans says: "Drawing in architecture is not done after nature, bur prior to construction; it is not so much produced by reflection on the reality outside the drawing, as productive of a reality that will end up outside the drawing."[29] This is precisely what Charney challenges when he evokes the idea of constructing images, as if reality is to be found in the drawing itself. The drawing becomes the architecture in a certain way. While Gianni Contessi looks at architectural drawings as seismographs, meditations, or commentaries on the discipline – or even as literary works,[30] In Charney's works, the images, the constructions,

LEFT | 2.6 Melvin Charney, *The Canadian Tribute to Human Rights*, 1986–90.

RIGHT | 2.7 Melvin Charney, *The "Tribune," Column No. 11,* CCA garden, 1987–89.

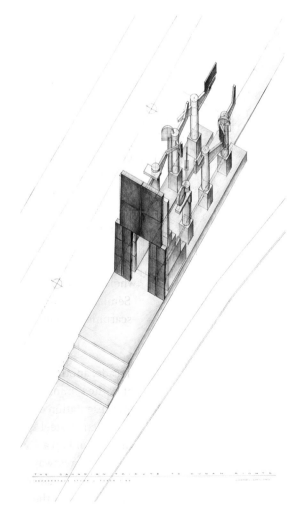

2.8 Melvin Charney, *Parable, No. 4 ... Segesta*, 1990.

the fragments, and collections of figures speak to us of the city and of the world. The passage from the text to the image, to the construction, and vice-versa, is the product of a displacement in which imagination and memory require the invention of an unending narrative of the architecture of the city. The recent work of Melvin Charney – layering photography, drawing, and painting, and superimposing different relations to reality – expresses the hope that here or elsewhere, we still need architecture to inhabit this inescapable urban world.

NOTES

1 Translation by Nancy Dunton, revised by James Leahy and Louis Martin.
2 Chapter 39, 419–24
3 See the question asked by Phyllis Lambert: "First of all, I would like to know how you view yourself as an architect?" at the beginning of her interview with Melvin Charney. Phyllis Lambert, "Interview with Melvin Charney, 12 March 1991," in *Parables and Other Allegories: The Work of Melvin Charney, 1975–1990*, ed. Alessandra Latour (Montreal: Canadian Centre for Architecture, 1991), 25. See also Melvin Charney's response to Yasmeen Siddiqui: "It is difficult to categorize what I do. Even though my activities are not all that complex, the available words are too blunt, as if an ossification of nomenclature has taken place in the face of change" (see Chapter 40, 432).
4 Chapter 39, 419–20.
5 Michel Foucault, *The Archeology of Knowledge* (London: Tavistock, 1972).
6 Reyner Banham, *Age of the Masters, a Personal View of Modern Architecture* (New York: Harper and Row, 1975), 5. For the intellectual context of architecture in the 1950s and 1960s, see "Challenges to Modernism in Europe 1959–1967" and "Challenges to Modernism in America," the final two chapters in Harry Francis Mallgrave, *Modern Architectural Theory: A Historical Survey, 1673–1968* (Cambridge: Cambridge University Press, 2005), 355–403. For a more in-depth study of the theoretical debate, see the thesis of Louis Martin, "The Search for a Theory in Architecture: Anglo-American Debates, 1957–1976," vols. 1–2, PhD dissertation, Princeton University, November 2002.

7 Alfred Schütz, *Essais sur le monde ordinaire*, trans. Thierry Blin (Paris: Le Felin, 2007), 77.

8 Chapter 39, 420.

9 Claude Lévi-Strauss, *The Way of the Masks*, trans. Sylvia Modelski (Seattle: University of Washington Press, 1982), 144.

10 Chapter 25, 264.

11 Chapter 34, 342–60.

12 The text by Nathalie Sarraute appears in *Les Temps modernes* (February 1950): "It would appear that not only does the novelist barely believe in his characters but that the reader cannot bring himself to do so. So we see the character in the novel, deprived of this support and of the faith in him of both the writer and the reader – those very people who stood him solidly upright and placed the weight of history on his shoulders – vacillate and fall apart." It is tempting to see in this a literary metaphor describing in a certain way the condition of the architect and of architecture of that same era. The text is reprinted in English translation in Nathalie Sarraute, *The Age of Suspicion: Essays on the Novel* (New York: George Braziller, 1963): 84.

13 Giorgio Grassi, *L'architecture comme métier et autres écrits* (Bruxelles: Pierre Mardaga, 1979), 161.

14 Alan Colquhoun, "Form and Figure," *Essays in Architectural Criticism: Modern Architecture and Historical Change* (Cambridge, MA: MIT Press, 1981), 202.

15 Johanne Lamoureux, "De la construction ou la traduction des modèles," in *Melvin Charney: Parcours de la réinvention / Parcours about reinvention*, ed. Jean-François Chevrier, Johanne Lamoureux, Jun Teshigawara (Caen: Fonds régional d'art contemporain de Basse-Normandie, 1998), 69.

16 Françoise Nicol, *Braque et Reverdy, La genèse des pensées de 1917* (Paris: L'Échoppe, 2006), 16–17.

17 Chapter 33, 338.

18 Jean Duvignaud, *Lieux et non lieux* (Paris: Éditions Galilée, 1977), 50.

19 Chapter 39, 419–24.

20 Rosalind Krauss, "Sculpture in the Expanded Field," first appeared (by great good fortune for critics) in the journal *October* in 1979 and is also included in *The Anti-Aesthetic, Essays on Postmodern Culture*, ed. Hal Foster (Seattle: Bay Press, 1983), 31–43.

21 Julie H. Reiss, *From Margin to Center, The Spaces of Installation Art* (Cambridge, MA: MIT Press, 2000), xiii.

22 Sarah Bonnemaison and Ronit Eisenbach, *Installations by Architects: Experiments in Building and Design* (New York: Princeton Architectural Press, 2009). It is surprising that the authors make no reference to the series of 1980s *Constructions* by Melvin Charney. Undoubtedly they see this as the work of an artist as opposed to the work of an architect.

23 Hans Ulrich Obrist, "Installations Are the Answer, What Is the Question?" *Oxford Art Journal* 24, no. 2 (2001): 93–101. Invoking Bruno Latour's idea of *laboratory*, Obrist makes no real distinction between artistic experimentation and architectural experimentation. One could say that installation transforms the idea of art as much as it does that of architecture.

24 Banham, *Age of the Masters*, 6.

25 Chapter 37, 380–7

26 Georges Didi-Huberman, "Quand il pense son œil s'étonne … (He thinks with an eye that is astonished …)," interview with Muriel Pic about the second volume of *L'œil de l'histoire* entitled *Remontages du temps subi* (published in 2010 by Éditions de Minuit) in *Critique* 762 (2010): 931–8. In this interview, Georges Didi-Huberman, recalling the unknown minor players of history, quotes Adorno writing about Siegfried Kracauer: "He thinks with an eye that is astonished almost to helplessness but then suddenly flashes into illumination. The oppressed may well become master of their sufferings with such a gaze." This idea of the imagination going from that which one perceives to that which one understands, from the invisible to the visible sheds light on these "remontages du temps." The work of Melvin Charney would unquestionably appear even more luminous when approached from this angle.

27 See "A Garden for the Canadian Centre for Architecture," 396–416.

28 Robert-Jan Van Pelt, "Into the Suffering City: Considerations of the *German Series*" in *Parables and Other Allegories: The Work of Melvin Charney, 1975–1990*, ed. Alessandra Latour (Montreal: Canadian Centre for Architecture, 1991), 41.

29 Robin Evans, *Translations from Drawing to Building and Other Essays* (Cambridge, MA: MIT Press, 1986), 165.

30 Gianni Contessi, *Écritures dessinées: Art et architecture de Piranèse à Ruskin* (Gollion: Infolio, 2002).

3

Montreal on My Mind: Melvin Charney and the Invention of "Montrealness"

RÉJEAN LEGAULT

Montreal is one of those world cities where a sense of destiny is vividly ingrained in its physical urban demeanor.

Melvin Charney (1992)

Cities have long been read as possessing distinct personalities, and their physical forms are often taken as the outward manifestation of underlying character traits.[1] New York, London, Paris have all been portrayed by means of their urban forms; the idea that Montreal, too, possesses a distinct architectural identity has become so widely accepted as to seemingly warrant no further questioning. Represented in a series of urban figure and building types – its streets, its squares, its greystone buildings and brick triplexes – this identity has now become part and parcel of Montreal's image.

The construction of the city's architectural persona is the result of a long and complex process that is no doubt difficult to unravel. Yet many observers of architecture have pointed to one text as the most compelling formulation of this representation: "The Montrealness of Montreal" by Montreal architect and artist Melvin Charney.[2] Appearing in a special issue of the British journal *The Architectural Review* dedicated to Canadian architecture in 1980, this article offered Charney the opportunity to both describe and explain the uniqueness of Montreal's urban architecture. It also made Charney the central figure in ongoing efforts to articulate the distinctive architectural character and image of Montreal.

Given the impact of this essay, it is worth asking: what is the place of the city in Charney's intellectual trajectory? Looking back at his earlier contributions on Montreal, I examine the roots of his intellectual and personal engagement with the city. Looking forward, I consider the place of this text within Charney's later thinking and work – both in architecture and in art – and probe its critical reception within the cultural and intellectual milieux involved in the study of Montreal's identity construction. In taking on this task, I must point out from the outset that the essay that follows is neither a biographical study nor an intellectual history. Based primarily on published sources and design works, its goal is to recover the key premises and various iterations of a discourse that has profoundly marked architectural thinking and practice in Montreal and beyond.

The Discovery of Montreal

Very early on, Montreal as a physical and architectural entity was on Charney's mind. The city was the focus of his first ventures into the world of artistic expression as evinced by the black and white photographs he took in the mid-1950s.[3] In a retrospective reading of his youthful years, Charney was eager to identify both the objects and the deeper meaning of his initial forays:

> In my early teens I began to photograph Montreal in a somewhat more systematic way, reversing figure and ground. Streets, the spaces between buildings, steam shovels and railway engines drew my attention, as did the processes and conventions of photography. What I had stumbled upon at that time were fragments of new urban formations emerging in the interstices of an evolving city – the transformation of the urban structure of a metropolis into a regional sprawl.[4]

Yet if his later discussions of these photographs would be wilfully theorized, the images themselves are revealing of an early preoccupation with the settings and constructions that were soon to be given an iconic status, first among them the space of the streets and the grain silos.[5]

It was only following Charney's return to Montreal, after many years of study and work outside the country, that his interest for the city's urban character was manifested in print. Published in 1964, "The Old Montreal No One Wants to Preserve" was the first article where he specifically addressed the topic of the city and its architecture.[6] Written right after Old Montreal had been classified as a historic district by the

3.1 A street of Montreal, 1964. Photo by Melvin Charney.

provincial government, his article highlighted the misconceptions about the architecture and urban structure of the old city. Its perimeter had just been defined by the Jacques-Viger

Commission, a body created in 1962, whose mandate was to "study all questions connected with the conservation, in Old Montreal, of the historical character of the district."[7] Charney deplored that the delimitation of the "Old Town" enabled the demolition of a wealth of buildings, both monumental and ordinary, that fell outside of the perimeter. More importantly, however, the essay offers a reading of the district's architecture that focuses on the contribution of vernacular types in the construction of the city. Dividing Old Montreal's development into four stages from the seventeenth to the twentieth centuries, Charney focused on the importance and significance of the undervalued nineteenth-century buildings, offering a framework through which they could be appreciated: "The development of the office building archetype, group housing, and the recently popular 'Functional' style happened in the nineteenth century."[8] He also paid special attention to the grain elevators, an industrial building type that he would repeatedly return to throughout his career.[9] Yet most fascinating in this review is the way Charney jumps over the imaginary wall of the old city to venture into the Saint-Laurent borough and beyond, describing the "urbanity" of the late nineteenth-century brick-faced housing type along Rivard and Berri streets. Challenging the territorial limits imposed by the cultural intelligentsia, Charney proposed instead to envision this terrain as a continuous – if torn – urban fabric.

Modern Montreal and Megastructures

Charney's concern for the "preservation" of Old Montreal ran parallel to his genuine interest in the analysis of the city's modern architecture.[10] His 1965 review of the newly completed Place Victoria attests to this fact.[11] The model he applied was the one he had just developed for reading Mediterranean vernacular architecture.[12] For Charney, the vernacular offered an interpretive model in which architecture is understood as a dynamic system, as the result of technical and social processes, rather than as a system of forms. Applying this conception of architecture to the analysis of Place Victoria, he was particularly impressed by the way in which the architect Luigi Moretti and the engineer Pier Luigi Nervi strove to express the logic of the building through the articulation of the three blocks of floors, the materialization of the corner pillars, the display of the diagonal braces and the treatment of the curtain wall. For Charney, the expression of each of these elements conveyed the fact that the tower resulted from a complex process of construction rather than from simple formal decisions. He also underscored the extent to which the architectural treatment of Place Victoria differs from that of Place Ville-Marie and CIL House, two new towers that appeared up the hill along Dorchester Street (later René-Lévesque Boulevard) during the same period. In Charney's opinion, the latter two attested to a formalism that sought to conceal rather than reveal their structural and mechanical complexity, unlike "Place Victoria [which] makes no aesthetic excuses for itself."[13]

His interest went beyond individual buildings, for he also focused on the logic of the new city centre as a whole. This attention was translated in an enlightening sectional drawing he made of the new city core. Charney described this drawing, first published in 1967, as a "North-south section through Montreal from Mount Royal through the central area, indicating the way in which the new buildings are heaped up on an underground network of walkways, Metro, car parks and basements."[14] Given that in the new modern core, users could go down as much as they could go up, this section shed light on the vertical stratification of this multi-level environment.

Although Charney's interest in modern Montreal would continue well into the next decade, his political turn in the early 1970s (about which I will have more to say later) would

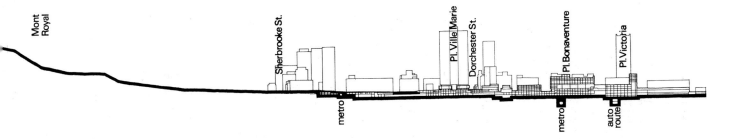

significantly inflect the content of his reading. By then it was the public character of the recent modern buildings that was to take centre stage in his writings. In "Understanding Montreal," an essay published in 1974, the entire discussion of the modern city core revolves around the status of public space.[15] Charney was most concerned about the type of civic space provided by the new urban complexes: "All the *Places* of the core transform the public function of the city into pseudo-public commodities."[16] Making reference to buildings like Place Ville-Marie and Place Bonaventure, he deplored the way they usurped the notion of *Place*: "Even the word *Place* was co-opted; it signifies a public square, and not a building." This essay also shows the section drawing that first appeared in 1967, but it now serves to support the insight that "the internal 'streets' are in effect basement-like shopping corridors buried under man-made platforms built above the fall of the land, negating their public function."[17] This drawing brilliantly revealed the fact that a large part of the new underground city core was actually above ground level.

Charney did not reject all of this architectural production. Place Bonaventure, for one, was considered to respond better than other *Places* to this new urban context. But this new urban type, with its distinctive low volume that covers an entire city block, only underlined the contradiction between architecture and its packaging as real-estate commodity. It is the complex

3.2 A section showing Montreal's new underground network drawn by Melvin Charney.

least recognized as architecture, however, that captured his imagination: Plaza Alexis-Nihon, located at the western fringe of the downtown area across from the Forum. Focusing on the spatial and functional characteristics of this multi-use complex organized around a central open place, he enthusiastically declared: "All that is lacking are some boom cranes perched on top of the elevator shafts to complete this home-grown futurist vision."[18]

As this discussion is clearly leading, Charney's discourse, though critical of the architecture of the modern city core, ran parallel to, not along with, that of the preservationists. Further proof of this discrepancy was revealed soon afterwards. In his 1976 book *Megastructure: Urban Futures of the Recent Past*, Reyner Banham devoted an entire chapter to Montreal's megastructural experimentations at Expo 67 and in the new downtown.[19] Heavily indebted to Charney's own reading of the modern core – Banham called him a "home grown" analyst who spoke with "inside knowledge" – the section on the new downtown paid special attention to the "pedestrian plumbing" and transportation connections of this subterranean city.[20] Banham concluded that in Montreal, "megastructures moved off the visionaries' drawing boards" to become a buildable building type, a position that was antithetical to any concerns for historic preservation.

Montreal as a Political Terrain

During the 1960s, Charney published almost twenty essays, constituting a coherent body of work that addressed architecture and the city viewed as the result of social processes. The new decade brought about not so much change as a radicalization of his position. He began to insist on the political dimension of architecture, an affirmation that burned through the pages of his provocative essay "Towards a Definition of Architecture in Quebec."[21] Published in 1971,

the essay appeared at a crucial moment in the economic and social evolution of Quebec, a period marked by numerous events and social movements that would transform the political landscape in a lasting way. Echoing this political agitation, the conclusion of his text was unequivocal: "The future of architecture in Quebec, or anywhere for that matter, depends on the resolution of these questions. Technically, we can build almost anything. Solutions lie in a social and cultural evolution where architecture becomes part of the struggle of people to control their own lives."[22] And he went on to add: "This means that the liberation of the architect depends on the political and social liberation of both the individual and the community." From this point on, he would no longer conceive of architecture as a simple act of design, even as a socially constructed one, but more than ever as a profoundly ideological gesture.[23]

3.3 Melvin Charney, *The Main, Montreal, St Lawrence Boulevard between Ste Catherine Street and René-Lévesque Boulevard*, 1965.

It was during the same period that he began to distance himself from architectural practice, turning instead toward art as the most appropriate means for disseminating his ideas on architecture as both a social and political fact. His first collective endeavour in this realm was Montreal Plus or Minus?, an exhibition he organized for the Montreal Museum of Fine Arts in 1972.[24] In this curatorial project, Charney brought a range of artists, activists, and community workers into the orbit of the museum to reflect on the city's social and material transformation.[25] His catalogue introduction explains that the exhibition "tries to say that the future of the city is found not only in urban growth, in technological innovations, or in the exercise of planning and design talents, but in the social and cultural evolution of Montreal."[26] The event addressed the city by means of a series of politicized conceptual-art projects. In his visual contribution to the catalogue, Charney presented a photographic survey of "St Lawrence Street, between Ste. Catherine and Dorchester Streets, November 16, 1965, 4:15 pm."[27] Though the photographs had been taken in the mid-1960s, this panorama did fit well within the vision of the city propounded by the exhibition: it was a work about people instead of buildings, or rather, about buildings traversed by people.

These political concerns also underlie his curatorial work for the now famous Corridart exhibition organized in the context of the 1976 Montreal Olympics.[28] Based on a detailed

ABOVE | 3.4 a and b *The Main ... Montreal*, detail east side.

BELOW | 3.5 a, b, and c *The Main ... Montreal*, detail west side.

inventory that described and deciphered what Charney called the "morpho-history" of Sherbrooke Street, the exhibition sought to highlight by means of documentary and artistic interventions the possibilities inscribed in its configuration. Titled *Les maisons de la rue Sherbrooke*, Charney's contribution to this collective exhibition was a "construction" that challenged both the physical and social condition of the street. Mirroring the facades of two nineteenth-century greystone townhouses located on the opposing corners of the intersection, the work – a plywood construction hung on a tubular scaffolding – alluded to the symmetry of baroque urban spaces with their axes terminating on an urban monument. This ephemeral construction pointed at once to the ruinous state of the site as well as the virtual urban form revealed by its remaining traces, creating a critical narrative about the architectural nature of both the street and the city.

The Montrealness of Montreal

Four years after the illicit nocturnal dismantling of the Corridart exhibition, Charney published an essay that, not unlike *Les maisons de la rue Sherbrooke*, left a mark on the imaginary construction of the city. Appearing in 1980, "The Montrealness of Montreal: Formations and Formalities in Urban Architecture" sought to describe and explain the specificity of Montreal's urban architecture.[29] With the introduction of the expressive neologism "montrealness" in the especially memorable title, Charney managed to encapsulate in a single expression the uniqueness of the city's identity. Emulating the title of Nikolaus Pevsner's famous study, *The Englishness of English Art*, in which the author attempted to circumscribe the identity of English art,[30] Charney's article was written at a critical moment in the process of defining the Québécois identity. As its subtitle indicates, the article focuses on the examination of both the processes and the customs at play in the formation of Montreal, offering an enlightening synthesis of the various traits that shaped the city's urban and architectural ethos.

As with all of Charney's discursive production, this essay did not stand alone. Rather, it was the outcome of an ongoing intellectual reflection on Quebec architecture begun many years before. Central to this continuing project was his 1971 groundbreaking essay, "Towards a Definition of Architecture in Quebec," in which he forcefully argued his deep-seated belief in the *savoir-inné*, the innate knowledge, of its inhabitants.[31] This idea was clearly spelled out when he wrote that "the sources of contemporary architecture are to be found in the so-called 'popular' architecture of Quebec, and in the tradition of the Québécois builder, rather than in the stylistic evolution of buildings expressed by established elite."[32]

Yet if that 1971 essay set the stage for a discussion of the agency of "the people," most of the content of "The Montrealness of Montreal" was derived from his preceding text on the city, "Understanding Montreal" of 1974.[33] Published within a guide to Montreal's architecture and urban form, this essay was as much about the present state of the city's architecture as about its history. At the outset, Charney characterizes the city as a physical and social entity: "Montreal is one of the few North American cities related to its geographical situation. No matter where you are in the city, a mountain appears close to its centre; its edges are marked by the broad expanse of a river. These define a presence ingrained in the sense of place, and are a source of vitality and delight."[34] Here Charney fully developed his interpretation of the way the urban form came out of the interactions between the inhabitants and their limited resources: "Much of the human character of present day Montreal has evolved out of an expedient adaptation of existing conditions, hammered out in a rough climate by the resilience of people to alien surroundings, modifying the physical substance of the city."[35] These transactions and interactions are key to explain the built forms of the *quartiers populaires*, with their mass housing that dated from the city's first phase of large-scale industrialization between the 1880s and the 1920s.

The concept of innate knowledge is equally central to an understanding of the logic of the urban grid. After asserting that the transformation of the *quartiers* evolved out of the rural immigrants' adaptation to life in the city, Charney writes: "The street grid was differentiated into *avenues*, *rues*, and *ruelles*, each assuming a distinct connotation and form."[36] In this process, the sole agent appears to be the people themselves. There are no traces of specialized actors or experts, like land surveyors, who could have played a role in the adaptation of precedents and models of land subdivision. Moreover, this interpretation implies a clear separation between the urban models – in terms of both origins and configuration – implemented by the elite and those developed by the people, thus suggesting the mutual isolation of the two main sociolinguistic groups that formed the city's population of the city.[37]

But there are also significant differences in these texts. One of them has to do with the tone.

"Understanding Montreal" almost reads like a political pamphlet, with its recurring denunciation of the dominating elite. By contrast, "The Montrealness of Montreal" adopts the guise of a disciplinary essay. Introduced with a discussion on the changing models employed to conceptualize the city (i.e., from biological to semiological), this text reads like a more objective account of the city's formation and form. Another difference, though one which is barely perceptible, has to do with the facts. But it may hold the key to a significant shift in Charney's interpretation and, thus, conceptualization of Montreal.[38] This difference is located in his explanation of the origin of the urban grid. It is worth quoting this passage at length:

The essential structure of Montreal is found in the plan of the initial settlement. This plan can be seen to be an instance, one of many in the Americas, where the organization of a town was adapted from devices found at the roots of classic planning which appear throughout history, particularly in the creation of new urban centres. The device itself was less a "model" than a series of reproducible relationships based on an undifferentiated grid. The grid subsumed the potential structure of a town: a tacit representation of "knowledge" of town organization.[39]

Making reference to the Zahringer new towns established in the eleventh century, Charney suggests that in both cases the dynamic "may be found in an 'open' relationship between the town and the surrounding countryside: the continuity of the town structure in a system of rural land division."[40] It is this comparison – or analogy – that enables him to assert that "beyond Montreal, a system of *rangs* – long narrow lots perpendicular to access roads – reproduced a rural configuration of the city grid, unique in North America."

The primacy of the *rang* in the development of the Montreal grid was by this time a well-established fact. Urban planners, among others, had already made reference to the link between the long and narrow farm lots typical of the *rang* system and the city's elongated urban plots.[41] Moreover, the rural origin of the *rang* had been well documented by geographers.[42] Backed by these interpretations, Charney was at ease in affirming in 1974 that the "*quartiers* grew out of the original patterns of land settlement – the *rangs*."[43] Yet in his 1980 "Montrealness" essay, Charney now claimed that the system of *rangs* "reproduced a rural configuration of the city grid." Downplaying the accepted interpretations of geographers, he chose instead to assert the precedence of the city grid over the rural subdivision. The *rang* had now become a product of the urban grid. The city came first.

Though subtle, this change was central to the entire argument about the "Montrealness" of Montreal. For if the city was to possess an identity of its own, this identity had to be found, or founded, in its plan. Looking at the 1672 plan of the city, he wrote: "The rudiments of an orthogonal grid, and a tight alignment of buildings defined by and defining the street, plot the main elements of the city."[44] The source of Montreal's urban grid was thus to be located in the configuration of its original settlement – which was itself an iteration of classical planning – not in some local adaptation of a seventeenth-century system of rural subdivision.[45] This anchoring of the grid in an ancient urban model was essential for an argument that privileged the urban character of its architecture: "The plans of numerous American cities were also derived from the linear grid. But the difference in Montreal is found in the sustained development of an urban architecture based on the predominance of the street as a physical entity which subsumed individual buildings."[46]

Charney's focus on the street as the generator of Montreal's urban form was undoubtedly

3.6 Aerial view of an urbanized *rang*.

connected to his teaching activities at the School
of Architecture of the Université de Montréal,
especially those centred on his Atelier d'architecture urbaine – the Urban Architecture Unit –
established in 1978. Yet the main topic of "The
Montrealness of Montreal" cannot be explained
by this fact alone. A synthesis of many years
of reflection on the search for an "authentic"

architecture, this essay proposed an original
interpretation of Montreal's urban and architectural forms. With its confident interweaving of
descriptions and explanations, the essay had the
convincing tone of a proper historical narrative. But its documentary sources were thin and
precise references rare, putting it at variance
from conventional historical discourse. Yet more
importantly, it is its interpretative model that
sets it apart from disciplinary history.[47] While
contemporaneous research in urban history
tended to focus on the complex links between

actors, agencies, and contingencies in the production of the urban environment, Charney instead privileged a historical narrative that gave the primary role to the collectivity itself.

While "The Montrealness of Montreal" is no doubt a historically minded text, it may be more accurately defined as a descriptive work. Charney himself often referred to the useful methodological distinction between description and prescription.[48] In an essay addressing the epistemology of the descriptive act, the historian André Corboz pointedly explained: "A description is never complete, that is to say absolute and this for a very simple fact: a description is never 'pure' because it is motivated by an intention that is often implicit."[49] What was Charney's intention? I believe it was to propose a new narrative on the foundational character of the city. Challenging the prevailing interpretation of Montreal as a city constructed by the mostly English-speaking commercial elite, Charney offered an alternative model that strove to assert the cultural and popular – mostly francophone – character of the city. Combining the innate knowledge of the people with the urban forms inherited from long-standing practices, Charney's discourse was that of a mythical refoundation that "naturalized" a historical phenomenon. In its attempt to recast the character of the city as a popular and cultural urban fact, "The Montrealness of Montreal" proved to be an engaging, and ongoing, work of description. It would soon be followed by its strategic counterpart, that of prescription.

The City within the City

Charney's new emphasis on the ancient origins of the city structure was not confined to his explanatory work. A contemporary essay, "On Interpreting Montreal: The 'City' of the City," is revealing of the way this rereading of Montreal's beginnings permeated his entire production.[50] Though unpublished, this text offers an enlightening view into Charney's subtle shift from urban history to urban psychoanalysis.

The essay begins with a description of an eighteenth-century map of Montreal. (See Pl. 35.) One learns that, like many cities created *ex novo*, Montreal's underlying structure is a rough, orthogonal grid that extends both inside and outside the walls "as some primal order of human settlement."[51] Pondering the meaning of this map, Charney was drawn to a series of composed and enclosed gardens, "the form of which represents the primary grid as fragments of an ideal, paradisiacal city."[52] For him, these fragments "call forth biblical images of Eden and of the Temple of Jerusalem, configurations which enjoy the presence of Heaven on earth," bringing to mind Joseph Rykwert's interpretation of architecture's origins in his well-known *On Adam's House in Paradise*.[53]

This hermeneutic reading of the map is key to Charney's evolving conception of the city and of his own artistic production: "Here then is an essential ingredient of Montreal, and one which informs my work. Not only is there a strong, urban order inherent in the basic structure of the city, but implanted in its physical structure are also the traces of a surfeit of self-reflexive and idealized representations of its existence as a city."[54] He continues: "What intrigues me is that in the balance between reality and the representation of reality, the physical traces of this city are clearly on the side of the 'spirit' and of desire, often wishful, naïve and illusory, but tempered by the rigors of life." He goes on to describe four works that illustrate his vision, among them his *Maisons de la rue Sherbrooke* and a slightly later work, *Museum Construction* of 1979. The conclusion of this brief piece makes no secret about his call for figural imagination and the need to reinvent reality: "These constructions appropriated and transformed the existing traces of the city. Its urban strata were transcribed in an attempt to evoke both history and a sense of immanence. Ideal, meaningful, useless, truthful and illusory figures were superimposed so as to elaborate the human impulse to reinvent reality."[55]

This text is also revealing of Charney's newly defined attitude toward Montreal: that of an "architect" whose ongoing project is the *reinvention* of the city.[56] This focus on reinvention and the role of figural imagination brings to mind the theoretical work of Aldo Rossi. That Rossi's thinking and projects permeate the work of Charney is obvious.[57] Though Charney himself never refers to Rossi explicitly, the latter's analysis of the city as a *fait urbain* – "urban fact" – is a direct precedent to Charney's own conception.[58] Yet any mention of Rossi's import is bound to be problematic, first because of the accessibility of his work in translation – his main opus, *The Architecture of the City* published in 1966, became available in English only in 1982 – and second because it underwent significant changes during the 1970s.[59] Moving away from the "scientific" approach propounded in *The Architecture of the City*, Rossi developed a project – the Analogous City – that elevated the role of imagination in the conception of the city.[60] Viewed in this light, Charney's call to reinvent the reality of the city is not unlike Rossi's fostering of imagination in the Analogous City.

Charney's dual process of reading and reinvention also made full use of insights provided by psychoanalysis. His 1982 article "To Whom It May Concern" is a case in point.[61] This manifesto-like essay was illustrated with a series of photographs taken by architecture students that were deemed to be "significant manifestations of contemporary architecture" in Quebec. Presented under the title "The City of Knowledge," a pair of images is described as follows (see Figs. 34.13 and 34.14):

In Montreal, there still exist two cities: that of urban knowledge, a city of quartiers and that of architecture, buried in that other city that is the metropolis. These two cities live one inside each other like Freud's analogy of the collective psyche, which he based on an image of Rome where all the buildings of every era existed together. It could be said that Montreal's libido, its life, exists still in the city of urban knowledge where ruins project its future.[62]

The thought that an imaginary, libidinal city lived within the existing city was reiterated in his contributions to the Pliny exhibition at the Montreal Museum of Fine Arts in 1983.[63] Centred on the *concours d'émulation* on the restitution of the famous roman villa described in a letter to Pliny, this exhibition offered Charney an ideal context to reassess this psychoanalytic view of the city. This idea is referred to in "Of Temples and Sheds," his essay on the purported meaning of the exhibition.[64] It is also alluded to in *Pliny on My Mind*, his installation constructed inside the walls of the museum. Describing one of the two works comprising the installation, he wrote: "A Roman villa is reconstructed out of the fragments of a Montreal tenement, a process that establishes a contemporary register of former objects."[65] Here again, Montreal's urban form provided the material substratum for this transhistorical reinvention.

This will to reinvent, in which the existing city offers itself as a subject of analysis, found its most compelling embodiment in his project for the CCA garden inaugurated in 1989. (See Pl. 38.) Built on a derelict piece of land across from the CCA museum, the garden offered Charney the ideal occasion to pursue his decipherment of the city. Given the complexity and richness of its design, which included an arcade, cadastral walls, eleven allegorical columns, as well as plant material, he felt the need to describe at length both the conceptual process and the resulting meaning.[66] Yet by his own admission, this rationalization was not meant to fool anyone:

The project for the CCA garden was tightly argued, but in its supporting logic, it is a pure creation. In the end, these dreams do not exist. As with the idea to haul the nineteenth-century industrial city onto the belvedere: if one looks carefully from the belvedere toward the city below the hill, there is almost nothing left to see. One has to really push the imagination.[67]

3.7 Melvin Charney, *Villas of Pliny*

But this void in the view did not mean an absence from the mind. In fact, all the building types of Charney's early discovery of Montreal – the grain elevators, the industrial buildings, the triplexes – are there, monumentalized in these rows of allegorical columns. It confirmed, if

confirmation were needed, that this summoning of the imagination process was as much about the analyst as it was about the subject analysed.[68]

Towards the "School of Montreal"

As mentioned above, the publication of "The Montrealness of Montreal" coincided with the creation of the Urban Architecture Unit at the Université de Montréal.[69] Though Charney was only one of three professors teaching in this studio, his writings were central to the development of the Unit's discourse and methodology. During its twelve years of existence (1978–90), the Unit proved to be a formidable vehicle through which his continuing work of description of Montreal could be translated in terms of architectural prescription.

At the very beginning, the focus of the Unit's work was the analysis of the existing city. The students were initially strongly discouraged from drawing. Figuration, however, came back with a vengeance in the early 1980s. This radical change was brought to light in two exhibitions of student work. The first of these, *Intervention en contexte montréalais*, which was shown in an art gallery in 1982, highlighted the "reintroduction of architectural figuration" and the "return to architectural drawing as a visionary instrument."[70] Two years later, the second exhibition was organized under the title *Lieux et figures: Montréal – neuf projets d'architecture*.[71] It presented a series of works in which the city was subjected to a kind of hermeneutic reading through the act of drawing. Focusing on Montreal's urban spaces, the projects illustrated the need for a "construction of the city" in a spirit that recalled Léon Krier's manifesto for the reconstruction of the European city.[72] Yet the students did not limit themselves to a single figural model, their graphic representations evoking sources as diverse as Rob Krier's *Urban Space* (1979), Colin Rowe and Fred Koetter's *Collage City* (1978), and Rem Koolhaas's *Delirious New York* (1978).

In 1992, the work of the Unit was presented in a retrospective exhibition, *Montréal en projets: Dix années d'architecture urbaine*,[73] and recorded in the accompanying bilingual catalogue, *City, Metaphors, Urban Constructs: Urban Architecture in Montreal 1980–1990*.[74] The students' primary focus of attention as stated in the catalogue – "The specificity of Montreal, the persistence of an urban structure unique in North America, was both the subject and object of the work of the Unit" – was clearly indebted to Charney.[75] The same is true of the Unit's changing approach over the years, a change that can be read as a record of his own semiological turn.[76] In his retrospective assessment of the Unit's history, Charney wrote: "The textuality of urban form present in the work of the Unit and its focus on precedent as a conceptual

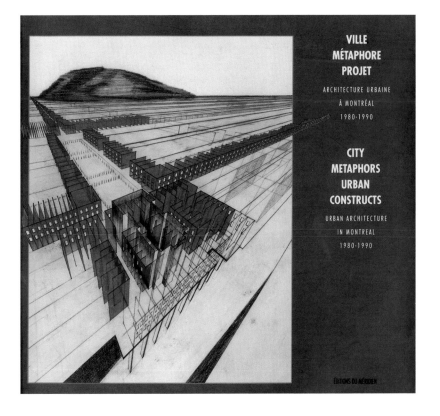

3.9 Cover of *City Metaphors, Urban Constructs: Urban Architecture in Montreal, 1980–1990*, 1992.

device introduced slippages in the design process, between precedent and analogy, between analogy and metaphor."[77] While precedents, analogies, and metaphors were key to his own work, it is to the last term that he gave the central role.[78] In echo to his own practice, Charney remarked that "in a third and final stage, the work of the Unit turned to metaphor as a generative tool of urban architecture."[79]

Be that as it may, by the end of the decade, the student works had indeed become highly metaphorical, and the Montreal depicted appeared more and more as an imaginary city. The slippages alluded to by Charney were such that Montreal's unique urban structure proved to be a palimpsest rather than a simple manuscript. As such, the exhibition offered a clear demonstration that the Unit's approach to architectural prescription had more to do with representation than about mere reconstruction.

While the twelve years of the Urban Architecture Unit offered Charney a student laboratory to foster the exploration of architectural figuration, his own venture into the realm of urban prescription was to have a markedly different outcome.[80] The core of this endeavour was the production of a report on the Faubourg Saint-Laurent for the Service de l'habitation et du développement urbain of the City of Montreal. This was the first consulting work Charney had ever received from the city administration. Focused on a heavily damaged neighbourhood immediately north of the old city, the report bore the subtitle "D'un savoir urbain à une vision éclairée du développement du faubourg."[81] Completed in early 1990, the report was commissioned by the administration of Mayor Jean Doré, who had made an election promise in 1986 to approach city development from a fresh angle after the long years of speculative urbanization.[82] The context was thus ripe for the production of a study that would establish the basis of both a new understanding of the city's urban form and a new methodology to guide urban inter-

ventions. Divided into three parts, the report examines first the character and urban structure of the faubourg, second its current dynamic, and third the proposed strategies of development.

At the outset, Charney cites widespread recognition that the city possesses a unique urban character, a belief he was instrumental in putting forth.[83] Responding to the rhetorical question "what constitutes, specifically, the urban character of Montreal?" he answers: "It is obvious that we refer to nothing other than the traditional city, which we chose to call the 'classical' city: the structure of the city of neighbourhoods existing within the structure of Montreal between 1850 and 1925. The remaining traces of this structure clearly demonstrate the existence of an 'urban project,' of an *innate knowledge* inscribed within the physical form of the city."[84]

This brief passage asserts the two pivotal notions on which the entire study is based. The first is the idea that both the structure and the components of the *quartiers* resulted from the implementation of a *savoir inné* – which can be translated as immanent urban knowledge. Developed in his writings of the 1960s, and specifically applied to his readings of Montreal in the 1970s, this idea reached its ultimate expression in the report. Yet contrary to the earlier essays, where "the people" are invoked at length, the report is strangely mute about the social body that incarnates this immanent urban knowledge. The second is the idea that while Montreal has gone through four stages of development, one of the stages is that of the *ville "classique."* Adapting the interpretive model proposed in his "Montrealness" essay, Charney associates each of these historical phases with a specific urban model. The model of the *ville "classique"* corresponds to the moment when the city – following the logic of its immanent "urban project" – has reached its highest level of coherence and completion. But the quotation marks added to the word *classique* cannot fail to underline the ambiguous usage of the term, a multi-layered meaning that points to an "established model or standard" while also hinting at the idea of "lasting significance" as well as that of a specific historical period.

Going beyond the mandate he was given, Charney chose to write a report that was didactic rather than simply prescriptive, offering an authentic "method" to rebuild the city. Central to this method was the identification of the "irreducible elements of the general plan" in order to formulate "a grammar and an ontology" of the urban form of the neighbourhood.[85] Based on the description of a series of "typical" elements – the block, the street, the square, the boulevard – Charney's urban grammar sheds light on the morphology and syntax that structure the existing city. Given the diversity of the city's formal components, this grammar tends somewhat to oversimplify the complexities of both the formation process and the existing forms of Montreal's neighbourhoods.[86] But it no doubt offers a powerful means to make sense of the city's intricate structuration.

The method proposed by Charney was to build the city by means of its main public spaces – its streets and squares – and the last section of the report is illustrated with drawings that represent the different interventions envisioned. Based on the close reading of remaining fragments, these interventions proposed a kind of architectural restitution emulating the types identified in the urban "grammar." One of the drawings, titled "Le faubourg reconstitué," is an axonometric that shows the whole neighbourhood as it would appear after the proposed urban interventions. Taking into account the two scales of the existing city – the classical and the modern – this graphic reconstitution has an eerie, even disturbing, quality – that of "an ideal city, homogeneous and timeless," to quote the architect Pierre Beaupré.[87]

This view of the "reconstructed" city was in sharp contrast with the figural explorations and metaphorical constructions conceived within

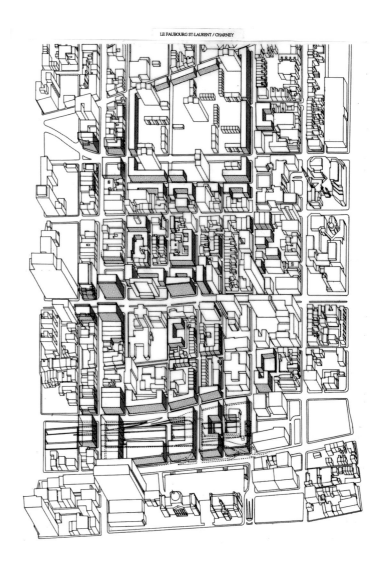

3.10 *Le Faubourg St-Laurent*, Pl. 63: A plan of the reconstituted Faubourg, 1990.

the school's Atelier. Yet both types of graphic representations were linked by the same ethos, one that posited the city as a form rather than as an idea, or, more precisely, as an idea of the city embodied in a form. In effect, the report is essentially based on the reading and production of graphic documents (maps, plans, axonometrics, and so forth) from which human presence and agency are totally absent, depicting a world where processes and forms appear self-motivated and self-generated.[88] Given that the methodology adopted for the report was heavily indebted to the morphological and typological studies produced by European advocates of urban architecture, this absence of actors should not come as a complete surprise.[89] These studies were, after all, primarily concerned with the formation and form of the city. Yet some of them were not averse to taking into consideration the practices of the urban dweller as well as the sensory experiences of the viewer/user.[90] The answer to this discrepancy, if there is one, may lie elsewhere: that beyond the idea of a collective agency, Charney may have returned to the view that urban architecture as a practice rested, ultimately, on the enactment of a formal gesture guided by the expert hand of the architect.

Nevertheless, Charney's report had a direct impact on the urban fabric of the neighbourhood. The most tangible was the construction of the Place de la Paix in 1994. Built on the traces of the former Place du Marché on St-Laurent Boulevard directly in front of the Monument-National theatre, the Place de la Paix was erected on the same stretch of street that had been the subject of Charney's first photographic panorama a quarter of a century before. His report also had a major impact on the way the city administration envisioned urban development. The Service de l'urbanisme adopted his precepts of urban architecture, commissioning a number of studies intended to regenerate targeted Montreal neighbourhoods.[91] Some of these reports were undertaken by Charney himself. In 1991, he completed a study on the city's Faubourg Québec located on the eastern edge of Old Montreal.[92] Pursuing the hypothesis that public spaces are the generators of the city, the report contained a proposal for the reconstruction of the Carré Viger, a mid-nineteenth-century square that had almost vanished from both the urban fabric and the city's memory. The same year, he contributed to another study whose mandate was to rethink the configuration of the rue de la Commune in Old Montreal, thus returning to the site of his very first essay on the preservation of the old city.[93]

A few years after the submission of the report, both the student projects of the Unit and Charney's own consulting work would be reunited under a single umbrella, that of the so-called "School of Montreal."[94] Identified and discussed during the 1994 colloquium Montréal: Agir dans la ville, the "School of Montreal" was the crowning achievement of Charney's engagement, over more than twenty years, in the decipherment and reinvention of the city.[95] By the time the importance of this "School" was finally recognized, its concrete embodiment as a living entity had already ceased to exist. But its knowledge and methods were to have a lasting impact on the practice of urban design in Montreal.[96]

From "Montrealness" to *Montréalité*

By the beginning of the twenty-first century, Charney's dialogical encounter with the city began to decline, a change that coincided with his retirement from teaching at the Université de Montréal. Interestingly, it is at this very moment that his idea of "montrealness," the one that encapsulated better than any other metaphor the specificity and uniqueness of the city, was to acquire a new life of its own.

In an important essay published in 2003, Luc Noppen and Lucie K. Morisset, architectural historians at the Université du Québec à Montréal, revisited the idea of "montrealness," launching an inquiry whose impact is still being felt. Titled "La montréalité de Montréal, ou l'invention du paysage montréalais," the study sought to reframe Charney's contribution within the context of the debate on urban identity.[97] The crux of their argument is that after many years of attempted conceptualizations of Montreal's identity, it is Charney who had finally managed to give it a "material form."[98] Called *montréalité*, this newly defined identity was not only a characterization of the existing city; they claimed it also served to formulate a *projet d'édification*, a vision of a desirable future. The authors were nevertheless skeptical of Charney's portrayal, questioning the lack of precision of the traits identified: "It seems that a tangible characterization is still wanting if we have the ambition to think of the city as a form rather than as an idea."[99] In spite of these reservations, however, the pair of architectural historians wholeheartedly adopted the term *montréalité* to discuss the city's architectural identity, thus giving it a broad appeal within the field of urban studies on Montreal.[100]

Yet if Charney was the clever author of the expression "montrealness," he had little to do with its French alter ego, *montréalité*. As a matter of fact, the 1992 French translation of his memorable essay bore the succinct, straightforward title: "Montréal."[101] In this revised version, the expression *montréalité* is nowhere to be found. In fact, Charney seems never to have published anything using this expression. Aware of this fact, Noppen and Morisset suggested instead that the French version of the term should probably be attributed to the architectural historian Yves Deschamps, who had published an essay entitled *Montréalité* in 1998.[102] But Deschamps's piece refers to works of postwar modernism, not to Charney's vision of an urban vernacular. To complicate matters further, the French expression was used long before, but in discursive contexts that were markedly different.[103]

Nevertheless, Noppen and Morisset played a leading role in putting the term *montréalité* on the academic map. Since then, the expression has had an extraordinary critical fortune. Following their example, a number of scholars from various fields – among them history, sociology, anthropology, and literature – have adopted the notion of *montréalité* as a component of their interpretations.[104] But the "montrealness" of Charney may not be the same thing

as the *montréalité* of Noppen, Morisset, and their followers. While Charney's use of the term emerged out of his thinking about urban architecture, that of Noppen and Morisset was linked to their concern with urban identity and the characterization of the built landscape. As we have seen, Charney's conception is rooted in the belief in the existence of some innate knowledge, in something immanent. By contrast, that of his interpreters is primarily indebted to theories of representation, to something that is socially constructed. This distinction is revealed in the way the notion was put to use in a subsequent contribution by Noppen in which he analyzes the "metropolitan" character of architectural projects designed by local architects.[105] In this context, *montréalité* is mobilized to discuss the identity of the architect's work, not that of the city's essential form.

This difference may seem minute, but it is key to understanding the slippage in meaning from "montrealness" to *montréalité*. This shift was made explicit in the work of one of their students. In an ambitious urban studies dissertation, Alena Prochazka placed the concept of *montréalité* at the centre of her investigations on contemporary architecture in Montreal.[106] Moving away from the idea that "montrealness is in the street pattern,"[107] she implies instead that *montréalité* is to be found in the architecture itself. The stated goal of the study, which examines a series of projects realized between 1992 and 2003, is to "understand how architecture and urban design projects are invested with the idea of *montréalité*."[108] To do so, the author distinguishes between three types of *montréalité* – the "progressive," the "preservationist," and the *melvinienne* – thus breaking up this unitary concept into distinct ideological paradigms. To refine this approach further, she also develops a sophisticated method by which to identify and analyze the traits – or "indexes" – of *montréalité*. Notwithstanding the heuristic potential of such a method, the concept of *montréalité* developed in the wake of Noppen and Morisset's teaching has reached a point where it has little to do with Charney's original conception of "montrealness."

Epilogue

"I have been interested in the phenomena of the city for a very long time," Charney declared in a 1989 interview. "I saw it as a kind of encyclopaedia of existence."[109] In this compendium, Montreal no doubt took up the most pages. That Charney's personal, intellectual, and creative trajectory was deeply anchored in Montreal is self-evident. His Montreal was not always a comforting place. Transformed, if not violated, by the radical interventions of the postwar period and beyond, his Montreal was rather a *cité souffrante*, a "suffering city," to evoke the image conjured up by Johanne Lamoureux.[110] But it was also a Montreal in which he found hope, however timid, for a better future.

As we look back at Charney's work on Montreal, it would be tempting to divide its trajectory into two broad periods, the first devoted to description, the second to prescription. This significant shift could be conveniently articulated around the publication of "The Montrealness of Montreal" – the essays in architectural description coming before, the student Atelier and the consulting work coming after. While this view could no doubt be substantiated, I would argue instead that Charney's engagement with Montreal was part and parcel of a unique project – not merely an architectural project, but a project conceived in anthropological terms, that is, as a *fiction opératoire*, an "operational fiction," following the definition given by Jean-Pierre Boutinet in his celebrated *Anthropologie du projet*.[111] A key aspect of Boutinet's operational fiction is the continuous, thoughtful attention toward something that remains elusive: "To conceive the project as a fiction is to affirm, if one understands fiction according to its etymology, that there is creation, there is fashioning by the mind

of something that the mind will never be able to inscribe fully within the real world: something that goes beyond reality, that escapes it, while continually focusing its attention."[112]

Charney's unrelenting Montreal project was conveyed through many different media and expressed in many different ways: historically-minded essays, critical manifestos, consultant reports, student explorations, photographic works, ephemeral installations, and permanent constructions. They are testimony to the fact that Montreal was always on his mind. And, in the end, although Charney's Montreal may have been an imaginary construct, it is a work of fiction that left a deep impression on the perception and construction of the contemporary city.

NOTES

The writing of this essay was supported by the Fonds québécois de la recherche sur la société et la culture (FQRSC). My thinking greatly benefited from many discussions with Louis Martin. I would like to thank him for his rigour and commitment to bringing this project to fruition. My appreciation also goes to Cammie McAtee for her balanced criticism, editorial scrutiny, and constant support. I dedicate this essay to Claude Lamoureux.

1 See Julien Gracq, *La forme d'une ville* (Paris: José Corti, 1985).
2 Chapter 33, 332–41.
3 For a discussion of Charney's photographic work, see Pierre Landry, ed., *Melvin Charney* (Montreal: Musée d'art contemporain de Montréal, 2002).
4 Chapter 40, 426.
5 See the black and white photographs taken in 1956 in Landry, *Melvin Charney*, 22–35.
6 Chapter 8, 88–93.
7 "By-law creating the Jacques-Viger Commission," no. 2760, City of Montreal, 16 August 1962. The Historic District of Old Montreal was established by a Quebec government bill dated 8 January 1964.
8 Chapter 8, 91.
9 Commenting on this building type, he wrote: "It always takes some imagination to appreciate 19th century grain elevators as architectonic monu-

ments of our new cybernetic society." Chapter 8, 91. See also chapter 18, "Grain Elevators Revisited," 169–78

10 For a discussion of Charney's approach to modern architecture in the 1960s, see my essay "'Pour une définition de l'architecture …': Melvin Charney et la modernité architecturale dans les années 1960," *Trames* 15 (Université de Montréal, 2004): 25–52.

11 Chapter 10, 117–19.

12 Chapter 9, 108–16. For an analysis of this model, see my essay "Pour une définition de l'architecture."

13 Chapter 10, 119.

14 See Norbert Schoenauer, "The New City Centre," in *Architectural Design* 37, no. 7 (July 1967): 311.

15 Melvin Charney, "Understanding Montreal," in *Exploring Montreal*, ed. Pierre Beaupré and Annabel Slaight (Toronto: Greey de Pencier, 1974), 14–27.

16 Ibid., 22.

17 Ibid.

18 Ibid., 23.

19 Reyner Banham, *Megastructure: Urban Futures of the Recent Past* (London: Thames and Hudson, 1976). On this issue, see especially Inderbir Singh Riar, "Montreal and the Megastructure, ca. 1967," in *Expo 67: Not Just a Souvenir,* ed. Rhona Richman Kenneally and Johanne Sloan (Toronto: University of Toronto Press, 2010), 193–210.

20 An argument supported by a reproduction of Charney's section drawing of the new downtown. See Banham, *Megastructure*, 119.

21 See chapter 25, 246–64. For a discussion of this essay, see Legault, "Pour une définition de l'architecture."

22 Chapter 25, 264.

23 Charney's critical position was close to that formulated around the same time by Alexander Tzonis in the introduction to his book *Towards a Non-Oppressive Environment: An Essay* (New York: G. Braziller, 1972). It is worth mentioning that during this period, Charney worked on three different manuscripts, each dealing with aspects of the political dimension of architecture in Quebec. Though unpublished, these manuscripts reveal a deep commitment to this approach. See Louis Martin, Chapter 23, 223–35.

24 Chapter 27, 271–5.

25 See Johanne Sloan, "Conceptual Art Meets Urban Attitudes: Melvin Charney and the 1972 Exhibition *Montréal Plus ou Moins*?" (paper abstract, 25 January 2011).

26 Chapter 27, 271–5.

27 This panorama recalls the photographic work of Edward Ruscha entitled *Every Building on the Sunset Strip* (1966). See Fig. 21.12.

28 On Corridart, see chapter 31. See also Hélène Lipstadt and Michèle Picard, "Corridart: Public Space Destroyed and Remembered," in *Architecture and Ideas* 2 (Fall 1998): 76–91.

29 Chapter 33, 332–41.

30 Nikolaus Pevsner, *The Englishness of English Art* (London: Architectural Press, 1956).

31 On this foundational approach to Charney's thinking and work, see Louis Martin, Chapter 23, 224–26.

32 Quote from typewritten preliminary version of "Towards a Definition of Architecture in Quebec" found in Charney's archive.

33 Charney, "Understanding Montreal."

34 Ibid., 14.

35 Ibid., 15.

36 Ibid., 17.

37 In response to this enticing yet debatable interpretation, I have tried elsewhere to show that the Montreal grid and its associated urban form were the outcome of a process that entailed subdivision models that were shared by the professionals of the city's two main sociolinguistic groups. See Réjean Legault, "Architecture et forme urbaine à Montréal: le développement du quartier Saint-Jean-Baptiste de 1870 à 1914" (master's thesis, Faculté de l'aménagement, Université de Montréal, 1986).

38 At this juncture, I am tempted to refer to Paul Veyne, who reminded us that in historical narratives, there are no facts, only interpretations. Paul Veyne, *Comment on écrit l'histoire* (Paris: Seuil, 1971).

39 Chapter 33, 333.

40 Ibid.

41 See especially the essay by Michel Barcelo, urban planner and professor at the Université de Montréal, "Montreal – Planned and Unplanned," *Architectural Design* 37, no. 7 (July 1967): 307–10.

42 See Max Derruau, "À l'origine du 'rang' canadien," *Cahiers de géographie du Québec* 1, no. 1 (1956): 39–47.

43 Charney, "Understanding Montreal," 15.

44 Chapter 33, 333.

45 In an essay published in 1978, Charney argues that Montreal's orthogonal street grid, which followed the alignment of the *rangs*, attests to a continuity that can be traced from Etruscan origins to the Roman cardo, to the medieval tradition that produced the Zahringer new towns of the eleventh century, and to the nineteenth-century

typology of the city. See chapter 32. It is only in the 1980 text, however, that he makes reference to Paul Hofer's essay in R. Hager, ed. *The Zahringer New Towns* (Zurich: Swiss Federal Institute of Technology, 1966).

46 Chapter 33, 334. In his exhaustive study of the origins of North American's city plans, John Reps shows that they were always based on the implementation of some pre-existing model. See Reps, *The Making of Urban America A History of City Planning in the United-Stated* (Princeton: Princeton University Press, 1965).

47 See especially Paul-André Linteau, "L'histoire urbaine au Québec: bilan et tendances," *Revue d'histoire urbaine* 1 (February 1972): 7–10.

48 In addition to these two terms, Charney sometimes also referred to the triad description–prescription–implementation.

49 André Corboz, "La description: entre lecture et écriture," in *Le territoire comme palimpseste et autres essais* (Paris: Éditions de l'Imprimeur, 2001): 251; my translation.

50 Melvin Charney, "On Interpreting Montreal: The City of the City" (unpublished essay, ca. 1981), n.p.

51 Charney, "On Interpreting Montreal," 1.

52 Ibid.

53 Joseph Rykwert, *On Adam's House in Paradise: The Idea of the Primitive Hut in Architectural History* (New York: Museum of Modern Art, 1972).

54 Charney, "On Interpreting Montreal," 2.

55 Ibid., 5.

56 It is the notion of *réinvention* that is at the core of a book published in conjunction with an exhibition on Charney's work, *Les Paraboles*, presented in France in 1997. Jean-François Chevrier et al., *Melvin Charney parcours de la réinvention = about reinvention* (Caen: Fonds régional d'art contemporain de Basse-Normandie, 1998).

57 Georges Adamczyk, among others, has stressed this connection in his essay on Charney's student atelier at the Université de Montréal: "The teachers of the Urban Architecture Unit often refer explicitly to the writing and projects of Aldo Rossi and Giorgio Grassi." See G. Adamczyk, "The City as a School," in *City, Metaphors, Urban Constructs: Urban Architecture in Montreal 1980–1990*, ed. Irena Latek (Montréal: Éditions du Méridien, 1992), 11.

58 See Aldo Rossi, *The Architecture of the City* (Cambridge, MA: MIT Press, 1982).

59 Before the 1982 English translation, his writings and projects were known primarily through pub-

lications like the special issue dedicated to Rossi by the Japanese journal *A + U* 65 (1976).

60 On the shifts in Rossi's work and the importance of his project for the Analogous City, see Jean-Pierre Chupin, *Analogie et théorie en architecture* (Gollion: Éditions In Folio, 2010), 127–81.

61 Chapter 34, 342–60.

62 Chapter 34, 350.

63 The Villas of Pliny and Classical Architecture in Montreal. Organized jointly by the Montreal Museum of Fine Arts and the Canadian Centre for Architecture, the exhibition was presented from 14 October to 11 December 1983

64 Charney writes: "It is not so much that Pliny's villa can be discovered lurking in the structure of this quartier [Hochelaga-Maisonneuve], as evidence of fundamental order that gives form to the city as an urban construct: the figure of a city within the city." Chapter 37, 386.

65 In Alessandra Latour et al., eds., *Parables and Other Allegories: The Work of Melvin Charney, 1975–1990* (Montreal: Canadian Centre for Architecture, 1991), 137.

66 See "A Garden for the Canadian Centre for Architecture," 396–416.

67 Louis Martin, "L'architecture comme roman: entretien avec Melvin Charney," *Parachute* 56 (Oct.–Dec. 1989): 11; my translation.

68 On the allegorical columns and their oscillation between document and monument, see Jean-François Chevrier in *Melvin Charney parcours de la réinvention = about reinvention* (Caen: Fond Regional d'Art Contemporain de Basse-Normandie, 1997), 173.

69 Officially established in 1978, the Atelier d'architecture urbaine was directed by professors Melvin Charney, Denys Marchand, and Alan Knight.

70 Louis Martin and Claude Lamoureux, "Projets d'architecture urbaine," *Intervention* 18 (1983): 26–7; my translation. The exhibition was presented at the Articule Gallery in Montreal in August 1982.

71 The exhibition was presented at the Optica Gallery from 5 September to 29 September 1984. See Claude Lamoureux, "Architecture urbaine: innover dans la continuité," *Continuité* 22 (1984): 23–4.

72 See Robert-L. Delevoy and Anthony Vidler, *Architecture rationnelle: la reconstruction de la ville européenne* (Bruxelles: Éditions A.A.M., 1978).

73 MONTRÉAL EN PROJET: Dix années d'architecture urbaine, an exhibition presented at the

Centre de design of the Université du Québec à Montréal from 21 May to 28 June 1992

74 Irena Latek, ed., *City, Metaphors, Urban Constructs: Urban Architecture in Montreal 1980–1990* (Montreal: Éditions du Méridien, 1992).

75 Charney, "Foreword," in Latek, ed., *City, Metaphors, Urban Constructs*, 7.

76 For an in-depth discussion of Charney's "semiological turn," see Louis Martin, chapter 23, "Other Monuments," 232–3, and chapter 35, "The Image and Its Double," 363–71.

77 Charney, "Confrontations in Urban Architecture," in Latek, ed., *City, Metaphors, Urban Constructs*, 101

78 In 1977, Charney wrote: "What began in 1970 with the *Memo Series*, which deciphered contextual metaphors including some drawn from events in the news media to compose a museum, evolved by 1976 into Corridart, a museum which built contextual metaphors into the public domain." Charney, "Other Monuments: Four Works, 1970–1976," in *Vanguard* 6, no. 2, The Vancouver Art Gallery (March 1977): 3–8.

79 Charney, "Confrontations in Urban Architecture," in Latek, ed., *City, Metaphors, Urban Constructs*, 102–3.

80 Between 1980 and 1990, as many as 250 students worked within the Unit. See Latek, ed., *City, Metaphors, Urban Constructs,* 125.

81 Melvin Charney, *Le Faubourg St-Laurent: d'un savoir urbain à une vision éclairée du développement du faubourg*, Étude préparée pour le service de l'habitation et du développement urbain de la Ville de Montréal, 14 March 1990.

82 The report was most likely commissioned by Serge Carreau, associate director of the Service de l'habitation et du développement urbain de la Ville de Montréal and former professor at the School of Architecture of the Université de Montréal.

83 Charney, *Le Faubourg St-Laurent,* 22.

84 Ibid.; my translation and my italics.

85 Ibid.

86 The weakest component of this grammar is the attempt to describe the morphogenesis – the formation process over time – of these types, especially the urban block, proposing an interpretation that was not grounded in any substantial historical evidence. See "Pl. 10 Un type de la densification de l'îlot," in Charney, *Le Faubourg St-Laurent.*

87 I borrow this description from Pierre Beaupré's review of the report. See Beaupré, "Aux portes du Vieux-Montréal," in *ARQ – Architecture Québec* 56 (August 1990): 21–6, at 21.

88 This absence of social life and its contradictions was well noted by Beaupré, who wrote: "Les brisures, les antagonismes sociaux, les hiatus s'effacent par la magie du prince." Ibid., 21.

89 See Philippe Panerai et al., eds., *Eléments d'analyse urbaine* (Bruxelles: Éditions A.A.M., 1980); see also Jean Castex et al., *Lecture d'une ville: Versailles* (Paris: Éditions du Moniteur, 1980).

90 See for example Jean-Charles Depaule, "La pratique de l'espace urbain," in Panerai et al., eds., *Eléments d'analyse urbaine*, 127–52.

91 In addition to the reports prepared in 1991–92 by Alan Knight, a professor of the Unit who was then working within the city's Service de l'urbanisme, many studies were written by outside consultants who had been influenced by the teaching of the Unit.

92 Melvin Charney, *Le carré Viger / Le faubourg Québec*, Étude réalisée pour la Société d'habitation et de développement de Montréal, 15 March 1991.

93 *Promenade de la Commune. Plan de réaménagement*, Service de l'habitation et du développement urbain de la Ville de Montréal, July 1991. The other architects who contributed to the study were Aurèle Cardinal and Peter Rose.

94 Louis Martin, "De l'école à la ville: la naissance d'une école de Montréal," in *ARQ – Architecture Québec* 83 (February 1995): 8–13.

95 Organized jointly by the Service de l'habitation et du développement urbain de la Ville de Montréal, the Société d'habitation et de développement de Montréal, the Faculté de l'aménagement of the Université de Montréal and the Canadian Centre for Architecture, the colloquium, Montréal: Agir dans la ville, was held at the CCA 11 and 12 November 1994.

96 A recent report by the City of Montreal documents the influence of the UAU ideas and methods on the practice of urban design in the city. See Gabriel Bodson, *Figures, syntaxe urbaine, projets: architecture urbaine à la ville de Montréal 1990–2001*, Division de la planification urbaine et de la réglementation, Service du développement économique et urbain, Ville de Montréal, 2001.

97 Luc Noppen and Lucie K. Morisset, "La montréalité de Montréal, ou l'invention du paysage montréalais," in *Réinventer pays et paysages*, ed. P. Dieudonné, L.K. Morisset, and Jean-François Simon (Brest: Centre de recherches bretonnes

et celtiques, 2003), 71–101; see also Luc Noppen and Lucie K. Morisset, "Entre identité métropolitaine et identité urbaine: Montréal," in *Identités urbaines: Échos de Montréal* (Montreal: Éditions Nota bene, 2003), 157–79.

98   Noppen and Morisset, "La montréalité de Montréal," 87.

99   Ibid., 101; my translation.

100 Some of their students played a key role in the dissemination of the notion. See especially the contributions of Alena Prochazka: "La montréalité dans tous ses états," in *Montreal-Glasgow*, ed. Bill Marshall (Glasgow: University of Glasgow, 2005), 31–52 ; "La mutation des traits de la *montréalité* contemporaine: le cas des couronnements architecturaux," *JSÉAC* 32, no. 2 (2007): 13–28; "Learning from Montreal?" in *Designing 21st Century Cities in Canada*, An Urban Design Lab University of Calgary Publication, 2008, n.p.

101 Charney, "Montréal: Formes et figures en architecture urbaine," in Latek, ed., *City, Metaphors, Urban Constructs*, 17–30.

102 Yves Deschamps, "Montréalité," *ARQ – Architecture Québec* 102 (April 1998): 12–13.

103 See Alain Stanké, "Montréalités," *Liberté* 28 (July–August 1963): 348–50. More recently, it also appeared in Guy Bellavance, "Développement culturel: montréalités," *Possibles* 11, no. 3 (printemps–été 1987): 53–72; Francine Couture, "L'exposition comme lieu de construction indentitaire: la montréalisation de l'art contemporain," in *Produire la culture, produire l'identité?* ed. Andrée Fortin (Quebec: Les Presses de l'Université Laval, 2000), 87–103.

104 See especially the contributions of Ignace Olazabal, "Le Mile-End comme synthèse d'une montréalité en devenir," in *Les Cahiers du Gres* 6, no. 2 (Winter 2006): 7–16; Kenza Benali, "Les représentations médiatiques d'un quartier en processus de gentrification: le cas du Plateau Mont-Royal à travers la presse francophone" (PhD dissertation, Université du Québec à Montréal / INRS-Urbanisation, 2007); and Jean-Sébastien Barriault, "De la montréalité: L'émergence de Montréal comme lieu de référence" (master's thesis, Département d'histoire, Université Laval, 2007). By 2010, the notion had even reached new shores, informing the work of scholars in countries such as Germany. See Nadine Klopfer, *Die Ordnung der Stadt: Raum und Gesellschaft in Montreal (1880 bis 1930)* (Köln: Böhlau-Verlag, 2010).

105 Luc Noppen, "Les architectes montréalistes: la quête du caractère métropolitain dans le projet architectural résidentiel contemporain," in *Patrimoines pour le XXIe siècle. Regards du Québec et de la Bretagne*, ed. Lucie K. Morisset and Patrick Dieudonné (Quebec: Éditions Nota bene, 2006), 61–115.

106 Alena Prochazka, "Le projet urbain vu comme un catalyseur identitaire: analyse de contributions récentes à la montréalité (1992–2003)" (PhD dissertation, Université du Québec à Montréal, 2009).

107 Noppen and Morisset, "La montréalité de Montréal," 91.

108 Prochazka, "Le projet urbain vu comme un catalyseur identitaire," xxxv.

109 Louis Martin, "L'architecture comme roman: entretien avec Melvin Charney," *Parachute* 56 (octobre–décembre 1989): 9–11; my translation.

110 Johanne Lamoureux makes reference to Robert-Jan Van Pelt's essay, "Into the Suffering City" (Latour, *Parables and Other Allegories*, 35–53) in Lamoureux, "De la construction, ou la traduction des modèles," in *Melvin Charney parcours de la réinvention = about reinvention*, 55.

111 Jean-Pierre Boutinet, *Anthropologie du projet* (Paris: Collection "Quadrige" PUF, 1990).

112 Ibid., 363–4; my translation.

PART TWO

Beginnings

"Beginnings" brings together seven essays which were originally published between 1962 and 1966. In these early texts, Charney searched in precedents for valid principles for contemporary architecture. His essays on pre-modern Mediterranean traditions revealed a tension between the practice of collective space making and the formal images transmitted by the architectural tradition. In the other essays, he studied contemporary phenomena such as the emergence of pop art and the recent architectural mutation of Montreal. His essays on Montreal highlighted the opposition between technological process and formalism in contemporary architecture and established a dialectical reading which is re-formulated throughout this collection. This section is illustrated with a selection of photographs taken by Charney in Montreal and abroad during the 1950s and 1960s.

4

Beginnings

LOUIS MARTIN

Melvin Charney belongs to the first generation of architects who learned the tenets of modern architecture in schools of architecture. While it was imperative to be modern in the 1950s, schools of architecture faced a pedagogical problem: the modern movement bequeathed a body of exemplary works but no unified doctrine for teaching architectural design.

During his studies at McGill from 1952 to 1958, Charney was exposed to a pedagogical system inspired by the teaching methods of the Bauhaus, which had been implanted during the previous decade under the aegis of John Bland. In those years, the school's faculty promoted the architecture of Mies van der Rohe in a manner that Charney found superficial and provincial: modernism at McGill was merely a style pasted on old plans, the last eclectic style of the nineteenth century. But one of his professors, Stuart Wilson, proposed an alternative approach which, echoing the 1950s discourse of the British journal *The Architectural Review,* suggested that the sources of the functionalist tradition were found in vernacular and industrial architecture.[1] This

meant that one would learn more by studying the backyard additions to houses in east end Montreal than by drawing the composed facades of Westmount.

Following the suggestion of Peter Collins, Charney pursued his graduate studies at Yale's school of art and architecture in 1959. Yale proved to be a stimulating environment where he could rub shoulders with the leading figures of the day in both the architectural and the art worlds, the more memorable being Louis I. Kahn, Philip Johnson, Paul Rudolph, John Johansen, Vincent Scully Jr, and James Stirling. During that year, he drew three projects directed respectively by Johnson, Kahn, and Johansen. These professors belonged to the second generation of modernists who, caught in a double bind, faced the dilemma of either imitating the formal language of the masters of modern architecture or of imitating the masters' creative freedom in inventing their own individual language of form.

With his promotion of Mies van der Rohe, Philip Johnson had been a prime advocate of the first option during the postwar period. But, in the second part of the 1950s, he developed a critique of the international style he had himself invented in the early 1930s. Bored with aesthetic puritanism, Johnson advocated a return to historical precedents to legitimize a functional eclecticism admitting more sensuous, if not arbitrary, forms. While Johnson identified, in his speeches of the period, the shortcomings of the functionalist doctrine he had learned from Gropius and Breuer at Harvard in the 1940s, the design method he proposed was hardly an innovation since it derived from the beaux-arts study of precedents.[2]

In contrast, Kahn chose the second path, like Paul Rudolph, John Johansen, and Eero Saarinen, the so-called "form givers" promoted by Yale's architectural magazine *Perspecta*.[3] Among these, Kahn was most influential on Charney.

Kahn and the Brutalist Image

As early as 1955, the British critic Reyner Banham associated Kahn's work with the new brutalism, the radical trend raging in England after the phrase was introduced by Alison and Peter Smithson in the December 1953 issue of *Architectural Design*.[4] Banham provided a pedigree and exposed the principles of the British brutalist "movement." According to him, the brutalist object had three characteristics: "(1) formal legibility of the plan, (2) clear exposition of structure and (3) valuation of materials for their inherent qualities 'as found.'" But ultimately, the decisive quality of a brutalist work was precisely its brutality. In this connection, Kahn's Yale Art Center could not be included in the brutalist canon because, in spite of Kahn's honest handling of materials, Banham argued, its detailing was "arty" and did not match the under-designed eloquence of the Smithsons' school at Hunstanton. The brutalist quality of the Smithsons' building resided in the ruthless and unashamed logic of its *image*. Banham wrote:

One of the reasons for this obtrusive logic is that it contributes to the apprehensibility and coherence of the building as a visual entity, because it contributes to the building as 'an image.' *An image* – with these two words we bridge the gap between the new brutalism as a descriptive label covering in varying degrees of accuracy, two or three buildings, and the new brutalism as a slogan, and we also go some way to bridge the gap between the meaning of the term as applied to architecture and its meaning as applied to painting and sculpture. The word *image* in this sense is one of the most intractable and most useful in contemporary aesthetics and some attempt to explain it must be made.[5]

Banham agreed that "image" seemed to be a word that describes anything and everything, but ultimately, he maintained, it meant something "visually valuable, but not in the standards of classical aesthetics."[6] The classical ideal supposed beauty was "that which seen, pleases," whereas the image was "that which seen, affects the emotions, a situation which could subsume the pleasure caused by beauty." Precisely, the brutalist image *perturbed*: it was radically anti-art or, at any rate, anti-beauty, in the classical sense of the word. For Banham, what was equally important was the nature of the cause for this specific reaction: what pleased in the classical was an abstract quality, beauty, whereas what moved a new brutalist was "the thing itself, in its totality, and with all its overtones of human association." According to Banham, these ideas were close but not entirely similar to recent anti-academic aesthetics, such as Michel Tapié's concept of *un Art Autre*. Nonetheless, "this concept of *image* [was] common to all aspects of the New Brutalism in England." And in architecture, the concept of image was quite precise: "Basically, it requires that the building should be an immediately apprehensible visual entity, and that the form grasped by the eye should be confirmed by experience of the building in use. Further that this form should be entirely proper to the functions and materials of the building, in their entirety. Such a relationship between structure, function and form is the basic commonplace of all good building of course, the demand that this form should be apprehensible and memorable is the apical uncommonplace which makes good building into architecture."[7]

The new brutalism was evidently an heir of functionalism. Its ethical message meant to restore the functional integrity of the object and the truthful expression of construction which is encapsulated in the phrase "what you see is real and true." But, as Banham's conclusion confirms, "memorability as an image" was the prime and necessary quality of brutalist architecture and what distinguished it from routine functionalism.

If Banham's partisan promotion of the new brutalism had undeniable effects on the propagation of the trend in the second part of the 1950s, it is more difficult to assess the real significance of his concept of image in the evaluation of contemporaneous architecture since the word does not seem to have generated any significant debate. Retrospectively, the perturbing image of the new brutalism appears an idiosyncratic and underdeveloped concept, at best a transitional term opening architectural discourse to issues related to the meaning of form. So, it is most probable that students of architecture, who like Charney were aware of the new brutalism, integrated the "image" more or less consciously in the horizon of their preoccupations.[8]

The Lessons of Louis I. Kahn

When Charney met Louis Kahn at Yale in 1959, his professor had acquired the stature of a master builder of international reputation. In effect, that very year, Kahn was invited to deliver the concluding discourse at what would be the last Congrès Internationaux d'Architecture Moderne (CIAM) meeting, an event organized by Team Ten at Otterlo.[9] In contrast to the other "form-givers," Kahn offered more than new forms and experimental structural concepts: he proposed new words, a new vocabulary to probe the essence of architecture, past and modern. The CIAM meeting was for him an excellent platform to expose his evolving philosophy; and in the context of the current study, the transcripts of his speech enable us to grasp what the master taught his students at the time.

In this talk, Kahn made a distinction between design and architecture. In Kahn's own words, design proposed formal solutions to a problem formulated a priori in the program, whereas architecture started with the "realization" of a problem. Kahn's criticism of design was twofold. First, the program, when conceived as a set of normative, budgetary, or aesthetic requirements, was a hindrance since it did not express the "real thing," by which he meant "the real job of architecture" as both symbol and specific design. Kahn illustrated this condition of architecture with the example of a house: "A house has to answer … 'house,' symbolically house, it has to answer 'a house' which is the problem … But the architect lies in his ability to make house, not a house."[10]

In addition, designers tended to impose order with exterior forms. Consequently, designers inevitably had to make compromises in order to make the thing work. This was the wrong approach. In contrast, Kahn believed an architect had to feel the "existence will" of a need and of the form lying undeveloped within that need, as a plant is already within a seed. The architect had to "realize" what the thing wanted to be. This way of thinking enabled the architect to grasp the underlying sense of things. Kahn illustrated his point with a number of examples.

For instance, a street was not merely a road with buildings on each side: the street wanted to be a building, and that was "realization."

In Kahn's philosophy, the city was made up of "institutions." By extension, urbanism was the study of institutions: housing, school, city hall, movement, "the institution of anything you like." Architecture created "institutions" in changing the given program in order to make the program alive to the very "existence will" which started an "institution" in the first place. He said: "The spirit of the start is the most marvellous moment at any time for anything. Because in the start lies the seed for all things that must follow. A thing is unable to start unless it can contain all that ever can come from it. That is the characteristic of a beginning, otherwise it is no beginning – it is false beginning."[11]

This is why Kahn valued archaic form, which was form still loaded with possibilities. He believed that there existed more life in what he called "preform" or "protoform" than in anything that followed. In studying beginnings, the architect realized the essence of things, something he could not achieve if he was thinking of "exterior forms" and of "all kinds of extraneous things."

While design was a mere solution to the given program, architecture was a natural extension of the realization of the problem, the product of an intellectual process rather than a mere preconceived vision. For Kahn, "realization" was the way to answer the new problems of architecture. The new demands were not concerned with style but with new discoveries which would create better institutions. Architecture went to the essence of things while design was concerned with the circumstantial, visible aspect. Using an analogy with music, realization in architecture was akin to composition, and design, to interpretation; Kahn explained: "What material you use is circumstantial; it is a design problem; it is a practical absolute problem. The design is the making of your composition, so that you

can play the music. That is all very important. It is imagery. It is the first thing you see. It is the tangible thing."[12]

Design, as imagery, was seemingly one possible expression of an architectural composition, which was itself triggered by a realization – that is, the discovery of the essence of an architectural phenomenon.[13]

In conclusion, Kahn argued that searching for the root principles of architecture helped one to solve the problem of stylistic imitation and constituted the best approach to keep tradition alive and meaningful: "If you copy Le Corbusier's design you are somewhat of a thief. But if you take that which is in essence architectural from him, you take it very freely, because it does not belong to him either. It belongs to the realm of architecture."[14]

Clearly, Kahn's understanding of design *imagery*, as materialization of the essence of architecture, was completely different from Banham's anti-classical, shocking, and aformal brutalist *image*. However important, the formal imagery produced by design was not the central objective of architecture since it remained for Kahn the circumstantial outcome of a perpetual process of inquiry into the nature of things, the real task of architecture.

The Lessons of Vernacular Architecture

After graduating from Yale, Melvin Charney followed Kahn's advice and probed the beginnings of architecture. This search led him to travel in the eastern Mediterranean countries. In looking at how ancient cultures answered architectural problems, the contemporary architect could learn how to get to the core of the emerging new societal demands. Studying the origins of architecture in search of principles was apparently motivated by a belief in the existence of an architectural essence which by definition could be grasped in both ancient and contemporary examples.

Charney's first publication conveys his feeling when he encountered Istanbul: estrangement, a feeling of unfamiliarity which was, according to Kahn, the first condition of learning. Significantly, the very first paragraphs established that he experienced the city as a series of images: "The unfamiliarity of an environment can sharpen reactions; the people, the way of life, the way the buildings occupy thoughts. These thoughts are examined, image by image, as pages in a journal."[15]

But street life made it difficult to see the architecture, whose illusive and frozen image had to be reconstructed in the mind: "Buildings and streets are dense with people, who spoil the moment, and you wish that they would all go away … Imaginary figures of people are adjusted by the mind's eye to illusive and sudden images, and a sequence of chimneys, and the pattern of dark openings in the wall of a street become buildings. People are always the measure. Ancient work sits empty, alone and cool, as the sculptured image of an architecture."[16]

Venturing into the streets, Charney found what Kahn conceived as the "existence will" of collective space: "The length of this interior street is a building which includes both shops and a street." Urban space revealed itself as a sequence of open-air rooms. Charney's words described precisely what his eyes saw, moving through a doorway, to a city square, to a mosque. The mosque appeared, made of similar parts assembled in a hierarchical montage. As religious building, the mosque created symbolically the "image of a desired heaven on earth"; its interior was the real facade of the building. Separation of small and familiar elements was the rule of the architectural game. According to him, the buildings retained "a sense of process"; consequently they had meaning for a contemporary architecture similarly made of small, prefabricated industrial elements.

The architecture of Istanbul embodied "construction," based on the principle of "piling up" material. In contrast, the troglodyte architecture of Cappadocia was based on the principle of "excavation," by which material was removed from natural rock formations to create inhabitable spaces. In rock-cut architecture, needs dictated the creation of space. As in Kahn's recent projects, servant spaces surrounded served spaces. Use thus dominated expression, just like in contemporary plastic architecture.[17] An order was imposed inside the rock, which maintained its exterior, eroded, natural shape. Without exterior architectural expression, these dwellings inserted into the natural landscape symbolized the confrontation of man and nature. Yet, the landscape of Cappadocia was also characterized by the presence of the discordant image of "constructed architecture" imported by the Christians during the eleventh century. Charney wrote: "The rock-cut dwellings were indigenous to these valleys as an architecture with its own manners and rules. It is the religious environment which here presents a discordant formalism of special interiors cut into the rock."[18]

While the "plan of a rock-cut dwelling began with the cutting of its spaces," religious architecture "began with an image," the image of a known style, of previous examples.[19] Ironically, this "construction" was merely sculpted decoration, a mere image of "construction." "The column shaft, the capital, and the row of beams under a heavy cornice are the parts of a construction. This portico presents a construction. But nothing here was constructed; there is no structure and the columns do not hold anything in place. Constructed architecture was sculpted into the rock with delicate and finished lines."[20]

What separated the indigenous dwellings and the religious environment of Cappadocia was not a difference of principle – both were realized by way of excavation – but the exact difference between architecture and design theorized by Kahn. Formalism began with a preconceived image, which in this case represented a structure of posts and beams that contradicted the very process of excavation. The traditional architecture of Cappadocia thus illustrated the tension between a truly functional vernacular architecture and the formalism of an official architecture essentially preoccupied with monumental expression.

Charney's interest in vernacular architecture was symptomatic of the period's search for an alternative to the received history of architecture which focused almost exclusively on monuments. What was an underground movement became part of the mainstream in 1964 when the Museum of Modern Art in New York presented Bernard Rudofsky's exhibition Architecture without Architects.[21] Charney was critical of this show, which proposed a catalogue of images but no interpretation of construction and symbolism. He was highly aware that the vernacular traditions based on pre-industrial building methods were doomed to disappear.

In his analysis of the trulli of Apulia, he focused on the symbolism of this archetypal form without neglecting their mode of construction. The circular plan of megalithic origin echoed both the protecting wall surrounding the fireplace of the primitive hut and a sacred burial place. It evolved into a standardized form, a circular stone hut, which was used both in the fields and in the construction of villages. The significance of the trulli for contemporary architecture was that it constituted a "clear and strong environmental system … a system that can make functional variations within a standard building method."[22] In addition, this example showed how vernacular architecture created the formal vocabulary of monumental architecture just like vernacular industrial forms preceded the invention of modern architecture. He wrote: "The circular base and conical dome can be considered as a basic form response that can be found in a variety of vernacular traditions. The architectural monuments of a civilization cannot be separated from these basic vernacular responses

which in the first instance nurture a vocabulary of forms. In this sense, modern architecture arrived when architects were able to discover the vernacular forms of industrial technology which had evolved despite them."[23]

The New Tradition Revisited

In his other essays of the early 1960s, Charney examined the recent developments of modern architecture in Montreal as he witnessed the spectacular mutation of the city in that decade.

The frenetic modernization of Montreal led him to ponder the disappearance of large sectors of the Victorian city. What replaced those houses, which were not necessarily rubbish in the first place, were often disappointing commercial structures that caused a rupture in the city fabric. The violence of destruction was symptomatic of the lack of knowledge about the architectural contribution of the nineteenth century. Charney pointed out that the commercial architecture of the second part of the nineteenth century not only prefigured the all-glass structures of modern architecture but also displayed a higher degree of visual clarity inscribed in the careful handling of proportion which was lacking in contemporary buildings.[24]

A detailed analysis of Place Victoria indicated the semi-successful insertion of tall skyscrapers in Montreal. Situated to the west of old Victoria Square, the tower overtook the square "and usurped its name."[25] The new structure symbolized the transformation of a traditional city of streets and squares into a city of dense, vertical clusters of buildings. Moreover, Place Victoria and its siblings, such as Place Ville-Marie, presented a special environmental problem: "The interior circulation spaces – arcades, lobbies, corridors, stairs and elevators – are part of the private building, yet because of the size of the building complex they really serve the public as streets and are in a sense an extension of the public city. In Place Victoria, as in other similar building complexes, this dichotomy is not clearly resolved in the planning."[26]

Yet Place Victoria was superior to the other recent Montreal high-rise office towers because it emphasized "a sense of process set up both in the grouping and in the phasing of the elements of this building." "From both far and near," Charney argued, "a sense of physical clarity in the architecture of this tower separates it from the others." By comparison, I.M. Pei's Place Ville-Marie and Skidmore, Owings, and Merrill's CIL House exhibited "an overt formalism and a two dimensional composition of parts"; their architecture followed a "packaging ideology" which had "all semblance of cool integration" of technology. "However, in Place Victoria," Charney concluded, "integration has in itself become part of the form; the technology of this tower is realized in the architecture, and, as architecture, technology here becomes a human factor."[27]

The World of Pop Art

In these early texts on architecture, Charney showed his mistrust for the formal imagery projected by architects and designers. He did not, however, discard the image altogether. In a rare piece of art criticism, he found in the recent production of American pop artists an alternative and critical handling of the image.[28]

What led critics to see a "movement" in the independent work of these artists, he explained, was their appropriation of a common source of imagery found in the "mechanized landscape of the urban sprawl."[29] That choice was based not on a simple acceptance of mass-produced objects but on an awareness that communications media maintained "a ready-made reality for the populations lost in an urban sprawl." He explained: "The ... urban sprawl itself presents a visual sludge of manipulative images that are devised to be read with the least effort by the largest number of people. Pictures, signs, and symbols tell us to turn, to yield, to stop, to buy pills for relief, beer for thirst, and tires to keep us on the move. It is this visual technocracy that the pop artist confronts. He uses its popular images and he is involved with the means of communication that made these images popular."[30]

For Charney, one could trace the origins of pop art back to Dada and especially to the work of Duchamp. But, he argued, the irony of pop artists differentiated their work from Dada: "Dada was a revolutionary movement; the self-conscious slogan 'épater les bourgeois' dominated the art. There was shock value in exhibiting the ready-made and commonplace object as art ... The contemporary pop artist is no longer assertive. He is, with an ironic detachment, at ease with the banality of his world. He fearlessly uses its popular imagery, and accepts the ready-made and the commonplace for what they are."[31]

Charney suggested that pop art was characterized by an attitude and "a growing idea" rather than by the search for an aesthetic. There was among pop artists "a strenuous allegiance to plain descriptive and deadpan realism, and to the choice of random but archetypal events and objects."[32] He clarified these two aspects of pop art with two literary references. First, pop realism was akin to the French *nouveau roman*: "The pop artist's attitude to reality and his predisposition to the commonplace and banal of our environment have affinities to the French 'anti-novel.' Pop, like the work of Nathalie Sarraute, can be considered to be a refusal to recognize a priority among objects, feelings, and events; as with Sarraute, the status of reality is allowed only to the 'small true fact, the true detail.'"[33]

Second, beyond the choice of the objects, the techniques of pop art defamiliarized the familiar and revealed the hidden mythology underlying the everyday landscape of the urban sprawl. He wrote:

The images the pop artist uses are so looked at that they have become unseen. This built-in alienation from looking at the commonplace of our visual milieu silences at first one's encounter with pop art, and especially with the work of Roy Lichtenstein ... He isolates, enlarges, and fragments these images in his work. He presents them in an impersonal and direct manner without sentiment or emotion ... The effect of this presentation of the subject matter is that of a shock treatment. One is forced to consider these images with an attention never given them before, and they are seen real and intense as if for the first time. "Pour la première fois mise à nu, la réalité mythologique des visions quotidiennes," noted Alain Jouffroy in the catalogue for the Lichtenstein exhibit held in Paris, June, 1963.[34]

These two aspects – the sensitivity to the "small true fact" and the uncovering of the mythological and archetypal realities of pop imagery – did not offer an explicit program for a pop architecture, yet, as discussed below, they played a decisive role in Charney's criticism of architectural monumentality during the 1970s.

If pop art shared with brutalism an interest in the ineloquence of reality and the things themselves, Charney's analysis pointed out significant differences between the two approaches. The techniques of pop art were in part antithetical to the brutalist desire to stir emotion with the brutal fact. Its ironic detachment and analytical precision revealed the unconscious mythology of daily life, of a modern world dominated by technology and money. Pop art thus reflected critically the imagery of the urban sprawl.

There existed no architectural equivalent to pop art's criticism, although Robert Venturi and Reyner Banham speculated on the possibility of an eventual pop architecture.[35] For his part, Charney valued process over formalism,

integration over representation, assemblage of parts over ideological packaging, environmental systems over buildings. In this connection, John Johansen's library at Clark University illustrated what a "post-packaging" design could look like.[36] The parts of the building were uncoupled, separated, and assembled freely to create an "environment" rather than an "object." It was precisely this search for an alternative to traditional architectural imagery that oriented Charney's further investigation into technology during the second half of the 1960s.

NOTES

1 Some of the articles published in the *Architectural Review* are collected in J.M. Richards, *The Functional Tradition in Early Industrial Buildings* (London: Architectural Press, 1958).
2 These included "The Seven Crutches of Modern Architecture"(1954) and "Retreat from the International Style to the Present Scene (1958). See Philip Johnson, *Writings* (New York: Oxford University Press, 1979).
3 See in particular *Perspecta* 7 (1961).
4 At first, the Smithsons' polemics intended to promote an unsentimental attitude which acknowledged the aesthetic qualities of bare brick, concrete, and wood. Later, they argued that this attitude was essentially ethical rather than stylistic. The Smithsons never developed a real theory; Banham's intervention was therefore crucial in the definition of the brutalist credo. See Reyner Banham, "New Brutalism," *Architectural Review* 118 (January 1955): 354–61, and Alison and Peter Smithson, "The New Brutalism," *Architectural Design* (April 1957): 113.
5 Banham, "New Brutalism."
6 Ibid.
7 Ibid.
8 In this connection, Denise Scott Brown's essay, "Learning from Brutalism," in *The Independent Group: Postwar Britain and the Aesthetics of Plenty* (Cambridge, MA: MIT Press, 1990), 203–6, establishes that during the 1950s Louis I. Kahn "had emerged as a quite unexpected American confirmation of Brutalist ideas, owing chiefly to his Trenton Bath House" for the students of the Architectural Association in London. And quite

interestingly, it is precisely with the concept of "image" in mind that Scott Brown, Robert Venturi, and Steven Izenour later developed their semiological critique of orthodox modern architecture in *Learning from Las Vegas: The Forgotten Symbolism of Architectural Form* (Cambridge, MA: MIT Press, 1977).

9 It is interesting to note that, Oscar Newman, the editor of the transcripts of CIAM '59, designed the Cité des jeunes with Charney at Hull during his stay in Montreal in the mid-1960s. (See Fig. 15.4.)

10 Louis I. Kahn, "Concluding Remarks to the CIAM Congress, Otterlo, 1959," in Oscar Newman, ed., *CIAM '59 in Otterlo* (London: Tiranti, 1961), 208.

11 Ibid., 207.

12 Ibid., 213.

13 It was in his questioning of what a scientific laboratory wanted to be that Kahn realized that working spaces should be surrounded by the servant spaces housing the technological components of the building.

14 Kahn, "Concluding Remarks," 214.

15 Chapter 5, 62.

16 Ibid.

17 Charney was interested in the potential of plastics as a building material. Here, he referred implicitly to "the house of the future," a moulded plastic prototype designed by Alison and Peter Smithson in 1956. See chapter 13.

18 Chapter 6, 76.

19 Charney's distinction between an authentic, quasi-natural vernacular and an architect's architecture echoed a point made by Adolf Loos in his essay "Architecture" of 1910. See Roberto Schezen, Kenneth Frampton, and Joseph Rosa, *Adolf Loos: Architecture 1903–1932* (New York: Monacelli Press, 1996).

20 Chapter 6, 76.

21 Bernard Rudofsky, *Architecture without Architects: A Short Introduction to Non-Pedigreed Architecture* (New York: Museum of Modern Art, 1964).

22 Chapter 9, 115.

23 Ibid., 113.

24 Chapter 8, 92.

25 Chapter 10, 117.

26 Ibid., 119.

27 Ibid., 118–19.

28 During his stay at Yale, Charney developed first-hand knowledge of the emerging tendencies in American art and began producing artworks of his own after graduation.

29 Chapter 7, 81.

30 Ibid., 81.

31 Ibid., 82.

32 Ibid., 82.

33 Ibid., 82.

34 Ibid., 82–3.

35 Reyner Banham, "The Spec-Builders: Towards a Pop Architecture," *Architectural Review* 132 (July 1962): 43–6; Robert Venturi, *Complexity and Contradiction in Architecture*, Museum of Modern Art Papers on Architecture 1 (New York: MoMA, 1966).

36 Chapter 11, 120.

5

A Journal of Istanbul: Notes on Islamic Architecture*

Architecture is now at a beginning, a beginning which realizes the terms and scale of multiple-man. It reacts to his will with crude forms. Everything else has become history, everything a curiosity to be looked at and tasted, to be experienced, accepted, or discarded. Buildings and cities, ancient architectures, pleasing hand-crafted work, sheds and cathedrals are all part of another world – a huge anonymous collection which one can still visit to find origins and motives of architecture, and delight in its forms.

There are no more far-off places. There is no more exotic; New York is as exotic as Baghdad. It is exotic desires that find exoticism in strange situations and histories. The unfamiliarity of an environment can sharpen reactions; the people, the way of life, the way the buildings occupy thoughts. These thoughts are examined, image by image, as pages in a journal. The environment and the buildings evoke questions. Questions by their very nature have in them the seeds of an answer. And the journal is of any city.

Look at that building, but you are pushed aside in the hurry of people. Buildings and streets are dense with people, who spoil the moment, and you wish that they would all go away. Movements, faces, odours, which distract. These people are active in the voids, the space left over; they force their way in and assert themselves. Imaginary figures of people are adjusted by the mind's eye to illusive and sudden images, and a sequence of chimneys, and the pattern of dark openings in the wall of a street become buildings. People are always the measure. Ancient work sits empty, alone and cool, as the sculptured image of an architecture.

Travels are underlined by the sea, the Mediterranean is never far away. A blue, blue strip vertically out to the horizon.

Thousand years of activity reads in the residue of buildings, and history is the continuum where cities are dust and villages have become the metropolis. The travel is east to Turkey, to Istanbul and the Cappadocian plateau of Asia Minor.

* From *Journal of the Royal Architecture Institute of Canada* 39, no. 6 (June 1962): 60–5.

The landscape of Thrace eases you into Turkey. At a river the line is crossed to the rattling accompaniment of a bridge. Lined with trees, and it moves off to a Roman city – Hadrian's city. Now it is the town of Edirne.

A profile of minarets. Shafts tapering to the sky, the round of domes below and an edge of houses. The forms of fifteenth- and sixteenth-century mosques dominate the town. Their presence, their architectural sophistication, is unfamiliar; as yet there are no terms of approach. A reality of people is more immediate, as is an environment of language and streets. At evening the people mill about in an open street of shops. The street is filled with dark figures, dark figures in a long hall where the walls of the hall are shops, and the ceiling is a sky.

A recess, shadowed in the wall, is a cafe of men at tables. The sinuous shape of a tea glass catches the eye, and the shape fits comfortably into the hand. From the line of shops stand out large entrances. The entrances lead inside, to an inner street, which has a vaulted roof and shops that fit into a repetition of masonry hays. The length of this interior street is a building which includes both shops and a street.

Shops set the mood and scale of this inside street. Long, empty exterior walls, and projecting entrances invited other shops to occur about the building. It is a building, which allows other similar buildings to become part of it, and it evokes a density in the town pattern and a special environment. Which buildings contrive to receive other buildings in an urban grouping?

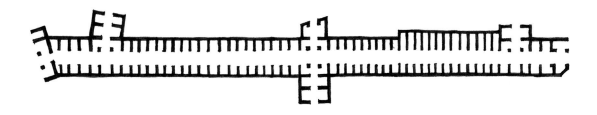

5.3 Galata bridge over the Golden Horn; the bridge runs into an ancient city, into Constantinople, which after 1453 became the capital of an Ottoman empire. The city in 1961 is still as shown in this photograph of 1890, only now the clutter is more cluttered; at the left edge is the mosque of Hagia Sophia and next to it that of Sultan Ahmed I.

If there are no densities in a town, what is to be an open space?

To Istanbul the road follows the contour of a wide plain, with the landscape it dips abruptly into each scooped valley. The road abuts a large airport, and in the manner of the new it becomes a wide throughway rushing you at the scale of its own landscape to the walls of the city. These walls remain formidable in spite of the road, but the new road effortlessly cleaves the masonry and a wide street enters. An edge of the city is still defined by walls, walls powerfully constructed and inevitably taken.

Drab wood and stone buildings crowd the streets of Istanbul. There is a Victorian air about the city, like a musty old house cluttered with exotic curiosities and things hidden in dark corners. The rush of a rattling tram forces you against a building. Through a gate between buildings is an alley of pedestrians, glaring bulbs illuminate the shops which stagger downhill in vertical strokes. The pavement widens for a kiosk. At the bottom of the hill a bridge leads traffic cut over water, over a wide street of large ships and flecks of boats.

The bridge crosses to Stanboul to that part of Istanbul, which was the centre of Byzantium and the Ottoman empire. People and vehicles move into the spaces about the Yeni Valide mosque, the spice bazaar, and the narrow streets. Streets of trade with peddlers hawking. The beasts of burden are porters who transport a world on their bent backs padded with straw. The crowds of people are indifferent, an indifference where the unfortunate have a definite place in the scheme of things. Life is on more crude terms. At one time super-sensual indulgence existed for the few. Now for the many there is sticky sweet pastry, the delicate lace of rose petals in syrup, music which, like old Kufric script, hovers and vibrates – a throaty thigh and belly music, and dark-eyed bosomy women. But it is not as yet the world of the many. Men pass their days sitting in cafes, crowded cafes where they click backgammon, stare out to the street as if bored for the last hundred years, and finger nervous bead chains bead by bead, one by one, over and over, as a Sisyphus easing his life with raki and tea.

Stanboul extends over a large area of hills to an edge of sea and Byzantine walls. Its pattern is both dense, tight, and open. The tight areas grow in on themselves, and the city is open where buildings have disintegrated to dusty fields.

Several streets converge on a square inhabited by taxis. About the square are the university gates and Beyazit Mosque. At the side of the mosque the ground rises, the mosque stills the noise of the street, and walls and trees shade an area in which a disarray of tables is a cafe for students. Behind the mosque is a yard, where worn books aligned in stalls and on the pavement make it a quiet and curious realm. The yard narrows, turns between two stalls down a stair into the tumult of the bazaar. Here everything is a shop or a conduit of movement; a man's arms, the niche in a wall, a narrow between two buildings, vaulted and dark interiors, all become shops; and movement is from light to dark through tunnels of shops, to alleys, to little streets, to wide openings, a peopled and cluttered labyrinth. Between houses, a low wall of regulated openings encloses a disarrangement of

thin stones and tufts of grass, and children playing. What a perfect place to play, stones which can hide, and some earth to dig in. A graveyard has become a fascinating playground where noisy delight is heard among the turban headed stones. Each space in a crowded city evokes a use, and fills with people in its pattern.

Lines of slender minarets catch the eye. The narrow street moves off to an open square, and there is the adjacent mosque. The mosque of Sultan Suleyman dominates this square defined by its outbuildings, and absorbs the space of the square in a sequence of courtyards, the square itself is as a courtyard. Banal life of the street is shut out. The main precinct of the mosque is delineated by a low screen wall, within are figures resting in the shadows, and diagonal paths to an entrance standing separate and dominant in the facade of a forecourt. The porticoed forecourt is an atrium, a delicate ablutions fountain sits small and commands the space. Views of the sky, and of the main hall, are framed by lines of minaret. Minarets, forecourt, and main hall are in sequence the parts of a mosque. There is a conscious putting together of these parts, the minarets still seem tacked on, and with the forecourt are as from another tradition the addendum on a building similar to Hagia Sophia. The parts are unrelated by the rhythms of the architecture, each is articulate in itself and as a separate building. The tall minarets are at the corners of the forecourt, and the void framed between these easy shafts stands airily against the hard working weight of the main hall.

The plan and constructive system of the main hall relate directly to Hagia Sophia, but something else is evoked, a different spirit is at work. The large dome is dominant, it rises high, and radial ribs move out to fasten the dome to a lower structure of arches. About the arches small domes dance as cupolas. These main arches are shallow and thin lines attenuate their mass. Four columns, at the springing of the arches, stand with stepped buttresses as structural walls into the building. But the columns are all capped with cupolas, they become part of the play of cupolas, and their weight reads as a hollow. Thin lines edge and separate the cupolas sitting them like cardboard hats on a space. The scale of the daring construction is played-off with a preference for lighthanded effects and picayune elements. At the lower edge of the building, where there are people, small tightly contained

5.4 Sultan Suleyman mosque was completed in 1557 to the plans of the architect Sinan. Prolific Sinan was at the head of an empire of architects. The dome has a diameter of 86 feet and a height of 156 feet. Drawing by Melvin Charney.

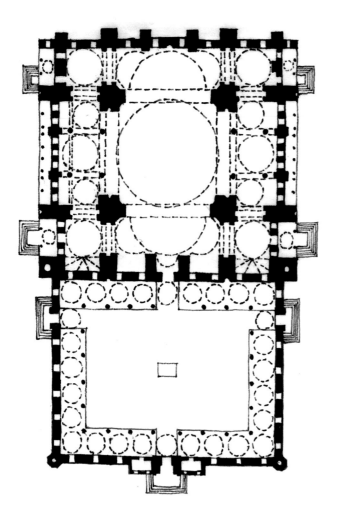

rhythms proliferate. The small is always consciously performing before the big, and the building shifts uncomfortably from one scale to another. "A taste for titillating little pleasures put into the architecture," wrote Henri Michaux of the Alhambra at Grenada. And Sultan Suleyman's mosque was the delight of Turkish poets.

The interior is a great sweep of space, the curve of the dome slides into that of half-domes and to the columns. The dome rises from a square of masonry arches. This square of arches on four columns is a structural frame, a clear and simple skeleton from which the dome, half-domes, and walls recede. Cupolas belong to the small and secondary spaces at two sides of the hall. There is only one dominant scale – that of the large space. The small, often repeated, is contained in the patterns, which play on all surfaces. A profusion of glass lamps hanging just above on a metal thread from high up are part of these patterns. Many openings light the interior.

In a small cafe the nervousness of the streets subsides. Trees shade the cafe. High above branches the delicate minarets of Sultan Ahmed Mosque thin out. A light forecourt can be seen in the depth of an overlay of screen walls. From a wall projects an entrance frontpiece, within is the porticoed forecourt and a fountain and second frontpiece door on axis. The dome of the main hall caps a build-up of half-domes. Against the base of the dome stand out four columns. Cupolas are somewhere below and withdrawn behind a thin line of verticals. The effect of the exterior is still so lighthanded. Out from the side of the forecourt, in the mosque precinct, are a few wide limbed trees and the inevitable figures of people cast into the shadows. The ground is uneven, there is a sense of other buildings underneath this site where once stood the hippodrome and the imperial palaces of Byzantium. Hagia Sophia is just beyond.

Lines of repeated openings tighten the exterior planes of the mosque. Walls of regulated openings build up planes of depth and planes

5.5 A repetition of minarets aligns Sultan Ahmed Mosque, the main mosque of the city. It was completed in 1616 with a plan based on an earlier mosque by Sinan.

of darkness. You see through, you see in, void is part of the building. The openings in sequence are rhythms. Rhythms play on your eyes – AAA/BB/C/BB/C/BB/ minaret – the minarets are part of it and the dark openings are part of it. Minarets and buttresses are the solid strokes in the sequence of openings, these solids then step up from the hollows to do their work above. The scale of each opening relates the lower building to people, the repetition of openings balances the large which can breath freely. Each element of the building occurs in some degree of repetition. Rhythms skilfully move you from part to part of the building, the collection of parts – minaret, forecourt, main hall – works together as a mosque.

The openings draw the eye into the building. Through openings can be seen figures of people in an inner courtyard, people become part of the building. There is a sense that you can participate in the spaces even though you have not come upon them as yet. The architecture directly implies voids to be used. Hollow and depth are archetypes in the expression of an architecture; how well Le Corbusier knows how to use this.

The inside of the dark voids are light, light openings which illuminate and float an interior. Exterior planes of screen protect, in their depth, a transparency of wall. The interior space is centred on itself by the structural frame which now stands sure on four massive rotund columns. From this structural frame the building expands in all directions, pulling tight into rounded and domed spaces. The buttress walls are as flying buttresses which move out from the columns with the skin of the building.

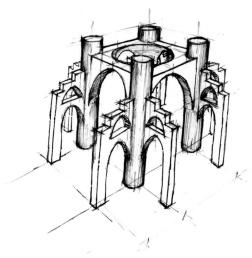

LEFT, ABOVE | 5.6 Sultan Ahmed Mosque drawn by Melvin Charney

LEFT, BELOW | 5.7 Axonometric drawing of Sultan Ahmed Mosque's structure drawn by Melvin Charney.

RIGHT | 5.8 The interior of Sultan Ahmed Mosque seen from a high point of view; the columns are 16 feet in diameter, and the floor is far below. The mosque is popularly known as the Blue Mosque for the blue tiles of enamelled faience that adorn the walls of its interior.

Lines and patterns play on the surface and relieve the white light. A play on the lines of structure divides the surface into thin attenuated panels. Repeated openings are part of the patterns; where the buttresses interfere, the windows are carefully painted as in a stage set. The discs of Koranic script are now part of the surface.

A building for religion is dominated by its own world, its image of a desired heaven on earth to be evoked by an architecture. For Hagia Sophia

it is an interior world, an expansive world where space moves away into dome and half-dome tightening the surfaces. This taut interior is the facade of the building, the structure does its job elsewhere. It is an interior of light and dark, at the centre of it all the main dome floats in light, and it is dark behind a screen of columns which shadow side aisles and galleries. Figures and hieratic symbols inhabit the mosaic surfaces of the interior. The architecture of Hagia Sophia is employed in Sultan Suleyman Mosque, the mosque uses it with clarity to its own intent, and the building becomes something else. Bones have moved out from the walls, they delineate the interior space and arc a structural frame from which the walls expand. Vestiges of Hagia Sophia remain part of this building: the plan is directional with secondary side aisles, infill walls stiffen the structural frame, in spirit the massive of the columns is still part of the walls. The screen of columns has moved outside, there are no darkened spaces. There is no room in the mosque for figurative imagery, geometric patterns texture the walls, many openings are part of the patterns and an even strong light illuminates the interior.

Sultan Ahmed Mosque is the great singular space. The plan has become central on itself, a square with radiating domes. The bones stand out sharp on four drums of massive column. All darkened and shadowed space is outside, screen walls are the exterior elements carefully manipulated to relate the parts and the scale of the mosque. It is an interior of light, the frame, the weight of the columns dissolve in light. Through large openings you can see out beyond the Bosphorus to a horizon.

The interior of an Ottoman mosque has no more walls but surfaces, thinned by lines of pattern, which pull out away from a structural frame left standing. It is as in a tent with the fabric billowing out from masts of support. The main columns, the four masts, extend from the top with buttresses as guy wires. In this manner

of a tent, the structural frame articulates the architecture of the building within and without. And as in the encampment the floors are covered with carpets. The strong light dissolves all interior substance, the building is no more, and space recedes far into distance. You are back outside, back in an atavistic space where steppe and desert are in the light of an open sky with the horizon at a far edge. It is the loved open space of the early Muslim, the nomad, to whom city enclosure was illness and death.

In the environs of the sixteenth-century mosques are groups of outbuildings. Religion was one with the state, and these were buildings for the public – for the faithful. And as buildings, they withdraw behind low and simple facades, behind continuous walls which are the background for a dominant mosque or an open space. The formal aspect of the facade sets the ambient mood.

It is the vigorous profile of the roof that vibrates in relation to the animated insides of the building. Shapes alternate and repeat in sequence to spaces below. The domes sit lightly, a large dome on a large space, and chimneys punctuate the rhythm. A tight exterior wall restrains an exuberance which shows itself at an upper edge, and the wall is as the tight rules and

5.9 An upper edge of walls of the outbuildings of Sultan Suleyman Mosque from the same period of the mosque.

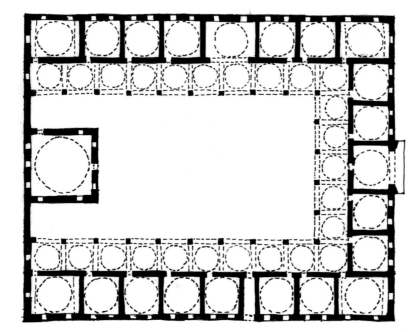

5.10 The plan of a medrese, an outbuilding for students of the Koran and other aspects of scholarship. The medrese of Beyazit Mosque dates from 1504. Drawing by Melvin Charney.

regulations which, at that time, circumscribed the emotions and violent energies of the Turk; spirited geometric decoration is always contained in an arrangement of tight panels.

Masonry walls and stone columns describe square bays and rectangles, and each is topped by a dome. The spaces repeat, collect about a courtyard, and evoke a building of use. The open and closed spaces change in sequence and become a convent, a home for the poor, a lodge for travellers, and these buildings are grouped together.

To articulate each building, to identify a door, a wall, an opening, a repetition of similar parts is used. The after image, the montage of visual impressions compounded from visits to these buildings and to the mosques, is of a hierarchy of architectural elements manipulated to achieve various buildings and effects, where everything is restrained, repeated, and contained to allow the mosque to inflate its singular billowing forms. On visiting another building a spatial arrangement might be new, but familiar pieces

are at work and you recognize a door and use it without thinking of what that aperture is, and by the emphasis of the entrance you know the status of the ensuing space. With parts familiar to people, the presence of a building recedes and does its work quietly. These elements were used, each more separate, by the Seljuk Turks in the twelfth and thirteenth centuries, and they occur in Persian architecture. In the work of sixteenth-century Ottomans these elements retain vitality as a vocabulary, but time and their formal definition quickly harden the idiom and it loses meaning, and in later buildings these parts are the bored appliqué necessary for the proper *mise en scène*.

Elements are units which can be put together in an architectural game to make anything you like. By observing the rules of the game, i.e. a door as a door, a building may be accomplished, adjusted to change, or distorted to suit a whim. How did the Turks play their game in these sixteenth-century buildings? The rules, by that time, had an established history according to which stone blocks and masonry were put together in terms of a build-up of elements. On a square of walls sits a dome, thin lines edge and separate the dome from the walls, yet the dome of masonry is just these walls arching out to enclose the space. This deliberate separateness is an aspect of the Turk's desire to have his architecture as a build-up of small and familiar parts. A repetition of similar parts is the very essence of the building, each part occurs over and over like the clicking of a bead chain. Each space, with repetition, is one of the elements. The repeated dome is a topping element, concluding and centring the space below; it can be a truncated pyramid, a cone, vault, or flat roof all according to the demands of the lower space. The wall is most skillfully used as an element. It is a continuous wall defining a within and without, and within is a courtyard, a special precinct, or the constructed volumes of a building. As the function of a building the wall is structurally load bearing, but it reads as standing separate, it is the facade – what a good facade – presenting a well mannered exterior to the street. And to the street the wall is always the formal background for other activities. The surface of the wall is tight, openings are carefully proportioned and regulated to reoccur in exact size and rhythm. Transparency of the wall varies, openings become larger until the wall is a light frame; the wall as a screen stands in front of the mosque of Sultan Ahmed. The wall marks a transition from one ambient to another, and passage through the wall is an event. And the event is set into the wall as a prominent door element which projects out, and projects above the facade. It is an entrance standing on its own two feet. In Seljuk work this can be seen in a building which is a magnificent entrance with something behind – the Ince Minare Medrese at Konya dating from 1267. The door element grows to make an entrance important, much energy is often expended on the decor of this frontpiece as the pièce de résistance of the facade which

tells of splendours inside. The buildings retain a sense of the process of this game.

And for contemporary work the idea of elements in the process of a building has much meaning, it is the very nature of industrial techniques to produce multi-repeated parts. The parts used in buildings are still too small.

On the hill dominating the waters of the Bosphorus and Golden Horn now stands Topkapi Palace, an empty Sultan's palace. The affinity of the Turk to open landscape is part of the building, large courtyards, gardens, and a hunting ground are contained within the surrounding walls. There is nothing of an acropolis about this place which was the site of the Byzantine stronghold. The palace is a curiosity. It is hard to discern an architectural order in the collection of buildings other than buildings delineating courtyards, or standing small in a courtyard. State ceremonies took place in the large courts, but the only part of the building which relates in scale to the space is a strong rhythm of conical domes on top of the pastry-cooks kitchens. The hareem was closed. The Cinili kiosk, a pavilion set in the gardens, was one of the first buildings erected by the Turks on their arrival, and the beams and columns of stone are cut and joined in the manner of wood members. There is a transient quality about the building; "The Turk carried something of his nomadic ways about him, and fashioned his life accordingly," wrote Nehru.* The kiosks of the inner palace are as too sweet pastry in their little delights between tight pools and planting. Their interiors are carpeted, cushioned, and temporary as those of a tent. But the view is out beyond the Bosphorus to Asia Minor, beyond the Balkan haze of Istanbul to where the air is light and clear.

* Editor's note: Jawaharlal Nehru, *Letters from a Father to his Daughter,* first edition, 1930.

6

Troglai: Rock-Cut Architecture*

In the familiar world architecture is a construction. A frame and pieces are put together to the measure of a build-up. Hollows are caught between the materials of the build-up, these left-over voids accommodate people. Building after building disposes these voids in the landscape of a city.

Rock-cut architecture belongs to another realm where the morphology of the city is that of a natural geologic formation. In the existent configuration of rock a hierarchy of needed spaces is excavated. A wall of rock is cut into, the debris is removed from the hollow and a void remains. One void and then another and another are cut, each space subtracted from the matrix of rock to accommodate people. An impulse common to all men motivates these people to make a place for themselves, but their reaction to the physical conditions about them invoked a different architecture. A visit to this architecture is a trip into a looking-glass world where you are transposed. Words and responses which have been conditioned by a familiar constructed environment are brought to the surface of your reactions; they are reflected by the walls of rock and an inner dialogue hurries you on.

If the Greek landscape in which you are aware of yourself in an elemental ambient of mountain, plain, sea and sky is taken to be the measure, then in Cappadocia you are aware of the horizon – a long horizon always distant at the next hills. Empty plains and mountains interchange but you are fixed and immobile, hardly moving as you slide over the landscape of a never ending and indifferent steppe. To move on is the same as to stop; the plain has the breadth of one's curiosity. To the south, the Taurus Mountains separate this high and central plateau of Asia Minor from the Mediterranean coast. Naked mountains stand out, but the steppe dominates. From Kayseri, ancient Caesarea, the extinct cone of Erciyas Dagi (Mount Argeus) follows you as you move along a wide depression and up a height to the region near the town of Ürgüp. Here erosion has altered a table of volcanic tufa into deep basins of rock verticals. A bare and mountainous relief map, lacking in horizontal scale, was carved out of the

* From *Landscape* 12, no. 3 (1963): 6–12.

layers of tufa. You fall into a density where space is closed in between a multitude of rock monoliths and walls. The dry beds of streams are the natural roads and corridors through the circus of rocks. The formations of eroded tufa stand out as objects presented for the sake of their own intensity; you cannot separate yourself from their sculptural presence. Each shape and twist catches the imagination: a flow of drapery, medieval towers, various creatures and men.

Clear light etches the eroded configuration. There is a severe grain to the disposition of the forms. From the height of the plateau, folded cliffs radiate descending pinnacles and thin skeletal valleys to a lower plain which slides out to the edge of a river; columns and cones grow out of the receding plain where a cap of hard rock has slowed the process of weathering. Surfaces of the fragile tufa were blown smooth by the wind. The surfaces fall and turn into one another in a soft, rounded motion. The colours: buff yellow and red, dry dusty white, with blue and a few tufts of green.

The rocks both hide and expose cavities where people have lodged themselves. A cave found under the cornice of a high ridge was a convenient place to hide; tufa is easy to cut and manipu-

late, and the inside walls could be adjusted with crude tools. The many rock walls offered expedient, high and dry places to live in an area where there is little wood. The Hittites had inhabited Cappadocia. It is as if people have always lived in the holes and clefts of those rocks.

Part of the rock monolith has fallen away exposing an interior of hollows one above the

ABOVE | 6.1 Old photograph of the tufa landscape of Göreme in the Cappadocia region.

LEFT | 6.2 Inhabited conical rock formations, Göreme.

LEFT | 6.3 A home in an eroded rock, Göreme.

RIGHT | 6.4 Interior of a rock-cut house, Göreme.

other. These exposed chambers have the measure and the character of a place that people inhabit. These chambers scale the presence of the monolith, and the rock becomes a building – a conical Gaudiesque building. In another rock formation the exposed openings reveal a second building, a third and a fourth are found among the faceted remains in the walls of a ravine. With the many exposed chambers the rock landscape assumes the guise of a city of buildings. At the beginning of the eighteenth century, Paul Lucas described in the notes of his journey what he thought to be the ruins of an ancient city.* And you see the city: long undulating buildings, a cluster of towers and a row of towers, steep dusty streets and alleys descending between

* Editor's note: Sieur Paul Lucas (1664–1737) was a French antiquarian to Louis XIV. He travelled extensively in Greece, Turkey, the Levant, and Egypt, in three major voyages: 1699–1703, 1704–08, and 1714–17.

pinnacles. A few towers are out in the fields as in a suburb. The city is full of hidden places and is secretive; all straight lines, the lines which dominate our familiar cities, belong to its interiors.

There is a willed interior in a horned rock. Anything within the limits of stability could have been cut into the friable tufa, but in this rock there is nothing haphazard. The exactness of the cutting is the note of regularity to the deformed monolith. An order was imposed inside the rock. You have to fit yourself in, examine each space and involve the architecture with your presence.

The figures of boys scale the volume of an abandoned chamber. Much rock has fallen away from the wall of the ravine and sunlight filters into this hollow; the colour of the stone tints and diffuses the light to a warm consistency. The volume of the chamber is both spacious and comfortable, the aspect of this interior relates to you in personal terms. Men had worked the easy material to their accommodation, voids were cut in, and rock was left to stand out. Alcoves, steps, and seats happen as if their very raison d'être had drawn these objects out of the rock. Years of use have worn a pattern into the stone. The imprint of cutting tools marks the walls; now exaggerated by weathering, these marks look cruder. It is so easy to imagine people carrying on with their lives in this empty room, their trace is everywhere.

The very effort of the rock cutter made the space. The on-the-earth builder begins with all of space and defines what is needed in a construction; he is involved with space through the intermediary of a structure. Nothing in the rock-cut interior was determined by structure. It was a void that was hewn into the rock; the space was placed lightly in the weight of the existent material.

The void of the chamber has a rectangular configuration, but there is none of the hard linearity of a construction. The grainy texture of the tufa has softened all edges, corners are rounded and shadows attenuate at the slow turning of a surface. It is as if the very sweep of the arm of the cutter rendered one stone surface into another. Walls and ceilings turn into each other and are one. The continuous surface describes the space with an effective ease, the surface slides and turns and the space is plastic. It is where people walk and climb that gives the rounded interior its sharper turns and quick repetitions – what a man can do with his feet is dimensionally limited. People stand fragile in any architecture.

Through openings in a wall there is another chamber. Space slides into tile other with a turn of stone. Your movement to the next void is free and easy. On the way there is a narrow pass, levels change, and you step up or down. In passing from one chamber to another there is a hesitation, you have to perform a varied step – a dance which alters your altitude. This transition marks a separateness. You then enter the next void and arrive at a space of different configuration and comfort from the first. The next void was cut to accommodate something else. Movement through the sequence of chambers is from void to void where each is a special event.

A group of these chambers is a cluster of voids in the rock. Each cluster is like a collection of balloons in which an end balloon anchors the group to the exterior, and the other balloons of void float off into the rock. Gravity is not part of their architecture. The voids meet and stand away above, below, beyond the first according to the ordered disposition of an inner plan. There is no end to the group; each void is finite but the continuity of voids terminates where it once had to; it could go on – the "building" is endless.

In the hierarchy of voids, the primary spaces are those through which you move. Secondary spaces are the servant spaces which relate as an order of niches to the primary volumes. These secondary spaces vary from large alcoves to slots; the slots for wall-climbing are small niches often repeated. The effect of these rock-cut interiors is that each chamber of niche occurs just where it was needed. These interiors are cool and detached, places which relate to use rather than expressive of use as is much of contemporary plastic architecture.

From the earliest times of Christianity the eroded landscape attracted anchorites. Their eremitic affinity for the rocks was part of an austere life shared by colonies of disciples. The nearby town of Caesarea was the most important town of Byzantine Cappadocia; the ascetic monk was one of the national heroes and a large number of religious communities flourished in these valleys. Near the village of Maçan a church had been cut into the rock under the pointed cap of a towering cone; the portico of this church was suspended above the landscape. For the monks of this church there was the ascetic comfort of sitting high as a stylite penitent on the top of his column, as well as the comfort of a holy place in the hollow of the rock. The church was both their cave and column. The vigorous landscape which first attracted the monks was later their refuge when the Arabs overran Asia Minor in the seventh and eighth centuries. Monasteries were hidden behind small and dark openings.

The History

The Seljuk Turks arrived in the eleventh century. And in the rocks is a multitude of cells, refectories, halls, small chapels and churches now empty and still difficult to find. These monasteries are sited with a sense of drama which is a part of the *mise en scène* of existing Greek monasteries at Mount Athos and at Meteora in Thessaly: perched high on ledges of rock between the earth and the sky these were "holy mountains," and then places of defence and inaccessibility in a land occupied by Islam.

The Christians brought with them into the rocks their constructed buildings. The more significant the aspect of a particular chamber was to be, the more it was carved to resemble a place known to have effective communion with the heavens. The rock-cut dwellings were indigenous to these valleys as an architecture with its own manners and rules. It is the religious environment which here presents a discordant formalism of special interiors cut into the rock.

The portico of a church situated in the walls of a ravine. Behind this arcade are rounded windows and two doors into a nave; inside are an apse and an altar throne. The moulded bandeau which runs along the line of arches is similar to the mouldings in the fifth-century St Simon Stylite monastery at Kalat Seman in Syria. From a distance the shadow of two cylinders on the top of the column ties the lines of moulding into that of the column shaft, but, closer to the facade, it is these cylinders which hinder the movement of lines. The capital is in Ionic order which has reverted to its essential geometric parts – the two cylinders help the column accommodate the bottom of the arch. The column shaft, the capital, and the row of beams under a heavy cornice are the parts of a construction. This portico presents a construction. But nothing here was constructed; there is no structure and the columns do not hold anything in place. Constructed architecture was sculpted into the rock with delicate and finished lines.

The configuration of figure 6.5 belongs to a constructed church. The plan of a rock-cut dwelling began with the cutting of its spaces, this church began with an image, and a relief depicting a known style and manner was cut deep enough to walk in. Robert Boulanger notes in a guide for the area: "All the various styles of architecture in use in Anatolia during the Byzantine period are to be found here as well as

6.5 Partial view of the arcaded porch of St John the Baptist Church showing a column, arches, and dentils, Cavusin, Cappadocia, Turkey

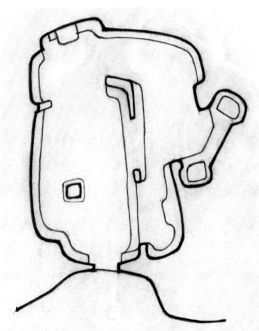

Armenian and Syrian influences … also several local types, a two-naved church."* Figure 6.6 is of the double-naved church; it was found by Sir William Ramsay in the valley of Göreme. In the rock the constructive sense of this plan is fragmented, and the nave, apse and second nave stand away from each other. Figure 6.7 has much less of a constructive sense in the disposition of the spaces; columns and a vault are indicated in the plan, but the caprice of their arrangement could only occur in a rock-cut interior. In the realm of rock-cut architecture, the more authentic interiors are those of the chapels of Byzantine hermits which have been found in Apulia, Southern Italy, in a region of a similar soft rock. Figure 6.8 could only be rock-cut; the space turns with a continuous surface from the width of a church into different and more sacred niches, levels change from seats to shelves to an altar and the furniture becomes part of the walls and floors.

Figure 6.9: The nave of a church in the valley of Göreme. A barrel vault and cupola alternate

* Editor's note: Robert Boulanger, *Turquie* (Paris: Hachette, collection Les guides bleus, 1958).

CLOCKWISE FROM TOP LEFT

6.6 Plan of a double-nave church in the valley of Göreme drawn by Melvin Charney.

6.7 Plan of another rock-cut church drawn by Melvin Charney.

6.8 Plan of a third rock-cut church drawn by Melvin Charney.

6.9 The collapsed nave of a rock-cut church in the valley of Göreme.

in the tunnel-like interior. These parts have no inherent relation other than that each part once belonged to a constructed church. The lower facade was derived from yet another manner of construction. The blind arcade of horseshoe arches and pilasters is similar to the facades of Sasanian brick buildings. In the rock these arches became flat, each arch varies in size, and the band has an air of whimsy not part of the original. The door, the row of holes, and the toothed window are the work of recent inhabitants who found this exposed nave to be an attractive front for their dwelling.

Lines of red and blue decorate the interior of this church. The decorations play on the shapes: a zigzag trims the curve of an arch as *dents de scie*, checks square the cupola, joints of stone masonry are drawn on the barrel vaults. Nothing is figurative. Churches with this geometric decoration were cut as historians have indicated, during an iconoclastic controversy of the eighth and ninth centuries. There is a compulsive vigour to the pattern on the decorations, quick jagged motifs and impatient strokes of colour dart about on the surfaces and hurry each sculpted shape along their design. The later inhabitants had added a splash of yellow ochre and a few appropriate doodles

Now the inhabitants of these eroded valleys gravitate to towns and villages. The towns are found to collect about large and prominent rock forms which stand conspicuous in the landscape. The town of Ortahisar is at the foot of a high tower pitted to its very top with exposed cuttings and openings to deeper insides. The rock commands the town as some unfinished tower of Babel with workers' houses scattered about; a minaret for a mosque is so arranged that from the main street the thin needle touches in perspective the height of the rock. The houses of Üç Hisar climb up the side of a high monolith; Maçan lies low about tall cones; Ürgüp, the most important town of this region, extends down from the sides of a long cliff. These dominant rocks about which the towns gather are hollow with the remains of chambers from an earlier town; the large rock belongs to an historic core and origins now forgotten.

The houses of these towns are both on and in the rock. Dwellings cut into the rock were extended out to the street with a construction. The constructions present their facade to the streets and the rock-cut parts belong to the inside chambers; often the rock was cut to resemble a constructed facade. In these towns the rock-cut dwelling is a secondary sort of place easily influenced by the built forms. It is out away from the towns that a dwelling of a character more indigenous to rock-cut is found. Away from the towns, an exposed collection of chambers in a wall locate the troglodyte dwelling. The process of erosion which first carved the wall has now exposed its insides, the dwelling retreated deeper and an earlier cross-section becomes the facade. The new chambers are just inside the surface of the rock. Here time has not changed, the carefully hand-worked fields are silent, the small dark openings are silent, people have disappeared into the rocks and you pass in the quiet of a ravine.

The village of Cavusin is sheltered in the bowl of a ridge which is broken and faceted by the remains of cuttings; a few of these cuttings pass through the rock to the sky beyond.

Much rock has crumbled away, the houses sit on debris of rock and openings. A constructed village of boxes peers out of the amphitheatre. Each box is geometrically blunt and dominated by the right angle, and each is the extension of a cut dwelling. Narrow alleys climb between the houses; house upon house forms the articulate arrangement of rectangular stones between piles of rock and twigs. As a typical Cappadocian village, it is flat-roofed and built out of the very material it sits on. The village has the colour of the surrounding rock. The sun tones the walls with gradations of light and shade and the village stands out of the landscape – a crisp profile of boxes to the demented profile of the ridge at the sky.

The house of figure 6.11 is on a white street in the town of Ortahisar. It is all one house both in the cut hollows of the rock and in the hollows of the construction. The different parts cohere in all inevitable composition; one part fits into the other, the openings are aligned,

LEFT | 6.10 The village of Cavusin.

RIGHT | 6.11 A house in the town of Ortahisar.

LEFT | 6.12 Detail of a
conical house.

RIGHT | 6.13 A house in the
village of Cavusin.

stairs carry up and through the collection. These constructed parts were made by a build-up of small blocks of tufa put together, one bearing on the other – an addition of geometric increments. Everything about the construction speaks of a simple geometry, of finite line, plane, and circle. Both the ribbed vault and the box are typical of a tradition of building which is indigenous to this region as is that of the rock-cut; the two systems derive from an addition or subtraction of the same material.

Figure 6.12: One dwelling above another in a conical rock. A stair turns up the side of the cone. There is nothing about the stair which is constructed, nothing is planar. A supple surface moves down into the shapes of the stair and runs off along the curve of an overhang to a wall. This cut surface reacts scrupulously to a use. The geometry of this surface can be described by a multiplicity of continuous lines where each of the many lines follows a changing contour – as in a Henry Moore drawing which plots the volume of a sculpted figure. It is the first geometry of one block sitting on another which is familiar to us rather than that implied by a more plastic and moulded environment.

A facade between houses in the village of Cavusin. A bizarre house as one of the houses along a street. The facade is falling apart; two blocks prop up an old eye, hollow eyes stare blankly, the overhang is a forehead, and there is a mouth. This facade was cut by erosion. Erosion then blended some man's cut openings into the stone and they as well have become an inextricable part of its slow swirl. No recognizable geometry orders the contours of this surface; nothing speaks of the hand of the man. In the places made by man, the very act of making a place evoked an order and a geometry which resolved itself in terms of the process. His place may assume an unfamiliar configuration, but there is always the recognition of a human mark. It is erosion which cut the unreal, the fantastic and grotesque, into the tufa.

7

The World of Pop*

The ancients began their work with an invocation to the muses; the medieval artist began and closed his work with an envoi to his Prince. We, the moderns, invoke technology, the masses, and the God Mammon to make a statement about the contemporary world.

In this age of technology the world has become denser than before. The communications media maintain a ready-made reality for the populations lost in an urban sprawl. The mechanized landscape of the urban sprawl itself presents a visual sludge of manipulative images that are devised to be read with the least effort by the largest number of people. Pictures, signs, and symbols tell us to turn, to yield, to stop, to buy pills for relief, beer for thirst, and tires to keep us on the move.

It is this visual technocracy that the pop artist confronts. He uses its popular images and he is involved with the means of communication that made these images popular.

His art, pop art, as it is now known, is essentially an American development even though the term pop was first used by the British critic Lawrence Alloway in the early 1950s to describe the work of several artists in London. Alloway then explained that pop art was based on the acceptance of mass-produced objects, just because they are all around us, and on the urgent quest for the unadorned or common reality. However, much of the British pop work took a more romantic and self-conscious view of pop culture than the Americans did. The Americans went beyond inspiration into vigorous painting.

Within a short period the American work was accepted and classified as a full-fledged "movement." This rapid classification is in a sense the most natural thing that could have happened to pop. Both our intellectual and commercial worlds digest reality in terms of hastily secreted images, and pop, in the first instance, was partly devised to deal with this phenomenon. The art scene is as well specially tuned to the sequence of movements.

In 1960, in America, there was no pop group and no movement. Rather, a number of artists

* From "Le monde du pop art," *Vie des arts* 36 (1964): 30–8. Translated to French by Jacques de Roussan. This essay is published in English for the first time from the original (English) manuscript.

were working independently of each other (as independently as the art mags permit) but with a common source of imagery. Within two years several of the artists had important shows in the larger New York galleries, they were lumped into a category, and, in December 1962, a symposium of distinguished critics and museum curators was held in New York.* The symposium acknowledged the label pop art; slides were shown of the relevant work by Jasper Johns and Robert Rauschenberg – two significant artists who stand outside the mainstream of pop but who can be considered to be direct precursors – and of the work by the now high-pop painters Roy Lichtenstein, Robert Indiana, James Rosenquist, Andy Warhol, Wayne Thibaut, Claes Oldenburg, James Dine, and Tom Wesselman. The discussion of the symposium served to set out the basic tenets of the movement; and, as one of the participants noted, "this is instant art history, art history made so aware of itself that it leaps to get ahead of art."

The symposium rejected the term neo-Dada for the work in question because it bore only a superficial resemblance. But, clearly, one can trace the sources of pop in modern art, and especially find sources in Dada – for example in Schwitters's *Mertzbilder*, and especially in the work of Duchamp. Dada was a revolutionary movement; the self-conscious slogan "épater les bourgeois" dominated the art. There was shock value in exhibiting the ready-made and commonplace object as art. When Duchamp exhibited his urinal, it served as his hermetic weapon in conflict; he was, as well, careful to insist that it was significant because he, Duchamp, had chosen it. The contemporary pop artist is no longer assertive. He is, with an ironic detachment, at ease with the banality of his world. He fearlessly uses its popular imagery and accepts the ready-made and the commonplace for what they are.

A growing idea and a common attitude dominate pop art rather than a fixed, single aesthetic. This pop attitude can be seen to emphasize the detachment of the artist; feedback, perhaps, from the American era of Zen, pot, and hipsterism. There is a strenuous allegiance to plain descriptive and deadpan realism, and to the choice of random but archetypal events and objects. He gladly allows chance to play with his picture. In his picture the pop artist uses the most common and massively projected images of our time. This insistent impersonality in the work is carried through to the signature that is left off, to the use of anonymous colouring – no colour or bright unmixed colours, and to techniques which are inventive facsimiles of industrial reproduction methods.

The pop artist's attitude to reality and his predisposition to the commonplace and banal of our environment have affinities to the French "anti-novel." Pop, like the work of Nathalie Sarraute, can be considered to be a refusal to recognize a priority among objects, feelings, and events; as with Sarraute, the status of reality is allowed only to the "small true fact, the true detail."†

The images the pop artist uses are so looked at that they have become unseen. This built-in alienation from looking at the commonplace of our visual milieu silences at first one's encounter with pop art, and especially with the work of Roy Lichtenstein. Lichtenstein singles out the printed world of the comic strip, the advertising poster, and the popularized reproductions of the art of Picasso. He isolates, enlarges, and fragments these images in his work. He presents them in an impersonal and direct manner without sentiment or emotion. The images are flat on the canvas, colour is kept to a minimum,

* Editor's note: The symposium was organized by curator Peter Selz at the Museum of Modern Art. The proceedings were published a few months later in "A Symposium on Pop Art," *Arts* (April 1963): 36–45. The participants were Henry Geldzahler, Hilton Kramer, Dore Ashton, Leo Steinberg, Stanley Kunitz, and Peter Selz.

† Editor's note: Nathalie Sarraute, *The Age of Suspicion: Essays on the Novel* (New York: George Braziller, 1963).

and hard edges and precise textures simulate the printed page. The effect of this presentation of the subject matter is that of a shock treatment. One is forced to consider these images with an attention never given them before, and they are seen real and intense as if for the first time. "Pour la première fois mise à nu, la réalité mythologique des visions quotidiennes," noted Alain Jouffroy in the catalogue for the Lichtenstein exhibit held in Paris in June 1963.*

Lichtenstein minutely reconstructs in his paintings the mechanical patterns of the commercial reproduction techniques. The printer's screens appear as parallel lines of dots; hard-edge overlays of flat planes and hard black outlines are laid on the canvas as if with an offset plate of a press. The simulation of an exaggerated mechanical process fragments the image into a calligraphy of anonymous blots and lines, and again one is pushed into unvisited visual terrain.

In Lichtenstein's work comic-strip vignettes become terrifying icons. The comic strip is essentially a healthy device, a popular morality tale where the good always win, and where archetypal evil in the form of a cat, a Martian, or a "dirty-red-commie" is met face to face and vanquished. Lichtenstein catalogues the iconography of sex, death, and violence that illustrate these popular tales and he plays with the current collective dreams and fears of man. Even in his painting *Girl with Ball* (1961), which could be a travel poster – an all-American girl in an all-American play situation – there is an ominous sense of desperation. One is not certain from the gesture of the figure, or from the expression of the mouth, if she is playing a game, defending herself, or sinking into the sea: "You thought that I was waving, but I was merely

7.1 Roy Lichtenstein, *Girl with Ball*, 1961.

drowning" are lines by the English poet Stevie Smith that aptly fit this enigmatic scene.† Even though the pop artists draw from a common source of imagery, the style, the decisions, and the message of each artist is unmistakable. No

* Editor's note: *Lichtenstein, 5 juin 1963*, texts by Alain Jouffroy, Ellen Johnson, and Robert Rosenblum (Paris: Ileana Sonnabend, 1963). Translation: "The mythological reality of daily images is revealed for the first time."

† Editor's note: Stevie Smith, *Not Waving but Drowning* (London: Andre Deutsch, 1957).

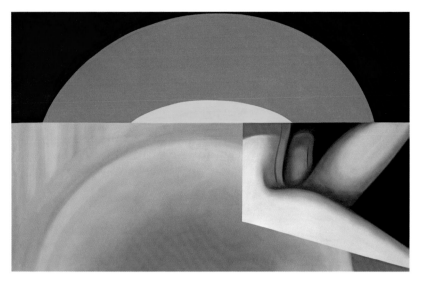

LEFT | 7.2 James Rosenquist, *Brighter than the Sun*, 1961.

RIGHT | 7.3 James Rosenquist, *Nomad*, 1963.

matter how close to anonymity the artist may desire to emulate the material of his inspiration – the anonymous mass world – he cannot ironically eliminate the personal gesture of art as an activity or of himself as an artist.

James Rosenquist paints with billboard realism a montage of images taken from the grand themes of advertising. A shiny car, the lips of a woman, a bowl of spaghetti … images that are part of the daily stream of visual consciousness are recorded in his work. His colours are the jarring colours of the outdoor billboards; he uses vibrant "Day-Glow" paint with a single-minded aplomb. The mechanical process of billboard reproduction is emphasized in the painting by the separation of planes of colour. Space, in the paintings, consists of flat planes that slide one over the other as a sequence of billboards that one passes quickly in an automobile, or the quickly turned pages of a magazine. The scale in the paintings is both that used in Big Sell adver-

tisements and that of fragmentary memories that have the size of one's imagination – Rosenquist floats peanuts like Zeppelins over the roof of a house, and a slice of tomato engulfs a car.

Rosenquist uses in his work the iconographic formulas of advertising to which we have been conditioned. He juxtaposes caustic fragments to emphasize the symbolic content of the images. But the messages of his paintings are his own. For example, in a series of paintings Rosenquist uses the erotic content that underlies much of advertising. The painting *Brighter than the Sun* (1962) is frankly sensual, a love story composed of the images of silk stocking legs and of the fragments of curved and supple shapes that are flashed before us in mass ads that promote and cash in on desires.

A recent painting by Rosenquist, *Nomad* (1963), is a large montage of things seen and remembered by a traveller – picnic furniture, parts of signs and of drive-in restaurants. Hanging from the top of the painting is a plastic bag streaked with the colours found in the work, and on the floor below the painting are several wooden sticks and boards spotted with paint. The bag of colours and the sticks and boards (pallets and brushes) present the raw materials and the tools of the artist. These objects are part of the composition and they imply that the actual painted panel is as well only an indifferent object that the artist left behind.

From the very beginning pop art has been involved with the object. The pop work charged

7.4 Robert Indiana, *Black Yield Brother*, 1964.

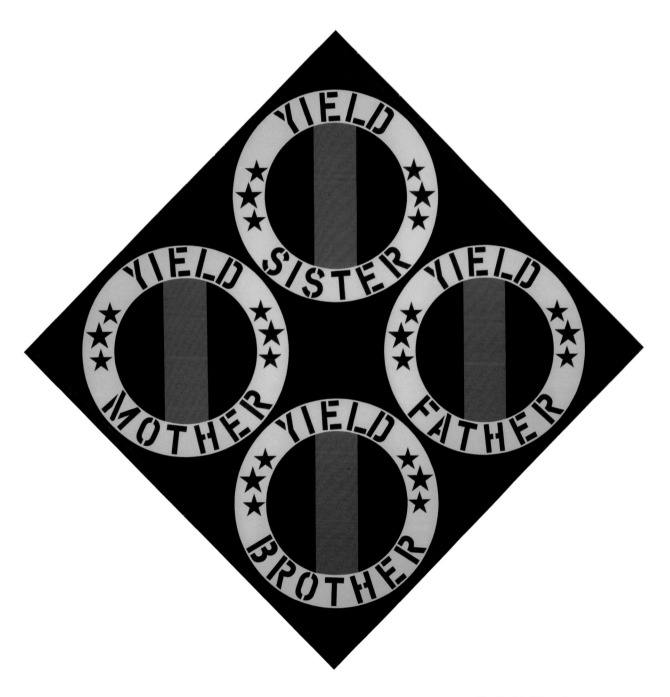

objects with an environmental presence, and the pop paintings and sculpture refer as well to their own presence as objects. For example, Robert Indiana's *Black Yield Brother III* (1964), which is a painting of road sign motifs, is rendered by the artist as a sign. The painting, however, can itself be seen as a sign, and as a sign it becomes an emblem that exudes the environmental presence of a roadside landscape. Pop art work, as objects, project an aura that they were always part of the environment: the artists merely pointed to them.

Much of pop work involves ready-made objects in a constructed environment. James Dine's *Child's Blue Wall* (1962) consists of a fragment of a papered wall sprinkled with stars painted on a canvas; at the side of the panel is a light switch, and in a corner stands a table lamp. With the switch one can turn on the bulb, and the stars glow forever on the paper heavens of the wall. One's participation in the work, no matter how reluctant, is direct. The ready-made

elements that project beyond the canvas draw the viewer into the accessible milieu of the canvas, and its banality reigns supreme.

George Segal casts life-size plaster figures, blanched of colour, into tightly composed environmental situations constructed from ready-made objects. The scale and space of his work are continuous with that of the viewer. The situations are taken directly from life: a group of people sitting on bus seats; a girl at a table painting her fingernails; a woman at a window; a man playing a pinball machine. These anonymous vignettes, small and true details, are fixed in time by the artist. It is as if these people were always there and the artist merely pointed to them at a certain moment in their lives. In the film *Jules et Jim* Truffaut stops the sequence of the frames that animate the actors on the screen, and the gestures of the actors are suddenly fixed in terms of the drama of the film. Segal's fixed scenes are the remembered fragments of specific gestures and specific faces

7.5 Jim Dine, *Child's Blue Wall*. 1962.

of the anonymous entities with which we inhabit our anonymous urban milieu. Each gesture, frozen in time, becomes painfully real and in itself absurd.

Segal's people are caught in a world of objects. They are dominated by the material scene in which they find themselves. In *The Gas Station*, a figure is standing with an oil can in his hand; he is surrounded by rows of oil cans and a rack of tires, and framed by a store front; another figure is sitting on a Coke box, with a Coca-Cola in his hand, between a rack of empty Coke bottles and a bottle dispensing machine. These mummified inhabitants become themselves ready-made blots of silent and disposable matter like the objects that engulf their lives.

It is difficult to like pop art. It dramatizes contradictions in the name of ambiguity so that the very nature of art becomes problematic. The subject matter of pop is banal. The cold presentation of this subject matter brutally exposes a slice of reality that one would prefer not to see, and any reconciliation it offers is harsh. The vulgarity of the subject matter makes high demands on the artist and it often overwhelms and dominates the content and the style of the work.

7.6 George Segal, *Gas Station*, 1963.

However, the artists' involvement with pop affirms man's contemporary world. He has no illusions that he can create, nor the ambition to imitate what he sees. He is, as Robbe-Grillet says of the role of the contemporary writer, "someone who has nothing to say."* That is, rather than being involved with general statements about life, he is involved with reality as it is. For most people the only tangible contact with reality is conditioned by the second-hand world of the mass media, and the pop artist deals in second-hand images. He uses the most reproduced images for an art which emphasizes above all the value of the unique object. A light bulb, a wall, a storefront, a sign, a bottle … the small, real, and true milieu of man is made special.

* Editor's note: Alain Robbe-Grillet, *Pour un nouveau roman* (Paris: Éditions de Minuit, 1963), 42.

8

The Old Montreal No One Wants to Preserve*

Like our ancestors we tend to reject the immediate architectural past.

In order to look at old and not-so-old Montreal let us set out a simple framework with which to proceed. Let us divide the buildings and streets of Montreal into four groups that correspond to the four unique stages that can be distinguished in the development of this city.

The first group belongs to the eighteenth-century town that once hid behind medieval stone walls. "Vieux Montréal"; narrow, ill lit streets; rough stone walls pierced by hard, rectangular, trimmed stone openings; the distinctive cornice and eave are all of this period which is now nostalgically regarded as the mythical time of innocence when life was simple and direct. Public lip service to old stones attests to the ever present ancestral image of the eighteenth century.

The second group of buildings and streets belong to the nineteenth century; that is the period after the 1820s to about the First World War. The city then moved out from the walls to

the east, to the west, up to the mountain, and across the river on the first iron bridges. The archaic stone buildings of the eighteenth-century town were replaced as some discarded garments that no longer fit. The general disregard for the earlier buildings was in keeping both with the original spirit of the population in leaving their ancestral lands in coming to this country, and with the nineteenth-century orientation towards the future. The growth of the city; dignified, tree-lined avenues; long streets of two- and three-storey tenements; the influx of immigrants; the beginnings of industrialization determined the character of the nineteenth-century city. It is this character that still marks the genius loci of Montreal as we know it.

The growth of the city and the industrialization that began in the nineteenth century accelerated rapidly in the twentieth. The subsequent distinctive group of buildings and streets belongs approximately to the first half of the twentieth century – the third phase in our game. The earlier city was pushed and pulled to accommodate the stirrings of the New Age. This period, as far as Montreal is concerned, was not

* From: *The Montrealer* (December 1964): 20–4.

equipped as yet to handle large buildings, a large population, nor the innovations of technology. The stone-bearing walls of the buildings of the nineteenth century now became walls of stone cladding supported on steel skeletons. Auto-mobiles gradually filled the streets that were originally planned for the horse and buggy; streets were widened, sidewalks were made narrow, and trees were removed. In keeping with the earlier spirit of the place, there was a total disregard for the old buildings other than by a few knowledge-able eccentrics.

A sterility characterizes many of the build-ings of this third period. Local historians have apologized that this architecture belonged to an "Economic Period." But the emptiness of the work and the inability to cope with reality in an imaginative way is difficult to defend especially in the presence of some nineteenth-century examples nearby. The big buildings of this third period look like small buildings that got out of hand as a mouse with a giraffe's neck. However, in a more recent phase, the builder-designers learned how to make big things big; for example, the recent Bank of Commerce building does not look too tall, it is tall!*

The contemporary period at which we have arrived is a fourth phase in the development of Montreal. The city as it was known is being dismantled. Unlike other periods when old buildings were demolished, in this new phase the very idea of a city seems to have become obso-lete. The growth of the place has now accelerated to the point where Montreal is no more a city within identifiable limits but a region whose boundaries have spread out far beyond the ori-ginal island (viz. the annexation problems of the once remote suburbs). The car now determines the modus operandi of the place. The express highways that are being built through the region

8.1 St Paul Street. The flat stones facades of commercial buildings, punctured by few windows, gave way in the nineteenth century to transparent stone skeletons. The extensive use of glass and the presence of an elevator, which have now become synonymous with office structures, were first introduced in these buildings.

of Montreal are cutting the city into disparate sections and tying it together as a patchwork of large and small groups of buildings connected by the roadways.

With the new expressways, the develop-ment of "centres" marks the new building type that belongs to the fourth phase of Montreal. The well-known shopping centre was the first prototype centre that appeared: a dense group of buildings surrounded by roadways, one can only get to it by car, and once there the car has to be left behind and one proceeds on foot in a town full of canned delights. The Place Ville-Marie complex is a centre of this sort with a daytime population that exceeds that of the old walled Montreal; the inside streets of Place Ville-Marie are as narrow as in a medieval town.

The new Trans-Canada Expressway that will cut through Montreal in a trench along Vitré

* Editor's note: The Imperial Bank of Commerce headquar-ters, inaugurated in 1962, was designed by British-born architect Peter Dickinson.

8.2 Commercial Palaces, 64 St Paul W. One notices the strong, repetitive rhythms of the stone, and a vertical emphasis controlled by the projecting horizontal bands which are stopped at the sky by the cornice. The cornice projects out to the street. Projections at the top of vertical elements articulate the facade with a flourish and create an event at each important joint in the construction. And, from the street, one experiences a rich, modulated, and sure architecture.

Street will lop off and isolate the old part of the city along the port. The proximity of the expressway, the density of buildings, narrow streets, marks this area as a "centre" in the new Montreal. The rise of popular preservationist sentiment that coincided with the fourth phase has already assured that a good part of the older buildings will here be embalmed (Bonsecours Market, for example). The influx of shopping + culture + old world charm will as well assure the commercial success of this new "Old Town Centre."

The older part of the city that is thus in the process of being salvaged in a historical centre is located between the streets of McGill, Berri, Craig,* and the waterfront, approximately the area of the eighteenth-century town. Few buildings remain from the eighteenth century, as most of them have been demolished or altered, but the tight texture of the earlier streets remains. The main square, and most of the buildings, date from the nineteenth century, when this part of the city was the "Old Town" where the administration, law courts, and commercial palaces were situated. However, the main centre of gravity of this nineteenth-century city was situated to the north-west.

It is in the major part of the nineteenth-century city outside of the old town that contemporary urban rebuilding, renewal, and removal is taking place. Most of the buildings that are now being junked belong to this epoch, as do most of the old buildings that still manage to hang on in the new urbs. We know very little about the architectural contribution of nineteenth-century Montreal. There is a sense of vengeance in the disregard, speed, and ease with which these buildings disappear. Many seem to be junked for no other reason than for clearing a piece of land of their presence. No one likes the buildings of their immediate predecessors: for most people the nineteenth century is still an

* Editor's note: now Saint-Antoine.

old and embarrassing garment that they want to shed, and not as yet the tattered but revered remnants of some ancestral vestment.

As most of the buildings done in the present, the buildings done in the past are for the most part speculative rubbish. Any society can insist on the replacement of its buildings. There is not one building that is not expendable; man-made, they are subject to his needs and often outlive their usefulness. But what is interesting is that some of the old buildings were not rubbish, and that everyone has more or less agreed that the continuance of urban life depends on the preservation of some part of the built structures of our cities as cultural vestiges. Usefulness, as well, is a complicated notion having to do with the collective needs of man as with his material expediency. Even though much of nineteenth-century Montreal has been demolished, there still remains a number of excellent representative buildings, and clearly some thought has to be given on what to keep and what to junk.

In nineteenth-century Montreal one can find the first examples of building types that have now become familiar in our contemporary city. These earlier buildings stand as witnesses to a period of ingenuity and vigour that did not hesitate to invent, with an architectural élan, new kinds of buildings for needs which were then very new. The development of the office building archetype, group housing, and the recently popular "functional" style happened in the nineteenth century.

The remarkable grain elevators that line the waterfront were developed in the nineteenth century, although built here at the beginning of the twentieth, using techniques that have only recently been applied to the building industry. The great European architects of the first quarter of this century expressed their admiration for these grain elevators, which represented for them the architectonic potential of a new age; in 1925, for example, Le Corbusier included

several photographs of Montreal grain elevators in his influential book *Vers une Architecture.** It always takes some imagination to appreciate the nineteenth-century grain elevators as architectonic monuments of our new cybernetic society. Montrealers have generally remained blind to these structures. Perhaps in the face of current sentiment that the grain elevators block Old Montreal from the port, a save-the-grain-elevator campaign will soon have to be initiated.

The first development of the contemporary office stack can be seen along St Paul Street. Commercial buildings dating from the mid-nineteenth century were the first to use an all-glass facade for maximum interior lighting, and an open interior plan that lends itself to a flexible arrangement of partitions. The facades of several of these buildings have a larger area of glass than the Place Ville-Marie tower. The solids of the facade explain with a pristine clarity the structure of the building – a simple cage of beams and columns. To emphasize the clarity of the buildings, the builder-designers modulated the parts and proportions of the building according to their height and placement in relation to the observer in the street; in Place Ville-Marie, a detail on floor 1 is identical to that on floor 31.

The streets east of St Denis, north and south of Sherbrooke, date from the nineteenth century. Here houses were built in series by speculators. A group along Rivard Street presents a taut, flat masonry facade to the street that is typical of the Montreal style of that period for low-cost housing. A somewhat later example of the same type of housing is a series of houses along Berri Street. Both series were built in the same manner – masonry-veneered wood boxes. However in the latter example we can see high nineteenth-century spirits at work. The street facade was visually enriched by the

* Editor's note: Le Corbusier, *Vers une architecture* (Paris: Crès et Cie, 1923).

8.3 The Functional Spirit, 415–419 des Récollets. An austere stone frame and glass infill, reduced to its bare essentials, relates this building to the great architecture of nineteenth-century Liverpool and the Chicago School. Among the essential aspects was the careful articulation of the proportions of its parts, of the base at the sidewalk and of the profile at the sky. The "Miesian" clarity of this architecture anticipates the style of the later international modern movement.

careful placement of ornamental elements. In both groups of houses, people were stacked on the ground at the rate of 200 per acre; a figure surprisingly higher than some of the recently proposed cure-alls for the world's housing ills.

The buildings on St Paul Street, the group of houses on Berri Street, and other nineteenth-century remnants show the involvement of the buildings with the street as an important place in the life of the city. According to this lingering

Renaissance manner, the facades of the buildings were invented to be seen from the street. All the excitement of the building was turned on for the passing inhabitants of the streets, and it told them what was going on inside. The nineteenth century very much enjoyed decoration, and details rich in carved motifs were placed for the passerby's eye. This decorative libido was defined and contained; austere walls would at special controlled places become exuberant, as

around a window or a door. The profile of the roof line, usually serrated, was used to bring the sky into the upper part of the building. One had to use one's eyes when looking at the streets of this city.

These nineteenth-century buildings have a sense of animated bravura about their iron, stone, and wood. There is a strength and visual delight in the work that reflects an optimistic belief in man's finite world, in science and in the good life. Now we know that science, for example, has a double edge that can wipe out life as easily as it can make it better. And our buildings, thin skinned, anonymous, endless, affirm our world.

LEFT | 8.4 Housing group on Berri Street. The dense collections of flats were grouped in two-storey units that enclosed the run of the street. The interiors of these houses are simple and comfortable; the energy of the architecture is spent on the environment of the street as a social entity. The street facade is composed of a repetition of identical elements, yet the total effect is visually rich in variation.

RIGHT | 8.5 Bijou style. The building was primarily composed of a pastiche of decorative vignettes according to taste, which said that everything important in the building had to happen somewhere off-centre. The insides were usually spacious and carefully worked out. The image illustrating the original essay is lost. This old postcard shows the house at the beginning of the twentieth century; it was demolished during the 1960s.

PHOTOGRAPHIC REVELATIONS

Photography is a central cognitive device in Melvin Charney's work. It played an important role in his art and in his inquiry into the social role of the image.*

When he was ten years old, he borrowed a camera and began to look at his surroundings through a photographic lens. The images that appeared in the shadows of his improvised darkroom revealed things that were not visible to the everyday, distracted eye. Photography, he later explained, was his means of assimilating the expanding urban and industrial world around him. At this young age, he also started collecting photographic images of cities and machines he found in various publications.

A few years later, the camera played a central role in his architectural education. During his studies at McGill University, he took pictures of Montreal, scanning his neighbourhood, the Mile End, the old parts of the city, and the industrial landscape of the port. At a time when photography was still considered an objective documentation of the real, he realized that this medium transformed space into an image of itself and thus taught an alternate way of seeing the city: the streets of his neighbourhood became linear gardens; the street as a physical entity subsumed individual buildings; the colossal grain elevators were part of a gigantic transportation system at the scale of the continent.

After completing his master's in architecture at Yale University, Charney followed the advice of his mentor Louis I. Kahn and travelled, during 1961 and 1962, in Mediterranean countries in search of the beginnings of architecture. Apart from the Greek temples of Sicily, he searched for timeless places rather than architectural monuments. Charney used many of his own photographs to illustrate his essays.

The photographs reproduced here are only a small sampling of the pictures he took in Montreal and abroad during the 1950s and 1960s.

* For a thorough analysis of the place of photography in Charney's work, see Pierre Landry, *Melvin Charney* (Montreal: Musée d'art contemporain de Montréal, 2002).

Pl. 1   Entrance to the Lachine Canal, Montreal, 1956.

FACING PAGE | Pl. 2 Lachine Canal, Montreal, 1956.

ABOVE | Pl. 3 Lachine Canal, Montreal, 1956.

Pl. 4 Grain Elevator No. 2, with Bonsecours Market,
Saint-Paul Street, Montreal, 1969.

Pl. 5   Temple of Poseidon, Segesta, Sicily, 1961.

Pl. 6 The columns, Temple of Poseidon, Segesta, Sicily, 1961.

THIS PAGE | Pl. 7 The columns, Temple of Poseidon, Segesta,
Sicily, 1961.

OVERLEAF | Pl. 8 Temple of Poseidon, Segesta, Sicily, 1961.

OVERLEAF | Pl. 9 Temple of Concordia, Agrigento, Sicily, 1961.

THIS PAGE | Pl. 10 Monasteries, Meteora, Greece, 1961.

Pl. 11 House under construction, east of Kirsehir, Turkey, 1961.

ABOVE | Pl. 12 Cappadocia, Ürgüp, Turkey, 1961.

FACING PAGE | Pl. 13 House on the road
between Konya and Aksaray, Turkey, 1961.

9

Architecture without Architects: The Trulli of Apulia*

The real history of architecture is for the most part a history of anonymous vernacular buildings. However, the study of architectural history was until recently confined to a few isolated monuments that belonged to the span of time and space deemed significant by Western man. As well as selecting only certain periods, architecturally history also counted the few buildings that belonged to the powerful and wealthy to the exclusion of all other kinds. This "official history" usually began with the Egyptian pyramids, it leaped to the temples of fifth century B.C. Greece and then unto Rome and the glorious Renaissance. Little deviation was allowed in the lineal progression of the stylistic development; Byzantine architecture, for example, was admitted without much enthusiasm because of its obvious Eastern influences. Some of the Islamic, Japanese, and Chinese architectural monuments were later allowed into the hallowed fold as "exotic" (i.e., foreign) elements.

Architectural history conceived in this manner, as a lineal sequence of periods and styles, made way for a style of architecture for our modern epoch; this history set out, in a sense, the context for the emergence and acceptance of a style of building appropriate to modern man as Roman architecture was stylistically shown to be appropriate to the Romans. Thus modern architecture, as the most recent of the styles, can be seen to fit the schema of the architectural historian, and an elitist attitude in regard to what is or is not important architecture has persisted well into this modern epoch.

This "official" architecture thrived on the work that could be attributed to an author and totally excluded vernacular buildings. The cult of style and personality, and of the isolated monument, was nurtured by the Romantic interlude of the nineteenth century. According to a social view of this period, the romantic attitude can be considered to be the reaction of the artist and the intellectuals to the beginnings of industrialization and of the mass anonymity of city-life.

* From "Trulli of Southern Italy," *Landscape* 15, no. 1 (1965): 32–3, and "Architectures sans architectes: les trulli de l'Apulie," *Vie des arts* 38 (1965): 54–7. Editor's note: This essay was published in abridged versions in *Landscape* and *Vie des arts*. It is published here in its entirety for the first time.

In this vein, the neoclassicist of that time can be seen to be the other face of the romantic coin of the period, and the modern movement of the first half of this century as the beautiful but final gesture of the romantic agony.

The modern movement was the ultimate reaction to industrialization and to the mass world; it still afforded the architect the possibility of making a manifesto and a personal gesture. However, the modern period also bared the problems of an architecture for the anonymous buildings of a massively populated world that had new technical means at its disposal. The modern architects looked to factories, warehouses, dams, and grain elevators – the anonymous industrial vernacular of the late nineteenth and early twentieth century – to find an architecture for their monuments. In the same way, they started looking at white houses in the villages on the Greek Islands in the Aegean as well as the Parthenon.

In the present world we are very much at home with mass technology and the anonymity of our sprawling cities. History is no longer accepted as a lineal, sequential succession of events but rather as a mosaic of evolving human impulses and techniques. Historiography and ethnography have broadened the base of architectural history.

As a young architect brought up in a milieu when anonymous vernacular architecture was not quite as yet accepted, one found oneself nevertheless attracted to these buildings. One's maître had pinned on the wall the plans of a fourth-century church which had subsequently been rebuilt several times; it was the sense of process and change in the plan that counted and not the finished, isolated building. With a sense of conspiracy, one shared with other architects the discovery of a well-composed row of nineteenth-century tenements on Lagauchetière Street in Montreal; the discovery in New York of sketches of the German anthropologist, Frobenius, of tubular Sudanese huts; and in

Paris, the exchange of impressions on visits to excavated towns in Cappadocia, and to the trulli of Apulia. The cognoscenti then shared the understanding that it was neither the picturesque nor the "exotic" that attracted one, but the thirst to experience and to learn about human environment.

This underground period is now more or less over. One of the events marking this was a recent exhibit at the Museum of Modern Art, in New York, called Architecture without Architects.* The exhibit brought together photographs that admirers of the anonymous vernacular had diligently culled from odd picture books and from their travels. These photographs were enlarged, catalogued, and exposed as a public polemic. This interest arrives at a time when, ironically, it is the beginning of the end for most of the architecture exhibited. Vernacular traditions represent for the most part pre-technological methods that have persisted until now despite industrialization, and it is inevitable that they will be replaced by the products of a central design office.

The vernacular traditions that are of special interest are those that have ancient origins. These buildings can serve as a major historical source; there is very little data available on the early developments of architecture and it is therefore surprising that the vernacular has until now been largely ignored. For example, a dramatic tradition that has persisted since the Neolithic period as a viable building system can be seen in the trulli dwellings of southern Italy. The trullo is a method of stone construction that results in a distinctive family of architectonic forms that are profoundly ancient, profoundly Mediterranean, and still in use. After visiting the ruins of Pompeii and the temples of Paestum, a

* Editor's note: Bernard Rudofsky, *Architecture without Architects: A Short Introduction to Non-Pedigreed Architecture* (Garden City, NY: Museum of Modern Art/ Doubleday, 1964).

secret part of the architect's "Grand Tour" has often included a turn to the east across Calabria with its hill towns to visit the trulli in the province of Apulia. Apulia is located along the Adriatic coast; it is the region of Italy that is nearest to the orient and throughout history it was at the cross-current of the Eastern and Western Mediterranean. The land is steeped in history; there are prehistoric remains, ruined structures that belonged to Magna-Graecia and to Rome, rock-cut cells of Byzantine hermits, as well as beautiful examples of Norman architecture.

The trulli can be found in a triangle of land formed by the city-ports of Bari, Brindisi, and Taranto; all three were once Greek towns. The landscape of this region is of rolling hills, olive and almond groves, cultivated fields, ochre-coloured soil, and outcrops of limestone. The stone outcrops have a narrow, banded stratification that fractures into flattish slabs several inches thick; these slabs are readily adaptable to be piled one on the other without further trimming. The stones cleared from the land form low walls that divide the landscape. The trulli begin to appear in the first rise of land above the sea; in the hills are the towns of Alberobello, Fasano, and Martina Franca at the centre of the trulli region. In the Istria valley, at the foot of Martina Franca, one has a view of innumerable trulli that dot the landscape with marked architectural strokes.

Between the fieldstone walls, a tighter enclosure of walls separates a cluster of conical stone domes – a trullo. Circular walls form the base of the cones, and the surfaces of the cones turn smoothly one into the other with a wave-like ripple that mounts one apex and then another. A part of the town of Alberobello itself consists of dense clusters of trulli along narrow streets. Parts of the exterior of inhabited trulli are painted white; the insides of the trulli are white in respect to an intimate family life, and the streets of the town are white in respect to

the life of the community – this is typical of the Mediterranean tradition.

Typical as well of the Mediterranean is the hard clear light of the region. The geometric forms of the trullo stand in the light and mark man's habitat. Yet the form of the trullo rises out of the earth with some difficulty: the lower walls tend to draw it back into the earth as they extend out to the fields from the base of the cones, and with height the cones attenuate – the attenuation is lengthened by a finial placed at the apex of the cone. The trullo, belonging both to the earth and to man-made forms that stand out of the earth, is very much in the Neolithic spirit.

According to archaeological evidence, the first human settlements of a permanent nature occur in the early Neolithic period at the beginning of systematic agriculture. The very stones cleared from the fields and arranged in a circle could mark off a place special and separate from its surroundings. The circle is the shortest line that can be used to enclose the largest area; and the circle affords as well, symbolic closure and a focus on a central point. The architectural historian Sigfried Giedion has pointed out that the circle around a fire had pride of place, and circular single roomed huts appear over the entire world as a primitive form of dwelling. These dwellings housed the living, the protective household spirits, and the ancestors – the dead were often buried under the floor. The lowest deposits of excavated settlements in the Mediterranean basin have shown the presence of circular beehive huts (*tholoi*). On the Island of Cyprus, for example, a settlement of several hundred tholoi has been discovered at Khirkitia; forty-eight were excavated, precisely recorded, and dated to the middle of the fourth

FACING PAGE | 9.1 Alberobello, Bari, Italia.

millennium – a relatively late date for tholoi dwellings.

The method of construction – stone on stone – is similar to other megalithic structures that are found in the Mediterranean, Northern Europe, Ireland, etc. In Apulia, along with the trulli, menhirs, cyclopean walls, and dolmens can be found. The marked relation of the trullo to the megalithic nuraghi of Sardinia is underlined by the presence in Apulia of proto-nuraghi towers. Stone towers found near Otranto are clearly of the nuraghi type and a variant of the nearby trulli.

The conical, hollow mound of stone – the form of the trullo – is related to the sacral tombs indigenous to the chthonic cults of the Mediterranean and of Asia Minor. The aegides of the gods were first invoked to protect the hut of a man, and later the hut itself became the dwelling place of the gods. The excavations of several ancient sites have shown that the circular form of the hut was superseded, once the settlements began to evolve, by rectangular constructions, and the circular hut subsequently came to represent a place that belonged to the ancestors. The archaeologist Seton Lloyd in his book "Early Anatolia" has remarked, in regard to the burial customs at Polatli Huyuk of the chalcohithic period, that circular tholos had been constructed in the empty space between two houses immediately above a stone burial chamber that belonged to a previous level of the settlement.* Circular buildings of this sort had been located at other sites, and the discovery suggests that they functioned as a funerary chapel built to mark the traditional location of a tomb.

The art historian Vincent Scully has pointed out that the Mycenaean and Minoan burial tholoi were related to a specific configuration in the landscape – the conical burial mound was usually placed in relation to a nearby horned peak.† The landform symbolized the body of the goddess in whose hollow enclosure the dead lords hoped to find permanence and a kind of immortality after death. He goes on to say that the conical hut itself may have been a place sacred to the goddess as can be seen in the trulli of Apulia where the markings of symbols resembling hers can be found: Scully found a trullo with a snake and horns symbol painted on the conical dome.

The resemblance of the present-day trulli to the tombs at Mycenae is very striking; for example, see the well-known tomb called the treasury of Atreus. The beehive form of the tomb, the articulated entrance (dromos), and the careful placement of the masonry can be considered to be a high art form of the tradition of construction that is still producing the trulli. The elongated rectangular entrance, the dromos, can still be seen to be part of some of the trulli clusters. The very sacral geometry of the Mycenaean necropolis – the circle and the conical dome – belongs to the tradition of the trulli. As a sepulchral monument, the conical dome on a circular base persisted for a long period; in Central Anatolia, several beautiful examples of conical tombs can be seen in the Seljuk architecture of the tenth and the eleventh centuries.

Pushing similarities of form yet further afield, the Stupas of India can be seen to have the same basic form order as the tholoi of the Mediterranean. One however cannot conclude that these similarities are entirely due to the migration of ideas; rather it would seem that given a certain material and climatic condition, people will tend to develop a similar geometry of forms. The circular base and conical dome can be considered

---

* Editor's note: Seton Lloyd, *Early Anatolia: The Archaeology of Asia Minor before the Greeks* (Harmondsworth, Middlesex: Penguin, 1956).

† Editor's note: Vincent Scully Jr. *The Earth, the Temple, and the Gods: Greek Sacred Architecture* (New Haven, CT: Yale University Press, 1962).

as a basic form response that can be found in a variety of vernacular traditions. The architectural monuments of a civilization cannot be separated from these basic vernacular responses which in the first instance nurture a vocabulary of forms. In this sense, modern architecture arrived when architects were able to discover the vernacular forms of industrial technology which had evolved despite them. The building tradition of the trulli thus belongs to an archetypal genre of Neolithic construction. And, in isolation, it evolved a regional type with a marked environmental system and visual character.

The horizontally stratified outcrops of stone that fragmented into slabs influenced the construction. The current type of construction of most of the trulli consists of thick walls composed of an inner and an outer layer of flat stone slabs with earth between. From the height of a man, the stones are corbelled, one row stepping in on the other, to cap the interior; and an outer skin of flat stone, laid like tiles, completes the cone, again with earth or rubble between the two layers.

The construction, the plan, and the vertical section of each trullo are very much the same: a standard vocabulary of forms is in use in response to environmental conditions. The usual plan of the trullo is a circular outside, with the interior invariably a square with apses or alcoves in the sides of the square as a Byzantine church plan. The height of the trullo varies according to the circumference of the base; the height at which the corbels begin remains constant. Entrances are treated in a standard way: a rectangular extension of one of the apses of the interior opens out to a shallow portico covered by an arch or corbel of stone – a truncated version of the ancient dromos. There is a standard method for finishing the apex of the cone, a prescribed method for painting parts of the trullo, as well as a consistent language of signs painted on the domes.

The trulli group consists of a cluster of the circular units that are linked in a uniform way. There are usually one or two dominant units about which the others accrete. The variation in height and size of the units in the cluster responds to an inner plan of use – the size and growth of the family can be clearly read according to the cluster.

The variations in the system of trulli occur in the grouping of the standard elements of construction. A defined spatial organization controls the relationship of these elements. There are three distinct zones, one above the other, in the organization. Plastically, each standard element is rich, and their controlled placement within a compositional framework serves to strengthen their context. The tripartite organization of the composition belongs, as well, to the classic tradition of stone construction.

The first zone above the ground is that of the field stone walls. These walls subdivide and control the landscape; they enclose large areas of cultivated fields, smaller compounds about the trulli, and become the tight, hollow, circular walls that thicken at the base of the conical domes of the dwelling. Roads and paths are localized by the walls, as are the points of entry and exit – a gate or a door that breaks the line of the wall. The main entrance to the trulli cluster usually strands somewhat higher than the walls and marks the main point of entry. The entrance is the only negative volume of the cluster; it is a shallow hollowing out, a concavity in the midst of rotund convexity.

The second zone is that of the cones. The stone is here laid as scales on a surface that undulates and slides with a wave-like motion. The third zone marks the profile of the cluster. Each cone is pinpointed by a finial that denotes an interior volume. The point of the cone thins and then flares out to a pedestal on which a finial is placed; the finial complements the geometry of the trulli with a sphere, a half sphere,

9.2 Trulli with coloured facade.

or a rectangle that has been cut in diagonally at
the four corners. This latter type of finial serves
to remind once again of the ancient origins
involved: the four-cornered rectangle strongly
resembles Minoan altars.

The location of the painted elements is related
to the tripartite organization of the trulli. The
lower walls at the base of the domes are painted
white as is the inside of the entrance; the conical
surface of the dome remains as a grey texture;

and the finial is rendered in white. The grey
stone of the cones serves as the background for
white signs; these are tilted to the sky and the
symbolic message is sent to the gods as well as
to fellow men. The iconography of these signs
reflects the historic and cultural influences
experienced on this tip of Italy; Chthonic, Latin,
Byzantine, and Cabalistic roots can be readily
discerned. Essentially these symbols belong to
the ancient preliterate traditions and graphically
illustrate the origins of the place.

The trulli can still be seen to belong in the
fields with the people who work the land. The

grouping of circular huts is a sculptural cluster in the round that can grow outward in all directions. Where a road approaches a trulli, the cluster can be seen in some places to have adapted to the linearity of the road with a rectangular facade that stands in front of the cluster as some artful *trompe l'oeil*. An example of a facade of this sort was found articulated in panels of colour; yellow was used for the large panels, blue for subsidiary panels, red trim about the entrance, and white trim for the secondary openings and for the frame – the colours, as historians have pointed out, that decorated classic Greek temples, used in a manner that is probably not unlike ancient polychromy. In the town of Alberobello, it can be seen how the clusters of huts have adapted in a crude way to a town organization. The trulli awkwardly arranged themselves to the disposition of the streets; the base of the trullo has become square, octagonal, or rectangular to accommodate the group along a street. There is no coherent order to the jumble of cones that are cramped for space – the cones heave and undulate as some primeval landform in a state of unrest. As archaeologists have shown, a rectangular building that lends itself to the organization of a street superseded the Neolithic huts in many ancient settlements that they have excavated.

It is the visual strength of the trulli as an architectural object, and the relation of the trulli to antiquity that attracts the aficionados to Apulia. The old Neolithic found here is particularly Italian: the primitive hut presents a "bella figura." But what is especially interesting for the architect is the clear and strong environmental system of the trulli, and a system that can make functional variations within a standard building method. Human values that have persisted despite change can here be experienced at a time when humanity is losing touch with its environment.

10

Place Victoria, Montreal*

A *Place* in a city used to be an open space surrounded by buildings. It was a focus of several streets and a gathering point for people and vehicles. Both its void and enclosure gave it meaning as an outdoor urban room.

Victoria Square was such a *Place* in Montreal. (See Fig. 33.6.) At its beginning the square was first a marshy piece of land to the west of the fortifications of the old town, and then a hay market. During the nineteenth century, the tight streets of the business district of the old city converged at this sunlit tract. The commercial palaces gave way to an easy row of trees, public grass, paths, benches, drinking fountains, and a public toilet. This sense of urban amenity was complemented by a bronze statue of Queen Victoria.

Now, Place Victoria is an imposing building complex, located to one side of the old Victoria Square. The building has overtaken the square and usurped its name. A tall, strong-boned, and well-wrapped tower stands forty-seven storeys above a lower block and a podium. The

* From *The Canadian Architect* 10, no. 7 (July 1965): 37–54.

lower block is articulated as separate elements, the tower itself has three equal divisions, and the whole complex reads as a cluster of similar blocks in a powerfully structured mesh.

The new Place has been set back by 80 feet from the line of the old square, and the area of the old square has been enlarged by 40 per cent. However the old square is now in effect, despite the proposed landscape design, part of the podium and the breathing space of a very large building. It is the building itself, as its name cleverly recognizes, that has become the urban focus.

Place Victoria, as an open square, belonged to the nineteenth-century city. The new Place belongs to a new Montreal that is rapidly expanding and reshaping the old city. The installation of a rapid transit system and the construction of expressways have dismantled the Montreal that was known. The heart of the city is being reconstructed in a dense vertical configuration that will serve as the centre of an expanding urban region. The *foci* of the new centre are building clusters such as Place Victoria and Place Ville-Marie. The scale of each of these complexes is equivalent to a district of the old town; in this way, Place Victoria is an effective physical link between the financial zone of old Montreal and the new commercial development along Dorchester Boulevard.* The Place will house a population equivalent to that of an important medieval town, but its inhabitants will vacate the town for the night.

The two elemental components of Place Victoria are the base of the building and the shaft of the office tower. The tower stands over the base which slides out beyond it to form a link for a projected second tower. The extended base forms plug-in points and links for a possible sequence of towers; even though only one tower is up, the system for the emplacement of another is set up.

The first scheme that Nervi and Moretti proposed for Place Victoria consisted of three towers in diagonal row above a base. In the second scheme, part of which has now been implemented, two independent towers are linked by a base. Both the first and second schemes are composed of a sequence of towers; but the first was more of a finished product, whereas the latter emphasizes a sense of process. The tower became, as well, more of an assembled element in the second scheme. The sense of process set up both in the grouping and in the phasing of the elements of this building engages the building in a dialogue that begins to answer some of the problems of this new urban type. Some of the answers shown by the architecture of Place Victoria are indeed very bold; one senses in the cluster of building elements some doubt as to the final destiny of the form even though each element is very complete in itself.

The high-rise office tower shares the skyline of Montreal with Place Ville-Marie, CIL House, and the Bank of Commerce building.† Neverthe-

less, from both far and near, a sense of physical clarity in the architecture of this tower separates it from the others. The articulation of stacks of floors, the expression of the bold corners, the exposed diagonal braces, and the taut, bulging curtain wall set off the physical and structural presence of this building.

The articulation of the corner columns and the diagonal supports introduce, within the scale of the total frame of the tower, the intermediate scale of a superstructure. The sense of process set up by the whole scheme is here carried out as well. The intermediate diagonal supports divide the total stacks of floors into three similar blocks, and these three blocks of floors appear as if inserted into the superstructure with the intermediate floors as a service plug-in link.

The blocks of floors are wrapped by a curtain wall that is treated as taut skin stretched between the corners. The smooth membrane bulges out to enclose the peripheral columns; a heavier metal rail is extended along the curtain wall on the line of these columns. At the top and bottom of the intermediate floors where the diagonal braces occur, and at the base, the curtain wall breaks and the edge is articulated by the ends of the metal rails that carry the glass plate; here, the two larger rails are pulled out. As in the rest of the design, the curtain wall is both well integrated and set off as an assemblage.

The office tower, as a piece of architectural hardware, has been evolving as a type since the nineteenth century. The anonymous nineteenth-century commercial buildings that can be found in Montreal, New York, or Liverpool, present in a very direct way the multi-use loft as an architectural type. Since that time there has been a steady development of its systems, and the interlude of modern architecture was, in a sense, only the recognition of a technological revolution that had already taken place. This type of building has become technically, a very complex piece of design integration. The two nearby towers of Place Ville-Marie and CIL House offer an immediate comparison to

* Editor's note: now René-Lévesque Boulevard.

† Editor's note: Charney refers to Place Ville-Marie by I.M. Pei and Associates; CIL House by Skidmore, Owings, and Merrill; and the Canadian Imperial Bank of Commerce by Peter Dickinson and Associates.

the tower of Place Victoria. Both were designed in association with large New York offices and are typical of U.S. corporate architecture. Both exhibit, by comparison, an overt formalism and a two-dimensional composition of parts. The physical gesture of the tower as an intricate structure does not penetrate their smooth skins. Rather than allow technology its logical game, as was relatively well played in Place Victoria, their architecture follows a packaging ideology which has all the semblance of cool integration. The tower of Place Ville-Marie is as well integrated a product of the type as can be found. However, in Place Victoria, integration has in itself become part of the form; the technology of this tower is realized in the architecture, and, as architecture, technology here becomes a human factor.

Even though the high-rise office tower is a known building type, it is the context of the tower that has very much changed. This context is no more the environment of a city street, but a cluster of buildings of which the tower is a part. In the case of Place Victoria, the components of the complex other than the tower consist of base buildings that extend five storeys above, and four floors below, the level of the podium of the tower. Here is where one arrives and departs, where one parks, and where the commercial life of the Place takes place. Each of the functions that can be found in this part of the building occupied in the old city a building of its own, i.e., the drugstore, the bank, the stock exchange. The shopping streets of the district of the city that was replaced by the Place have in a sense moved into this part of the building. Place Ville-Marie, which was the first complex in Montreal with an interior arcade, now has 80,000 people per day circulating through its shopping precincts. As in the old city where one district was connected with another, there is a system of tunnels now being constructed that will link Place Victoria with Place Ville-Marie, other important building groups, and with the Metro.

The base components of the Place thus present a special environmental problem. The interior circulation spaces – arcades, lobbies, corridors, stairs, and elevators – are part of the private building, yet because of the size of the building complex they really serve the public as streets and are in a sense an extension of the public city. In Place Victoria, as in other similar building complexes, this dichotomy is not clearly resolved in the planning. The interior shopping plaza is treated as a corridor, and the layers of shops and parking lots are not related to the podium in or to the nearby remains of the old square. The arrival and entrance by car is still treated as a very secondary affair even though the very existence of the Place is keyed into the new regional road network.

It is the clear conception of the tower of Place Victoria that carries the strength of the project. Inasmuch as the architects and engineers of Montreal who participated in this building understood the spirit of its vision, and the spirit of their craft, they contributed to its realization. If one is to judge from the design of the curtain wall, and from that of ribbed slabs that are said to have been worked out by the local associates, it is to these specialists that part of the success is due. However as Marshall McLuhan has pointed out, a specialist is one who never makes small mistakes,* and this can be illustrated by much of the local architecture of Montreal. It is the genius of Nervi, and that of Moretti, that are to be felicitated. Place Victoria makes no aesthetic excuses for itself; it manages to express by its very existence a building as an elegant human gesture. Its realization is an important architectural event, and it is indeed fortunate for Montreal that its centre should include a building of this calibre.

* Editor's note: "The specialist is one who never makes small mistakes while moving toward the grand fallacy." See "Housing: New Look and New Outlook," in Marshall McLuhan, *Understanding Media: The Extensions of Man* (New York: McGraw-Hill, 1964).

11

The Rear End of the Xerox or How I Learned to Love That Library*

In an issue of *Architectural Forum* concerned with the core of the city "where the action is," John Johansen's Clark University Library building sets off its architectural gymnastics in a void. A library is part of a university, and as such it is a component facility of a group of buildings that together make a campus. In the larger urban context a campus itself can be seen to exude its own sense of place where the educational action is. What is the environmental identity of the

* From: *Architectural Forum* 124, no. 4 (May 1966): 60–1. Editor's note: This essay was originally introduced with the following paragraphs from the editors of *The Architectural Forum*. "Three months ago (Jan./Feb issue), we published an article on the proposed Clark University Library, and a commentary on it by its architect, John M. Johansen. The architect's statement, 'John M. Johansen declares himself,' elicited a mixed response from readers around the globe – to put it mildly. Meanwhile, Mr Johansen had asked a number of well-known critics and historians to comment. Some did – but not for publication; others said they were rendered speechless by the design and/or by Mr Johansen's prose. Two respected critics, however, agreed to submit their reactions in writing and for publication. Their comments are reproduced herewith." The first critic was Melvin Charney, the second, Sibyl Moholy-Nagy.

Clark campus? How does this library relate? How do the circulation patterns tie into this cultural junction? It is obvious that these questions were not primary criteria in the design of the library. This building is interested in itself; it is involved in a library as a physical surrounding rather than in its surroundings.

Library architecture requires the skilful handling of large and small spaces plugged into a warehouse of books. Contemporary libraries are for the most part neatly packaged commodities that oversimplify and generalize wrapping and structure. The most up-to-date package calls for fragmented and accidental effects. Johansen's building can be included in this current trend; however, the fragmentation here is soundly based on post-packaging notions that commit the architecture to a true form dialogue. The parts of this building are uncoupled, separated, moved out into the campus and re-engaged so that the building becomes a free assembly and a "place" where something special happens, as well as an object. It is this environmental quality that marks this building as an important contribution to the present architectural scene.

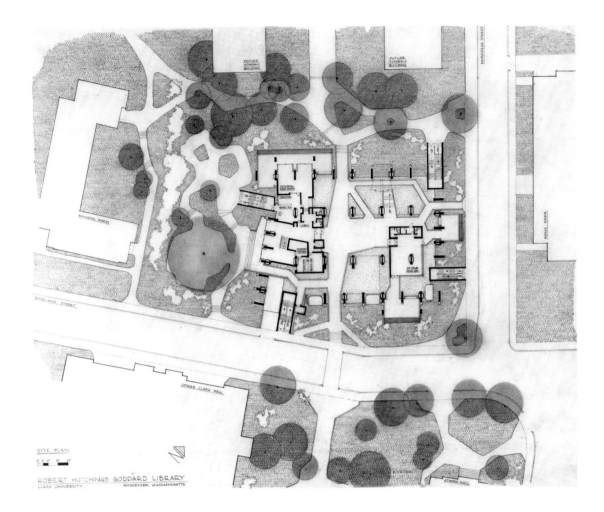

SITE PLAN

ROBERT HUTCHINGS GODDARD LIBRARY
CLARK UNIVERSITY.   WORCESTER, MASSACHUSETTS.

11.1 Floor plan of Johansen's Clark Library.

The Johansen building is designed from the inside out. The parts of the library that the students use for various activities with books stand out from a central book silo. Each of these parts is treated as a component with its own required configuration of space and material: the periodical room is very different from the reading rooms, which are in turn very different from the bent tube stairs or the snorkel ventilators. These components undergo further modifications according to light and orientation conditions. The total assemblage of these components is also concerned with use. The central box of books and ancillary elements are clearly related to the circulation conduits that feed up from a lower pedestrian plaza.

Despite Johansen's claim in his "Declaration of Independence" accompanying the photographs that this architecture just happened and that the building is "improvised" and "uncomposed" like the backside of a Xerox machine, there are traditional canons of composition evident in his work. In the assemblage the corners are made heavy, and the disposition of elements at the columns is articulated in a quasi-tripartite arrangement that sits firmly on a battered base with a sharp weight at the top against the sky. In this way, as well, this building is very much in touch with the times.

11.2 Clark Library, model.

The emphasis in the design of the library on the specific configuration of parts, and the whole as a frank accumulation of these parts, reveals to the observer a physical dialogue that clearly explains the nature of the building. The building reads as a committed place full of the objects and implications of a library; thus it becomes an identifiable density. In the totally urbanized environment of the city-lands in which we live, the nature of the architecture of a special sub-environment becomes an important message of this building.

PART THREE

Beyond Architecture

"Beyond Architecture" brings together ten essays which were published between 1966 and 1969. At that time, Charney examined the discourse of contemporary architecture about the anticipated effects of the technological revolution. He revealed that the masters of the 1920s saw Montreal's grain elevators not as the physical facts of a technological process, but as formal images of the beginnings of a new architecture. For him, a similar formalism characterized the utopian visions of the 1960s. A careful examination of the possibilities offered by new materials such as plastics and concrete led Charney to argue that future developments already existed in present possibilities. In tune with the optimism of Reyner Banham and Cedric Price, Charney saw in technology a means of individual emancipation which could transform building design into an environmental process. Rather than formal design, architecture could implement technological processes in such a way that users would interact with and transform their environment. Charney's entry for the Canadian pavilion at Osaka, which was conceived as a flexible, self-erecting building system to be shipped in containers, is the emblematic project for this section.

12.1 Melvin Charney, ca. 1967.

Beyond Architecture

LOUIS MARTIN

One finds the best formulation of Charney's critique of formalism in his essay "Grain Elevators Revisited," published in the July 1967 issue of *Architectural Design* on Expo 67.[1] In this seminal text, he reminded readers that Montreal's grain elevators were a source of inspiration for the pioneers of modern architecture. If the elevators were seen by modern architects as the prefiguration of a new geometric architectural language, he noticed that they were never studied as functional organisms. Similarly, contemporary architects looked for a new lifestyle in technology but were really interested only in the image of technology. For Charney, to learn something from grain elevators it was necessary to consider them as "a system, or part of a system, the mechanisms of which are dominated by movement." Consequently, as an analogy for architecture, the elevators could not be reduced to mere formal images. For him, it was "the process of which they are an image that is important. This process we must study if we believe that architecture is an involvement with human processes rather than with designed things."[2]

Towards New Environmental Systems

The way beyond "architecture as formal image" took the form of a search for new industrial environmental systems, which Charney conceived in terms of prefabricated kits of parts. In this connection, his conversations with Konrad Wachsmann provided important notions which corroborated his ideas. During the Second World War, Wachsmann had developed, with Walter Gropius, the "packaged house system" which consisted of prefabricated self-supporting panels with which it was possible to erect a house in nine hours. A commercial failure, Wachsmann's system represented for Charney more a contribution to an aesthetic of prefabrication than a real technological breakthrough. More important for Charney was Wachsmann's idea that all spatial projections were from the start geometrical projections, an idea which was confirmed by vernacular rock-cut architecture. To validate that intuition, Wachsmann talked about the "tacit dimension of knowledge," a notion that Charney immediately tracked down in the writings of Hungarian philosopher Michael Polanyi.[3] His travels had opened his eyes to the fact that vernacular architecture had an inherent architectural order; the work of Polanyi led him to assert that people possessed an innate knowledge of architecture.

The conjunction of prefabrication, new synthetic materials, and innate architectural knowledge suggested that the mass production of prefabricated industrial elements would enable people to build and modify freely the physical environment according to their needs. Inspired by the works of Buckminster Fuller and Cedric Price, Charney foresaw that "buildings" would become "systems-to-live-in" capable of generating "indeterminate environments that are geared to perform their required jobs. The design distinction between a general service infrastructure, and the components that specifically relate spaces to people, allows the designs to profit from both transient and the permanent conditions; the transient elements being clearly designated as expendable."[4]

A first synthesis of these ideas was realized by Charney's students in an architectural studio which probed how plastics could be used to create a portable environmental system to house workers in the arctic and subarctic regions of Canada. Among other requirements, the program specified that this system should be assembled by the workers themselves rather than by a specialized workforce. This experiment logically led Charney to reflect on two problems: prediction, or the architect's capacity to visualize future environments, and flexibility, or the degree of actual freedom an environmental system could provide to users.

Prediction

Charney addressed the issue of prediction in several essays. In "Notes on a Guide for Travellers to the Plastic Inevitable," an introductory essay to a thematic issue of the magazine *Parallel* entitled "Urbland," for which he was the guest editor, he embraced the recent tendencies toward open-ended systems and formless, anticipatory design because they broke with the fixed images of the supercity of past utopias.[5] Drawing on a number of recent publications, Charney depicted how the emerging form of the megalopolis was only a transitional stage leading toward a future urbland. The megalopolis erased the distinction between country and city, anticipating a totally designed landscape in which transportation systems would connect high-density pedestrian clusters of buildings. But the first-generation clusters, like Place Ville-Marie or Place des Arts in Montreal, remained inadequate ideological containers filtering the experiences of shopping and art. "The problem for the new architecture," Charney wrote, was "the creation of an instant environment that is compounded of willed and spontaneous life."[6] Such an environment was approximated in Cedric Price's Fun Palace, "a giant erector set with the potential of manufacturing spaces for all purposes; a kit of parts that can be animated to accommodate a political rally, a wrestling match or bingo fest."[7] He added: "One has here the sense of *urbland*: an environment of places at the nodes of the transportation systems. The *place* is a device which has a life-supporting structure, similar to a street-grid in the old city, about which a transient, parasitic and specific architecture, similar to buildings on old city streets, will work for people."[8] The editorial concluded confidently that urbland was the thing to come.

In his next essay on the issue of environmental prediction, "Environmental Conjecture: In the Jungle of the Grand Prediction," Charney noted that the latest anticipations of the future were less optimistic than the frozen visions of the megacities of the first part of the century.[9] After all, humanity had learned that science and technology could "serve any master and any set of goals." The proliferation of superarchitectures that predicted the inevitable urblands of the future raised the question "How do we get there from here?" But for Charney, that interrogation was unreasonable and biased because it was "a product-conditioned question that [was] seeking another and newer form of product."

Referring to George Lichtheim, Charney posited that prediction was based on the dialectics of extrapolation and demonstration: "In environmental design, prediction is not only a question of the extrapolation of existing trends and countertrends but also the demonstration of the environmental and symbolic potential inherent in the fantastic display of technologic capability current in other fields."[10]

The superarchitectures of the 1960s projected visions of a totally industrialized environment in which the recent developments in aerospace and armament gave the texture of the future machine to live in. But, for Charney, their anticipatory environmental hardware was far less radical than many existing systems like mobile homes, for instance, which he considered "a raw but operating model of predicted plug-insvilles." Charney framed the problem differently: for him there was a gap between the planners' ability to know what to do with the urban environment and current technological know-how. On the one hand, most predictions did not use technology but were "inherent technological evocations." On the other hand, the actual integration of technology into the building industry consisted, most often, in the adoption of new materials as substitutes to traditional ones and had consequently no impact on the structure of the physical environment, as when, for instance, a plastic version of the typical suburban bungalow was proposed by a leading corporation in aerospace equipment. In contrast, Charney argued that technology could produce new modes of organization capable of integrating unpredictability. For him, the experimental megastructure and the plug-insville architecture

were "not ready-made environments but simulations of the physical form of new processes of human organization which are evident both in the way people live and in the possibilities of technology. In terms of new technology this work seeks to redefine some of the fundamental values which have marked every form of human settlement."[11]

In this connection, the projects of Cedric Price not only were feasible – after all they implemented existing and conventional technological devices – they demonstrated that technology could create a physical organization that acknowledged human action. Rather than being a force to be feared, technology could be turned into a means of emancipation enabling "the engagement of the users of buildings in the active modification of the physical surroundings – as citizen architects."[12]

In the essay's conclusion, Charney pointed out that the new industrial environmental systems already existed and that they could potentially produce a new vernacular. He argued: "Anonymous architecture has always been 'there.' Technically most of the visionary projects referred to are 'there.' They are analogues; and as analogues, they can yield new concepts and be used to isolate some of the new elements which the future will comprehend. They are exciting because they oppose processes that inhibit the full articulation of technology."[13]

Process

The "cluster of ideas" about urbland remained the frame of reference for three other essays of the period in which Charney concentrated on "learning environments." The subject was topical, with the recent creation of the Ministry of Education in Quebec which, following the recommendations of the Parent Commission (1963–66), planned to implant a network of large-scale schools throughout the province.

Obviously, for Charney, these projected "learning centres" could be seen as a further realization of urbland: "Improved transportation has meant regional secondary schools, technical schools, and colleges that are now conceived as large, centralized establishments – virtual towns that accommodate 4,000 or more students."[14]

It was in this effervescent context that he reflected on the possible shape and appropriate building system for the realization of this ambitious government program. His research nourished two projects, the École Curé-Grenier[15] built at Notre-Dame-des-Laurentides (1964), and the Cité des jeunes de Hull, a concept for a large educational complex conceived with Oscar Newman (1966). (See Fig. 15.4.)

Being himself involved in the construction of a primary school, Charney realized first-hand that there existed no coordinated standards and no technological innovation in Quebec's school building. He studied the recent systems and prototypes diffused in British and American publications. In parallel, he was invited by the Schokbeton company, an emerging leader in precast concrete technology in Quebec, to write a paper about this innovative method which could speed up the building process.[16] Judging by the contents of that essay, there was apparently no doubt in Charney's mind that the new schools to be built in Quebec would benefit from innovation in planning and construction.

Entitled "An Environment for Education," the text was first published in a special issue of *The Canadian Architect* on educational facilities. Charney suggested that the new learning centres had to be interactive environments built with precast concrete components. In the first part of his text, he applied the themes of change, flexibility, and process to the planning of new schools. Changes were being felt in education, which was now considered a key to the economic growth of advanced countries. But, according to Charney, new schools would not only reflect recent changes in curricula and

teaching methods, they would embody change itself in providing a flexible environment in which students would actively participate in their education; in a literal sense, the building would become a learning apparatus. In the United States, the so-called "schools without walls" allowed for a flexible learning program based on a system of moving partitions which enabled the users to transform their environment. Education itself was thought of as a process which generated new conditions for the building of new types of schools; it also changed the perception of the man-made environment: the building became an environmental process.

In the second part of the text, Charney explained that concrete was "more a building process than a material." Precast technology enabled the production of standardized components which redefined buildings as component systems. Being a formless composite material, concrete could be cast into varied shapes which enabled the precast components to be attached to a structure or to be themselves structural, as in John Johansen's U.S. Embassy in Dublin, a project on which Charney worked after his student year at Yale.

If process was the overarching concept capable of unifying a planning approach and a building material, the question of environmental flexibility and of concrete construction were thereafter treated as two separate issues.

Flexibility

Charney's study of the publications of the Educational Facilities Laboratories of New York led him to distinguish two understandings of flexibility.[17] The first type of flexibility was prefigured in the American "schools without walls," in which movable partitions and mobile equipment enabled the users to transform their environment; this type of flexibility enabled choice, involvement, and participation. The second related to the kit-of-parts as building system. A building system was considered flexible when its components permitted a variety of edifices to be built. In school construction, the British CLASP system and the American School Construction System Development Project (SCSD) were in this respect exemplary, in spite of limitations in span and height that could be overcome with the introduction of precast concrete technology. These systems tended to borrow from the 1950s innovations in office loft architecture, with their integrated ceilings and demountable partitions.

But Charney also forecast a tendency to regroup learning facilities in educational centres, which transformed the traditional idea of the school as building. These could take the shape of a suburban campus, as in the Cité des jeunes, or could be conceived as small learning centres integrated into multi-functional vertical developments. Charney also speculated on movable classrooms, inspired by the mobile home industry, which would be used as portable urban infills. Extrapolating from Cedric Price's Potteries Thinkbelt project, he argued: "The development of flexible educational facilities in the urban framework can be regarded to follow the disengagement of the school from a city structure, and the subsequent re-engagement of the facility as self-articulating infill in an urban network ... As in the child's learning centre where the activity of the children is the source of 'design' in the organization of the immediate learning environment, so, at an urban scale, given a mobile and multi-functional educational infill, facilities can be generated by students and can generate students."[18] Ultimately, education was both a function and an instrument of social organization.

As a barometer of architectural culture, Charney's reflection on education was totally in tune with the most advanced trends of the period. Therefore, it is not a coincidence that he reviewed the little book *New Schools for New Towns*, in which different projects by Tom Vreeland, Cedric Price, and Robert Venturi illustrated the disintegration of schools into the city and the landscape.[19]

Precast Concrete

By 1968 Charney had become an authority in Canada on the questions relating to the architectural handling of concrete, and he was invited by the periodical *Architecture Canada* to edit a special issue on the subject.

His editorial succinctly exposed the different types of technical information available in the press about the production of concrete and the various building methods available. Once again, he stressed that concrete was first and foremost the result of a process. As a synthetic and industrial product, it was produced in two different ways. On the one hand, movable industrial equipment could transform the building site into a kind of temporary factory. On the other hand, another approach favoured the use of "standardized preformed components that could be factory fabricated and assembled on-site."[20] In reality, both ways were complementary and tended to merge.

But most important, Charney also noted that since concrete was a formless material, it was subjected "to the will of a designer who is concerned with the appearance of the product, and its image as a cultural artifact, as well as with its function." Therefore, one had to recognize that "the styling characteristics of concrete buildings" were "an integral part of the material system." These remarks were not inconsequential since they led to conclusions that Charney never exposed. In spite of the apparent freedom offered by concrete, this material created totally controlled environmental systems which could logically not be spontaneously appropriated and transformed by "citizen architects." In the process of producing concrete environments, it was the designer and not the users who determined the shape and style of the physical environment.

Moreover, if precast elements did fragment the building into standardized parts, they nonetheless did not constitute a really flexible kit of parts since they were put in place once and for all in a precise and permanent configuration. In the end, concrete buildings were buildings in concrete rather than a new process of human organization that challenged the very idea of a building.

A Self-Erecting Building System

In collaboration with Harry Parnass and Janos Baracs, Charney visualized the possibility of creating a flexible environmental system for the Canadian pavilion at the 1970 universal exhibition of Osaka, Japan.[21] This entry was conceived as a simulation of a possible environment in which technology provided a flexible environmental system. The project proposed to select a number of off-the-shelf industrial elements, such as escalators, cranes, and all the paraphernalia necessary for exhibition spaces. This equipment was to be shipped to the site in containers. The cranes would serve both to erect the elements and to support the pavilion. The containers themselves were meant to serve as versatile building units. At the end of the exhibition, this kit of parts would be dismantled, packed back in the containers, and shipped to another location. Significantly, concrete was not judged an appropriate building material for such a project. However, in proposing the fiction of a self-erecting building system, the project remained silent about the capacity of the users to transform the shape of the pavilion. It is perhaps this limit that led Charney to probe further the relationship between users and the technological environment.

Towards a Liberation of Social and Technological Possibilities

With the seminal essay "Experimental Strategies – Notes for Environmental Design,"

Charney pursued his search for an architecture of indeterminacy based on technology.[22] In this text, structured in nine parts, he restated many of his previous convictions as he elaborated on the following ideas: the future lay in the present; formalist design transferred imagery, not technology; indeterminacy led to the dissolution of the concept of building; design was only one part of the process of technological planning. The essay also introduced new ideas that refocused and radicalized his criticism of design.

At the outset, he modified his stance on anticipatory design. Quoting Erik Erikson, he stated that "rather than speculate on the possible futures that can be seen in trends," it was more important "to look at the ideological distortions that obscure our visions in regard to trends," because they were in part shaping the future itself. In this connection, Robert Venturi's recent inclusion in the imagery of architecture of "a Main Street vernacular of popular culture" was a point of contention.

At first sight, the polemic of Venturi and Denise Scott Brown was quite similar to Charney's criticism of formalism. They showed a similar interest in pop art; they noticed that the historical avant-garde was fascinated by industrial imagery, just as the neo-avant-garde was by the space industry; they showed a similar suspicion of the architectural image as total design. Yet, in Charney's opinion, they proposed a very selective idiom which reinforced the basic premises of architecture. Although their intent was ironic, they were still committed to find architecture when they visited Las Vegas. Consequently, in their work, "The Strip was turned into the fragments of some hieratic culture and into a system of forms in which there is no place for the user-consumer other than as the ideal spectator – the antithesis of the Main. Las Vegas was isolated and rendered 'anonymous' and 'common-place' so as to 'gain insights,' as was done with industrial buildings earlier this century."[23]

By focusing on the language of architecture, Venturi and Scott Brown created a parody which missed the fact that "beyond the frame of reference of a formal idiom, the physical environment of Main Street documents the consumer aesthetic of industrial technology and high styling which is in touch with the daily lives of people."[24] To illustrate his point, Charney referred to the Diner, "the pantheon of Strip architecture," which, in grafting synthetic industrial materials onto the prototypical form of a railroad car, embodied a classic example of "the cogent use of technology." If one was to learn from this "artifactual landscape of instant sensibilities turned on by technology," and be really revolutionary, one had to study the relationships between man and his commodities. In Charney's words, "the emphasis in design on the interaction of people and environmental artifacts comes closer to representing these artifacts correctly than any isolated view of the artifact itself."[25]

These observations led Charney to formulate a dialectical view of the physical environment as a product of design, a product which functioned "as a system of restraints on people" rather than as a landscape of visual symbols as Venturi and Scott Brown had proposed. He noted that there was a conflict in the development of large-scale industrial production "between the response of production to the growing satisfaction of needs and the imposition of repressive conditions of use." In effect, industrial production led to the "standardization of the aspiration levels and use patterns of consumers," and thus both determined and narrowed the interaction of the user-consumer with artifacts. Charney argued that "the constituency of the user [had to] evolve with an emerging user-orientation in industry" which would "determine the actual utilization of artifacts, but not limit their possible utilization." In environmental design, this meant a change of objectives: the designer would no longer be an intermediary between the user and his environment; he would instead provide participatory

mechanisms whereby users could organize their environments. As recent changes in educational facilities indicated, "the pluralistic design of the artifacts [tended] towards a further liberation of both social and technological possibilities." This orientation indicated that "the physical environment can be geared to set out mechanisms of self-organization not to liquidate authority (form), but to liquidate authoritarian structures (formalism) at a time when the existing methods and orientation of design are clearly inadequate to deal with the transformation of the physical environment."[26]

In this new formulation, Charney for the first time identified formalism with the inherent authoritarianism of the process of design. Technology was no longer considered a building system produced by the designer but something out there to be used and appropriated. In the end, the dialectic of environmental design was characterized by an ideological confrontation between the formalist design of objects and an emerging pluralistic type of environmental design. Architecture faced a choice: "Whether architecture will remain as the design of a few unique and one-off objects posited for the edification of a few ideal spectators, or whether it can further develop into the systematic design of the mass produced physical matrix of society."[27]

The dilemma of architecture lay in contradictory ideological motivations inherent in the desire for change, the leitmotif of the avant-garde since the 1920s. In its search for an *architecture autre*, formalist design was an image of change, not change itself, and therefore non-structural change. An alternative type of design was needed to structurally alter the conceptual system of architecture: one based on the realization that "the very material existence of built artifacts is transformed into service commodities in which the relevant social issues and time scale are critical to design."

"Environmental Strategies" constituted both a summary and the beginning of a closure of Charney's analysis of technology. During the 1970s, the idea that technological change would enable social change faded gradually as Charney's fascination with the underlying meaning of architectural images grew.

NOTES

1 Chapter 18, 169–78.
2 Ibid., 174, 177.
3 Michael Polanyi, *The Tacit Dimension* (New York: Anchor Books, 1967).
4 Chapter 13, 134.
5 Chapter 14, 137–42.
6 Ibid., 139.
7 Ibid., 140.
8 Ibid., 140.
9 Chapter 16. 152–60.
10 Ibid., 153.
11 Ibid., 160.
12 Ibid., 158.
13 Ibid. 160.
14 Chapter 17, 162.
15 Now École du Boisé.
16 Charney read his text at Shokbeton's factory in St-Eustache in January 1967. Established in 1962, the company developed methods of fabrication derived from the system developed in France by the engineer Raymond Camus.
17 The Educational Facilities Laboratories was an independent research organization established by the Ford Foundation in 1958. During its twenty-eight years of existence, the EFL spurred innovation in school architecture by distributing more than 2 million copies of its publications on research, experimentation, and emerging trends. See Judy Marks, "A History of the Educational Facilities Laboratories," http://www.ncef.org/pubs/efl2.pdf.
18 Chapter 19, 187.
19 Chapter 22, 217–20.
20 Chapter 20, 190.
21 A Self-Erecting Exhibit System: Project for the Canadian Pavilion, Osaka Expo 70, 194–201.
22 This essay was written for a lecture Charney gave at the School of Architecture at Rice University, Houston. It was first published in *Perspecta 12* at editor Peter C. Papademetriou's request. *Perspecta 12* was conceived as a critique of Robert Venturi's pop theses. Chapter 21, 202–16.
23 Chapter 21, 210.
24 Ibid., 211.
25 Ibid., 212.
26 Ibid., 215–16.
27 Ibid., 216.

Environmental Chemistry – Plastics in Architecture*

13

Plastics are now accepted building materials, but their present application, even though extensive, is still mainly confined to their use as a substitute for traditional materials in a traditional and usually non-structural context. The problem of the application of plastics to building is a twofold one in which there is, firstly, the question of the chemical and performance characteristics of the materials. Considerable progress is being made in this area by research, and, as the characteristics of plastics lend themselves very well to the production of the gadgetry with which we are surrounding ourselves, so we can expect that our buildings will be structured more and more out of these materials. However, it is the second aspect of the problem that is the less publicized of the two and the less researched, yet it is the one that we experience daily and that influences

the comprehensive use of plastics in a direct way. This aspect is one of context – the form of the physical environment in which we live and to which plastics are applied. The technology that created plastics also created the conditions for a new environment, our surroundings are being modified, and with the current restructuring of the environment, new ways of modifying technology are in turn being found.

With the industrialization of construction – a hitherto slow yet inevitable process – buildings, for industry, become assemblies and sub-assemblies of fabricated components.

From an urban point of view, buildings, as cities, have either grown vastly in size (Place Ville-Marie in Montreal), or they are being grouped into large infrastructures (Simon Fraser University or a suburban shopping centre) so that they are no longer definitive units but large assemblies or elements of a larger assembly. From an economic point of view, the parameters of building design are also changing so that obsolescence and change itself become dynamic environmental factors. As a result, the built environment, as the tendency of technology

* From *Journal of the Royal Architecture Institute of Canada* 43, no. 5 (May 1966): 105–7; translated and reprinted in *Architecture, Bâtiment, Construction* (June 1966): 39–43. Editor's note: This essay was originally illustrated with drawings of Charney's students.

itself, becomes a cybernetic study in systems, system analyses and man-machine relationships – the gamut of techniques current, for example, in the aerospace industry (in the 1930s, Buckminster Fuller had pointed this out in relation to the aircraft industry). It is interesting to note that with the passing of the recent rocket boom several aerospace companies have turned their systems methods on environmental problems such as mass transportation and housing.

In this context, a house can become an assemblage of packages of space and appliances which render life amenable; each package having its own renewal cycle – the kitchen package versus the heating/cooling units. These assemblies-to-live-in can be lodged in an infrastructure, keyed into a service network, and grouped according to social conditions that can analogically promote a backyard, a street, or a neighbourhood. The great architecture of history can be seen to have had its sources in indigenous constructions which first responded in a new way to new technology; similarly, in contemporary popular modes of building, one can find a response to a new environment and an indication of things to come. An operative example of the system-to-live-in is the mobile trailer home that is being produced in North America in large number.

These lightweight and compact housing packages on wheels are designed to be plugged into service lines in different cities; there are, as well, several high-rise "parks" being constructed with ten storeys of mobile trailers plugged into a concrete cage. If the manufacturers find it feasible, these mobile homes can be structured out of plastics and reinforced plastics without altering the design – in this context, wood and aluminum seem out of place. Educational facilities in this new tech world also become assemblies of space components serving groups of students plugged into audio-visual cores and circulation circuits. And a cultural centre, as has been shown in a recent project for London, becomes a machine-to-live-it-up-in where a service structure can

assemble a mobile system of prefabricated panels for the presentation of a three ring circus, a bingo fest, or a political rally.*

These "buildings" create indeterminate environments that are geared to perform their required jobs. The design distinction between a general service infrastructure, and the components that specifically relate spaces to people, allows the designs to profit from both transient and the permanent conditions, the transient elements being clearly designated as expendable. This new context accordingly implies new material needs and new performance criteria for which the unique properties of plastics offer direct answers. The ease with which plastics can be formed and shaped makes them naturally suitable for production techniques and assembly methods. The high strength-to-weight ratio of plastics becomes a dynamic design factor in a component building system. With the discontinuous loading conditions of plastic assemblies in a concrete superstructure, for example, the dimensional instability of plastics can be controlled.

Environmental and chemical architecture are both at the elemental phase of development where possibilities are inferred and diagrammed. The content of the new technology has only begun to be externalized into viable methods of organizing our physical environment. In this age, the emphasis of national wealth and energy is primarily expended on aerospace and military hardware; war and the fear of war are in this age, as in any other, the main motivation of technological advance. In Vietnam, for example, use is being made of warehouses structured out of inflated vinyl covered nylon skins that can be deflated, folded up, laundered, and shipped elsewhere. The use of filament-wound, fibre-glass-reinforced plastics illustrates this "sci-

* Editor's note: This is a reference to the Fun Palace, a visionary project designed by the English architect Cedric Price for English theatre director Joan Littlewood. (See Fig. 16.2.)

entific" gap in our environment – the distance between the capacity of how to do things and the knowledge of what to do: in rocketry, nose cones, fuel propellant cases, and thrust chambers are being structured out of filament winding techniques; the complex stress conditions of each component are programmed into the winding process. The same company that spins these impressive moon missiles, using the same techniques of winding glass fibres on inflated rubber mandrils, recently prepared a study for a house of the "future" in which a suburban family home, typical of any that can be found sprawled along the peripheries of our cities, was recast in its pristine glory in filament wound shells in a singularly impressive demonstration of what not to do.

Nevertheless, beyond the fringe of the main current of architecture a quiet revolution has transformed some buildings into industrial "design" products that are technologically conceived and produced. These building types are marginal to the construction industry, such as radar domes, polar and military shelters, and exhibit structures. For the most part, these buildings were conceived of, and made operative, as component systems structured entirely in fibreglass-reinforced plastics. The inherent expendability of these buildings, the need for a system of interchangeable parts, and reproduction in quantity were design conditions that were enough to set the problem as one removed from the pale of traditional construction. Also beyond the construction industry is the design of micro-enclosures such as bus shelters and telephone booths. These elements are being industrially manufactured in plastics as other equipment for human use like the telephone itself; these mini-buildings are human engineered and moulded to the configuration of the body for which plastics are especially suited. In the technologic modus operandi of these quasi-buildings, a faulty component is designed to be replaced, and the assembly conceived a

priori to redistribute the stress circuits at the removal of a member (the geodesic raydome is an example of this device).

New technology is extending man's environment into hitherto uninhabitable parts of the earth and extraterrestrial space with consequently new environmental conditions. The ease of mobility and the need of natural resources have, for example, opened the arctic and sub-arctic of Canada to settlement. The problem of structuring a place-to-live can here be approached by entirely new means as there is no existing context to limit possible solutions; the logistics of the problem imply new constraints and hence new possibilities. The light weight and high strength of the materials used, and a system of building components that can be easily produced, erected, and demounted are design requirements because of accessibility to the site by air, the varying size and the type of the necessary installations, and the inherent need of standardized and interchangeable building blocks. These requirements set out material and production parameters for which reinforced plastics are especially suited.

The housing of workers in sub-arctic conditions was the subject of a study conducted at the School of Architecture of the University of Montreal with the fourth-year students.[1] The objective here was to orient the students to the methods and content of future solutions, and this project introduced plastics, a new material with which to structure buildings, in the context of a new problem which cannot be solved in a traditional way. The study was called "Project Mini-Camp," and the problem was to design a demountable, transportable shelter system that could be adapted to varying terrain conditions, mining, scientific and settling operations in the remote areas of northern Quebec. The system was to be designed in fibreglass-reinforced plastics, and be completely prefabricated and equipped so as to minimize fieldwork. The basic camp cell was to sleep four men, and include

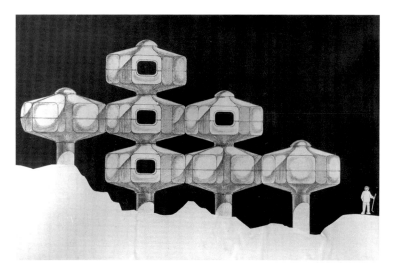

13.1 Camp cluster; fibreglass-reinforced moulded plastic panel system cantilevered from aluminum stair tubes. Student, Renata Jentys.

ancillary services required for their well-being. This cell was to be designed to be linked to other similar cells and to recreation and dining cells so as to form a larger camp unit.

A dialogue was set up with the students to program the design. The mobility of the mini-camp introduced the factor of weight control and the optimum design of all enclosed voids. The basic camp cell was both to be an extensible assemblage of components, as well as a component of a larger cluster, and linking conditions had to be studied. The use of fibreglass-reinforced plastics introduced stressed skin structures, interlocking surfaces, and a material that can be moulded to specific interior configurations – such as cast in beds – as well as to general structural configurations. The content of a housing environment was thus put to question; there were no possible traditional references, other than human use, that could be assumed without redefinition. For example, a window became a hole to be punched out of a stress panel, and consequently the shape, purpose, position, and the very need of a transparency and a light

source were put to question in such a way that new answers could be proposed. The study was limited to the phase of preliminary models that simulated possible solutions; it was intended that this project, as elementary research, be open-ended so as to encourage future development. Most of the students structured their systems out of shaped sandwich panels with honeycomb or foam cores; a few ventured to use filament winding techniques. The joining of components was found difficult; there was still a screwing, nailing and notching mentality at work and not enough inventiveness with PVC and butyl tapes, and adhesives – part of the chemistry of plastics.

The general feedback from the students was that, for architecture, plastics implied prototype and systems design techniques that in turn imply a different orientation than the one-and-only, non-repetitive building point of view. The study demonstrated that the successful use of plastics in building implied, furthermore, the need for the total uncoupling of the idea of a building itself as an environmental system so that it can be reprogrammed and restructured in a new way and in response to new needs and new material criteria. This problem of housing workers can be seen to be a special and reduced version of the larger problem of housing a growing urban population. Perhaps the experience of these new architectures (or non-architectures – really two sides of the same coin) will influence the structuring of the urban environments in a more dynamic way.

NOTE

1 This project was carried out under the direction of Professor Melvin Charney with the assistance of Professors Michel Barcelo and Serges Carreau, and the Fiberglas Company of Canada; Mr Eric Brown, of Polyfiber Limited, and Henry Finkel, industrial designer, participated on the final jury.

14

Notes on a Guide for Travellers to the Plastic Inevitable[*]

In the first quarter of this century – the end of the first machine age – the omnipotence of science inspired utopian dreams. The super architectures that were invented then implied new social orders emblazoned in the iconography of the great city dream: emotive images of men freely moving about in vehicles that glided on superhighways which in turn entered towering structures at several levels and emerged at several others; soaring, streamlined pinnacles and cigar-shaped aero vehicles. The public responded to these excursions with enthusiasm. They were on the way to a new world of plenty – a rebirth of the Garden of Eden.

These diverting excursions into the future are now part of the planning and decision-making apparatus of technologically oriented nations. The operational role of Futuribles – the activity of looking ahead – has been recognized as an indispensible tool, and long-range planning

groups are at work making models of the world to come.

The planning of any type of environmental hardware – a school or an autoroute – has been recognized to implicate a forecast for future needs. More detailed and complex anticipation procedures are now needed, and as Nigel Calder, the editor of *The World in 1984,* has pointed out, we are getting them, but in a disjointed way.[†] The "anticipatory design" of our future environment, as Buckminster Fuller, the guru of experimental environmentalists, calls it, has begun.

Urbland is an operative model that seeks to anticipate where we will live. Unlike the super-city architecture that was proposed earlier in the century, this model is disinterested in what things ultimately will look like. It is concerned with the possible organization of the new environment. Ideograms of probable patterns are suggested with probability itself acting as an active determinant. This built-in hesitation,

* From *Parallel* (March 1967): 19–24. Editor's note: Charney wrote this editorial statement as an introduction to an issue of *Parallel* entitled "Urbland," of which he was the guest editor.

† Editor's note: Nigel Calder, ed., *The World in 1984: The Complete New Scientist Series* (Harmondsworth/Baltimore: Penguin, 1964).

explained in terms of open-ended systems, is indeed the saving grace of contemporary proposals. Inasmuch as human action is recognized as the basic generator of organization, recent proposals are socially committed.

Not only has technology extended man's physical capacities – the inspiration of utopias of the first machine age – but electronics have now extended his nervous system so that utopias are no longer imaginary. Contemporary proposals for the future environment seem far less radical than actual implementations that we can find today.

Has there been a proposal for a system of mobile houses, plugged in and serviced like family appliances, that is as way out as the trailer home system which is actually in operation in the United States? Thin, lightweight metal and plastic capsules, equipped with chemical toilets, travel the highways like tandem missiles behind Ford Galaxies or Dodge Barracudas. One out of every six homes purchased in the United States in 1965 was a trailer.

High-rise mobile home parks built near several urban centres provide docking facilities for these capsules. The trailers are driven up ramps, backed into concrete pigeon holes and plugged into the telephone, plumbing, and electricity core. Here, then, is a raw but operational definition of the future plug-in architecture of *urbland*.

The form of Human Settlement is changing before our eyes. In a recent issue of *Scientific American*, devoted to cities, planner Hans Blumenfeld pointed out that the city is undergoing a qualitative change so that it is no longer merely a larger version of the traditional city but a new and different configuration.* We still think and act in terms of city and country when in fact these concepts have lost meaning.

Old cities have grown so that the hinterland of one has become the beginning of another. Vast urbanized regions are now emerging. The French geographer Jean Gottmann, in his study of the eastern seaboard of the United States, concluded that the entire region along the Boston/New York/Philadelphia axis is a thousand-mile urbanized band which he called megalopolis. It is not difficult to identify the emergence of other megalopoli (every important region of human habitation on the earth) and to conclude that the world is undergoing a process of megalopolization.† Farms and forests are amalgamated in the new configuration. The new landscape is a totally designed, contrived, man-made environment.

To see an actual megalopolis one has only to visit the Tokyo/Kawasaki/Yokohama conurbation which contains, within a radius of 60 miles, a population of 22,500,000. There is less than one square yard of open space per person in this fantastic, sprawling jungle of buildings. Jeremy Dodd, architect and planner working in Tokyo, has written about this Oriental megalopolis for our guide. He shows a new pattern emerging in Tokyo, an elaborate network of expressways, high-speed trains, and the world's longest monorail in a sprawl where only 23 per cent of the dwellings have main drainage.

The emerging form of megalopolis and the development of transportation systems are inseparable. New channels of movement and new terminals within the movement networks articulate a new order. Communication has always provided a framework of human contact – the life lines, so to speak – and the very raison d'être of settlement. The urbanist Kevin Lynch has explained that most people organize their impressions of the environment in terms

* Editor's note: "The Modern Metropolis", the essay mentioned here, was published in the September 1965 issue of *Scientific American*. The definitive version of it was included in part 1 of Hans Blumenfeld, *The Modern Metropolis* (Cambridge, MA: MIT Press, 1967).

† Editor's note: Jean Gottmann, *Megalopolis: The Urbanized Northeastern Seaboard of the United States* (Cambridge, MA: MIT Press, 1964).

of the "paths" which they travel.* *Path* has become an important contemporary means of organizing complex environments.

The planning of the transportation system for Expo 67 in Montreal has been used to connect the centres of the exposition in a greater degree than has been possible in any existing urban area. Expo can offer a live sample of an organized view from the road, and a description of the transport systems of Expo, written by A.I. Diamond, has been included in our guide to *urbland*.

Megalopolis is a transitional phase of human settlement. The ultimate form will be a world resettled in *urbland*.

In the megalopoli of North America one can see canals of transportation – autoroutes for the most part – cutting swaths of open space through the old fabric of settlement. The superroad systems have introduced a superscale and supervalue to land, and buildings are being reconstructed and regrouped into tighter, taller, denser clusters. The new building complexes are easily identifiable. They stand out as dense blots between the raw cuts of concrete expressways and are usually called *Centres*. What was once served in the city by one building, a public hospital, for example, is now served in megalopolis by an extensive cluster of buildings – often a virtual town in itself. Centres of this sort are Place Ville-Marie and Place des Arts in Montreal; hospital centres, research centres, industrial centres, sports centres, and so forth; the World Trade Center, Lincoln Center, and the centre of all centres, the Rockefeller Center.

These centres have become pedestrian towns. They have populations equivalent to important medieval towns, but here the town is occupied during only part of the day or night and the rest of the time resounds with the hollowness of an abandoned film set. The medieval town analogy is close to the texture of the place: one arrives by

car or train and once within, there are tortuous corridor streets, tight elevators, service alleys, blind corners, and even public pissoirs.

The internal pedestrian circulation systems of some of these centres have become important "intertown" sub-systems. In Montreal, for example, the pedestrian "roads" of one of the centres has branched out to other centres and is connected to a mass transit system. In the winter climate of this city, the daily routine of many people can be spent in a controlled atmosphere. This is not an underground city but megalopolis mechanisms creating multi-level development of circulation systems.

These new centres are the places in *urbland* where everything takes place; they are the Roman forums, the agoras, the corner drugstores, and the drive-ins of *urbland*. Architecture here – the physical containers and disposers of place – has to promote the presence of people and react to their will. It is a neo-city architecture in which architecture is only a small part of the total happening.

Although we tend to think of cities as natural phenomena, they did not grow naturally. They were built up piecemeal over extended periods of time in response to the needs and aspirations of a community of men. The problem for the new architecture is the creation of an instant environment that is compounded of willed and spontaneous life. How can a total human ambient be planned? One of the answers, at least, may be cans of sprayed-on city life; the patina of time, drying in ten minutes. Inasmuch as the Disneylands and 42nd streets of North America do manage to transmit a certain vibration, they can tell us about *urbland* to come.

The "culture centres" now being built in many of our cities can be used to illustrate the transition of *Old City* to *Megalopolis* to *Urbland*. We are all familiar with city theatres; the high, mid, and low cult, the Broadway, the off-Broadway and the off-off-Broadway, the clubs, and the Motown shows in run-down jiving halls. In megalopolis,

* Editor's note: Kevin Lynch, *The Image of the City* (Cambridge, MA: MIT Press, 1960).

the Culture Centre has become the place of spectacles – music, ballet and theatre; for example, Lincoln Center in New York and Place des Arts in Montreal. A group of fixed, pompous, concrete packages are usually set off on a quasi-religious podium. Inside, the audience is well protected from the stage; the spectacle is segregated on a platform. If there is any raison d'être to any art, it may be that it tells us something about ourselves or our world, but the audience in these theatrical museums are by the very configuration of the place protected from any message. In the same way as the shopping centres of megalopolis are really buying centres, since there is no real shopping for varied goods; the cultural centre filters culture. The medium here is certainly the message. And if we look for the message in the community, we find that for most people the event is the going to the place and the contact with others before, after and especially during the spectacle. It serves an important grooming function in our society, and it is this theme that can be a key to a machine to live it up in the style of *urbland*.

Joan Littlewood, the British director, with a team of environmental technicians, including the architect Cedric Price, have proposed the Fun Palace project. (See Fig. 16.2.) Their belief in spontaneity and audience participation led them to conceive of a zone of total probability in which participation in practically everything could be caused. The Palace was designed as a giant erector set with the potential of manufacturing spaces for all purposes; a kit of parts that can be animated to accommodate a political rally, a wrestling match, or bingo fest. And the whole fun machine is seen as a piece of urban hardware expendable in ten years. Reyner Banham described this fun machine: "Day by day it will stir and reshuffle its parts … sometimes bursting at the seams with activities, sometimes with only a small part walled in but with the public poking about, pressing buttons to make things happen themselves … even the simple business

of finding where to go next would be rewarding or stimulating."*

One has here the sense of *urbland*: an environment of places at the nodes of the transportation systems. The *place* is a device which has a life-supporting structure, similar to a street grid in the old city, about which a transient, parasitic, and specific architecture, similar to buildings on old city streets, will work for people.

This politic of creating within a transportation net a supergrid that will support environmental machines which are life-generating and responsive to people, has been the important guideline for many of the current ideas on how *urbland* will function and how it will look. The Archigram group of young British architects has advanced these ideas into the realm of possible environments. Their work is presented in this guide by one of their members, Warren Chalk. They present *urbland* where man is reinstated to a physical milieu that responds to his new and changing needs. A conscious effort is made to preserve human qualities that do not change with time, and redefine them in terms of contemporary technology.

At the same time as man reaches toward outer space, he explores the nature of his inner places. With the increase of population the globe has contracted: space has become both a limited commodity and one which is totally designed by some anonymous contriver for some anonymous inhabitant. The factors which determine the adequacy of inhabitable spaces have until now been informally conceived and poorly formulated. As a consequence of recent advances in knowledge they can now be described technically; proxemics has become the study of the relationships between man and the spaces he occupies.

The major proponent of the anthropology of space, Edward T. Hall, maintains that too

* Editor's note: Reyner Banham, "A Clip-on Architecture," *Architectural Design* 35 (November 1965): 534–5.

little attention has been focused on behaviour as a determinant of the types of space in which the human animal flourishes.* He illustrates the importance of behaviour understanding to environmental design by the concept of territoriality – the way a species lays claim to a given space and defends it. Without territoriality, life as we know it could not have evolved; each organism, no matter how simple or complex, has around it a sacred bubble of space, a bit of mobile territory which only a few other organisms are allowed to penetrate, and often only for a short time. Included in our guide to *urbland* is a contribution by a social scientist, Lionel Tiger, of the University of British Columbia and resident sociologist at the London Zoo, who is studying prehistoric patterns of animal behaviour (ethology) in order to further our understanding of the human species. Megalopolis is a crowded form of human settlement and crowding that, as the ethnologists have shown, leads to psychological and physiological aberrations. With new knowledge, *urbland* can mean the healthy redistribution of organized territories.

In combination with proxemics, ergonomics (human engineering), which is based on detailed studies of the physiology of the body, offers techniques by which mass environmental systems can be made to respond to specific individual and cultural needs. Ergonomics was developed during the Second World War from the need to put men in the tight compartments of aeroplanes and tanks. The weight of the machines' accommodation for men, and the use of equipment was here a question of life or death. These studies have been greatly advanced in the recent work being done on space medicine. In dealing with the large numbers of people in megalopolis, environmental ergonomics has also become a question of life or death.

* Editor's note: Edward T. Hall, *The Hidden Dimension* (Garden City, NY: Doubleday, 1966).

The human performance of an environment can also be programmed in *urbland* to feed back information so that the walls (if there are any) can correct themselves for varying conditions. The primary role of the architect will be territorial – in making places that can identify and serve human activity. *Place-making* implies a knowledgeable hypothesis about the way people live and interact, and about the way the human body functions, so that the built environment works for people.

One always fears the unknown. The new world of total urbanization and industrialization leads to fears of Big Brother and of the impersonal plastic intestines in which we live. Norman Mailer sees in the contemporary world a totalitarian impulse that not only washes away distinction but looks for a style in buildings and daily objects which diminishes one's sense of reality. Mailer is right. But in *urbland* we are looking for a post-totalitarian spirit where distinctions are redefined. If one important aspect unites all the contributions in this guide to *urbland,* it is the preoccupation with an environment that is keyed to active human participation and to a new scale of individualization of man. We have learned that technology indiscriminately serves any master, and that humanistic-oriented *urbland* is as possible as its opposite.

In the contemporary art scene there is an attempt to draw into the active process of the art those who, until now, were the passive spectators. The work of the painters Agam and Vasarely, the sculpture of George Segal, Oldenburgh, Tinguely, says that the spectator is not an outsider anymore but that he has to build his own work of art by his own participation. The same process is advocated in the theatre. In the spherical theatre project of Jacques Polieri, for example, the audience floats on suspended discs which are part of the show. In Joan Littlewood's Fun Palace, one's presence in the theatre itself is the spectacle. What is proposed in this guide is that in *urbland* the citizens will become architects and actively participate in making the kind of place in which they will live. In the way "hot-line" radio and TV have attracted extensive audiences – the passive listener becomes the active broadcaster – a form of "hot-line" architecture is foreseen. Every citizen, as an individual and as part of a collectivity, will be called upon to participate in an architectural experience.

The gradual evolution of our environment into one in which the citizen participates in the active modification of his physical surroundings is increasingly apparent. Schools are presently being designed with sliding walls so that teachers, within the envelope that controls climatic conditions (the outside walls), can make the appropriate spaces needed for different learning activities. It is the teacher who generates an instant architecture, and place-making becomes an activity that is part of the learning process shared by the pupils. Large workplaces (industry and administration offices) are being provided with walls and floors which can be moved at will. This flexibility can easily be extended to the total environmental system. The British architect Cedric Price has proposed a university for 20,000 students to be built around a road and rail network. His Thinkbelt will encompass an area of 100 square miles: faculty areas will occur at the main-line stations of the rail system, and slidings will provide rail-based mobile learning units. (See Fig. 16.3.) Thus the university, the "multiversity," becomes a highly flexible and responsive physical that can by its very definition serve the needs of education. This approach, coupled with an electronic communication system, is eminently feasible, and stands as an answer to the fixed concrete Neolithic monoliths presently being constructed.

Virtually all human history has been concerned with settlements on stable land masses and in temperate climates. As well as settlement in extreme climates, systems are being designed for the settlement of water areas and of outer space. The Japanese have envisioned the Tokyo megalopolis projecting across Tokyo Bay with a series of floating cities in the Pacific. In the United States, the Martin Company is working on a moon settlement, Douglas Aircraft on a spaceball complex, and General Dynamics on a linear spacetown. The premises for these projects are very OK. Human settlement will be expansive.

Urbland is the thing to come. In *urbland* the transportation networks will extend lines of human contact to all parts of the earth and beyond. Within the networks *place* will occur where human existence and values will be reaffirmed in the new terms of technocracy. Here, the operational systematic approach to an electronic and chemical architecture will be exploited. The future of human settlement is indeed changing, and it is to *change* that this issue of *Parallel* is dedicated.

15

Recent Directions in Canadian Architecture*

Rather than a forceful architectural stream within which or against which one works, forceful social, economic, and climatic circumstance influence design in Canada. If one considers the size of this country, its rigorous climate, its dispersed population divided by at least two cultures and two languages, occupying the larger but more frozen half of the North American continent that it shares with the United States – the all-pervasive super-country of the twentieth century – one has the sense of an architecture that has had difficulty finding itself.

This problem of identity is one that is now shared with other countries in this epoch of mass communication in which the influence of one architecture is infused with that of another. And, unlike other countries, Canada, because of its unique situation, can digest to some degree the dominant barrage of American architectural work and magazine propaganda, and can participate in the development of a new technological world that uses micro-circuits and vinyl without

becoming preoccupied with idiosyncracies such as "Coca-Cola" formalism.

The assimilation of the landscape in design has been important to the development of architecture in North America as some inevitable initiative phase. Even though the landscape varies considerably from one end of the country to the other, there is a sense of void that marks one's experience. In a recent book the well-known American writer Edmund Wilson notes that "as in early America the scale of humanity is so reduced ... that despite all of the scenery it appears to take place in a void ... for example from Ile d'Orléans in the St Lawrence, just above Quebec. From a high cliff, the wide smooth river and its flat opposite banks are of a magnitude quite dumbfounding ... such a prospect seems annuling to human assertion which can hope to make little impression."† In the U.S., Frank Lloyd Wright was able to make this sense of void part of his architecture; Wright would emphasize a

† Editor's note: Edmund Wilson, *O Canada: An American's Notes on Canadian Culture* (New York: Noonday Press, 1966).

* From *Cimaise* (Paris) (July 1967): 30–42.

place of human containment in an endless horizon. In Canada, this has happened, but in a new way that responds to new conditions.

As elsewhere, the phenomenon of total urbanization is evident. Along with a new form of urban living new technologies are generating totally new building programs and new building processes. The role of the architect, and the nature of architecture is changing. Research and development in many fields have opened up vast possibilities in the structuring of the human environment, and social scientists have demonstrated that hypotheses on the way people live, behave, and interact have a profound impact on design. Yet much that is being constructed in this country as in other parts of the world remains amateur.

It is in this state of affairs that we are trying to situate recent architectural development. The modalities of some of the new work can be well illustrated in the designs of several universities; with the new role of education in contemporary society, and the scale of the new programs, the design of a university has become a problem type that embodies the scope of much of current architecture.

Transition can be seen at the University of Manitoba, where individual buildings were originally set out as separate pavilions in a suburban, park-like setting. This planning, valid perhaps in the temperate climates of England, forced the students to negotiate the torturous cold winter weather between classes without even the compensation in the summer of a well-defined campus in the vast prairie of the Canadian midwest. As the university grew, these distances became larger, and a new "University Centre" has now been designed which is, in effect, a large central street that ties the different buildings together. Universities have become virtual cities, and this design recognizes the new urban implication.

A total university campus realized in urban design can be seen in the new Simon Fraser

15.1 Simon Fraser University, Arthur Erickson and Hart Massey, architects.

University located in Burnaby, British Columbia, part of which has now been constructed. The architects Erickson-Massey have succeeded in satisfying both the symbolic unity and the vast heterogeneity of the modern university. Flexibility, expansion, and the other shibboleths of what is considered to be the mainstay of the contemporary *Geist* in architecture are here given some design meaning. The mountain-top site of the university is especially dramatic, perhaps unnecessarily so; but it is indeed a very Canadian setting with mountains, water, sky, and lush greenery of the temperate jungle of the Pacific coast. The buildings are grouped and clustered in a dense sequence that confirms on the mountain top an atavistic sense of human scale and human use. The university is at once one building and a group of buildings; the principal "building" at the centre of the group is a large, covered mall – an agora and a place of meeting that confirms an urban presence.

Scarborough College, in Ontario, by the architects John Andrews and Page and Steele, is another demonstration of a college designed as one building which is in effect a pluralistic environment accommodating 6,000 people. Pedestrian access corridors have here become streets, and it is along these streets that all the specific sub-environments (i.e., buildings of the old university) are assembled. In Scarborough, the cluster is centric; from a centre where there is a meeting place and the crossroads of the University, the Science and Humanities wings bend away. In multi-functional, high-density contemporary architecture the vertical dimension has become important, and the section of this building steps up and out in marked profiles that manipulate an interior "sense of place" and the penetration of natural light. The use of concrete and plastics, and the integration of new electronic teaching techniques and mechanical services, are part of the translation of a new program and new conditions into significant architecture.

15.2 Scarborough College, John Andrews, Page and Steele, architects.

In Quebec, secondary and post-secondary education has been neglected for many years and the province planned regional campuses that centralized facilities. These Cités étudiantes, as they are called, offered a new program which could accommodate, in expanding facilities, 4,000 or more students. In the design of the Cité étudiante de Hull, for 10,000 students, the architects Melvin Charney and Oscar Newman

15.3 Collège de Chicoutimi, Paul-Marie Côté and Léonce Desgagné, architects.

developed the potential of this new architecture in an urban vernacular of interlocking elements that satisfied specific learning environments plugged into a circulation and service grid.

A university can never be a city, but the urban analogy was well used to yield new concepts and isolate the architecture of a new lifestyle. Here architects can exercise urban design aspirations which they have not been able to realize elsewhere. Montreal, however, has become unique on this continent for having built up during the last decade a multi-functional and

multi-use centre that does satisfy many of these current architectural aspirations; this, regardless of the architecture of the individual buildings. The individual buildings in the centre of Montreal include Place Victoria designed by Moretti and Nervi (it is said to be the world's tallest reinforced concrete structure); the Place Ville-Marie tower complex by the firm of I.M. Pei; an inconsequential office tower by the firm of Skidmore, Owings and Merrill; the Place Bonaventure by the local architecture firm ARCOP; and the work of many architects whose nationality represents the source of financial investment for the buildings. The bases of these complexes have spread out and interconnected in a network of interior pedestrian streets,

15.4 Cité des jeunes de Hull,
Melvin Charney and Oscar
Newman, architects.

transportation systems, parking facilities, shops, hotels, theatres ... all the amenities of a city life in a climate-controlled situation. To give one an idea of the size and complexity of the elements of this centre, Place Bonaventure consists of fifteen storeys of offices, shopping galleries, and exhibit halls, built over five acres with a 400-room hotel on its roof. The multi-functional performance of this large constructed block makes it more like a many-layered part of the city than a specific building. The Paul Rudolph

reminiscences and the dash of crude, so-called "brutalist" polemic in the design of the exterior envelope detract from the interest of the building, from its role, and from its bulk – a town in itself.

The American magazine *The Architectural Forum* (important because of its content and because Canadian architects are influenced more by it than by their own publications) published lead articles on Simon Fraser University, Scarborough College, and on the Centre of Montreal soon after construction was well under way. Of Scarborough they wrote (May 1966) "an important milestone in urban design in North America ... some of the new urban design theories

15.5 Photomontage of Montreal's centre (Place Victoria, Place Bonaventure, and Hotel Chateau Champlain)

15.6 Place Bonaventure, Montreal, ARCOP, architects.

(Plug-in Cities, Action Architecture, Service and Traffic Grids, etc.) will be given their first, practical workout." And of the core of Montreal, *Forum* (September 1966) exuded the following verbiage: "Montreal is about to become the first twentieth-century city in North America ... few people in Montreal seem to realize that they are building the most advanced urban core of our time." This reportage served firstly to situate the new Canadian architecture on the world scene, which its own publications could not do, and, secondly, to show that a country with an identity problem prefers to have its work confirmed by others. However, the younger architects who participated in the realization of the above work see it more as Canadian influence on the U.S. – feedback in an electronic epoch. After all, one can see that in world centres, such as New York,

that control the propaganda media, a sort of insular provincialism does set in; in Montreal, Canada, one has to be informed of what is going on elsewhere, and this worldliness does often come out in the architecture.

The "buildings" mentioned above react to new environmental requirements in a new way. They involve change, and with change the rhetoric of a very contemporary dialogue. The techniques of urban planning are at work within as well as outside of these building complexes. In the core of Montreal, traditional design canons have no meaning in the essentially interior architecture of large, interrelated building blocks. Even the elegant Nervi building, when seen from some distance, combines with the core as some series of elements plugged into vertical elevator shaft; Nervi heightens this effect in the design by dividing the tower into three fifteen-storey blocks separated by a mechanical and structural service floor. (See Fig. 10.1.) Inside has become outside in this new architecture in which buildings become open assemblages, non-architecture, and urbanistic place-making. And, in Canada, for the first time, there is some architecture that is not only good – i.e., competently designed, that can tell us what not to do – but an advanced architecture that can tell us where to go and what to do next.

In many other smaller buildings across the country, there are examples of architecture that go beyond the rudiments of ordinary competence. Some of the work of Etienne Gaboury, Wolfgang Gerson, Fairfield and Dubois, and Ron Thom can be cited here. Much of this work takes itself very seriously, and the sense of commitment that comes through the material of the building sets the general tone of some of the more interesting architecture across the country. In this sense, the necessary unreality of Expo 67 buildings sets its architecture apart.

The development of French-Canadian work has to be fitted into its own context or else it stands as some provincial, local aberration. The landscape, the spirit of the settlers and the voyageurs who opened up the North American continent, and the mobile, on-the-road mystique that is at the root of much of American life can be seen to infuse French-Canadian architecture. Despite language and cultural differences, its roots are profoundly American. These tendencies are expressed in raw, inarticulate gestures of an anti-city architecture that prefers and is nurtured by the indigenous landscape.

The work is on a frequency which many architects and critics find difficult to appreciate, since it is related to their inability to apprehend and work within the stream of popular architecture that has produced a rich, anonymous body of work on the North American continent.

When seen in this light, the work of the architect Roger D'Astous can be appreciated for its bravura and for its involvement in an American folk idiom that is heavily influenced by the work of Frank Lloyd Wright. D'Astous studied in Taliesin and imported Wright's well-known idiosyncracies such as the mystique of "natural" materials (whatever that may mean in this age of almost total synthetic production of the artifacts that surround us). The exaggeration of form beyond structural and material rationale can be well illustrated by his churches and private homes; it is a sort of folk architecture by a folk hero who felled the trees, hewed the planks, and cut the stone of his own buildings. The hotel Château Champlain, which he designed for the centre of Montreal in association with the architect Jean-Paul Pothier, uses elements derived from Wright's Marin County Administration Center. Yet despite the papier-mâché precast concrete, there is a strength to the overall building that is difficult to find in other contemporary hotel designs. However, in the typical work of such architects as Henri Brillon and Paul-Marie Côté, there is a lack of scale and control that can be found in the work of D'Astous. Here the aggressive architect's contrivance becomes a kind of mood engineering, and the function of the building itself has too often little bearing on the gymnastics of the forms. This spirit of conscious mood engineering brings us back to the spirit of the architecture that can be found on the roadsides of America.

Reaching out beyond the fringe of what is still accepted as architecture, one should mention the current vernacular architecture that still serves as a source, as it did for Gropius and Le Corbusier early in this century, of buildings that readily assimilate new technologies into direct environmental uses. The motels and the trailer homes that inhabit the roads provide crude but operative examples of a mobile, prefabricated response to human habitat. Also included in this category is the neon architecture in which myriads of colours are played into forms that use the latest electronic devices, and the important industrial vernacular such as the recent General Motors plant near Montreal, and the grain elevator system which stretches across Canada.

Also beyond the fringe of what has been traditionally considered to be architecture, a highly technical building industry is developing. In this industry, expendability, the need for a system of interchangeable parts, and reproduction in quantity are removing traditional work from the pale of architecture and transforming it into industrial products. The Triodetic Company, for example, markets a system that can be used to assemble any combination of structural members at any vertical and horizontal angle, and to vary the angularity to conform to various shapes and conditions; furthermore, the design analyses and production of these struts can be put on a computer, and the ultimate buildings need never be drawn. Atco Industries manufactures and assembles prefabricated housing and schools, and a plastics company manufactures folded homes that can be used for housing in the tropics. For the most part, these buildings are still used in marginal situations such as the construction of habitable human environments in climatic conditions of the sub-arctic. A good part of Canada is marginal territory, and the North represents new problems that have to be solved in new ways, offering the potential for new and rich architecture.

15.7 Hôtel Château Champlain, Montreal, Roger d'Astous and Jean-Paul Pothier, architects.

16

Environmental Conjecture: In the Jungle of the Grand Prediction[*]

These remarks are occasioned by the recent surfeit of plug-insville architectures, of walking cities, computer cities, helicoidal and cubed infrastructures, *villes spatiales*, *villes ponts*, and *villes flottantes* – the superarchitectures predicting the inevitable "urblands" in which it is said we will all live – as well as by a letter from *Landscape* magazine asking how do we get there from here.

The prediction of the unknown was once the art of augury and divination; if it was considered to be scientific, it was based upon the recognition of regular patterns traced through history. The unknown is always worrisome, and when prediction is framed in apocalyptic stimuli and couched in parascientific phrases, it generates responsive chords.

At the beginning of this century, the impact of technology and the changing fabric of social institutions inspired visions of soaring social edifices rendered in a hard (metal) or soft (concrete) edge geometry, depending on the disposition of its designer. A vision of technology was used in the design of buildings and new urban centres – for example, the paratechnology of the "international style." The public responded to these excursions into the shape of things to come (from Sant'Elia to Flash Gordon) with enthusiasm; they were on their way to a new world of plenty, a technological rebirth into an urban Garden of Eden.

It is now a commonplace idea that planning has become imperative for our times, and what used to be for the most part a diverting excursion into the future is now part of the decision-making apparatus of the technologically advanced nations. Looking ahead has become an indispensable tool; every design of environmental equipment – a road or a school – involves a prognostication of future patterns. Complex and detailed anticipation is now needed in order to deal with current problems. As Nigel Calder, the editor of *The World in 1984*, has pointed out, we are getting them [the future

* From *Planning for Diversity and Choice: Possible Futures and Their Relation to the Man-Made Environment*, ed. Stanford Anderson (Cambridge, MA: MIT Press, 1969), 311–27. Originally published in an abridged version as "For Design," *Landscape* 16, no. 3 (1967): 21–4.

patterns], but unfortunately in a disjointed way.[1] Planning groups in government, in industry, and in the universities are at work making "models" of possible worlds to come. These planning techniques involve the extrapolation of existing trends, the use of computers to organize and digest data, and what Daniel Bell has called "intellectual technology" – linear programming, simulation, and game theory.[2] Prediction, like other informally conceived spheres of human activity, has now assumed a formalized (i.e., scientific) role.

At the same time the optimism, the sense of wonder, and the fantasy are gone from prediction. Conclusions generally tend to be pessimistic. There is still a lingering fear of the future, which is coupled with what seems to be a latent paranoia. The probable scarcity of educated manpower, the decline in national intelligence, the control of mass behaviour, and the smooth plastic intestines in which we shall all have to live – these predictions have conjured up a world of lost sensibilities. We have learned that science and technology can efficiently serve any master and any set of goals. The magnificent electronic computers that are used to simulate future patterns reason according to the determinate logic of their bit memories, and the present distortion in the indeterminate relationships between social and political man and machines is all too evident in the kind of sensibly insensible output that surrounds us, such as "kill, kill for peace." The Garden of Eden was found, furthermore, to have plastic flowers and polyvinylchloride grass (Astro-turf, in the trade) in a spongy polyurethane landscape.

George Lichtheim pointed out that of those who are trying to sketch future trends, even the most empiricist are obliged to make projections that are not simply enumerations of abstract possibilities.[3] In environmental design, prediction is not only a question of the extrapolation of existing trends and countertrends but also the demonstration of the environmental and sym-bolic potential inherent in the fantastic display of technologic capability current in other fields.

It is no less commonplace to say that the present development of aerospace and armament technologies is far ahead of the development of any of the environmental technologies. Several agencies in the United States responsible for the research and development of the aerospace program have, in anticipation of the post-Apollo lag, turned their systems know-how to environmental problems. In developing the weapons he biologically lacks, the human animal has invented, as a by-product, the processes that have made his life better. Computers and human engineering, important to current environmental design techniques, are Second World War developments. We now know about defoliating sprays. How soon, then, will someone start to work on a re-foliating spray?

The environmental equipment that is being projected for the years to come must draw on present developments in armament and aerospace. It is, however, of less technical interest, less radical in its implications and less self-assured in its goals. So much is now technologically possible that one can, by simply making a photomontage of an aircraft carrier sitting in a wheatfield (as Hans Hollein has done) or by drawing people in on a photograph of a cross section of an air conditioning machine, predict the texture of a new place. (See Fig. 22.2.) We are so concerned with the total industrialization of our environment that any illustration of a machine to live in says something to which we are predisposed.

Among the British experimental architects, Archigram's Warren Chalk claims the ack-ack forts in the Thames Estuary, dating from the early years of the Second World War, as the respectable ancestors of their plug-insville projects; Arthur Quarmby's plug-in plastic capsule dwelling tower can be seen as a stacked, polyester version of the trailer home; and Cedric Price's "Fun Palace" installation uses the physical

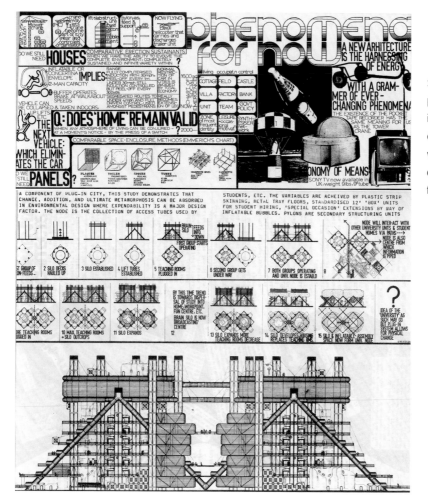

16.1 A typical slice of plug-in polemic; an assemblage of industrial, aerospace, and computer hardware and verbiage, designed in the name of a new technologic lifestyle; from *Archigram*, no. 6.

planning of a steel mill-cum-department store of about 1930.

Predicted environmental hardware is also far less radical than many systems now operative. A common example, but one worth mentioning, is the system of mobile homes that can be plugged into service lines like family toasters – a system much more technically sophisticated than that of the conventional home-building industry. Thin, lightweight metal and plastic capsules travel the highways behind a Ford "Galaxie" power unit like some tandem module in orbit. The figures for mobile homes are now well known: one out of every six single-family dwellings in the United States in 1965 was mobile. The attractions are low initial cost, low maintenance, and, since the mobile home is not classed as real estate, a tax-free existence. High-rise mobile home parks are being projected to provide docking facilities for these capsules close to the urban cores of several cities.[4] Here the dwelling capsules are driven up a ramp, backed into a concrete pigeonhole and plugged into a service core. Regardless of the slum-like "mobile ghettos" that do exist, and the fact that some of the mobile units make only one trip from the plant to their site because of road restrictions, the mobile homes show us a raw but operating model of predicted plug-insvilles.[5]

The current projects predicting the future environment, unlike the supercity architecture that was proposed earlier in this century, are generally uninterested in the ultimate shape of things. I suggest that their main interest lies in the possible new organizations of the physical environment that they imply. The plug-insvilles present the new human environment implied by technology, which, in turn, predisposes the physical environment to further technological development. In this light, these projects stand between our present technological know-how and our inability to know what to do with the urban environment.

This gap can be illustrated by the attitude of a corporation which developed aerospace equipment – nose cones and thrust chambers of rocket units and space module shells. These elements are constructed out of filament-wound, fibreglass-reinforced plastics, with the complex stress conditions of each component pre-programmed into the winding process. The same company that produced this hardware designed a house of the future: a typical suburban dwelling was recast in the filament-wound shells. Who needs filament-wound bungalows? What form of housing do we really need, and can it effectively use these stressed-skin components?

Another large corporation – General Electric – has been looking for a site on which to build the first of several new cities with a population of 100,000. The company already makes much of the equipment needed to build and maintain a city, from nuclear power plants through heating and cooling equipment and electric cars down to toasters. Big-city building for large corporations has evidently become simply a method of creating markets for new products.

In the current environmental design establishment, this gap is seen as the distance between its method and its products and the environmental processes involved. We now know that change, adaptation, obsolescence, and renewal affect any physical plan, and we are learning that these characteristics are not simple mechanisms but relationships with varying rates and reversible conditions. The professional design

16.2 The proposed "Fun Palace" for London, by Cedric Price. Two suspended auditoriums assembled by a travelling gantry crane that could later take them apart. The system clearly distinguished the transient potential of a technological environmental machine.

16.3 Monolithic integrated circuits in an electronic computer.

worriers have argued for the last fifteen years that environmental products are unforeseeable results of a process. If one looks at the plan of any town or building in use for several years, these remarks become self-evident. The form of any segment of the physical human environment is not fixed in time but moulded by life processes. Even though change has now become a fashionable word, the projects of several experimental architects, such as Yona Friedman and Cedric Price, are actually based on hard-core realities, far less fanciful than most current building and urban design.

Environmental design has now become technologically complex social hardware design. Engineered and electronically designed micro-environments have begun to appear in the form of quasi-buildings such as bus shelters, telephone booths, and hamburger stands, fitted and moulded to specific needs using mass-produced, interchangeable components. The promotion by the American Institute of Architects of "performance concept" – the operative feedback of materials and material systems performance data – and research in architecture indicate at

least some involvement of the established design profession.

The opened rear end of an electronic computer (see Fig. 16.3) can be used to illustrate the mechanical base of most current environmental projection: a firmly grounded superstructure carrying the trunk lines into which are plugged clusters of thousands of specific, parasitic microcircuits.

The microenvironments (microcircuits) of most designs utilize, with disarming ease, pods of fibreglass-reinforced plastics, expandable, inflatable, and disposable materials derived from current aerospace innovation.

At the scale of cluster and the supercluster of microenvironments we are no longer dealing with a strictly physical structure but with a process involving social and behavioural prediction. At this scale, the proposed future urban infrastructures are often brave visions of multi-dimensional networks containing many levels of response. However, urban organization involves extensive sequences of data and complex relationships, and the current masterminding of the complexities of this dimension result, all too often, in oversimplifications.

Since many of the experimental projects are at ease with technology and are models of new ways of organizing, operating, and redefining the objectives of urban structure, they can tell us more about current problems than much of the current planning work. These models suggest probable patterns with probability itself acting as a variable. This built-in hesitation is indeed the saving grace of most of this experimental work.

Modern technology is feared as a force that is arranging the world in such a way that it will be unnecessary to experience it in a personal manner. Norman Mailer sees in the contemporary world a totalitarian impulse that not only washes away distinctions but also looks for a style in buildings and in daily objects which diminishes one's sense of reality. If one important point is to be drawn from the work of Yona Friedman, the Archigram group, and Cedric Price, it is their involvement with a physical organization that acknowledges human action, and a new scale of individualization.[6] In their work there is a redefinition of distinctions.

These projects design situations where the inhabitants will be able to participate in the specific place making of the microenvironments. The British architect Cedric Price's "Fun Palace," which was prepared under the direction of Joan Littlewood, is an "area of probability" where spectators can come to interact with one another and with the machinery of the palace, an area capable of producing different spectacles. The "Potteries Thinkbelt," also by Cedric

Price, is a university for 20,000 students, to be built around an existing rail and road network, conceived as a highly flexible physical plant that can be assembled and reconstituted as readily as a freight train. Universities should initiate progress and change rather than attempt to catch up with progress; in "Thinkbelt" the environmental hardware is geared to initiating change. Price's design is an important commentary on university planning in a country that needs to increase its facilities in a time when the process of education is changing; in "Thinkbelt" there

16.4 "Potteries Thinkbelt," by Cedric Price, a proposal for a university using a mobile and dispersed organization.

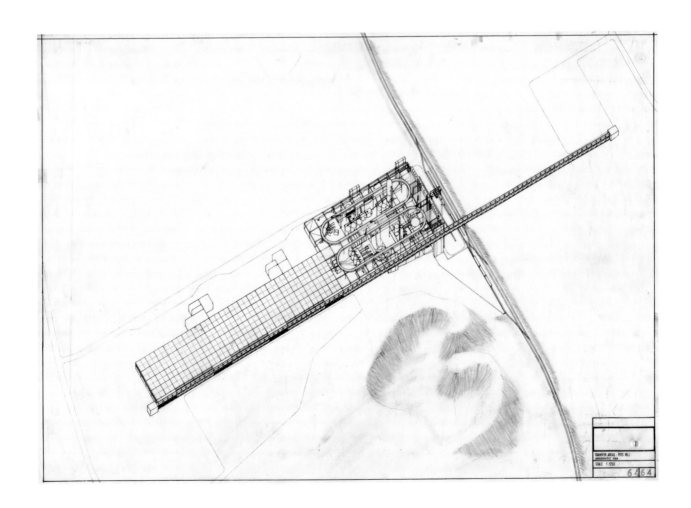

16.5 A "flying crane" helicopter transporting a mobile "plug-in" hospital pod in Vietnam; from *Life* magazine, 25 February 1966.

is a commitment not to permanent buildings but only to a serviceable installation that can be easily fabricated out of current technology. If there is anyone in the environmental field who is clairvoyant today, it is the man who can tell us what is possible with existing technologies.

The engagement of the users of buildings in the active modification of the physical surroundings – as citizen architects – is evident in some current work. In many primary and secondary schools now under construction sliding walls are being installed; the internal spaces can be varied for different learning activities, and the teacher can thus generate a form of instant architecture. Place-making becomes, in this way, an activity shared with the pupils and hence part of a learning process.

The design of adaptive equipment programmed to respond to varying conditions has been well advanced in the aerospace industry.

16.6 *This Must Be the Place,* by Roy Lichtenstein, 1965.

The moon probes, for example, open out and telescope on contact with the lunar surface. In a recent report on its F-111 jets, General Dynamics explained that "several pilots redesigned this airplane in flight." The parameters of operation within which this aircraft is effective can be varied in flight in response to specific conditions. An instant "architecture" is now being used by United States forces in Vietnam: "Flying Crane" helicopters carry surgical "pods" on medical missions near the battlefields; the pod is an emergency clinic, and a cluster of pods can be used as a hospital. Inflated, nylon-vinyl envelopes are in use for lightweight, transportable, instant supply depot architecture.

In painting, sculpture, and theatre, the passive spectator is also being transformed into an active participant. In the recent "Theatre and Engineering" spectacle at the Armory in New York, Robert Rauschenberg's *Open Score* was so composed as to be performed by the audience of five hundred; the crowd became a living canvas, so to speak. Art – from ladies' pottery classes to happenings – is, in many ways, returning to a form of communal psychodrama.

What I have tried to point out is that at best the experimental megastructure and the plug-insville architecture are not ready-made environments but simulations of the physical form of new processes of human organization which are evident both in the way people live and in the possibilities of technology. In terms of new technology this work seeks to redefine some of the fundamental values which have marked every form of human settlement.

It has been observed that the form of human settlement has changed and that we are moving into a post-industrial and post-capitalist era.[7] It is this new world in which most of these predictions operate. *They do not "use" technology, but are inherent technological evocations.* They speak of human organization at the nodes of transportation networks – the historic lifelines between settlements, the organization of parasitic micro-environments within servicing infrastructures, of new symbols, and of individual and communal responses that will structure the form of human settlement.

To ask how do we get there from here is unreasonable; it is a product-conditioned question that is seeking another and newer form of product – perhaps an instant futureville full of cosmoshapes. (See Fig. 16.6.) Anonymous architecture has always been "there." Technically most of the visionary projects referred to are "there." They are analogues; and as analogues, they can yield new concepts and be used to isolate some of the new elements which the future will comprehend. They are exciting because they oppose processes that inhibit the full articulation of technology.

NOTES

1 Nigel Calder, "Wells and the Future," *New Statesman,* 23 September 1966.
2 Daniel Bell, "The Future as Zeitgeist," *New Leader,* 28 October 1963.
3 George Lichtheim, "Idea of the Future," *Partisan Review* 33, no. 3 (1966).
4 David F. Lyon, "High Rise Mobile Home Parks," *Trailer Life,* October 1964.
5 See "The Evolving Strip," *Landscape* 16, no. 1 (1966), and a recent study published by Cornell University (*New York Times,* 11 April 1967) that reports: "At their present rate of growth, mobile homes could dominate the low-cost housing market by 1970, despite the fact that the mobile homes have as yet to be recognized as houses by many government agencies. Contrary to popular conception, the mobile home owners stayed in one place about as long as other home owners do, and the largest group of dwellers are young, lower middle class families."
6 See Warren Chalk, "Plug-in and After," in *Urbland 2000* edited by M. Charney, *Parallel* no. 6 (1967).
7 Lichtheim, "Idea of the Future."

17

An Environment for Education[*]

It has become a commonplace observation, but one well worth repeating – that industrially advanced nations of the world have, during the last decade, moved into a period of accelerated technological development. Concerning the changes in education, as the noted American economist John Kenneth Galbraith pointed out in an interview in London, in November, 1966, "one very important thing to bear in mind is that the education explosion of recent years is not some new enlightenment. To a much greater extent than we realize, education is a reflection of the needs of industry and technology."[†] Education is now considered as an important key to the economic growth of this country. It is interesting to note, furthermore, that it is through the initiative of an industry involved in building that this seminar on educational facilities is taking place.

We now recognize that any constructed environment represents an hypothesis on the way people live, behave and interact. Therefore a building designed for education is an hypothesis about the way people learn, and about the current and future needs of society. So, before examining precast concrete techniques with which we can build, let us briefly situate some of the new conditions that influence what we will build; principles on which we base school building today are dangerously obsolete.

The New Context

When we begin to talk about what is new, and the effects of change, we are involved with prediction. When we design a building, such as a school, with a life span of about thirty-five years, we are prognosticating the future whether we want to or not; this building will still be in

[*] From *The Canadian Architect* 12, no. 3 (March 1967): 30–3.

[†] Editor's note: Charney was probably referring to Galbraith's fourth Reith Lecture about the new industrial state which was broadcasted by the BBC on 4 December 1966. In this text entitled "The Role of the State," Galbraith stated: "When we realize that our new concern for education is the result not of a new enlightenment but a response to the needs of industrial planning, we shall begin to worry, I think, a good deal about the future of liberal and humane education." http://downloads.bbc.co.uk/rmhttp/radio4/transcripts/1966_reith4.pdf.

use after the year 2000. Prediction of the future, which used to be, for the most part, diverting excursions into the shape of things to come, has, in this period of change, become part of the planning and decision-making apparatus of governments and of industry; the operational role of looking ahead is now an indispensable tool. It has been found, furthermore, because of rapid change, that if there is anyone who is visionary these days, it is the man who can clearly see what is possible at this time. That is, when we talk about the future, we are talking about what can happen now. The extensive use of precast concrete technology in school construction, which is very possible today, implicates, in this way, future needs.

The period of rapid population growth that we are experiencing, and the change in the pattern of human settlement, means that not only more schools have to be built, but also new criteria for the location of these new schools. The total urbanization of human settlement is very evident; it is a qualitative change in which the urban pattern is no longer merely a larger version of the traditional city, but a new, man-made, regional configuration.

The new urban form and the development of transportation facilities are inseparable. Improved transportation has meant regional secondary schools, technical schools, and colleges that are now conceived as large, centralized establishments – virtual towns that accommodate 4,000 or more students. These educational towns can afford, because of size, the highly specialized teachers and facilities for the specialized training needed in our complex society. These towns represent a new form of constructed learning environments which, to date, are still being designed and built in archaic ways.

Elementary schools, on the other hand, relate to where families live and can seem to be fitted into the new urban megastructure as small, satellite teaching units. As housing is being developed into high-rise systems, these schools will eventually be integrated into the community levels of vertical neighbourhoods. In 1948, Le Corbusier put a primary school and a nursery on the top of his famous Unité d'Habitation in Marseille; here the children go up to school in a clear-sighted demonstration of things to come.

As well as the current needs of more schools and the need to integrate these schools into a new form of urban living, the process and the role of education in society have been radically altered by technological progress. With the shift from mechanization to electronics automation, developments such as cybernetics, data processing, and instant communication have changed our operational world. For example, as we all know, we have become more involved with processes, and in a simultaneous rather than fragmented approach to phenomena; in education, students want an active role in the learning process, and in construction, precast concrete is more important as a process than a material.

We are being warned that with increasing complexity the uneducated may soon be not only unable to get a job, but also be unable to function in society. The economist sees how education is becoming a basic industry, as central to the political economy of the future as mass production was to the past; electronic automation, which is causing the withdrawal of the present workforce from industry, will cause learning itself to become the principal kind of production and consumption in society. Currently, in the United States, the production, distribution, and consumption of knowledge account for 29 per cent of the gross national product of the country, and it is growing at about twice the rate of the rest of the economy. Paid learning is well on its way to becoming a dominant source for employment and the source of new wealth in our society.

In response to complexity, the process of education itself is becoming more technical.

Extensive research on the process of learning from automated teaching, to child behaviour, to the chemistry of the brain is now under way. New curricula, new teaching methods, such as team teaching, which improve teaching levels, and the deployment of teacher specialities and a greater emphasis on individual programmed instruction, mean that the requirements of school facilities have changed. Educational methods that emphasize the active participation of the children require a hierarchy of varied spaces for different learning activities – from individual children in a language laboratory, or with a teaching machine programmed to correct a personal deficiency, to a group of 60 or 125 for a film presentation. An example of a new synthesis of building and learning process can be seen in the so-called "Schools without Walls," several of which have been constructed in the United States.* The plan allows for a flexible learning program in which group participation may be left to the discretion of the child – i.e., if he reads better he can move off to an advanced group.

It has been recognized that change has become a permanent state of affairs in the educational scene. One answer to constantly changing demands being made on schools has been the recognition of the need to develop acceptable building systems that can easily be modified, enlarged or even scrapped if necessary. One answer to the need of highly varied learning spaces has been a flexible system of mobile partitions with which the configuration of the interior of the school can be changed without compromising the quality of the environment. The possibility to change the plan of the school while the school is in session is similar to the General Dynamics F-111 jet which can be redesigned while in flight – for different flight conditions the wing configuration can be altered. In a similar way, the teachers and children in a school with sliding walls make their own spaces as they need them and thus participate as

citizen-architects in the educational process, and in the world around them.

Not only are changes in the role and process of education giving us new conditions for a new type of school building, but also the change in the way we look at the physical, man-made environment has altered our concept of a building. Primacy is now given to a building as an environmental process. We have become aware of the built environment as man-made process in which mechanisms are brought to bear on the human animal, so that a set of relationships are set up between him and his surroundings.

The factors which determine the adequacy of inhabitable spaces can, as a consequence of recent advances in knowledge, be described technically. Various experiments are now under way to study how man uses the building spaces he occupies, and learning spaces can in this way be qualified.

The School Environments Research (SER) project of the University of Michigan should be mentioned here. This project sought to determine how the totally man-made environment affects the learning process. There is little known about the effect of total environment – space, sonic, thermal, luminous and social factors – on learning, and this study provided us with current data and guidelines for future research.

A psychologist, Daniel Carson, who worked on the SER project, has qualified the degree of complexity of an environment, and has found that children in elementary schools need an information-rich surrounding. For children, environmental impressions are as real as words and ideas. In an elementary school that I designed and that is now under construction, concrete structural columns are used as "information" for the identification of each primary teaching place.† Entering and leaving affect one's sense of

* Editor's note: *Schools without Walls: A Report from Educational Facilities Laboratories* (New York, 1965).

† Editor's note: See Melvin Charney, "Transitional Flexibility, École Curé Grenier, Notre-Dame-des-Laurentides," *Architecture Canada* 45, no. 3 (March 1968): 46–7.

place, and in this school each doorway is emphasized and the main entrance to the school is a special gateway – an arch of triumph to a special town. The school in this way uses a language of simple environmental elements that belong to the child's culture and with which he can actively learn.

The Potential of Precast Concrete Technology

Construction has undergone, as other phases of human activity, a shift of emphasis that gives primacy to process. How we build has become very important. Just as in education where more has now to be learned in less time, so, in school construction, we now need more buildings, higher quality, and lower costs.

However, the construction industry in general, and school construction in particular, have on the whole resisted significant technological innovation. Despite the great increase in the volume of school building, and the fact that collectively the school building market is large, schools in Quebec are built one by one; there are no co-ordinated standards, and there are few incentives offered to industry or to architects to encourage the development that is necessary. It is evident that innovation will have to be introduced if we are to meet educational requirements.

Technological advances that are currently underway in other sectors are showing us what may very well happen to construction. The research and development program in aerospace and in installations, for extreme climates, abounds with new innovations that are prerequisite to innovations in the science of building. Buildings, according to these developments, are assemblages of environmental hardware, plugged into service megastructures; construction means the fabrication and assembly of systems of interrelated components and sub-systems. This system reorientation repre-

sents an important step in the automation of design and the industrialization of construction. It implies interchangeable parts, human engineering, "performance concept" feedback, expendability and obsolescence, and the use of computer technology; at our School of Architecture for example, as well as computer training for students, we have added to our faculty, as a research consultant, an aeronautic engineer who directed an aerospace laboratory in the United States. The American corporations that accomplished the space research and development program are now entering the building field – they call it the environmental field – in search of new markets for their systems development know-how, and they may very well displace much of the traditional building procedures.

Concrete is, ideally, a technologic material par excellence in the sense that it is a composite whose characteristics can be controlled by varying the constituents according to specific design requirements. It uses reinforcing steel in tension, and one gets in this structural use of this metal the most force per dollar.

Precasting is the industrialization of concrete construction. Concrete is preformed into building components under controlled factory and laboratory conditions. Control is basic to the successful use of concrete; and, even after extensive experience, site control is still found to be difficult. Under industrial conditions, the temperatures, mixes, additives, the placing of the steel reinforcing, vibration, frequencies, forming, and especially curing can be carefully controlled.

For example, in the Schokbeton process, the casting takes place on shock tables that vibrate at 250 cycles per minute; a low slump is used, and, with no increase in the normal cement content, the result is a high strength concrete in the order of 10,000 psi, and denser concrete that is relatively impermeable – with a water absorption factor from 1 to 2 per cent. This method allows for the manufacture of concrete components with a high degree of precision, tolerance, low shrinkage, and a section that can be designed as narrow as 2".

It is important to note that precast concrete is more of a building *process* than a material. The material is formless and plastic, and can be cast into the varied shapes. This plasticity is both the beauty and the difficulty of the process since its discipline is directly related to the conception of a building itself as an assembly of components. This is nothing new, but still most of precast concrete is used in designs that are basically brick, wood, or steel construction. As an industrial product, the design, manufacturing and marketing of the precast concrete components greatly affect ultimate costs. Thus the future of precast concrete depends very much upon the redefinition of buildings themselves as components systems adjusted to modern technology.

It has been demonstrated in several countries that a standardized component systems approach to school building can encourage the necessary technological development. Furthermore, it has been shown in other sectors of industrial production that the standardization of components does not mean the standardization of buildings; components can be designed to allow for variable assemblies that respond to specific school and site requirements. That is, buildings can use the same language of components and say different things.

The pioneer work with building systems was done in England, where industrialized mass-production techniques have been successfully applied to 20 per cent of all school construction during the last twenty-two years. Several versatile systems were developed of which the most famous is the CLASP system; recently, CLASP has been adapted for export, and it is being used in Italy and France – a CLASP school was awarded a special prize at the last Milan Triennale. Building costs in this way were held down, construction time is cut, yet planning and design remained flexible.

The School Construction System Development Project (SCSD) is a recent American example of the component approach to school building that has resulted in both considerable cost saving and in the improvement of teaching environments. The project grouped together a number of school districts to provide a large enough market to enable industrial concerns to design, tool up for, and produce a series of interlocking building components. These components – the structural, lighting, thermal, and partitioning sub-systems – were selected on a proposal basis made by industry according to a set of performance standards that were established by SCSD after a study of educational programs. Presently there are thirty SCSD schools under construction; no two schools look alike, and their plans vary from campus to compact arrangements. The Lockheed Aircraft Corporation has used this system to build a large plant in several months and Rensselaer Polytechnic Institute is now studying the feasibility of this component system for schools in New York State.

Both the British systems and the SCSD system, which is a direct offshoot, use metal structural components. However, in England, it is now generally agreed that for flexibility in height, form and loading, and to secure adequate insulation against noise, temperature, and fire, concrete has substantial advantages: in its precast form it can be used to integrate the structure with a maintenance-free building envelope, and with other services. In the SCSD project it is the approach and the result that are significant, rather than the system itself. This system is only efficient for a one-storey school, which may be fine in California; however, when two-, three- and even six-storey facilities are now necessary because of the need of more efficient land and building use, concrete components can offer a more direct solution. With several storeys the sixty-foot span of the SCSD system has to be cut down, and concrete spans become more efficient. Furthermore, the costs in labour and other materials have risen during the past ten years while the cost of concrete work has remained the same. The signs now are that a great step forward in design and technology will come about as concrete, industrialized building processes are in more general use.

Although precast concrete construction is relatively new, it is now in extensive use as the subsequent projects will show. The current work demonstrates clearly the evident potential in the use of this process in school construction.

In countries where there were severe postwar housing shortages, precast concrete systems have been in use for over twenty years. The Camus system of bearing wall panels is in use in fifty countries of the world; it was developed in France, where there are several systems of which the Coignet system uses an important degree of industrialization in the manufacture of precast elements. In England there are several systems in use, as in other European countries; in Russia, entire room elements are being precast. The components of these systems are used over and over again for many buildings, and whether one likes the way these buildings look or not, they do represent for many people the difference between having a home or not, and for construction, an important phase in the development of economic techniques of mass-produced total-precast concrete construction.

Like another new building material, plastics, in which large-scale application has been very rapid, precast concrete is extensively used on this continent to replace traditional materials in a traditional context. Precast concrete cladding bolted to a structural frame is an important part of the current market of the industry since precasting offers integrated windows and a maintenance free facade which can be elegantly finished and formed into an instant architecture. Recent examples of precast "curtain walls" include the Place du Canada in Montreal.

However, it is in the use of precast concrete as an integrated building system that its logic and economies emerge; for the "curtain wall" a more feasible solution could be achieved using the precast components both as load-bearing and envelope. In the design of the U.S. Embassy for Dublin, Ireland, in 1959, a precast concrete component system was used in which the envelope of the building was structural, and floor slabs and interior bearing elements were keyed into it.* The building was designed from the beginning as an assemblage of components; the system was developed with a company which was chosen from several companies that were asked to submit bid proposals on the basis of a preliminary study. As construction is becoming technologically more complex, and related to industrial processes, it is inevitable that industry will have an important role in the design development of buildings.

The Police Headquarters building, completed in 1962, in Philadelphia, is another example of a concrete component construction where structure and envelope were synthesized; 2,000 concrete pieces were built out from a concrete spine.† In the new Stephen Leacock building at McGill University, a central core was first poured into which were fitted precast bays: the pouring of the core eliminated delay during fabrication of the components, and rigid joints were also eliminated in the precast components since the core took care of lateral stability.‡ In the construction of the men's residences of Loyola College in Montreal, a precast system of wall panels and channel slabs simplified the site work.§ These

---

* Editor's note: The U.S. embassy in Dublin was designed by Architect John M. Johansen. Charney worked for Johansen after his graduate studies at Yale and drew parts of this building.

† Editor's note: The Philadelphia Police Headquarters was designed by architect Robert Geddes.

‡ Editor's note: The Stephen Leacock building at McGill University was designed by ARCOP.

§ Editor's note: This residence was designed by Fred Lebensold of ARCOP.

projects used custom-made concrete components designed for a one-and-only building application, and even though they were competitively priced, these traditional designs do not reflect the true potential possible in school construction. These projects are, however, interesting in as much as both designers and fabricators learned how to use precast concrete. Joining methods and the reduction of piecemeal assemblies were found to be important design criteria. Transportation and handling methods were greatly improved and there was an increased precision in the casting of components.

In current work there can be seen a greater tendency towards precast concrete components integrating several building functions, and precast components which can be keyed to variable assemblies so that they can be used on several projects. Precast component techniques are now also in use in highly competitive apartment construction, and for hospitals, where costs are a primary factor. An extension to Brigham Hospital, in Boston, uses precast, prestressed components that are post-tensioned, and that integrate to some degree mechanical services.

As you can see, we are clearly involved in a new type of building situation. However, converging tendencies are discernible. It is now generally recognized that an industrialized systems component approach to school construction is inevitable if we are to meet educational requirements. At the same time, important developments have been realized in the economic use of precast concrete process. The use of precast concrete components predicates that a building be conceived of as an assembly of interlocking elements, and the conception of a school as a place of learning that is geared to the modern world is also tending towards an assembly of space components.

Both building technology and the environmental requirements of schools are becoming complex; for example, the form-releasing agents used in the manufacture of precast concrete must be chemically compatible with joint sealing compounds. Production and assembly schedules are critical to the cost of components, and have become contingent on a growing complexity of factors; for variable assemblies, the linkages and joining methods have become complex design problems that involve the careful prediction of all possible conditions. Future development of building design and production will be contingent on the use of computers to handle these increasing complexities.

Technology means complexity, but also the tools with which to handle it.

The present tendency towards a system, components-assembly approach to building production is in itself an effect of computer technology. A computer program can be used from the storing and retrieving environmental criteria, to the ultimate automation of the production of the concrete components. Computer graphics techniques can improve and speed up the design of assemblies components moulds.

In the automated production of precast concrete components, injection moulding is very possible with the improved moulds; these moulds could, of course, be written off on a mass production basis. Extrusion techniques now in use for the production of some precast elements are still crude, but they do offer another approach to the automation and the control of the process. With the constituent materials themselves, the development of lightweight cements, or ideally, polymer substitutes, would greatly reduce dead-load redundancies. Chopped steel fibres impregnated in the concrete may replace steel rod reinforcing in many types of components; in Russia, glass fibres have been successfully tested as reinforcing.

The structural potential of precast systems has only begun to be exploited. Prestressing, and post-tensioning techniques will further reduce the dimension of components. The increased precision of the casting techniques and computer-aided design procedures, can result in sophisticated concrete hardware. The engineer Janos Baracs has recently developed precast concrete space-frames using simple castings and joining methods. If, as the noted engineer Lev Zetlin has pointed out, the failure of steel space frames lies in the waste of labour in having to assemble thousands of pieces, then Baracs's system, in which the nodes are precast and complicated joining eliminated, is an important development. The spans of this precast structure, and the depth, offer some answers to the flexibility needed in school designs, as in the SCSD solution.

18

Grain Elevators Revisited[*]

The handling of grain was first mechanized in the mid-nineteenth century. Sacking was eliminated, and equipment was constructed to move the grain as a flowing substance.

The first steel elevator in North America was completed in Philadelphia by 1866. By 1911, the construction of reinforced concrete elevators was found to be cheaper than steel.[1] The design and the construction of the elevators were far from anonymous. Experiments in the design of bins in England and Germany, characteristics of different systems of construction, patents and the technical innovations of designers and engineering companies, were all published in handbooks and technical journals. From these one learns the names of the earliest designers. Max Toltz, a mechanical engineer with the Great Northern Railroad, designed the large elevator in Buffalo in 1897 and another in West Superior Wisconsin in 1899, on the basis of experiments that he carried out on the fluid pressures of stored wheat. The John S. Metcalf Co. and the MacDonald Engineering Co. of Chicago used

their patented system in the design of steel grain elevators throughout the United States and Canada. The engineer J.A. Jamieson, of Montreal, designed reinforced concrete grain elevators before the turn of the century. By 1923, there were in Canada 3,800 grain elevators, and the engineer-builders had by that time twenty years' experience in the construction of concrete silos using slip-form techniques.

The present system in Canada includes *transfer* elevators at the Great Lake ports where the grain arrives by railcar and is collected and loaded into ships, and *terminal* elevators, such as those in the Port of Montreal, which serve international shipping. At shipping berths, lifts, telescopic spouts, and mobile marine towers resemble the mobile launchers at Cape Kennedy.

The *transfer* and *terminal* elevators are themselves internal sub-systems of grain movement. The linearity of the transportation and handling equipment disposes the silos in parallel lines. The honeycomb of vertical drums is tapped top and bottom where distribution conveyors trip the grain into the bins for storage, and shipping conveyors collect the grain from hoppers. The

* From *Architectural Design* 37, no. 7 (July 1967): 328–34.

18.1 The port of Montreal is dominated by six groups of grain elevators, each of which consists of a cluster of interconnected silos, several of which (numbers 1, 2, and 5 shown on the photograph) are linked by fifteen miles of conveyors reaching out to twenty shipping berths. They stand out from the rest of the buildings of the city: round concrete surfaces, extended conveyors on spindly steel legs, diagonal piping and ductwork, mobile towers, and telescopic tentacles. In the foreground, Elevator No. 5 is composed of the original steel B elevator (1902), in the centre, of the concrete annex (1923), to the left, and of the long, concrete, B-1 addition, to the right (1959).

runs of the conveyors are connected by lifts that carry the grain several storeys above the silos to cleaning, drying, and grading machinery. Wheat cannot be stored in one place for any great length of time, and within the elevator it is transferred from one silo to another and aired on the conveyors.

The elevators are ventilated against dust explosions. Ventilation ducts interlock with the grain distribution conduits and terminate in bulbous fan units. The thin conduits of electrical control devices travel in clusters along the contours of silos and columns and introduce yet a third order of circuitry. Workmen were originally used to control the flow of grain and feedback information. But the recent automation of control devices has eliminated people from the machinery.

Vers une architecture

Early in this century grain elevators were "discovered" by architects; they were looked upon as exemplars of construction demonstrating the potential of a new machine age. Architects saw in the grain elevators a new anonymous architecture that would reflect in a new way, new industrial imperatives. They were more easily

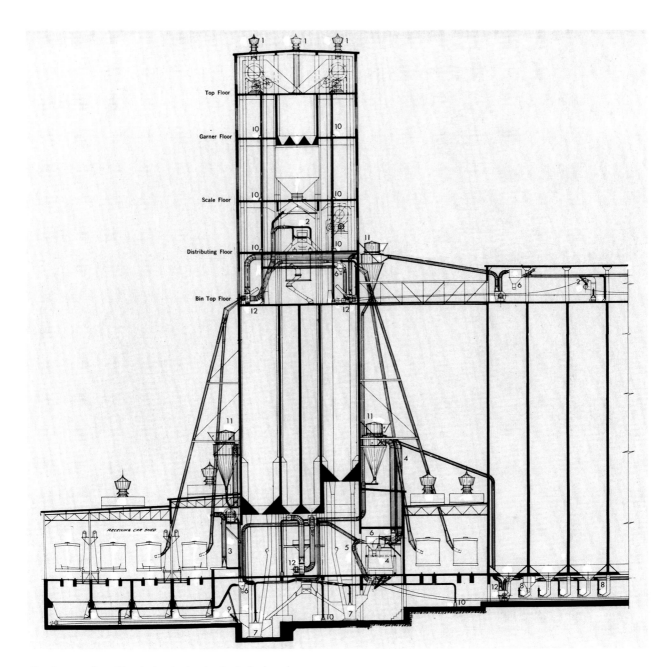

18.2 Cross-section of terminal grain elevator, track-shed, work house and storage annex, showing the dust control system.

Key

1	vents	7	boot hood
2	tripper suction assembly	8	belt loader hood
3	car dumper dust system	9	belt discharge
4	cleaner collectors	10	floor sweeps
5	main suction system	11	dual clone collector
6	grain trap	12	exhaust fan

18.3 Lakehead grain elevators at Port Arthur, Ontario, where wheat is trans-shipped to terminal ports for export.

assimilated into the canon of acceptable forms than most industrial artifacts because they resembled buildings; they could be seen as architectural compositions of large, formal elements with dimensions that physically echoed the heroic possibilities envisioned for the future.[2] They offered, as well, an image of new techniques and new materials. Furthermore, the hard-edge geometric simplicity of the grain elevators was the antithesis of art nouveau; the basic geometric forms related to the cubist vision of faceted planes of light. At the time that Cézanne observed that "everything in nature is shaped according to the sphere, cone and cylinder,"*

* Editor's note: Cézanne to Émile Bernard, 15 April 1904.

engineers were composing the grain elevators out of cylindrical drums and conical hoppers.

The earliest references to grain elevators in connection with the new architecture appeared prior to the First World War in German architectural publications.[3] Le Corbusier had only seen the grain elevators in photographs when he included them in 1923 in *Vers une architecture*. In the essay, "Trois rappels à MM. les architectes," his famous "bon mot" appears: "L'architecture est le jeu savant, correct et magnifique des formes assemblées sous la lumière,"[4] and accompanying this statement are illustrations of silos that loom large and without scale in a grey light.

The silo drums in these illustrations stand on a heavy base and are capped by rectangular, lintel-like conveyor galleries in a classic tripartite composition. The composition is thus familiar when in a subsequent essay one is confronted with a colonnade from Paestum, columns

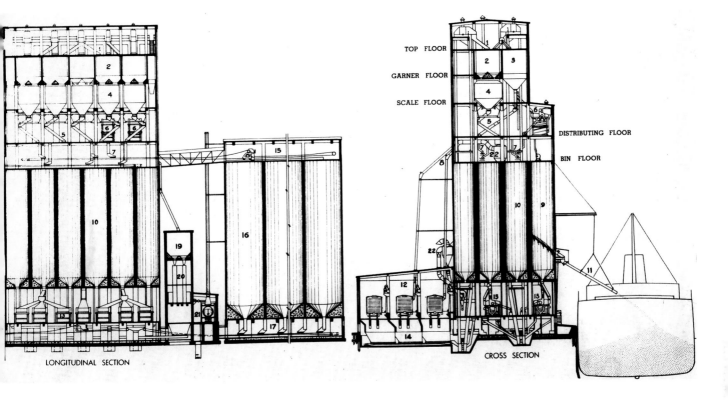

LONGITUDINAL SECTION

TOP FLOOR
GARNER FLOOR
SCALE FLOOR
DISTRIBUTING FLOOR
BIN FLOOR

CROSS SECTION

from the Parthenon, and even a photograph of a Parthenon metope, all recalling these elevators. The illustrations, moreover, are set between photographs of Pisa Cathedral and of the Belvedere Courtyard in the Vatican Palace by Bramante, giving to the grain elevators an unexpected historical significance. They appear in lieu of a new architecture, yet to emerge.

In 1929 the grain elevators appear in Bruno Taut's *Modern Architecture,* among the buildings called "Industrial." Here the American grain elevator has become modern architecture. Yet, Taut warns the reader of the shortcomings of the architecture – "Americanized to the extent of mere utilitarian or remunerative considerations."*

* Bruno Taut, *Modern Architecture* (London: The Studio, 1929).

18.4 Longitudinal and cross-section of terminal grain elevator showing dust control system.

Key

1 discharge spouts from elevator legs	10 workhouse bin
2 scale garner	11 boat loading spout
3 cleaner garner	12 car unloading shed
4 hopper scale	13 receiving separators
5 mayo and telescopic distributing spouts	14 receiving hoppers
6 screenings separator	15 storage cupola
7 loading spouts to storage belts	16 storage bins
8 car loading spouts	17 storage basement
9 shipping bin	19 dryer garner
	20 drier
	21 boiler house
	22 dust collectors

18.5 Grain Elevator No. 5, Montreal, with conveyor runs and mobile marine towers.

As interest in the machine cult waned, so interest in the grain elevators lapsed. They were never studied as functional organisms. Virtually none of the architects who admired them knew how they worked, and they were therefore unable either to appreciate their systems of organization or to draw conclusions that might have served them in their own designs. The grain elevators were upheld, if at all, as geometric compositions.

Vers une non-architecture

But they are physical facts that are neither beautiful nor brutal. They are part of a system that offers a specific service. As an analogy for architecture, the grain elevator can be taken to be a building, a system, or part of a system, the mechanisms of which are dominated by movement.

The structural techniques of No. 5 elevator complex are varied, some silos are built out of masonry reinforced with steel rings, the square bins are of steel with diagonal bracing, the circular bins are of steel and of reinforced concrete. Elevator B was the first large steel elevator built in Montreal, and in a period of sixty-five years, the original installation has been increased to five times its capacity; new conveyors, new ventilating ducts with high velocity air intakes, and automated controls have been introduced.

This system was not designed to change. But because it was first conceived as a process of handling wheat rather than the design of a specific machine, new requirements and technological innovation have been readily integrated.

The latest generation of elevators has new components that fit the system as a logical outcome of the process.

Seen and experienced first-hand, elevators such as No. 5 at Montreal are too large to be comprehended as single physical events. The whole cannot be seen; it remains almost as abstract a concept as that of the mass of people the wheat inside is destined to feed. Moving through the complex, one experiences an environment of repeated elements and groups of elements – a consistent vocabulary that results in visual wholeness, a story and even a history. But the concept of "elevator" as a design is not readily to be grasped. Functionalism here relates to the action of each part, but more especially to the complex interaction of all the parts. There is a sense of fitness in the clustered silos as satisfying as that evoked by the more simple, easily comprehended clusters of Neolithic granaries.

But the Montreal elevators are infinitely more complex and deserving of deeper study if they are to be properly comprehended and allowed to influence our architecture. Para-symbols, the latest forms of technological innovation, are used still to give an up-to-date image to strictly traditional building. Architects look, as ever, for a new lifestyle in technology. But they are interested only in the image. We are stirred by the structures at the Kennedy Space Centre. In the January–February issue of *Forum* the steel structures and ductwork of the mobile launching platforms and the vehicle assembly buildings were profusely illustrated, rather than the

LEFT | 18.6 Interior of Elevator No. 4, Montreal.

RIGHT | 18.7 Mobile Launcher for the Saturn V Rocket at the Kennedy Space Center.

Apollo vehicles or details on the design of their "life-supporting" systems that might really influence our environmental imperatives. Again, as in Le Corbusier's acclamation of the grain elevators, words like gigantic, fantastic, and phrases such as "implications for new architecture and a new urban technology" are used to persuade us.

But technology is happening, and new lifestyles are evolving. Even with the grain elevators we can opt for an understanding of the complexity of the organization rather than a simple appraisal of the design image. We *can* opt for the telescopic spouts, the mobile towers, the mobile cranes, the moving conveyor belts, the stack of

FACING PAGE | 18.8 and 18.9 Elevator No. 1, Montreal, built in 1903, a typical elevator that was illustrated in architectural texts of the 1920s. The lifts and conveyors were added to increase handling capacities.

LEFT | 18.10 The spout loading grain into the hold of a ship.

parts that can be inserted into the system when needed, the concrete silos as distended tubes in the conduits of movement, rather than the static and lumpish neo-monuments of yesteryear, but we must opt for them not as formal images. It is the process of which they are an image that is important. This process we must study if we believe that architecture is an involvement with human processes rather than with designed things.

In this way the grain elevators may yet again suggest to architects a way out of their self-imposed limitations.

LEFT | 18.11 Shipping side of Elevator No. 4, Montreal, built in 1956. It is 1,200 feet long, 233 feet high, and has one of the largest capacities in the world for a single elevator, with an unloading capacity of 140,000 cubic feet per hour.

RIGHT | 18.12 Baie-Comeau, Quebec: elevator built in 1960. The angle of accumulation of falling grain determined the slope of the storage components on the right; on the left, steel bulk tanks are used to supplement the storage.

NOTES

1 Milo S. Ketchum, *The Design of Walls, Bins and Grain Elevators* (New York, 1911), chapters 15 to 17.
2 Eric Mendelsohn, *Amerika* (Berlin, 1926).
3 Walter Gropius, "Die Kunst in Industrie und Handel," *Jahrbuch des Deutschen Werkbundes* (Jena, 1913), 21–2.
4 Le Corbusier, "Trois Rappels à Messieurs les architectes 1. Le volume," *Vers une architecture* (Paris: Crès et Cie, 1923), 16.

19

Learning Environments:
Planning beyond Flexibility*

The notes assembled in this study deal primarily with flexibility. There has been much written on the modes of flexibility in school design, and some flexible schools have been built. These notes intend to develop some of the premises implicit in the design of flexible educational facilities, and to suggest a responsive environment that goes beyond physical flexibility. The material is organized into three parts, each of which deals with a specific scale of flexibility. The first and second treat the educational facility of the child, age two to eight, and that of the student, age eight to sixteen, respectively (flexibility from within), and the third is on the educational facility itself as a sub-system of new urban forms (flexibility from without).

In the design of educational facilities, with all deference to the many issues involved, two operative attitudes should be distinguished. The first of these consists of a level of persistent

conditions. A drawing of a school, published in France in 1881, serves as a good illustration. This design shows a masonry building in which fixed components are imbued with an architect's sense of purpose and with his understanding of readily observable environmental criteria; for example, the openings of the classrooms are carefully oriented and are made to distinguish between the penetration of light and of sun.

The teaching methods that were current, inasmuch as they were considered to be design criteria, were similarly translated into building form. This concern with methods of teaching is manifest today in the common question "What are the architectural implications of educational reform?" This question presupposes that a viable design framework can still exist in which change can be assimilated; it assumes that a deterministic, causal working arrangement is still possible whereby reform in education is directly translatable into unique building forms.

This concern of the architect with reform in education is very real indeed. Society has become education oriented and this can be regarded as less of a question of some new enlightenment

* From: *Architecture Canada* 45, no. 3 (March 1968): 39–45. Editor's note: Several images that illustrated the original essays could not be located and are thus not reproduced in this publication.

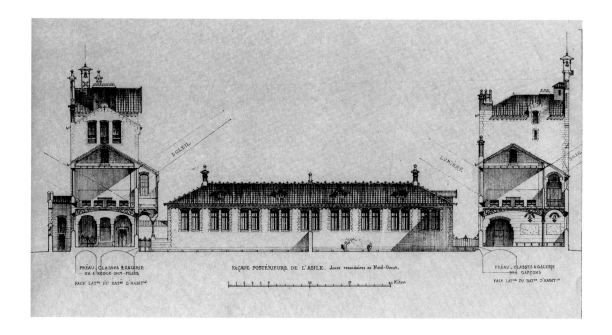

19.1 Competition design for an elementary school for boys and girls for Levallois-Perret (Seine) dated 1881.

and more as a response to the needs of technologic growth and social development, as John Kenneth Galbraith and others have pointed out.* As well as a concern with change, there has been in response to technology and to social development a commitment to change that has demonstrated the conditions of new learning environments, in which one is no longer dealing with a "New School" but with an emerging environmental "non-architecture" – the second operative level.

In the broadest sense, the emphasis now is on a technology for education: the engineering of the entire environment for the learning process; (see, for example, the report "Technology for Education" prepared by the editors of *Science and Technology*, August 1967). A part of the total educational environment that is being engineered is

*Editor's note: John Kenneth Galbraith, *The New Industrial State* (Boston: Houghton Mifflin, 1967).

the hard-shell containers that are the equivalent to what we know as school buildings. However, technology can also be seen as a way of thinking about problems, and the commitment is to control the distinction between real and desired output. These new imperatives are especially manifest in a concern with flexibility. That is, a concern with the adaptability of the physical environment and of the inhabitants to sustain and effect change.

Flexibility in a Child's Learning Centre

In order to tune into the spirits of change in education, a brief invocation: a general revision from lockstep, rigid schooling with the teacher leading the class at a time through a given curriculum, to the elimination of formal grades, to the emphasis on active participation, varying group activities and self instruction, and to the teacher as an advisor and as a manager of learning resources with the hard shells of the learning environment as one of the resources to be managed. In building these new kinds of educational facilities, it has, however, been easier to proclaim this spirit of independence than to create a spirit of flexible independence.

In primary schools and pre-school centres for children from two to eight years old, the development that begins to indicate this change is the building of schools that enclose large packages of continuous space containing three to five groups of thirty children and their teachers. In the report *Schools without Walls*, published by Educational Facilities Laboratories in 1965, the recent use of a non-differentiated large space in which "school takes place" was attributed to the introduction of non-graded teaching methods.* To show how an open space can effectively serve small as well as large groups, and how individual work is possible in a background of ambient noise, the report chose two examples, the first of which was the open offices of a banking floor where ranking executives hear out prospective customers, and the second example showed diners in a pretentious, candle-lit restaurant. Instead of this demonstration of class solidarity, it would have been much closer to the point to have observed children, for example, in the mobile patterns generated by children in any play (i.e., learning) situations in an open area.

The dominant concern that emerges from this report is a preoccupation with acoustics. This may be simply explained by the fact that sound levels as those of light and temperature are easily quantifiable. However, of the many environmental characteristics that interact in a place of learning, sonic conditions have generally received inordinate attention. Along with the tendency towards informal learning and space use, the idea persists that learning takes place when children are quiet; in the "open schools" there has also been some transference of the noise disciplining syndrome from the children to the buildings in which the floors are punished with carpets.

* Editor's note: *Schools without Walls: A Report from Educational Facilities Laboratories* (New York, 1965).

In these "open schools" the external shell of the environment was disengaged from the learning activities and withdrawn to a neutral perimeter. The shell can provide thermal and light conditioning, and offers a spread of protected floor for a working surface. Ideally, within the shell, an infill of learning activities can generate permissive spatial and grouping configurations, as required by the limitations set by the participants.

Consider, firstly, the disengaged shell as a flexible enclosure, and observe two "open school" buildings:

1. The Granada Community School in Belvedere Tiburon, California. The internal space is built up from a cluster of interlocked enclosures that open to each other; the school itself is composed of several of these clusters. Within the cluster, it is possible to identify large and small areas that can be used together or apart. The angled, faceted sides generate working corners and surfaces, and the additive assembly implies, in a direct way, growth and contraction. The scale of the structure also is related to, and can be identified with the spaces within which different groups can gather.

2. The Satellite building. Public School No. 219 in Queens, New York. The rotund, with its nerved beams and low dome, dominates the interior void. Within the dome, the fix of the circle, a fixed concentric inner circle, and a central mezzanine preform and stiffen the open space with an exaggerated vertical dimension and the feeling that someone up there is watching you. But this school does, at least, show that an internal large space can have a vertical dimension.

Having disengaged a durable and serviceable macro-shell from the specific infill – the immediate learning process – the objects that are left within the space such as storage units, chairs and tables are now separated from the walls and stand free. The learning environment now depends very much on the re-engagement of this equipment; this can be seen, in a negative way, in the case of the 219 School. With potential mobility, this equipment can affect and be affected by the flux and variety of the children's activities.

Consider, then, a gamut of learning activities: Joseph Featherstone, in a recent article in the *New Republic*,* has described a non-graded primary school (K-2), located in Leicestershire, in action: "If you arrive early, you find a number of children already inside, reading, writing, painting, playing music, tending pets. Teachers drift in slowly, and begin working with the students … some small groups … but mostly children are on their own, moving about and talking quite freely. The teacher sometimes sits at her desk, and the children flock to her for consultations, but more often she moves about the room, advising on projects, listening to children read, asking questions … rooms, open out onto the playground which is also very much in use. A contingent of children is kneeling on the grass clocking the speed of a tortoise which they want to graph against the speeds of other pets and people. Nearby are five year olds finishing an intricate tall tower of blocks … there is a quieter library nook for the whole school. The rooms are fairly noisy … paint spills, a tub overflows … usually the children mop up and work resumes … there are no individual desks and assigned places. Around the room there are different tables for different kinds of activities: art, water and sand play, number work … a library alcove with a patch of carpet and an old easy chair … a corner with dolls and furniture for playing house … a dress-up corner with castoff clothes … a makeshift puppet theatre and a stage for dance dramas that involve lots of motion … there is no real difference between one subject in the curriculum and another or even between work and

play … the extent to which the children really work purposefully is astonishing."

Here the flexibility of the environment has to do with choice, involvement, and with participation. Sections of wall, corners, parts of the floor, shelves, platforms, tables, soft and hard chairs, boxes, blocks, and books are drawn into the process of learning. In the description, reference is made to classrooms, corridors, and outdoor play areas – the traditional elements of a school building. Yet, despite the traditional configuration of the plan, a spirit of spontaneity and participation animates the children. The plan is transcended by the activities and by the equipment which transform the rooms and corridors into so many different learning situations. Even though some of the equipment referred to is furniture, its use also transcends the intrinsic nature of "furniture."

In order to articulate this learning equipment, a platform which places several children above others so that they are in a position to be seen and heard can be considered to be a learning device. Accordingly, a platform which a group of children can assemble and under which, or on which, they can work together is as much a learning device as are doll's houses, Cuisenaire rods, or logic blocks. And scales can be devised whereby objects are intrinsically charged with information, identity, possibilities of selective combination, and mobility. Flexibility can, in this way, mean the specific commitment of the physical environment to the child. The proposed equipment represents an instrumental architecture at the scale of fit immediate to that of the learning process. It can act as the permissive surrogate of floors and walls, and can be used to create corner conditions. Because a high degree of variability can be introduced into the design, a wide range of accommodation is possible. The generating source of energy in organizing combinations of this equipment, as in the learning process, rests with the children and with the teacher.

* Editor's note: Joseph Featherstone, "Schools for Children: What's Happening in British Classrooms," *New Republic* 157, no. 8/9 (19 August 1967): 17–21.

Further, the conception of this equipment as fragments of the environment that can be actively engaged means that the child can personalize a part of his surroundings to his needs. As an individual, or as part of a group, he can engage his surroundings by his actions, and, in "place-making," he can participate in a cultural process. Intelligence is born of action, and any fact of intelligence consists of carrying out and co-ordinating operations, noted Jean Piaget. This child can then emerge conditioned to the responsive control of at least part of his environment.

The Student's Facility

The well-known program of the School Construction System Development (SCSD) that was set up in California, in 1964, defined four modes of flexibility that still summarize the scope of current planning: (1) Variety of space sizes and functional capabilities to provide options in the use of the facilities. (2) Operative methods of reducing, multiplying, or expanding spaces for different activities in the day-to-day operation of the school. (3) Long-range changeability of the interior divisions to facilitate changes in the educational program, with electrical and mechanical systems, floor materials, and furniture to back up possible rearrangements. (4) The orderly

expansion of the facilities with the possibility of closed, functional systems at each successive stage.*

The definition of these modes depends directly upon a breakdown in time of possible changes. As the feasibility study by Alan Green points out, they can be seen to follow a time scale; the minute-to-hour in-process changes, the day-to-week program changes, and the term to year changes in planning. The dimension of probable change is more difficult to deal with as it depends on the pre-programming of a design according to an extrapolation of known tendencies.

The subsequent SCSD buildings assimilated the above program. The system consisted of a one-storey horizontal sandwich with a thick central layer of usable space that could be divided by demountable and operable panels set between a fixed floor layer, and ceiling roof layer which was in itself a sub-sandwich containing adjustable electrical and mechanical systems.

* Editor's Note: *SCSD: The Project and the Schools. A Report from Educational Facilities Laboratories* (New York, 1967).

19.2 SCSD planning system. Structural planning is on a five-foot horizontal and two-foot vertical module. Partitions may be located anywhere on the four-inch planning module.

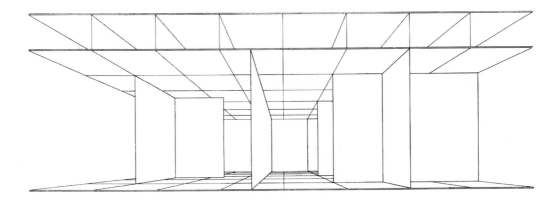

19.3 El Dorado High School (First increment). Placentia, California, architects William E. Blurock and Associates.

Observe two of the SCSD schools completed in 1966:

1. The "English Wing" of the El Dorado High School in Placentia, California. Even though the traditional elements of a school are pulled apart by the building system, the internal arrangement is conditioned by a persistent classroom block plan down to the double loaded corridor. In a 25' × 110' corridor, fourteen carrels for individual study are found, and from this central space there are 10'–35'-wide doorless openings to rooms on either side; two operable panel walls divide three of the classrooms. The spaces are confronted by the edges of walls and the projecting edges of corners in a cornered-off arrangement of panels.

2. Sonora High School in Fullerton, California. Under a floating horizontal plane visually held down by thin columns and held up by masonry walls, panels inserted into the ceiling grid divide an endless flow of space. The containers thus formed are assigned to be compartmented rooms. Again, the spatial elements with which one is accustomed to experience a "School" are both there and not there. A flexible system does not in itself generate flexible use. The flexibil-

ity of the SCSD system consists of a "universal space" device of a great room with an expedient provision for internal rearrangement.

Its hardware is borrowed from office loft architecture of integrated ceilings and demountable partitions developed in the 1950s; the rectangularity of the file cabinet adjustments that can be made with the partitions responds to so many modules of rental increments and to desks and sheets of paper that had to be accommodated. (See Fig. 19.4.) However, with the use of this flexible hardware, mechanisms were set out whereby a number of plan relationships can be developed by rearrangements. The educational facility geared in this way to use an industrialized hardware, and to give some operational form to environmental feedback, can engender habits that are more important than the system itself. The clarity of the edged and lined components in these SCSD schools (the equivalent of production and assembly tolerances), and the ease with which the components fit together, show that the voids thus enclosed lack a similar coherent working relationship. The environmental distinctions that can form the basis of sets of relationships have here been eliminated. The internal homogeneity of the components tends to dilute the articulation for accessibility, for a group or an individual, or for transition or common ground, which are all basic environmental bits of information necessary to the flexible use of an education facility. For example, the movement of students through a school can be used to define the facility in terms of periods of stop and go, and of fluctuating distribution and collection patterns of mobile increments. The accommodation of the mobile students, each with a varying mix of stop periods according to both programmed and non-programmed activities, can constitute a working criterion for flexibility; time and place are linked by scheduling. The SCSD definition of the design problem ignores movement as an organizational constraint (30 per cent of the total area in many cases); it is based on a fixed building into which movable elements are introduced, which is a costly premise to start with. The necessity to distinguish between fixed and less fixed conditions when dealing with environmental flexibility has been demonstrated by the "infill strategy" that has been suggested in many experimental projects during the last few years; circulation and movement have been shown to be part of the long-term organizational structure of facilities. This suggests that fixed spaces related to specific educational needs can be used in a flexible mix of a facility – the use of fixed spatial configurations is occurring with the introduction of electronic and audio-visual teaching devices.

The selection of learning devices that are now incorporated in educational facilities includes electronic hardware for the storing and reproduction of sounds and images. The use of these media generates variable group sizes, and directly involves the students in sets of relatively precise environmental conditions.

19.4 Interior, Connecticut General Insurance Building, Hartford Connecticut, architects, Skidmore, Owings and Merrill.

The fixed optimal range of these conditions has meant that flexibility of the kind that calls for demountable and folding partitions can easily restrict the use of the media. Therefore, facilities that can both accommodate media and permit some intermittent regrouping of students as learning situations develop, and self-contained "media-modules" that can be moved as the students move, have been designed. The viewing angles of the display equipment determine angular configurations that allow tight geometric packing of usable space and more surfaces on which to project or to work. The walls and floors of a facility have in this way been integrated into the equipment systems.

The use of media renders the student immobile before a screen or between a pair of headphones which effectively turn him into a passive receiver. As a fixed receiver, his particular anthropomorphic and perceptual characteristics can be measured, and a closed, measurable loop can be considered for study. A total learning environment is complex, but this simplified model has been used to set out some relationships between the student, learning, and the environment. These relationships are all inferred from performance. More sophisticated design models can now be structured by set generating strategies to qualify the interaction of the learning infill with the physical environment.

Learning or teaching devices function as communication systems or aids in the communication processes. Accordingly, a scale of communication mechanisms can, as in the case of the child's learning centre, include printed matter, chalkboards, tackboards, floors, walls – the wall panels of the SCSD system served as chalkboards, as well as video systems, motion pictures, film strips, slides, cathode displays, and reproduction equipment. The total physical facility can be scaled in terms of communication input not only for direct participation in the learning process, but also for environmental information – indirect learning.

Research in psychology has shown how environmental factors influence man's information handling capacities. Overall findings indicate that there is an optimal range of preferred input, and that information coefficients can be attributed to a given environment to qualify the amounts of stimulus, uncertainty, sense deprivation, and information overload. The well-known experiments of D.O. Hebb have shown the degree to which alertness depends on a constant regimen of dealing with environmental diversity. The demonstrated importance of a complex, information rich environment for the development of human capacities has a direct influence on the educational facility, which is that fragment of the built environment created for the "development of human capacities."

To physically structure the environment that is to be charged with complexity, the building technologies that are being developed tend more and more to use materials and assemblies that can change, be moved, and adjusted: disposable materials with varying life cycles; light sensitized materials that vary transparency with intensity; folded, rolled, inflated or demountable components: fold-out, portable media modules, etc. With these mechanisms the hard shells of the environment can begin to respond to their designed purpose.

The introduction of computer-aided instruction (CAI) has coupled media with electronic data handling devices, and has demonstrated that direct feedback loops that engage the child in a two-way dialogue is possible. Similarly, an operable environment that could be computerized could change the configuration of the room, or, as Dr Warren Brody has pointed out, the lighting or the lessons, or the mix of spoken words, picture, and alphanumerics, or colour, or two- or three-dimensional display, and request the teacher to appear only when the child-computer system encounters difficulties.

The student and the educational facility can be regarded as object and environment for each other. With servo-mechanisms for correction strategies, a two-way environmental dialogue can generate likely change, provided that these changes can be pre-programmed. With self-reinforcing feedback loops, the environment could learn from each student, develop with the user and take part in his development. The place of learning can become a place that learns about learning and about the structure of its environment.

Urban Flexibility

It is no longer possible for an educational system to exist independently from its economic, physical, and social contents. Different learning media do not function as isolated systems in an educational facility; similarly, the facility itself cannot survive as an isolated environment fragment. The introduction of new teaching hardware depends on shared programs, and the industrialization of building technology depends on a consortium of schools. In this way, along with the individualization of the educational process, some of the conditions for change are based on a larger planning unit.

It can be observed that education has emerged as one of the determinants of changing urban form, and in response to new imperatives we are experiencing a redistribution of facilities. More is required out of land use and this has meant that facilities are being treated as part of a denser urban packing. The regrouping of facilities can be seen in the development of educational quarters such as the secondary school campuses that are being built in Pittsburgh and Quebec.

A multi-functional vertical development can be seen in projects in which the upper levels are designed for housing and the lower levels for community facilities, schools, and shops; the air rights over transportation arteries are being used for schools as in the proposed linear city over an auto expressway in Brooklyn, New York, for example. The structures of existing buildings are being treated as extensions to the urban service grid into which school facilities can be placed as specific infill; for example, an abandoned warehouse and a telephone exchange building in Chicago are being converted to educational use. School facilities as portable infill have been realized in the use of re-locatable classroom containers in many cities; a quick erection system based on the experience of the mobile home industry – project tactics – is now under study in Chicago.

Flexibility in office loft architecture was achieved by disengaging the internal space divisions from the building structure into independent, self-supporting component systems. The development of flexible educational facilities in the urban framework can be regarded to follow the disengagement of the school from a city structure, and the subsequent re-engagement of the facility as self-articulating infill in an urban network.

Design sources can in this way be tapped at their origin. As in the child's learning centre where the activity of the children is the source of "design" in the organization of the immediate learning environment, so, at an urban scale, given a mobile and multi-functional educational infill, facilities can be generated by students and can generate students.

This allows students to participate in and derive the maximum benefit from a life style in the process of dynamic change. It allows the student greater involvement not only with his social context, but also with research and industry as extensions of the education process. In the end, education, for any society, must be seen as a function and instrument of social organization.

20

Concrete: A Material, a System, and an Environment*

It has become a standard feature of the architectural press to pay at least annual homage to concrete as the dominant building material of the time. However, the commitment of the press to the singular role of the architect as a creator and "Master Builder" of unique, interesting shapes that somehow relate to people has tended to cloud many of the basic issues involved.

Rather than report on the variety of recent concrete buildings or products, which are well illustrated in any case in advertisements, the following pages deal with several conditions in the conversion of concrete into built form in an attempt to suggest a few of the neglected issues that affect design.

The basic characteristic required out of concrete is its strength and stability. Structural developments are particularly emphasized and well documented elsewhere, and they do not need to be reiterated. Nonetheless, it is inevitable that the essential structural character of the material pervade the text.

It is also inevitable that the emphasis here is on process. That a sense of process imbues the physical state of the material with a sense of form is one of those truisms which, unfortunately, has to be repeated from time to time as some banal aphorism that resists becoming fact.

In an environmental design sense, concrete has no existential nature of its own. It is a composite, plastic material that is subjected to forming, reinforcing, machine handling, and chemical change. It is subjected, furthermore, to the will of a designer who is concerned with the appearance of the product, and its image as a cultural artifact, as well as with its function.

The concept that a composite material has qualities that are better than the components alone, or radically different from any of them, has acquired a broad significance in modern technology.[1] In this sense, reinforced concrete, as one of the first composites to be extensively used in construction, represents a modern materials system. The variables in the system allow a control potential; the degree of control depends on the extent to which the mechanisms of the process can be qualified and quantified.

* From *Architecture Canada* 45, no. 6 (June 1968): 41–4.

This control potential predisposes the system to the development of a diversity of materials, fabricated components, and systems of varying performance characteristics. A composite is also predisposed to concepts of industrial technologies that have recently been developed which, in turn, allow further innovation.

The extensive use of this building material in competition with other materials, the tendency towards the scientific formulation of empirical building techniques, and the subsequent "600 percent improvement in the performance of reinforced concrete achieved in recent years"[2] has resulted in an overwhelming quantity of technical information. Developments have tended to expose new problems and spawn more development. Perhaps the major innovations may be the quantity of data on concrete that is currently being put on paper. Handbooks have either become too specialized, too complex or too simple-minded about problems (four parts sand, one part lime, one part cement, etc.). The information overload is psychologically threatening and the role of the designer as a "Master Builder" who sports a comfortable overview offers a safe retreat.

In order to begin to find some coherence there are several themes which could be developed. Recent innovation in the technology of material systems – from the restructuring of molecular bonds to the introduction of the computer – tends to be submerged in production and fabrication. Therefore, one could begin by drawing on recent research on the chemistry of concrete. Despite the familiarity, antiquity, and the extensive use of this material (consumed, in 1963, at the rate of one ton for every human being, which places it second only to man's use of water), major advances in the chemistry of concrete have been made only in the last two decades. As in many other industries, theory has tended to follow application.

A second theme could be drawn from the recent developments in forming and handling

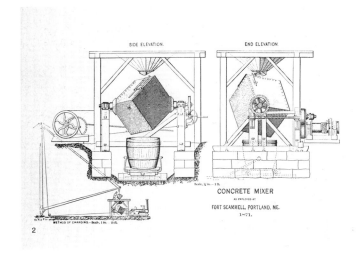

ABOVE | 20.1 A concrete mixer used at the end of the nineteenth century; turned by steam power.

BELOW | 20.2 A concrete mixer first employed in 1871. As is common with most early concrete mixing vessels, a cube shape was used.

methods – concrete as a production technology. There are two basic and diverse tendencies that can be distinguished. Construction processes have tended towards on-site mechanization very early in the use of reinforced concrete (see Figs. 20.1 and 20.2): slip-form construction using a

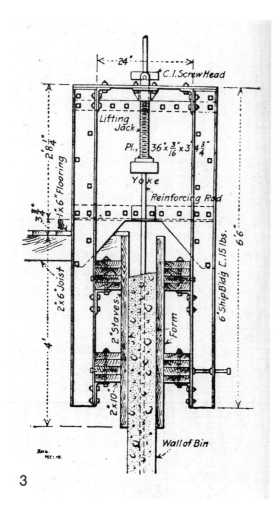

3

20.3 Lifting Jack in slip-form construction used by the Canadian Stewart Co. in the construction of the Fort William Grain Elevator completed in December 1910.

standardized preformed components that could be factory fabricated and assembled on-site as finished units. Both these tendencies – on-site mechanization and off-site fabrication – are tending to merge into processes which affect the change from concrete construction to concrete production. Both merge into production systems, which depend on a sizable market base and on the translation of buildings into industrial artifacts. This requires a direct involvement of industry, as well as a user-orientation in design.

In the same way that a system's view of the production of an artifact destined for the market would include styling considerations, so in the production of concrete artifacts the styling characteristics of concrete buildings can be considered to be an integral part of the material system. The process by which concrete is turned into built form can be considered from within the design process itself. No one designs in a vacuum, yet styling is one of the unmentionables of current architectural discourse, even though design is, by its very nature, oriented to the filter of changing sensibilities that determines the look of concrete and the look of the appropriate image of technology itself.

Other themes can be developed: the impact of computer technology on design and production; the forecasts of material resources that indicate the further innovation in the composite nature of concrete – the introduction of new constituents such as lightweight resins and high-strength fibres. The major use of concrete in the so-called "non-building" category of the construction industry could also be noted. Tunnels, bridges, dams, highways, airport runways, wharfs, streets, piles, and foundations form a superstructure of concrete within which are found smaller environmental artifacts that are specifically fitted to human needs. This simplified overview offers a vision of concrete as the dominant material system which structures large urban organization.

lever or screw jack system was innovated at the beginning of this century in the building of grain silos (see Fig. 20.3), a sidewalk paving machine that extruded slabs behind it, and a concrete pump that used compressed air were introduced in 1909.

Currently, the almost total on-site mechanization is bringing many factory conditions to building – in some cases portable factories themselves. Concrete construction has tended also towards the reduction of buildings into

In the design of the physical environment current events are ahead of current design. Design depends on concepts with which the designer comprehends conditions immediate to him and renders them instrumental in his work. Buildings and application can be found in the existing fabrication techniques, and concepts of milieu that exemplify attitudes are as yet to be incorporated in the working style of building design. Concrete was the "new" material of modern architecture which was oriented in its goals to the state of technology at the beginning of the century. Habitual gestures reminiscent of these goals, rather than the goals themselves, have tended to persist, and, fifty years later, concrete

20.4 An on-site portable factory used in the construction of Marburg University. The panels and columns can also be cast in the form of boxes, but the process is essentially the same.

is still being used to demonstrate contemporary design. Accordingly, the material has not lived up to design expectations; new innovations in concrete systems have also exposed new problems, and, in turn, new "potential." In the current generation of designs in which concrete is extensively used, however, new attitudes can be distinguished. Regardless of the styling in some buildings, or because of it in others, there

is a change in the use of concrete that reflects a fragmentation of the material into systems and varying networks of use. For each solution there are alternative systems using other materials which are economically and technically feasible, and reasonably applicable. This has tended to shift the design emphasis onto relationships between the use of the material and environmental conditions. Further change can now be found in the design breakdown of environmental problems such as urban housing and educational facilities. It is in this redefinition of the physical environment in which real innovation is found

in the use of the concrete. And it is in this context that the architect can make an important contribution.

Postscript

The April 1964 issue of the magazine *Scientific American* attracted attention because of a study that it published on hallucinogenic drugs. However, the excursion into the "inner spaces" of matter for which this issue is noted is found in an article by two scientists of the Portland Cement Institute on research into the chemical

ABOVE, LEFT | 20.5 Total mechanization of "non-building." Slip-forming of the San Luis Canal in 1967. Four machines – a rings trimmer, a modifier liner, a joint inserter, and a finisher – pave at a rate of 600 yards per hour, i.e., the capacity of a batch plant. One operator controls the movement of the unloader.

ABOVE, RIGHT | 20.6 Factory casting of "architectural" concrete still involves slow production runs.

RIGHT | 20.7 On-site mechanization using automated casting and crane rigs. This process still involves hand-made connection systems.

reactions that occur when concrete sets. One of the authors has updated this article for this issue of *Architecture Canada*.

Material systems have developed to the point where alternative solutions are feasible. The capacity of producers exceeds demand, and they are actively promoting the competition of materials and the expansion of their markets. Both the producers of cement and of the chemical additives have taken an initiative in research into the chemistry of the system so as to improve and develop concrete products. This can be seen in an article prepared by a leading company in the field of development and manufacture of concrete admixtures. It can also be seen that producer-based research tends to emphasize the properties of the material rather than the composition of the system.

The importance of chemical "admixtures" as one of the basic constituents which controls the quality and performance of concrete is described in an article prepared by the Building Research Division of the National Research Council. It is interesting to note the attitude of government based research in addressing the hardcore content to the architect/designer as if he were as a delinquent spec-writer; the article is more telling of the approach of the NRC than that of the problems of the designer working with a complex materials system.

Ordinarily, the aggregates in concrete composites are considered to be inert. However, research at Rensselaer Polytechnic Institute has shown that aggregates are affected by cold weather, and the freeze-thaw cycle is challenged as the reason for deterioration in concrete. It was thought important, because of the Canadian climate, to reprint a report on this study which appeared in *Concrete Construction*.

Even though concrete has had an important role in contemporary architecture, the recent popularity of concrete in design dates back ten years. At that time, the magazine *Progressive Architecture* planned the first of several issues devoted to the problems of concrete construction and building design. Whether their first issue predicted a design tendency, or whether it was itself a symptom of that tendency which it helped to confirm is difficult to say. However, the magazine did contribute to the setting of the style, and the editors of *P/A* were asked to reconsider their findings for *Architecture Canada*. By definition *P/A*, as other similar magazines, is architect oriented, and what emerges is a vivid description of some of the agonies of the designer in the face of technologic complexity, the change in the scale of his work and role.

NOTES

1 Anthony Kelly, "The Nature of Composite Materials," *Scientific American* 217, no. 3 (September 1967): 96–110.
2 W.O. Alexander, "The Competition of Materials," *Scientific American* 217, no. 3 (September 1967): 254–68.

A SELF-ERECTING EXHIBITION SYSTEM

Project for the Canadian Pavilion, Osaka, Expo 70*

Competition project based on the system below; March 1967. Credits: Melvin Charney, MRAIC and Harry Parnass, Architects, in collaboration with Janos Baracs, P.Eng. and Marcel Pageau, P.Eng.

The system describes a way of selecting components and assembling these components into a variety of exhibit machines for a variety of expositions and trade fairs. These exhibits are usually limited to a maximum duration of six months; the exhibits and exhibit "buildings" are usually fabricated in Canada, and assembled at the site of the show. Because of these contingencies, the system is based on the processes of fabricating exhibit "buildings" and on the techniques of shipping. It uses ready-made, mass-produced, and interchangeable components, readily available on the market. These components are chosen for their plural use potential in order to maintain high reuse and salvage options.

Assembly

Tower cranes and crane modules are interlocked in a post-tensioned structural matrix. This matrix supports exhibit enclosures which are designed as fold-out shipping containers. It houses the visitor distribution system and the trunk lines of the environmental servo-systems. The self-assembling cranes assemble themselves and the structural matrix. They are used to install the exhibits and, if so programmed, to reassemble the exhibits on several occasions during the show. At the end of the show, the cranes dismantle the exhibits and themselves. The components are then shipped elsewhere for another show, or sold as marketable equipment with a high salvage value rather than second-hand building materials.

* From *Architecture Canada* 46, no. 3 (March 1969): 34–6.

Systems Aesthetic

The ready-made components and the assemblies are not "designed" but designated for a particular exhibit. Upon the termination of an exhibit, they are replaced in other situations – perhaps put into a different "non-architecture" future. The components possess no intrinsic significance beyond their utility. It is difficult either to project into them extraneous qualities, or for them to be appropriated for personal needs or for symbolic, transcendental values.[1] The assembly of the crane modules, the swinging arms of the booms, the taut cables, and the enclosures are "scaffolding" for the participation of people in the light, sound, and movement of an exhibit.

NOTE

1 Dan Flavin, *Pink and Gold*, exhibit catalogue (Chicago: Museum of Contemporary Art, December 1967).

LEFT │ Pl. 14 Self-assembling tower cranes, and crane modules.

RIGHT │ Pl. 15 Shipping containers.

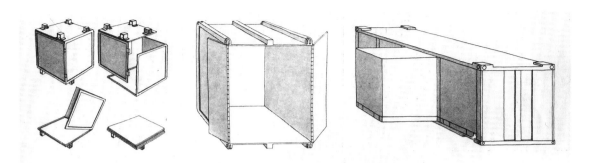

ABOVE | Pl. 16 Fold-out shipping containers.

BELOW | Pl. 17 Walks and ramps – powered and non-powered.

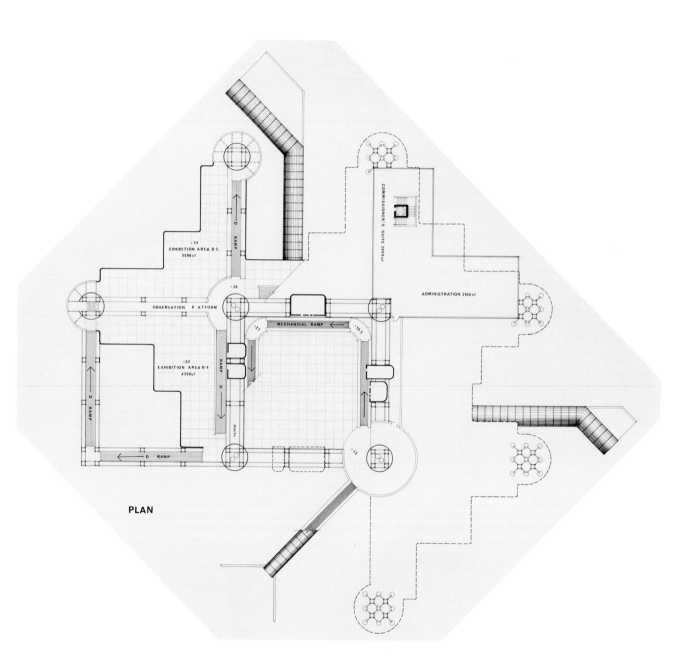

PLAN

Pl 18 Lower-level plan.

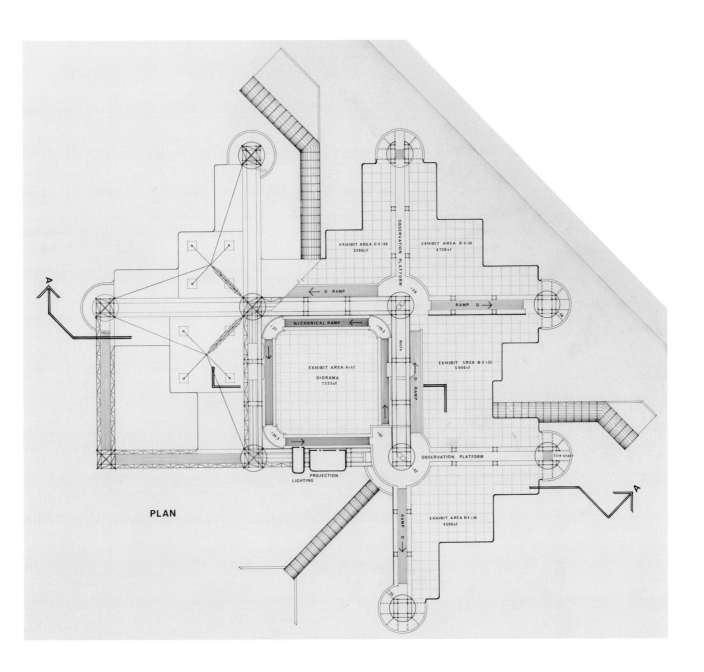

PLAN

Pl. 19 Upper-level plan.

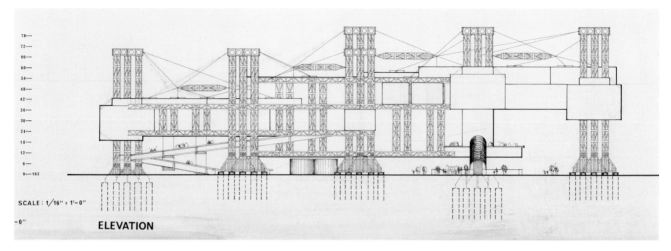

78
72
66
60
54
48
42
36
30
24
18
12
6
0 — 163

SCALE : 1/16" = 1'-0"

—0"

ELEVATION

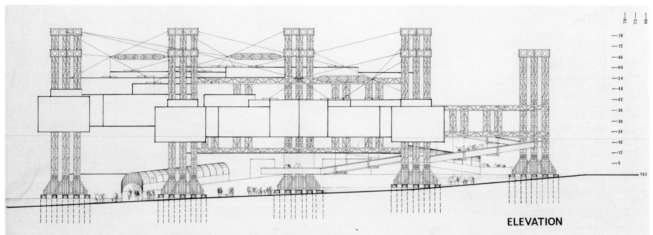

78
72
66
60
54
48
42
36
30
24
18
12
6
163

ELEVATION

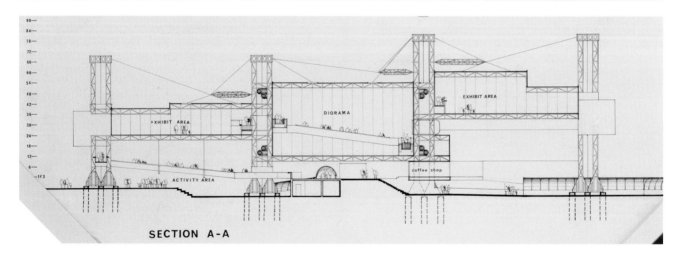

90
84
78
72
66
60
54
48
42
36
30
24
18
12
6
—1f3

EXHIBIT AREA

DIORAMA

EXHIBIT AREA

ACTIVITY AREA

coffee shop

SECTION A-A

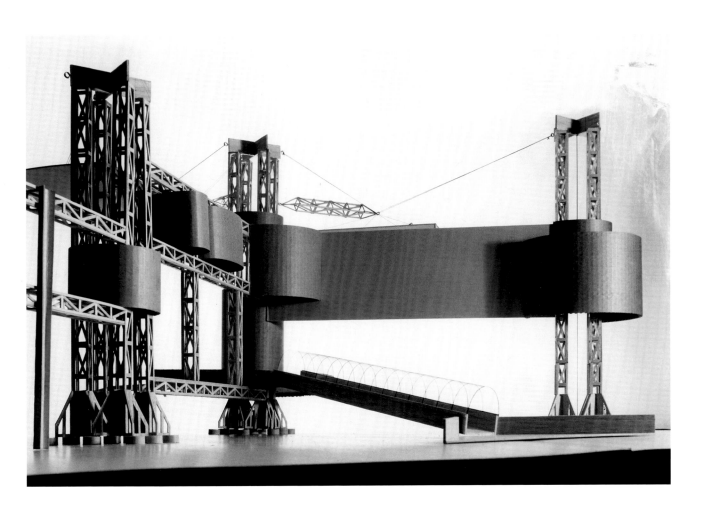

FACING PAGE, ABOVE | Pl. 20 Main elevation.

FACING PAGE, CENTRE | Pl. 21 Left-side elevation.

FACING PAGE, BELOW | Pl. 22 Section.

THIS PAGE | Pl. 23 Entrance to the "Travelator."

21

Experimental Strategies: Notes for Environmental Design*

Any environmental artifact is designed in the present for a future use, and even if it were possible to define the present, the uncertainty of the future is implicit in the design process.

1. Volume V of the working papers of the Commission on the Year 2000 includes a letter from Eric Erikson to Daniel Bell, chairman of the Commission, in which Erikson explains that rather than speculate on the possible futures that can be seen in trends, as the Commission had proposed, he felt that it may be more important to look at the ideological distortions that obscure our visions in regard to trends, since we must assume that we are actively in the process of helping to make the year 2000 what it will be.[1]

In the act of designing the physical environment with which we surround ourselves it is obvious that we are making the future in part what it will be, and, rather than speculate on design trends, it may be worthwhile to follow Erikson's suggestion and examine attitudes in regard to these trends.

2. Design depends on the concepts that the designer can use to comprehend and objectify the conditions in which he finds himself and to which he is trying to respond. He assigns concepts to events and to things so as to render these conditions instrumental in his work. Thus, in sequence, current events are ahead of current design, and it is in the nature of design to seek out in the existing environment conditions that bridge the present and the future.

A concept with which the designer objectifies his work is at best an "'objective fact' only in small part, in larger part it is a survey of possibilities."[2] Rather than suggest futures by describing design scenarios, or depicting visionary projects which tend to be single episodes, an approach can be developed that can suggest the basis of many possible episodes. Emphasis can be put on the perimeters of possibilities – the constraints that structure

* From *Perspecta 12 The Yale Architectural Journal* (March 1969): 21–9. Translated into German and reprinted in *Deutsche Bauzeitung* 103, no. 8 (August 1969). Translated into Japanese and reprinted in *Formalism, Realism, Contextualism,* ed. Hajime Yatsuka (Tokyo: Shokokusha Publishing), 1979.

the physical environment – as well as on the possibilities themselves which can mean different things for different people.

The emphasis in design on technology and on formal sensibilities can be oriented to favour an operational approach that does not polarize these ideals from each other and from the social reality of the inhabited physical environment as some science or art fiction.

3. In the visionary designs of the last fifty years, architects experimented in transposing marine and aerospace hardware into physical environment in order to focus attention on the emerging conditions of total dependence on technology. New environmental dependencies were inferred in this way.

Recent projects such as aircraft carrier cities, hovercraft office buildings, and plug-in plastic tenements[3] still borrow lumps of new hardware and dish them out in an architectural context – a context oriented to start with "The Shape of Things to Come." These anecdotes are delineated in a graphic medium that is commonly used to demonstrate real building conditions. In responding to the media the observer is directed to question how do we get there from here, as if there was a real "there," and the essential ana-logic role of these images tends to lose itself in irrelevant details of technical feasibility.

These projects promote new visions while maintaining a traditional frame of reference. They tend to underline dependencies on the past in their use of formal devices – a city, a building, and a tenement, in the above typical examples – in the same manner as Ledoux and Boullée drew upon historic forms.[4] As in the earlier work of the eighteenth-century French "visionaries," realization depends less on technologic innova-tion in the hardware sense – technically they are immediately feasible – than on the development of the social organization of human resources in the framework of a production system that could respond to the scale of these projects. This can be seen in the influence of the French vision-

aries on the subsequent federal architecture of the burgeoning industrial states that emerged in the latter half of the nineteenth and the first half of the twentieth century. Recent visions tell more about the plight of the contemporary designer as a sender and receiver of images of new technology than about the transfer of advanced technology to the built environment; the environmental logic that is represented by the aerospace and materials technology used in these studies resists this level of design transfer. The success of these projects is found in their demonstrations of a new set of images that are readily absorbed in the current styling of built artifacts. Even though old frameworks are maintained, they are at least experimented and the relevance of these studies, as opposed to their success, ultimately lies in the insight they provide about the present.

4. The expectation of finding art in a fixed design has recently given way to the conception that art can be found in indeterminacy where a final design may or may not be foreseen.

It is no longer easy to see this revelation as intellectually revolutionary. Even though it takes new realities to suggest new possibilities, environmental objects have always been the convenient intermediaries of our surround-ings; chronologically, buildings obviously have a future of their own, and conditions of change are at least as evident in the history of the physical environment as conditions that have remained fixed for long periods of time. It is especially difficult to accept vestiges of deter-ministic attitudes in regard to fragments of the immediate past of modern architecture. In the description of the Zonnestraal Sanatorium of 1927–28, by Bijvoet and Duiker, that appeared in a recent issue of *Architectural Design*,[5] it is not the "power that is still visible" in the building despite changes that is the important psycho-logic fact, but rather it is the changes themselves that measure the "authentic authority" of this building. That a hospital designed in 1927 for

Figs. 21.1 and 21.2 | Transplants of hardware at the scale of new technology have been part of the existing landscape for over a half-century. Yet montages that displace and exaggerate objects in a landscape are needed to tune design sensibilities to the new scale, and to suggest to the designer to go to the things themselves.

LEFT | 21.1 Steel Mill and Company Houses, Birmingham, Alabama, 1936.

RIGHT | 21.2 Hans Hollein, *Carrier City in the Landscape*, 1964.

TB patients should not have undergone alteration by 1968 is inconceivable; medical science for its part has at least learned to cope with TB. The catalogue of changes that were possible is most encouraging about the building – such as its transformation into a geriatric unit, and the additions to its mechanical systems. As a bit of the present, the details of the original building are intelligible.

Indeterminacy, as a condition of use determined by change, shifts the emphasis in design to the generic service function of built artifacts. Solutions to a given problem tend to be divergent rather than convergent; the designer can no longer accept the fixed value system that protects his position as the singular determining agency of built form. This leads to the further dissolution of the material nature of the concept of a building, and consequently to the further disposition of its service function to technology – such as the translation into design of the replacement cycles of industrially produced bits of the built environment, for example.

5. While indeterminacy has been recognized in design as an operative condition, in technological planning the principles of a theory of change are being developed.

A number of recent studies on technological planning have established its role as the "basis of a scientific arm of planning." For a clear and enthusiastic review of the state of the art see *Technological Forecasting in Perspective* by Erich Jantsch;[6] among the assumptions and commonly used terms here defined, it should be noted that technological planning refers to the development of intellectual concepts concerned with the active implementation of technology transfer from one level or sector of technology and human activity to another.

Jantsch shows that the distinction between forecasting and planning is somewhat a tautological but necessary articulation of the process. The two have an inherent tendency towards integration, which, by the 1970s, may result in the disappearance of forecasting as a distinguishable discipline. He also notes a parallel consequence

in the change from "production-oriented" planning to "function-oriented" planning, and the subsequent necessary adoption in planning of high-level social goals.

As described by Hazan Ozbekhan,[7] new planning strategies delineate a commitment to the reality of many possible environments (i.e., architectures). In the earlier model of planning (i.e., design), choices were basically concerned with the feasibility of techno-economic alternatives rather than with ends. What we can do has expanded vastly and, what this kind of feasibility tends to define is no longer the issue. As a planning tool, feasibility is redefined as relevancy, as well as expediency.

These developments in planning recognize that technology has become more critical with regard to the human situation than with the scientific, with which it tends to merge. However, the emergence of an emphasis on "goals" in no way forces socio-political issues. Jantsch optimistically speaks of the future integration of fundamental research and the social environment that will serve in formulating guidelines.

The impact of systematic planning on environmental design is all too evident. Not only do the institutions which developed the planning technologies in the first place have an important role in determining the urban environment, which has already happened, but the development of

the planning techniques constitutes a basic elaboration of the design process. If planning can be said to define modes of action, then design is formulated in the midst of the action. Furthermore, the exigencies of large-scale industrial production of the built environment tend to merge design with technological planning.

6. The active implementation of technology is characterized by the development of new attitudes. Jantsch describes the current development as a change from "product-orientation" to "function-orientation." On the most general level, this emerging emphasis can be considered to be a shift from subject to activity; from the primacy of products (buildings) to an identification with the user and with services (the interaction of people with environmental artifacts).

These attitudes generated by recent technology are as critical to the underlying basis of environmental design as the industrial mechanization of the late nineteenth century was to modern architecture.

If several of the evocations that Le Corbusier used in his book *Vers une architecture* to infer by analogy the emerging sensibilities of an industrial world are now used to infer in a similar way changing sensibilities, then in place of a photograph of the Delage automobile of 1921, "Grand Sport," juxtaposed with a photograph of the Parthenon as some Parthenon on wheels,

Figs. 21.3 and 21.4 | The analogy with the machine (1): The obsolescence of machine aesthetics

LEFT | 21.3 Delage "Grand-Sport," 1921.

BELOW | 21.4 A photograph, dated 1927, of a hydraulic press compacting the chassis of a scrapped automobile attests to the early development of a replacement cycle in the auto industry.

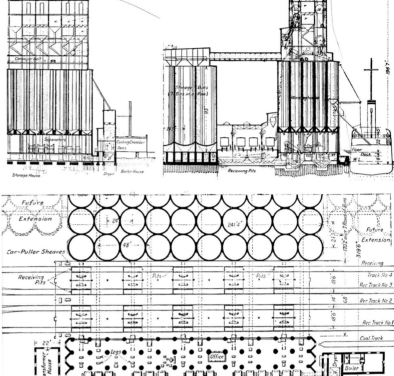

LEFT | 21.5 "Canadian Grain Stores and Elevators" illustrated in *Vers une architecture*.

RIGHT | 21.6 Plan and transverse sections of the grain elevator illustrated in *Vers une architecture* that appeared in *Engineering News*, 23 February 1911, p. 221. This elevator was completed in December 1910, using reinforced concrete slip-form construction; Fort William, Canada.

one could substitute a photograph, dated 1927, of the hydraulic press at the Ford plant compacting the metallic carcass of an auto like some Parthenon that has outlived its useful tenure (or its advocated uselessness).

Instead of an exterior view of a grain elevator, circa 1910, that shows a cluster of silo drums in a neo-Hellenic assemblage at the scale of a "Heroic Modern" building, one could substitute the plan and section of this grain elevator which show the silo drums as the distended tubes of a distribution machine that was used to move grain to world markets. As part of a transportation system, the measure of capacity of the machine and its finished components are turned to the internal voids, and, as an analogy, the machine can be used to illustrate the recent report on urban transportation prepared by the Stanford Research Institute: "Transportation is a service function … it does not exist of and for itself."[8]

In the first example, the auto industry initiated mass production techniques that were later adopted by other industries, and it was rightly championed by the moderns. However, comparisons of automobiles to buildings have generally failed. The analogy served in many cases as the

basis of a transplant of methods rather than a transfer of technology at the level of appropriate concepts.

Early in its development the industry evolved a replacement demand based on the life expectancy of the machines it produced. This shifted the material value of the artifact to the service that it rendered. The idea of expendable artifacts and inexpendable service offers a device for the ultimate liberation of architecture from the physical constraints of buildings, yet the question of expendability is still generally considered by designers to be a "moral" issue as if it offends their sense of property or undermines the objectives of their profession.

If one is to take Le Corbusier's words in regard to the Delage of 1921 – "if the problem of the dwelling and the flat were studied in the same way that a chassis is ... by industrial production

ABOVE | 21.7 Construction of the Commonwealth Apartments, 900 Lake Shore Drive, by Mies van der Rohe, June 1957. The envelope of the building was fabricated in large sections of anodized aluminum to save on assembly and joints. These sections, however, were each made to look like an assembly of catalogue components.

FACING PAGE, ABOVE | 21.8 One-line assembly jig in the manufacturing of Alcan Universal Homes. Production techniques were borrowed from the mobile home industry; a capacity was developed for 2,400 homes per year.

FACING PAGE, BELOW | 21.9 A "model" Alcan home on site; one of several available. The subdivision housing "industry" has always been committed to the ready-made styling of housing units. Alcan's styling was designed to exploit the existing market. These units are sold through a network of franchised dealers; the selling price of the furnished and equipped package includes lamps and curtains.

Figs. 21.8 and 21.9 | The production and market styling of factory-built homes

... defensible forms would soon appear" – and then look at a recent Ford or General Motors product, as was done in *Perspecta 11,* or at an Aston Martin, it is evident that one message for the designer is his role in the style engineering of identifiable bits of mass-produced artifacts. Many other design roles are probable and possible, such as the assemblage of off-the-shelf hardware according to user specifications, development design and systems research, but the role of the "visualizer" of symbols does offer a place for the designer in the industrial environment.

In a recent article on the "state of architecture," Peter Smithson continues the analogy of the automobile and compares the 1920 Bentley to the work of the Constructivist/Sachlichkeit faction with their composed display of machine products, and the 1960 E-type Jaguar with the 900 Lake Shore Drive of Mies as highly integrated and smooth machines "modeled in some universal material."[9] Even though he affirms that architectural design has stood close to the fashionable view of the machine, he begs the question that this position depended on styling, and that the "unique and one-off" 900 Lake Shore Drive is made to look like routine catalogue stuff.

The auto industry has also demonstrated that mass production in the form of an assembly-line-computer-hook-up offers some large scale response to the specific needs and desires of users. According to Ford: "The line is now tuned to serve the needs of the buyers who have options and colour preferences. All special data on car make ... is fitted into a production schedule." According to Ford every car is a "custom job." General Motors claims that it can produce in one year as many variations as its total production run. As a "custom job," this sales gimmick represents superficial assembly modifications. It exploits the vulnerability of the consumer. But it does show that production can be geared to diversity, and that it is not indus-

trial technology that is holding up the development of pluralistic environmental conditions.

7. Architectural imagery has recently swung out to include in its design repertoire a Main Street vernacular of popular culture in which we are all immersed. The early days of the modern movement had a similar populist edge that included a vocabulary of street signs and large store-front display windows. But this earlier idiom was adapted from the main streets of cities, whereas the recent idiom is drawn from the American "main drag" – the strip version of a super Main Street generated by and for the automobile.

Categories in architecture tend to persist, and even though new inclusions introduce new idioms they reinforce basic premises. As architecture, the recent idiom is inclusive in a very selective way that accepts only a very special part of Main Street phenomena.

One of the most inventive exponents of the Main Street approach, Robert Venturi, recently visited Las Vegas, and in the description that followed this visit, the "grand tour" mannerisms that are used to examine the formal complexities of the Strip appear as a pop parody of the "architect" himself – cast in his own words[10] rather than in the plaster of a George Segal assemblage. His commitment was to find architecture. The Strip was turned into the fragments of some hieratic culture and into a system of forms in which there is no place for the user-consumer other than as the ideal spectator – the antithesis of the Main. Las Vegas was isolated and rendered "anonymous" and "common-place" so as to "gain insights," as was done with industrial buildings earlier this century. A similar description of Las Vegas by Tom Wolfe is inhabited by the creatures of the Strip.* Even though Wolfe abuses people and drowns them in their own trivia, at least

* Editor's note: Tom Wolfe, *The Kandy-Kolored Tangerine-Flake Streamline Baby* (New York: Farrar, Straus and Giroux, 1965).

they are there. He presents the real life designers and fabricators, such as Vaughan Cannon, who are consciously working in the Strip on its own terms. Furthermore, many of these Las Vegas buildings are architect designed. It is not that the names are important in terms of personalities, but for the personification of design sensibilities.

Beyond the frame of reference of a formal idiom, the physical environment of Main Street documents the consumer aesthetic of industrial technology and high styling which is in touch with the daily lives of people. The spin-off from aerospace has had a significant effect from the direct incorporation of surplus, to the use of new materials such as adhesives and plastics, to the application of ideas and images. These "self happenings" are the technologic equivalent of the more well- known and important organizational inventions of the Strip such as shopping centres, state universities, motels, Disneylands, etc.[11]

The cogent use of technology can be illustrated with the classic example from the pantheon of Strip architecture: the Diner.

LEFT | 21.10 Early diner: a converted railroad car at the side of the tracks, Oakland, California.

RIGHT | 21.11 Later diner; Duchess Diner, New Haven, Connecticut.

Monel metal and stainless steel kitchen, wood and linen photo-simulated laminated plastic tables, sheet aluminum panels and extruded trim, the linear organization of a short-order cuisine, and the railroad car prototype developed into a lightweight kit-of-industrial-parts that can be seen assembled across America. The Duchess Diner in New Haven is a particularly fine specimen; it stands in contrast to the nearby striated concrete buttresses of the Yale Art and Architecture building which looks as if they were extruded out of the bedrock. If Kienholz moved the interior of this Beanery into the Museum, how soon will someone move the Museum into the Diner?

Fabrication techniques in plastics such as vacuum and thermo forming, injection and blow moulding, new colour binders and metal coated vinyl powder formulations make possible the up-to-the-minute styling of the disposable bits of Main Street landscape. Years of research on the effects of ultraviolet radiation on PVC molecules went into these tableaux. In a design sense, the existential nature of these new polymeric materials tends to disappear into the complex fabrication processes, and into the use of the artifacts as media. From "Les Voix du Silence" of the plastic horticulturalists, to the reconstituted natural wood paneling, to the lustrous high-gloss finishes, and the "Corsican Cremo Marble" of laminated plastics, one has an artifactual landscape of instant sensibilities turned on by technology. The buildings of the Street form an extension to this media either as some walk-in multimedia, or as a neutral shell within which things take place.

If one is to follow Husserl and go to the things themselves, or heed what Venturi said, that learning from the existing landscape is a way of being revolutionary for an architect, then the only way out in this "natural" world is through the artificial, through exploitation, and through the subjective relationships between man and his commodities. But Main Street is built on the industrial production of environmental commodities. Similarly, the design translation of the built environment into consumer-based, industrially manufactured commodities will obviously have to deal with these relationships.

8. The physical environment can be considered to function as a system of restraints on people, and the emphasis in design on the interaction of people and environmental artifacts comes closer to representing these artifacts correctly than any isolated view of the artifact itself. This confirms the role of these artifacts as cultural devices that can tell us something about ourselves, and the world around us, as well as affirm that truism that dissolves all too quickly in the design process: it is people who give the physical environment its substance.

FACING PAGE, ABOVE AND CENTRE | 21.12 The Strip with buildings as the walk-in extensions to the graphic media of the signs. From *Every Building on the Sunset Strip* (1966), an endless photographic foldout showing every building block and corner on both sides of the Strip, by Ed Ruscha.

FACING PAGE, BELOW LEFT | 21.13 The gas station "Service Station" as the essence of Strip architecture. Light, graphics, uniformed attendants, and a dispensing machine are integrated in the media of a readily identifiable service into which the "building" as such disappears. In the thin plastic and enamelled metal skin, and the thin detailing of the enclosure, are built-in the possibilities of shedding one wrapping for another; the identification and attention span in the designed look is critical since the product that is dispensed remains essentially unchanged. The copy for the above photograph reads "nothing stays the same any longer than it takes to improve it." The recent clip-on myths range from the above hard-edge packaging, to the stone siding and cedar shingle version of a neo-frontier pony-express station. The periodic updating of the station's look does, in a sense, allow it to maintain a front-edge engagement with on-going sensibilities. To say that these sensibilities are trivial, contrived, and part of the big commercial put-on is to raise similar issues with much of current architectural design.

FACING PAGE, BELOW RIGHT | 21.14 The absurd mannerisms of "Architecture" as the packaging of expendable Main Street media (1965).

Any physical environment that someone has used in a personal way, or that has been activated by a group, communicates a degree of specific incidence that anonymous design can only infer and approximate. Both levels of engagement – the anonymous and the specific – have an obvious function. But design interpretations of industrialized building have tended to articulate the anonymous component, whereas technology offers the only real means for the production of a pluralistic and personal environment. In the development of large-

scale industrial production, a conflict is readily apparent between the response of production to the growing satisfaction of needs and the imposition of repressive conditions of use. Increased production does mean the standardization of the aspiration levels and use patterns of consumers; those at the receiving end are assumed to become more and more malleable in an escalating series of "trade-off" ratios. From the position of the user-consumer, the question is not whether his constituency is a collective one, but rather how it is controlled. As the constituency of the user should evolve with an emerging user-orientation in industry, so the

LEFT | 21.15 Street of housing in Manduria, Italy (1960). The walls of the street were first built to define the structure of the town. Behind the facades, party walls divide the lots. Within the walls, each tenant family could structure their own home with available resources. Similar indeterminate forms can be traced through the past in the history of architecture.

RIGHT, ABOVE | 21.16 An abandoned car lot in the Congo as an instant bidonville. A panelled truck was transformed into a bar, and a bus became a meeting hall.

RIGHT, BELOW | 21.17 Housing in the abandoned car lot: The goodness of "non-fit" that does not limit possible utilization of artifacts.

environmental bits as consumer commodities will be subjected to agencies that can protect the user and define his needs. For example, the instruments of productivity may determine the actual utilization of artifacts, but not limit their possible utilization.

The design emphasis on the interaction of people and artifacts frees design from the self-imposed limitations of its commitment to buildings. Techniques such as "advocacy architecture" can mobilize the public in a dialogue with the designer. According to the role of the designer which is based on the rapport between an architect and a client, the anonymous client is given some semblance of his traditional form and content. A "real" client is brought into the studio and to the construction site, and he is asked to define his needs and life styles.

This relationship still fixes the position of the designer as the intermediary between a user and his environment, and leaves the question open in regard to the traditional commitment of this working method, and to the participatory mechanisms whereby individual users can, if they wish, also organize their environment.

A possible translation of environmental artifacts into community equipment can be demonstrated in the design of educational facilities.* Education is changing from rigid schooling to the active participation of children and students in varying activities, in non-graded programs, and in self-instruction. Observations on a variety of school buildings that use these new methods of instruction show that the learning activities transcend the buildings and furniture regardless of their planned use, and that flexibility in these facilities has to do with choice, involvement, and with participation.[12] This tendency can be seen in the current design of school buildings as open packages of space in which the "architecture" is stopped at the macro-shell of the building and the indeterminate interior is left void.

It is in this void where the "school" is really taking place. Here, a platform which a group of children assemble, and under which they do something together unseen by others, or on which they are in a position to be seen and heard by others, can be considered to be a learning device as a doll's house or logic blocks. With this idea for equipment, expendable artifacts intrinsically charged with information, identity, use, selective combination, and mobility can be developed for a wide and permissive range of "school" accommodation. In engaging this equipment, the generating source of the design of the specific organization rests with the chil-

21.18 The logic blocks of a "citizen architect."

dren and the teachers.[13] The macro-shell of this equipment can be many things, and at an urban scale these "schools" can be located anywhere in response to local requirements ("store-front schools," etc.).

Even though the design of a responsive environment does not depend on complex technology, this equipment may be further developed with electronic media, and extended to the programming of the urban artifacts themselves. In this way, educational facilities can be generated by students, and can generate students. And design sources are tapped at their origin in an ultimate commitment to the basic premises of the role of education in society.

If these recent changes in education are less of a question of some new enlightenment, and more of a response to the needs of technology and social change, it then follows that the pluralistic design of the artifacts tends towards a further liberation of both social and technological possibilities. The physical environment can be geared to set out mechanisms of self-organization not to liquidate authority

* Editor's note: These remarks are taken from a study published as "Learning Environments – Planning beyond Flexibility," *Architecture Canada* (March 1968) by Melvin Charney. Reproduced in this book as chapter 19.

(form), but to liquidate authoritarian structures (formalism) at a time when the existing methods and orientation of design are clearly inadequate to deal with the transformation of the physical environment.

9. If the desire for change can be singled out as one of the motivating spirits of modern architecture, then not only is change now assumed to be commonplace, but it is also an Establishment issue, and the rhetoric of change tends to obscure the basic transformations which have or have not taken place.

Whether architecture will remain as the design of a few unique and one-off objects posited for the edification of a few ideal spectators, or whether it can further develop into the systematic design of the mass produced physical matrix of society, all semblance of traditional form has disappeared. The collapse of traditional systems has been the axiom of vanguard architecture during the last fifty years. One difference may now be found in the realization that the transfer of technology does not transform old buildings into new kinds of buildings, but that the very material existence of built artifacts is transformed into service commodities in which the relevant social issues and time scale are critical to design. The form of the built environment is obviously a vehicle for cultural communication, and the difference between "structural" and "non-structural" change has also been recognized, but the context of transactions, whether instructional or metaphorical, has radically altered.

In the search for new design formulations, given this total dissolution of genres, rather than "une architecture autre," another basis for architecture as a conceptual system is emerging.

NOTES

1 For the text of this letter, see the Volume V of the working papers of the Commission on the Year 2000 of the American Academy of Arts and Sciences, privately printed (Brookline, MA, 1966). This letter was sent in lieu of a memorandum that Erikson was invited to submit on the possible futures that can be seen from trends in the modes of conduct of youth.

2 Werner Heisenberg wrote in *Dialectics*: "What we establish mathematically is 'objective fact' only in small part, in larger part it is a survey of possibilities"; as quoted by H. Marcuse in *One Dimensional Man* (Boston: Beacon Press, 1964), 150.

3 The work of Hans Hollein, Peter Cook, and Arthur Quarmby, respectively.

4 This can well be illustrated by the recent proposals for Toronto, and for Harlem, New York, by Buckminster Fuller.

5 *Architectural Design* (December 1967): 552.

6 Erich Jantsch, *Technological Forecasting in Perspective* (Paris: OECD, 1967).

7 Hasan Ozbekhan, "The Triumph of Technology: Can Implies Ought," in *Planning for Diversity and Choice: Possible Futures and their Relations to Man-Controlled Environment*, ed. Stanford Anderson (Cambridge, MA: MIT Press, 1968), 208–10.

8 For example, in 1967, the Battelle Memorial Institute research on urban transportation, prefabrication in the building industry, and housing: Aerojet General and General Electric on housing; Stanford Research Institute on Urban Transportation; Systems Design Corporation on Urban systems.

9 Peter Smithson, "The Rocket," *Architectural Design* (July 1965).

10 Robert Venturi and Denise Scott Brown, "Learning from Las Vegas," *Architectural Forum* (March 1968): 37–43.

11 Reyner Banham, "The Missing Motel," *Landscape* (Winter 1965): 66.

12 For example, the description of a school by Joseph Featherstone in "Schools for Children," *New Republic*, 19 August 1967, 17–21.

13 In this example, the child, as some primitive "natural" being still consciously integrated into his physical surroundings, is not exploited in a romantic sense, but rather used in the social sense of finding design coherence in our alienation from our physical surroundings. We are all dispossessed.

22

Review of *New Schools for New Towns*[*]

This little paperback volume is a report of the fourth annual Design Fete sponsored by Rice University School of Architecture.[†] The Fete consisted of a two-week design marathon conducted by six architects, each directing a team of students. Included were such well-known architects as Charles Colbert, Robert Venturi, and Thomas Vreeland of the U.S., Cedric Price of London, and Hans Morganthaler of Atelier 5 in Switzerland. They were backed up by a group of research participants representing some of the most interesting names in the R&D of educational facilities, and received the support of Educational Facilities Laboratories.

The explicit purpose of each architectural team was to translate into design a program for a "new town" and its educational system in order to "develop new concepts." But, since new urban areas and new educational systems do not read-ily lend themselves to singular design visions, the episode of this Fete as a whole has less direct bearing on the concepts of "New Schools for New Towns" than on architecture itself as a system of concepts dealing with environmental problems.

In order to look at the work of the Fete one has to distinguish between the world of design and the "real" world. Design operates on its own level of vested reality removed from the problems of urban schools, and the real drama of an event that sets out to "develop new design concepts" lies in the resolution of seemingly incompatible realities.

The rhetorical language and the format of the report add to the distortion. The projects of the individual teams are cut up into a pastiche of sections on "underlying themes." The educational programs on which the work is based are only vaguely suggested. However, the design work speaks for itself, and if one can disregard the static a reasonable coherence emerges.

In this light the resulting projects are both interesting and discouraging at the same time: interesting because they do present an excellent sample of current design attitudes; discouraging

[*] From *Architectural Forum* (October 1969): 70–1.
[†] *New Schools for New Towns* was published by Educational Facilities Laboratories and Rice University School of Architecture, Houston, Tex., 77001. 60 pp. 5 ⅞ by 7⅜ in. Illustrated. Free.

because of the evidently primitive state of design and educational planning vis-à-vis the complexity of urban educational problems.

Paul Kennon's program involved a "university town" in which all distinctions between "town and gown" were to be eliminated, creating instead a "gown-town" down-town. The design integrates all community and educational facilities in a "Giant Educational Concourse" so located that the town residents can "encounter learning in their daily lives" and be "included and invited to join classes." The rationale here is that "educators and planners would do well to apply the same criteria of accessibility to facilities for commerce." So, along the downtown spine of this town are found a supermarket, a physics department, and a shoe shop.

What emerges is a beautiful example of a grand parti of a finite town manifest in the current "with-it" regalia of building design. All the familiar bits are there: a "tree" organization; a central activity spine; the sweeping, sinuous lines of residential branches fitted into the cardboard contours of a sloping, non-existent site; eight-storey drums at the node points; a carefully arranged haphazard composition; a lineup of Vierendeel trusses and battered, stepped-up walls of linear masonry, mesmerized in concrete.

If Kennon's project can be cited as an example of the styling of containers conceived in the image of architecturally designed things, and trapped in its media, the project of Charles Colbert represents the professional styling of buildings and gadgets in the image of the corporate establishment. Colbert proposes that educational facilities "be given equal stature with those of business." By "stature" he seems to mean building size and building style. Accordingly, SOM-like towers are shown in zoom-perspective sketches. A concern with the facade grid, the corners, and the bases of the towers is expressed with neoclassic remnants typical of the current styling of corporation buildings. This poor man's semiotic speaks of the poverty of environmental design rather than of the basis of environmental communication.

With the work of Thomas Vreeland and Cedric Price, the vacuous antics of the above projects are left behind. A photograph from Vreeland's project, of two children listening to a transistorized, hand-held receiving unit, clearly articulates the difference. With a readily available design these children are "in school," in direct contact with the world around them, without a building or an architect between them and an accessible educational environment.

The program of Vreeland's project involved a depressed area of 50,000 inhabitants living within a large urban region. He develops an educational environment from bits of hardware presently on the market to supplement and upgrade existing educational structures. He uses these bits as the elements of a system that can generate many plans. The types, quantities, and costs of the components are set out: decal graphics, transistor radio, street-corner "telephone booth" study units, a convoy of VW travelling "schoolrooms," mobile-home child day-care centres, SCSD prefab learning centres, a Roux-Dorlut incremental multi-storey building system for adult learning centres, and "Mes-Tex" prebuilt vocational shops. These are distributed throughout the community, and are connected to a central "Town Brain" which transmits educational messages. Rather than buildings for education, facilities are provided in the form of equipment for education. This equipment is industrially mass-produced, and totally interchangeable. The mobility of the system, conceived as a function of the environment, goes beyond the idea of flexibility of buildings.

Many of the ideas on which Vreeland based this work were developed by Cedric Price in such well-known projects as the "Fun Palace" and the "Potteries Thinkbelt." In the Fete, Price handles these ideas with facile enterprise. He goes further than Vreeland in engaging the total matrix of the community in his design. In Vreeland's

ABOVE | 22.1 A school bus converted into a learning environment. Project by Cedric Price.

BELOW | 22.2 A mobile library. Project by Thomas Vreeland.

The IESC and the CESC are the Industrial and Commercial Educational Showcases that spell out to the passing public the processes and products of industry, displaying foods and information not normally available for inspection, and dispensing educational services in self-service machinery. The AL is an Auto-Link, and the RTS a Rapid Transit Service – both provide media for commuter education; for example, the back seats of buses become miniature, electronically telemetered study carrels. The major element is the HSS, the Home Study Station, a self-contained cubicle filled with electronic media placed within existing homes or added to them, to replace the schoolhouse for most educational communication. The ITT, an Infant Teach Toy, resembles a travelling circus with several trailers and lightweight extensible enclosures easily relocated to serve a shifting age group. If, somehow, the educational messages do not come through, there is an LC, a Life Conditioner drive-in educatheque which straddles the expressways leading to and from major areas of the community, in which programs for "inquiry, tutorials, group instruction, and investigation" are provided for all age groups. Education is, effectively, everywhere: it is not simply accessible, it is there, so to speak. It pervades the very nature of the physical setting.

Even though this design is projected twenty years into the future, it is entirely structured out of familiar hardware and existing systems; for example, the RTS has been in use for a number of years in Montreal. The design explains well the idea that it is not mainly the sophistication of a proposed technology that determines innovative potential, but the way in which technology is applied that constitutes a difference. It says, moreover, that it is in the nature of design to seek out in the existing environment the conditions of possible futures, not only because of changing life needs and lifestyles, and the spinoff from related technologies, but also because of responses to future environments that have developed outside the defined limits of design.

project, the educational components are type objects placed in the community, and, as such, are separate from it; they are identified with the symbol of an open hand. In Price's work, the attempt is made to extend the physical structure of the community.

The program (prepared by John Tirrell and Albert Canfield) projects a new town for the year 1990. As previously, Price's strategy begins with a totally decentralized kit of parts whose nomenclature reads like some multi-stage NASA system. It begins with the TB, the "Town Brain" that transmits data to a series of devices throughout the town and to the town itself.

An exercise in design based on the iconography of the urban environment is found in Robert Venturi's project. Typical to his design work, he seeks in the setting of Main Street indigenous architectural devices. Education as a service facility becomes in his project a drive-in educational "Service Station," without gas pumps but with a billboard that says *Learn* rather than *Shell*. This says an accessible educational environment does exist around us, and suggests that architecture tends to deny the indigenous physical setting of our urban culture.

The program for Venturi's project was based on a new town to accommodate 120,000 residents. The town of his scheme is composed of eleven townships, of equal populations, and each connected by a loop freeway system that runs directly through its centre. Along this central strip, Venturi places a mix of educational buildings and commercial establishments. All the paraphernalia of the suburban main drag is there: the billboards, supergraphics, drive-in vending machines, minitown shopping centres, etc. If Colbert's position was to imbue education with the style of big business, Venturi finds his appropriate setting in the structures of small business.

This project was proposed for the year 1970. It is then, supposedly, beyond the planning stage and well into construction. Venturi, accordingly, develops his design as a piece of current history. He knows well the problems and risks involved in the design of a town, and he avoids them in a parody not only of suburban "new town" design – Columbia New Town – but also of historical influence on town design and current design devices. This has less to do with the design of urban educational facilities than with the architectural edification of the designer. To this end, Venturi also parodies himself, his work, the Fete, and its program. However, given that this problem is real enough, his exercise in architectural gamesmanship is interesting, but, ultimately, redundant.

The problem common to all the projects of the Fete is the design of "accessible" education. It is one thing to say in a program that education should be accessible, and another to try to translate this into viable physical form. The former is a statement of intention, the latter a plan of action. An educator may say that learning should be readily available, but for a designer to put up a sign of an open hand or a billboard with the word *Learn*, is to play with analogues rather than to postulate plans. Similarly, to apply the criteria of shopping centres to places of learning questions cognitive processes rather than design procedure. One known factor is that accessibility does involve the freeing of education from the rigidity of existing institutions.

If anything of design value emerges from the project of the Fete, it lies perhaps in the demonstration of the intrinsic relationship between the form of the physical environment and communication processes. The designs that assume physical form as defined by the tradition of cities, streets, buildings, and masonry assume that people come to education. In the designs that shift the commitment of architecture from these traditions to a concept of education itself as the function of a physically responsive environment, education is brought to people with the ease of available media. This important change directly transfers the question of access from a physical design issue to a social and political issue where it belongs in the first place: How much and what kind of knowledge is available, or accessible, to people?

Moreover, the idea of a designer's commitment to environmental structures that do not necessarily involve buildings confirms the most generic purpose of architecture itself. It advocates its potential, and demands that architecture have its own technology. Perhaps one of the first technologies to develop is a systematic method of conducting explorative design studies.

PART FOUR

Other Monuments

"Other Monuments" is a selection of eleven essays published between 1971 and 1982. In most of these essays, Charney looked for alternatives to the dominant idea of the monument as emblem of the dominant structure of power in society. Probing the meaning of anonymous architectural images circulating in mass media, he proposed a redefinition of "heroic" architecture which made visible a dialectic between people's heroic struggle for survival and the institutionalized visions of architecture. Media images were Charney's starting points for works in which he brought to consciousness the relationships between people and the world of objects in which they find themselves. In the other essays, Charney develops an interpretation of Quebec architecture. For him, popular architecture was both an embodiment of a people's struggle for a place on the continent, and a means of resisting the colonial attitudes embedded in the official architecture of the bureaucracy and big business. In this period, Charney's work took a political turn as he argued that the anonymous built environment represented people's innate knowledge of architecture – a symbol which supplanted modern technology as both a means and an image of collective emancipation. The anchoring project for this section is *Les maisons de la rue Sherbrooke*, conceived by Charney for Corridart, the street exhibition meant to accompany Montreal's 1976 Olympics.

23.1 Melvin Charney at a symposium on Corridart, organized
by Normand Thériault at Média Gallery, Montreal, one of
several gatherings on the state of the arts held on the occasion
of the 15 November 1976 Quebec elections.

Other Monuments

LOUIS MARTIN

The turn of the 1970s marked yet another reorientation in Charney's probing of architecture. Two essays published in 1971 introduced new themes which, in the context of the rising separatist movement in Quebec, gave a political twist to his dialectical models of architecture. These essays opened two intertwined modes of criticism, one conducted by means of projects and the other by means of writing. Both modes were nourished by photographs found in all kinds publications, both denounced the authoritarianism of official architecture, and both attempted to reveal the content of daily life – particularly its repressed mythological dimension. In sharp contrast with the post-1968 criticism of utopia which put into question architecture's capacity to change society,[1] Charney developed a critical position which proposed that architecture became a means of collective emancipation when people were engaged directly in environmental design, as citizen architects.

Social Content

Entitled "On the Liberation of Architecture," the first essay described the *Memo Series*, Charney's entry to a Canadian competition for the design of an Air Force Memorial. This project constitutes Charney's most achieved approximation of a possible liberation of architecture from the dominant "conception that architecture resides solely in the design of a specialized object in the form of a building."[2] Charney proposed an alternate basis for architecture: rather than situate meaning in the look of the building, he suggested that "architecture is reflected in the meaning of a 'building' as found in the use we make of our artifacts." He explained: "To the extent that the relationships between people and physical things can be found mirrored in the 'things themselves,' the raw material of the architecture of an Air Force Memorial can be found in readily available artifactual bits known to materialize for people the remembrance of air flight and Air Force."[3] Quoting Walter Benjamin in the epigraph of his essay, Charney esteemed that "the tiniest fragment of everyday life says more than" a work of art.

One novel element introduced in this pivotal project was that these found artifactual bits were selected for their evocative power rather than for their potential as building material for the creation of a built environment. Divergent and inclusive, the design action – that is, "the process of selecting a suppressed range of access and experience" – openly contradicted the design intention of erecting a building. The series identified numerous scenarios (meetings in abandoned hangars, encounters with the site of a crash, virtual flights, etc.) in which people, in interacting with artifacts, discovered the history of air flight in various interactive experiences. By a process of proliferation and dissemination anticipating today's internet social networks, these appropriable resources were meant to create a low-cost, cross-country "memorial network" which would enable investment in real services, like social housing, rather than in a memorial building isolated in one part of the country.

For Charney, the active participation of people in the realization of the memorial network would ideally overcome the contradiction in contemporary architecture "between its elitist and repressive condition and its obvious origins in social content." As such, the *Memo Series* outlined an almost totally dematerialized architecture in which "design [could] assume its architectural condition by virtue of its granting existence to an architectural concept in the heads of people, where it really happens, and where it belongs in the first place."[4]

Yet design was not restricted to the patterns of resources proposed by the *Memos*. It included also the actions of the participants. For him, the reinforcement of these patterns by the users' selection constituted in itself "an act of design intervention and a deliberate political, social and aesthetic act." This new understanding of design as a political act of collective emancipation coloured Charney's criticism throughout the 1970s.

Innate Knowledge

The contradiction of contemporary architecture was the central feature of the second essay of 1971 entitled "Towards a Definition of Architec-

ture in Quebec," Charney's first manifesto about the architecture of his home province.[5]

In a provocative comparison, two images excerpted from official government publications were juxtaposed to illustrate the confrontation between elite and popular architecture. On the one hand, the picture of an architect's house found on the cover of a book on contemporary architecture in Quebec embodied the ideology and the failure of "architecture as an institutionalised system." Limited by aesthetic prejudice, the formal expression of that official architecture was, even in the eyes of Claude Beaulieu, the author of the book, "due to some outside influence as opposed to a national inspiration."[6] On the other hand, the photo of an anonymous house in the Laurentians, which illustrated an article by architect Marc Drouin denouncing the ugliness of Quebec's landscape, represented the other, repressive side of an elitist cultural institution incapable of seeing in this image "an authentic architecture born of real things and rooted in people's real lives."

A scrupulous description of the architect's house indicated that its ambiguous formalism detached the building from its environment. In its formal isolation, this house recalled "the language of an aesthetic myth": the house revived the past "by cloaking itself in a modern vocabulary." Unable to disengage from the past, it symbolized the cultural isolation of the French Canadian elite. Charney wrote: "The house seems to be in limbo – it could be anywhere at all, frozen in the mind of its creator. The American critic Edmund Wilson characterized in similar terms the fiction of Anne Hébert, who 'does take us into the maisons … And we are partly in a realm of dream …These old line French Canadians in their cultural enclave on the North American continent do not always quite know where they are.'"[7]

Found on the side of the road, the other house was, on the contrary, totally integrated to its environment. This anonymous house was "specific

to its occupants and to its place." Built of standardized, readily available industrial materials, it
did not display the academic and authoritarian
formalism of the first house. Its real significance
lay in the fact that it reflected "the condition of
those who had to struggle – with a minimum
of resources available – to find a way to house
themselves." For Charney, this house was representative of an authentic popular architecture,
the modernist version of Quebec's vernacular
tradition which, according to Ramsay Traquair,
at its best was "the work of the people unassisted
by academic architects." Charney added: "A tradition refers to an attitude towards building, an
attitude rooted in an innate response to the need
for organization of physical space and conditioned by the resources available."[8]

Just as when he saw in ancient vernacular
traditions the source for classical architecture
and in industrial vernacular building the source
for modern architecture, Charney maintained
that "the source of contemporary architecture in
Quebec [was] in popular architecture and in a
way of building that has shaped the relationship
between people and the built form that they
inhabit."[9] But in contrast with his assertions of
the mid-1960s, Charney did not speculate on the
design of new environmental systems: the kit of
parts was already there; the building industry
provided the materials that citizen architects
appropriated to erect an authentic and living
architecture.

In spite of similarities, Charney's conception
of the opposition of elite and popular architecture was quite different from that formulated
in parallel by Venturi and Scott Brown in their
apology for "ugly and ordinary architecture."
The authors of *Learning from Las Vegas* clearly
intended to "emphasize image – image over
process or form" in their criticism of elite
architecture, but their goal was to highlight the
"lack of correspondence between substance
and image" in "heroic" avant-garde architecture.[10] They judged irrelevant the deliberately

unconventional look of the late modern style
because it excluded popular symbolism from
the vocabulary of architecture. The expres-
sionist image of buildings like Paul Rudolph's
Crawford Manor suggested "the reformist-pro-
gressive social and industrial aims that [modern
architecture] could seldom achieve in reality."[11]
Their apology for the "decorated shed" meant
to justify a conventional and inclusivist architecture, which, in their opinion, would be more
relevant socially because it would communicate
information to a larger group of people. Under
the influence of semiology, architecture was for
them a system that communicated with conventional signs. By contrast, Charney situated
meaning in the interaction between people and
their environment. For him, "the organizational
system of the physical environment [constituted]
a *language* of interaction between people and
things."[12] In Quebec, people's "innate response
to the need for organization of physical space"
gave a "central role to the meaning of street
and square in the organization of towns and
cities." The current problem was "to translate
that understanding into coherent physical
form." Moreover, in recognizing people's innate
knowledge of architecture, Charney articulated
a much more radical position which amounted
to a quasi-revolutionary political program. His
essay concludes: "the liberation of the architect
depends on the political and social liberation of
both the individual and the community. And in
Quebec, this means that it depends on the assertion of a new and renewed Quebec identity."[13]

Written in the months following the crisis
that shook Quebec and Canada in October
1970, Charney's call resonated with the Front
de libération du Québec manifesto, which
envisioned that workers would liberate themselves from the slavery of foreign big capital in
appropriating the means of industrial production. In the field of architecture, Charney apparently believed that an analogous drive animated
the groups of citizens who united to protest the

destruction of their neighbourhoods and formed cooperatives in order to buy and collectively maintain their dwellings. For him, the appropriation of the *quartiers populaires* by their inhabitants inaugurated a fourth phase in the history of Quebec architecture, an age in which people could at last liberate themselves from the authoritarianism of the architectural institution.

Struggle for a Place

In the early 1970s, Charney worked on two substantial research projects. The first was a report on "the adequacy and production of low-income housing" for the Central Mortgage and Housing Corporation of Canada.[14] The other was a book project entitled *Struggle for a Place*, which used Quebec as a paradigmatic example of "the political signification of cultural practice … in a struggle for identity against the imperial forces of advanced capitalist production … on its home ground."[15] Sent to a New York publisher, the book was never published, its contents being judged too political. Yet the ideas developed in these texts were disseminated in Charney's subsequent essays that examined the production of social housing in Canada.

An essay published in 1972 diffused the conclusions of his research on low-income housing in Canada.[16] For him, the problems surrounding housing were not related to the capacity of production or to a lack of national wealth but to "the redistribution of resources and the control of resources in society." So he argued that "as long as this [was] glossed over, low-income housing programmes, no matter how efficient, [would] simply remain ineffective." Existing programs guaranteed high returns to the building industry but did not really produce affordable housing and led to popular dissatisfaction. Concerning the CMHC, he wrote: "The failure of the 1970 Special $200 Million Low-Cost Innovative Housing Programme did not reach the front pages of newspapers as did the guerilla activities

of the Front de Libération du Québec in Quebec. But the widespread politicization of the large number of families across the country who could not afford any of the so-called low-income housing, or were caught in an ownership trap of expensive and inadequate housing, may have as serious a long-term and widespread effect on the future of the country as the more visible terrorist actions."[17]

This conclusion was embarrassing for the CMHC, which emulated the programs in place in the United States. In spite of rather spectacular outputs in the number of built units, these programs institutionalized dependency, controlled behaviour, packaged poverty, and ultimately locked the poor in their condition. For Charney, governmental housing programs were emblematic of the oppressive and delusory use of architecture by authorities.

A second essay, published in 1976, introduced considerations which were central in the *Struggle for a Place* manuscript. Canadian housing policies, Charney argued, hid "a Machiavellian web of political intrigue" which repressed the cultural traditions of self-reliance and used housing as "political instrument for entrenching consumer values."[18] He denounced the neo-colonial attitude rooted in the ideology of capitalist development imposed by the political caste. His critique built on the central idea of the FLQ manifesto, according to which the political elite sold the nation's riches to foreign interests and enslaved Quebec's working class. Charney applied this model to his analysis of Quebec's architecture by opposing two modes of production of the built environment that illustrated the confrontation of people and government.

The first was symbolized by Montreal's *quartiers populaires*, where he found "the first truly indigenous construction to emerge out of the experience of this continent." Charney drew a parallel between the repression of militant action in these working-class neighbourhoods and the state of dereliction of the existing stock of buildings which provided the bulk of low-income accommodation in Montreal. While barely supporting the rehabilitation and maintenance of the *quartiers populaires*, the Canadian government subsidized deliberately unattractive and inadequate urban housing as if it wanted to "punish the poor."[19]

The other mode of production was symbolized by the single-family house of the suburban *villes champignons* promoted by the CMHC. Rationalized and produced in factories, the suburban house reduced the home to a commodity and its proliferation transformed the best farmland into suburbia. Here Charney again drew a parallel between the repression of the workers' unions and the imposition of a type of house totally inadequate for the rigorous climate of Quebec. While the workers' housing provided in company towns of northern Quebec was hard to distinguish from concentration camps, suburbia transformed the middle class into consumers. Charney wrote: "The *villes champignons* are evidence that housing has been refined as one of the instruments now used to maintain a relatively cheap, but well-fed labour force which has the means and the taste for the consumption of the middle-class, high-income goods, including the purchase of an expensive family appliance called a home."[20]

The two modes produced different environments, one ecological and collective, the other consumerist and individualist. The imposition of the second mode was repressive and an act of cultural denial, he argued: "In the earlier *quartiers populaires*, as in recent squatter settlements, a collective ecology of settlement emerged out of the political ferment of people seeking to make their lives bearable with whatever means were available: in the *villes champignons*, consumer packaging of housing is robbing people of the symbols of their collective identity."[21]

Beyond the symbolism of their respective image, the confrontation of these two modes of production encapsulated the tragedy of a people robbed, by imperial forces, of their cultural identity and of the means necessary to self-determination.

Mass Media

Political analysis was only one side of Charney's architectural criticism during the 1970s. In parallel, his practice took off in a series of original productions that challenged the conventional idea of the architectural project as prediction and anticipation.

Pivotal in more than one way, the *Memo Series* opened two large fields of inquiry which both derived from the pop fascination for everyday images. The first tracked the meaning of architecture in images found in print media that highlighted the interaction of people with their environment; this search for the "small true fact, the true detail," "the tiniest fragment of everyday life," led to the creation of the *Dictionnaire d'architecture*. The other found in these images a heroic content that demanded a redefinition of architectural monumentality that Charney reified in a series of small-scale constructions.

By the end of the 1960s, Charney started collecting printed images to illustrate his essays. The idea of "learning from the wire services" gradually enabled him to develop an understanding of architecture as a form of knowledge not restricted to the knowledge of forms displayed in *Learning from Las Vegas*. Architecture could be a means of understanding the dialectics of the built environment. Books, magazines, and mainly newspapers provided the raw material, the living archive of anonymous images depicting people's daily struggle against oppressive power. Because of their worldwide diffusion, these snapshots of reality participated in the formation of a global consciousness. Yet, paradoxically, their architectural content remained invisible unless they were isolated from the stream of everyday life, as was the case with pop art. The act of collecting retrieved them from the cycle of inattentive consumption and transformed them into monuments.

Most of these images were shocking, not because of their raw aesthetic, like the brutalist image, but because of their violence. Poor people taking refuge in prefabricated concrete pipes or making quasi-symbolic shelters out of scrap material; rioters erecting barricades; prisoners claiming space with rags; armed soldiers breaking into houses; old people evicted from their homes or sequestered in institutions: these scenes revealed that "every built fragment was taken to be an affirmation of denial of cultural, social and economic barriers."[22] Images of catastrophes (fire, earthquake, flood, war) revealed the geometric structure and the bare bones of the built environment; the spectacle of politicians, bankers, and architects showing off models of mega-buildings displayed the unashamed monopolization of resources in the hands of a ruling class; the images of citizens forced by soldiers to lie in a row, in the street, face down and hands on their heads exposed the architectural order of power. Proliferation and redundancy suggested a possibly inherent yet unrevealed structure to the dialectics of liberation and oppression of which architecture was both an instrument and a mirror. Ordering these images, at once specific and universal, created the *Dictionnaire d'architecture*, a learning device Charney exhibited in several versions over three decades.[23]

Myth

If the *Dictionnaire* drew attention to the "small true fact, the true detail," "the tiniest fragment of everyday life" hidden in the flow of daily images, it also confirmed an intuition of the *Memo Series*: that "every built gesture seemed to assume a monumental connotation."[24] The critique of traditional architectural monumentality became a central theme of Charney's

practice. In 1977, he explained the mechanics of monumentalization:

> The architecture that I do is preoccupied with monuments. The building of shelter is not merely a biological contingency, but involves the cultural transformation of utilitarian needs. A built gesture produces something that was not there before. As such, it cannot but idealize (make heroic) to some degree all those relationships that allow it to be conceived and materialized. But as Vitruvius would have it, monumental buildings reproduce the necessary forms of primitive construction in permanent and noble materials. And even though this attitude changed by the end of the eighteenth century, and it has been a long time since architects were paid by rulers to build noble temples and palaces, architecture still reflects its origins: the heroic content of building is reserved for the strategic embellishment of the lives of those who control the purse strings if not the privileges in society, and who desire the ultimate privilege: to see themselves privileged in their own eyes. The idea of the monument is still promoted as some atavistic emblem of class structure that dominates the practice if not the spirit of architecture.[25]

Here, driven by the irreversible process of improvement of known models, architecture, even modern architecture, inherently monumentalized the social content of life. Whether the architect intended it or not, architecture was the idealized reification of life.

In 1903, Alois Riegl made explicit that the task of the intentional monument was to commemorate – to keep a past event forever present to consciousness.[26] Monuments were conceived therefore as memory machines. As Charney put it, architects used "the language of an aesthetic myth" to commemorate power, its institutions, its wars, and its agents by means of buildings intended to survive the work of time. Architectural monumentality was monopolized by the ruling classes. But Riegl also pointed out that in the modern era, the concept of monumentality was expanded to incorporate artifacts which were not intentional monuments; these artifacts were monumental because they were historical documents of a bygone era. Charney gave a different meaning to the non-intentional architectural monument. His project was derived from Michel Foucault, who suggested, in *The Archeology of Knowledge*, that history transforms documents into monuments.[27] For Charney, all architecture was a document commemorating the heroic content of life. The dialectics of elite and popular architecture implied a dialectical understanding of architectural monumentality which was the site of a political struggle about memory.

Interestingly, heroism was a central trope of modern architecture's revolutionary mythology. While the Venturis rejected the heroism of brutalism and the late modern style, Charney defined a different critical position; he wrote: "In a special issue of *Architectural Design* in 1965, Peter and Alison Smithson defined the 'Heroic Period of Modern Architecture' as a series of buildings which appeared in Europe between 1915 and 1929 when 'a new idea of architecture came into being.' 'This period,' they wrote, 'is the rock upon which we stand.' They found nothing heroic in America."[28]

On the contrary, Charney found a heroic content in Quebec's popular architecture. That content was invisible to the cultural elite, and his creations searched for ways to render it manifest.*

A photograph found in Alan Gowans's history of Canadian architecture was the triggering element for Charney; it showed an anonymous building, built in Saint-Canut, probably in the 1910s or 1920s. (See Fig. 25.1.) Gowans used that image to assert that "in the French sections of its [Quebec's] cities and in its countryside appeared a hideous assemblage of structures that belong to no conceivable architectural tradition whatever."[29] The house, representative of the North American "boomtown" typology, was familiar: it was a sibling of a house in which Charney spent his summers as a young boy. (See Fig. 34.2.) For him, it was representative of Quebec's popular architecture, an example of people's innate knowledge, an unconscious monument of a people's struggle for a place.

An exemplary demonstration was needed, and Charney conceived it from a photograph found in a report about the urban renewal of Trois-Rivières, the once self-proclaimed world's capital of paper. (See Fig. 1.1.) A small building, presumably a domestic building, illustrated the type of construction the renewal plan found inadequate. The photograph triggered a story, that of the "Treasure of Trois-Rivières." For Charney, the image represented a worker's house built "in the shadow of a massive pulp mill." As photographs found in Charney's archive demonstrate, he visited the site. The house, Charney wrote later, was demolished in 1974 as a result of the urban renewal program.

Drawing over the image, as in radiography, Charney revealed the architectural substance that made of this anonymous construction a heroic building: its shape reproduced the form of a classic temple; its facade facing the street

* Editor's note: Charney's dualistic model may have been inspired by John A. Kouwenhoven's *Made in America: The Arts in Modern Civilization* (Garden City, NY: Doubleday, 1949). It is not clear when Charney discovered this book in which Kouwenhoven outlined the interaction between academic and vernacular architecture since the nineteenth century. In the third chapter entitled "Two Traditions in Conflict," Kouwenhoven argued that the vernacular tradition was transformed by industrialization, notably by the invention of balloon framing and prefabrication. According to him, the vernacular tradition was the real driving force of "an architecture indigenous to modern civilization" (95), an idea that Charney internalized and reformulated in his writings.

recalled meso-American architecture; a giant cross supported the facade. As in psychoanalysis, Charney's narrative revealed an architectural unconscious, indicative of a people's innate knowledge of architecture; he wrote: "This house was an uneasy discovery. Its classic forms suggest both the temple and sarcophagus. This contradiction permeates its scale, as if the figure of the house were both there and not there, at the same time. At the confluence of three rivers – the meeting of a trinity – some French-speaking Québécois whose livelihoods were caught up in a factory run by Anglo capital, and whose redemption was refuted by the church, built the figure of a house of death, and lived in it as if to expurgate their fate."[30] "Is this not architecture? Is not the ultimate idealization of our existence the libido at rest (death), and the perfect building the ultimate realization of Adam's House in Paradise (the tomb)? And if this architecture is refused its place in the consciousness of our culture, is it not because the culture denies the consciousness of its people?"[31]

Charney saw in the "Treasure of Trois-Rivières" an incarnation of the archetypal primitive hut which was the origin of architecture according to the Vitruvian myth. He discovered, in Joseph Rykwert's recent book *On Adam's House in Paradise*, an erudite interpretation of the meanings associated with the primitive hut in architectural theory which helped him to substantiate his interpretation.[32] The destruction of such an exemplary case by a blind political apparatus was an act of cultural repression that Charney wished to counterbalance by the creation of a monument intended to commemorate its heroic content. For him, "the act of physically assembling this building ritualized the figuration that gave it meaning. What emerged was a totem: a built effigy that reproduced the original documentation (see Fig. 30.4) as if it were the program of a building. This act reversed Vitruvius's dictum – it presented a monumental construction that reproduced the necessary forms of permanent and noble buildings in primitive materials; and it turned around the modern tradition noted by Colin Rowe – it put back meaning into the thing itself, rather than proposing its meaning in a project."[33]

The Freudian overtones of the totemic monument as substitute for the killed father are obvious: the displacement made visible what was impossible to articulate in speech.[34] Clearly, Charney's story gave meaning to an image generally thought to be meaningless.

Perhaps the most disturbing element of his story lies in the fact that the house was not demolished. Visibly, Charney did not oppose history to myth as Manfredo Tafuri's criti-

23.2 1085 Ste-Geneviève Street, Trois-Rivières, 1982.

cism proposed;[35] on the contrary, he filled the otherwise invisible images of the everyday with a powerful mythological content that awakened consciousness. As he later explained in a discussion about his project for the garden of the Canadian Centre for Architecture: "You can indeed read the piece on several levels. It is like riding a magic carpet: you never wonder how the carpet can float in the air so long as the logic that is inherent in the story holds up. That is, so long as 'image' and 'language' blend with one another."[36]

Architecture was there: the task of the architectural project, as built allegory blending image and language, was to make it visible. This Freudian logic of displacement became increasingly apparent in Charney's production of the late 1970s, starting with *Les maisons de la rue Sherbrooke*, his contribution to the street exhibition Corridart, infamously destructed by order of Montreal Mayor Jean Drapeau in 1976.

Traces

During the 1970s, Charney wrote extensively on Montreal and its architecture. Already in 1972, he had been invited by the Montreal Museum of Fine Arts to realize an exhibition on Montreal. His intention was to present an alternate view of the metropolis based on the citizens' perception of their own city. He wrote in the introduction to the catalogue: "The exhibition tries to say that the future of the city is found not only in urban growth, in technological innovations, or in the exercise of planning and design talents, but in the social and cultural evolution of Montreal."[37] In the aftermath of this major event, in which a larger number of Montreal artists participated, Charney transformed his architectural studio at the Université de Montreal into a study group examining the social and cultural content of Montreal's architecture.[38]

In 1976, he was invited to orchestrate Corridart, the cultural pendant to the Montreal Olympic Games. The program visibly intended to use works of art to embellish the city according to the dubious logic expressed by Mayor Jean Drapeau at the time of Montreal's Expo 67 when he said: "The ugliness of slums in which people live doesn't matter if we can make them stand in wide-eyed admiration of works of art they don't understand."[39]

Charney transformed Sherbrooke Street into an eight-kilometre-long museum-in-the-street exhibition which "explored the neglect and destruction of street life in the city."[40] For him, Montreal was unique in North America: it was made of streets and squares which were urban rooms where people gathered. He argued that "the physical traces of the streets define[d] a bond between people and the city as a collective, public artifact which subsume[d] individual buildings."[41] That was why, in addition to the insertion of contextual artworks by Quebec artists, he used Sherbrooke Street itself as exhibition material. The civic character and the urban form of Montreal were symbols of the collective identity of Montrealers. Corridart meant to bring this meaning to consciousness: "The main thrust of Corridart, therefore, was on the signification of the street. The container of the exhibition – the street – was to be contained within the larger meaning of the street in its urban context. Each element was to draw on the familiar language of the street, accessible to and understood by people. Traces of the civility of Sherbrooke Street were to be re-presented. But the representation was to attempt to depict its baggage of status and power in a changing role: a street whose significance now derives from a place that belongs to all people of this city."[42]

Inspired by the Italian film sets of Cinecittà, he built *Les maisons de la rue Sherbrooke* on a governmental site which had been vacant for nearly ten years. This installation consisted of a full-size plywood replica of the facades of two Victorian urban houses situated on the other side of the street. Re-presentation, by a mirror image, duplicated the real and created a monumental setting. Conceived with references to a series of precedents, Charney's allegorical narrative intended to demonstrate that the traditional city form of Montreal embodied an innate knowledge of the baroque principles of urban scenography. But in the context of the mid-1970s, when the heart of Montreal was full of fragments of a disappearing city, *Les maisons* had a political meaning. These plywood facades inserted new traces which reversed metaphorically the process of destruction: rather than ruins, old fragments of the city became emblematic of cultural resistance and the program for the reconstruction of the collective space of the street. Yet, the profound significance of *Les maisons de la rue Sherbrooke* surfaced, not without bitter irony, with their very destruction, which made tangible the conflict between power and popular culture previously theorized by Charney. The figurative content of this work and the images of its destruction acted as a catalyst which brought to collective consciousness the fact that the city was the battleground of a real struggle between a repressive power and cultural resistance. Charney wrote: "Therein lies the significance of Corridart. It affirms the strength of a well-aimed, figurative gesture in architecture as a means whereby we can come to terms with the way people understand the conditions of their lives. After all, autocrats still fear the power of an image."[43]

Retrospectively, the work also seems to have anticipated the imminent shift towards "contextualism" in Montreal architecture illustrated by the inauguration in 1979 of the new urban campus of the Université du Québec à Montréal (UQAM), a group of new buildings built around the spire and the side portal of a former neo-Gothic church, fragments which had been listed as historical monuments by the goverment of Quebec in 1973.

Yet the most remarkable aspect of Charney's act of urban activism was its worldwide diffusion under the form of a mass media image: the photos of *Les maisons de la rue Sherbrooke* acquired the status, and diffused the message, of the images collected in the *Dictionnaire*.

Signs

The postmodern moment culminated in 1980, at the Venice Biennale, entitled The Presence of the Past, with the alliance of a semiological architecture of conventional signs and a humanist apology for historical continuity stimulated by Christian Norberg-Schulz's concept of place, Aldo Rossi's concept of memory, and Colin Rowe's contextual theory.[44] Symptomatically, the postmodern critique, with its return to "history," valued the traditional city, its urban forms and architectural types, at a moment when these forms had been "reduced to mere abstract outlines, to ruins of their former selves."[45] Charney interpreted this spectacular shift in terms of a change of the analogy by which cities were conceptualized: "A mechanical, biologic analogy (organism, growth, tissue, heart, arteries) may be seen to be displaced by a semiologic analogy (vocabulary, signification, syntax, narration). It also suggests a structural displacement in the understanding of architecture as a societal practice, since semiology is based on the assumption that there exist shared referential links to which human artifacts convey meaning, and these links, be they biologic or established by habits of schooled recognition, are socially bound: society makes every use a sign of itself."[46]

This realization was the starting point of two texts on Quebec's architecture, the first on Montreal, the other on anonymous architecture.

In "The Montrealness of Montreal," Charney pursued an analysis begun in the early 1960s which examined the replacement of the traditional city core by high-density mega-clusters. According to him, one of the strongest features of Montreal's urban architecture was "the predominance of the street as a physical entity which subsumed individual buildings."[47] Since the 1960s, the inherited dialectic between official monumental architecture and the authentic city of the *quartiers populaires* had given way to an increasing tension between the interior private spaces of the superblocks, which transformed urban space into a commodity, and the exterior collective spaces of the traditional city, which were increasingly eroded and reduced to fragments. Yet two tendencies indicating the vitality of Montreal's urban culture were noticeable. On the one hand, the most recent superblocks tended to incorporate features of the traditional city such as a "square" in the case of Complexe Desjardins and historical fragments in the case of UQAM. On the other hand, renovation, insertion, and gentrification became common practices which helped in preserving the neighbourhoods. The introduction of the concept of sign helped to elucidate the new phase in the dialectics of elite and popular architecture. Charney explained: "Be it the introduction of an urban configuration in inner-city superblocks, or the strong identification with the urban architecture of the *quartiers*, public symbols of the city are seen to be alive and well in the cultural affirmation, if not the social articulation, of people. The resolution of these references in architecture is caught, however, between the total reproduction of large-scale urban interventions, with its tendency to automate and normalise sign systems, and the replication of things-as-they-are, emanating from small scale interventions in the *quartiers*."[48]

Charney saw the collage of historical fragments with the new superblocks as a transitional stage leading to "the introduction of textural urban figuration and typologies."

The second essay, entitled "To Whom It May Concern: On Contemporary Architecture in Quebec," represents another attempt "to put back meaning into the thing itself." This text interpreted an archive of a different kind. For several years, Charney asked his students to photograph examples of significant architecture in Quebec. Charney's selection illustrated how all built form was a form of representation, a sign in a semiotized milieu. Popular architecture, as some natural sign, represented the fundamental nature of architecture: true primitive huts "at once both primitive and metaphorical."[49] In other words, these examples were at once a true beginning and the symbolic reification of the Vitruvian myth of origins. Charney argued: "As other "primitive huts" in other periods of history have done, they serve as an essential model of architectural creation. They confirm the arrival of an architecture that finds its place in the new order of things and that is aware of the images of images, the symbols of symbols and the signs of signs. It is as if architecture starts by refusing to refuse, by wanting to affirm that continuity between art and life."[50]

An architecture of signs doubled reality with the alternate reality of the image and thus created a *mise en abyme*, a universe of signs endlessly reflecting each other.

NOTES

1 The criticism of utopia is a topos of the revisionist criticism of modern architecture and urbanism and characterizes theories as divergent as Colin Rowe's formalism, Venturi and Scott Brown's semiology, and Manfredo Tafuri's ideological criticism.
2 Chapter 24, 236.
3 Ibid.
4 Ibid. 237. Charney's understanding of "conceptual" architecture was quite different from Peter Eisenman's theory of "conceptual architecture." Like Charney, Eisenman believed in people's innate capacity to grasp the geometrical concept of architectural form. However, Eisenman's approach was based on a parallel between architecture and Chomsky's linguistic model and conceived architecture as a system of notation that transmitted information about the conceptual operations used by the designer to create an environment. Eisenman's theory was a most extreme formalism based on the belief that

the essence of architecture was revealed when form was self-referential. See Peter Eisenman, "Notes on Conceptual Architecture: Towards a Definition," *Casabella* 359–60 (November–December 1971): 49–57

5 Chapter 25, 246–64.

6 The author of the pamphlet, Claude Beaulieu, was one of Quebec's leading modernist architects of the 1960s. At the time, Beaulieu was an editor of the magazine *Vie des arts*, which published the translation of Charney's "The World of Pop."

7 Ibid., 249.

8 Ibid., 250.

9 Ibid.

10 Robert Venturi and Denise Scott Brown, "Ugly and Ordinary Architecture or the Decorated Shed," *Architectural Forum* (November 1971): 64–7. The whole quotation reads as follows: "We shall emphasize image – image over process or form – in asserting that architecture depends in its perception and creation on past experience and emotional association, and that these symbolic and representational elements may often be contradictory to the form, structure and program with which they combine in the same building."

11 Ibid.

12 Chapter 25, 262.

13 Ibid., 264.

14 *The Adequacy and Production of Low-Income Housing*, a Report prepared by Melvin Charney, M.R.A.I.C. in collaboration with Serge Carreau and Colin Davidson for the Task Force on Low-Income Housing, Central Mortgage and Housing Corporation (Ottawa, October 1971).

15 The chronology of this book project is hard to establish. A proposal entitled *After Architecture: On the Liberation of the Built Environment*, dated December 1971, seems to be the first outline of the book. An undated, more succinct but more precise outline entitled *Struggle for Place: Quebec, a Study of Cultural Conflict and the Control of Human Settlement* seems to be the second formulation of the project. Also undated, a third, 122-page document, entitled *The Struggle for a Place: A Documentary on Quebec. Transformations in the Architecture of Quebec: A Test Case for America*, is the most elaborate formulation of the book, which expanded the argument of "Towards a Definition of Architecture in Quebec."

16 Chapter 26, 265–70.

17 Ibid., 268.

18 Chapter 29, 281–90.

19 Ibid., 286. These words echo Michel Foucault. Charney was a fervent reader of Foucault, who had just published his book *Discipline and Punish: The Birth of the Prison*.

20 Ibid., 289–90.

21 Ibid., 290.

22 Introduction to *Struggle for Place* (unpublished manuscript), 3.

23 *Tracking Images: Un dictionnaire*, with texts by Melvin Charney, Jean-François Chevrier, Phyllis Lambert, and Manon Régimbald (Montreal: Canadian Centre for Architecture, 2000).

24 Chapter 30, 294.

25 Ibid., 291.

26 Alois Riegl, "The Modern Cult of Monuments: Its Character and Its Origin" [1903], *Oppositions* 25 (Fall 1982): 21–51

27 Michel Foucault, *The Archeology of Knowledge*, trans. A.M. Sheridan Smith (New York: Routledge, 1972). Charney acknowledged the decisive impact the work of Foucault had on him. In this connection, see Jean-François Chevrier, "Art as the Reinvention of an Urban Political Form" in *Melvin Charney, Parcours: de la reinvention / About Reinvention* (Caen, France: FRAC-Basse Normandie; New York: Distributed Art Publishers, 1998), 162–241; Luc Baboulet, "De document au monument," *Communications 71* (2001): 435–63; and Georges Adamczyk in chapter 2 of this book.

28 Chapter 32, 321.

29 Alan Gowans, *Building Canada: An Architectural History of Canadian Life* (Toronto: Oxford University Press, 1966).

30 Chapter 30, 299–300. Retrospectively, it is possible to see that this piece of Quebec's popular architecture was to a certain extent an analogue of the trulli Charney found in Apulia: it was a house in the shape of a tomb.

31 Chapter 30, 300.

32 Joseph Rykwert, *On Adam's House in Paradise: The Idea of the Primitive Hut in Architectural History* (New York: Museum of Modern Art, 1972).

33 Chapter 30, 300. Charney refers to Colin Rowe's essay "Chicago Frame" in which Rowe contrasted the American and the European conception of the structural frame of posts and beams. For the Americans of the Chicago School, the frame was a "fact," a solution to a specific problem; for the European modernists, the frame was an "idea," a manifesto for a new architecture. According to Rowe, the Chicago School failed to achieve a complete architectural revolution because

it lacked the ideological content found in the European approach. As this quote makes clear, Charney intended to put the unconscious architectural meaning back into the "fact" itself.

34 Sigmund Freud, *Totem and Taboo: Resemblance between the Psychic Life of Savages and Neurotics*, trans. A.A. Brill (New York: Vintage Books, 1946).

35 See Manfredo Tafuri, *Teorie e Storia dell'Architecttura* (1967, 1970), trans. Giorgio Verrecchia, *Theories and History of Architecture*, 1st American ed. (New York: Harper and Row, 1980).

36 Chapter 39, 421.

37 Chapter 27, 275.

38 Melvin Charney, "Confrontations in Urban Architecture, in *Ville, Métaphore, Projet – Architecture urbaine à Montreal, 1980–1990*, ed. G. Adamczyk (Montreal: Éditions du Méridien, 1992), 98–103.

39 Chapter 30, 304.

40 Chapter 31, 314.

41 Ibid., 315.

42 Ibid.

43 Ibid., 319.

44 See Christian Norberg-Schulz, *Genius Loci*: *Towards a Phenomenology of Architecture* (New York: Rizzoli, 1980); Aldo Rossi, *The Architecture of the City*, introduction by Peter Eisenman; translated by Diane Ghirardo and Joan Ockman; revised for the American edition by Aldo Rossi and Peter Eisenman (Cambridge, MA: MIT Press, 1982); Colin Rowe and Fred Koetter, *Collage City* (Cambridge MA: MIT Press, 1978; *Presence of the Past: First International Exhibition of Architecture, the Corderia of the Arsenale, La Biennale di Venezia, 1980, Architectural Section* (London: Academy Editions, 1980). Under the supervision of Paolo Portoghesi, the Biennale took the form of a stage set in the form of a street, the *Strada Novissima*. On 4 March 1981, Charney wrote a letter to Robert A.M. Stern, who was in charge of the North American selection of works presented at the Biennale, to indicate that he conceived Corridart with the same reference to the Cinecittà studios and that his work should have been included in the show. This letter was found in Stern's Fond kept at the Manuscripts and Archives collection at Yale University. My thanks to Léa-Catherine Szacka for sharing the information.

45 Chapter 33, 332.

46 Ibid.

47 Ibid., 334.

48 Ibid., 341.

49 Chapter 34, 360.

50 Ibid.

24

On the Liberation of Architecture: *Memo Series* on an Air Force Memorial[*]

The tiniest fragment of everyday life says more than ...
Walter Benjamin, "The Author as Producer"

Early in 1969, an announcement in the Canadian press invited architects to participate in a competition for the design of an Air Force Memorial. The competition called for a Memorial which was also to be a museum to air flight, and a place for meetings of Air Force veterans.

The program of the competition allowed for only one type of design solution: a building. Any other response to the problem, one which might, for example, involve modes of experience other than those circumscribed by the form of a building, was clearly beyond the scope of the competition. What would not "look like" a building most certainly would not reflect architecture.

Since these conceptual limitations are characteristic indeed of the condition of much of contemporary architecture, this competition offered as good an occasion as any to re-examine some of the underlying premises.

[*] From *Artforum* 9, no. 9 (May 1971): 34–7.

To begin with, even though new and important idioms have been introduced into contemporary architecture, to say the least, innovations have also tended to reinforce the existing conception that architecture resides solely in the design of a specialized object in the form of a building. Anything beyond these premises is largely situated as meaningless, regardless of the legacy of the constructivists, for example. Contemporary theory and criticism tend to mystify the existence of this barrier which fetters architecture to a repressive condition, refusing to acknowledge that architecture is reflected in the meaning of a "building" as found in the use we make of our artifacts.

To the extent that the relationships between people and physical things can be found mirrored in the "things themselves," the raw material of the architecture of an Air Force Memorial can be found in readily available artifactual bits known to materialize for people the remembrance of air flight and Air Force.

Proceeding in this way, existing artifactual bits recognized for their Memorial content are described and catalogued in a series of *Memos*.

These constructs describe the evidence of "object correlatives" of the Memorial, and the physical conditions that support this evidence. The *Memos* then extract from the constructs design propositions. In other words, the idea of the *Memos* is to expose the possible design of a Memorial, and hence its architecture, rather than impose a design.

These constructs are drawn directly from the community. They are not so much given, as they are taken out of a constantly elusive matrix of experience implicating different sets of physical things. They are said to come from the people, with the understanding that this means, for one thing, that different people experience "things" in different ways, even though the mechanisms of their experience may be similar. Since the relationship of people to the reality of their artifactual environment changes with time, regardless of consistencies in these relationships, and their conception of reality itself changes with time, the selection of *Memos* constitutes an ongoing process of continuous defining and redefining of the design experience.

This process tends to be divergent and inclusive. A proliferation of Memorial constructs strengthens the assumptions of a possible architecture, and brings to light conditions that would otherwise remain inaccessible.

The *Memos* then provide the sources of a design program. The subsequent implication of these sources in the actual external form of a Memorial depends upon some sort of communication; access to communication depends upon available channels, and the content of communication, on the expression of experience.

Given the best of intentions to design in the interest of the people and to have people participate in the design process, in the present limitations of architecture, the design action – the process of selecting a suppressed range of access and experience – contradicts the design intention.

If architecture is conceived of as creating the sources of design, people can be actively engaged according to opportunities they have to externalize their experience. Their act of externalization – their design – involves a selection of experience: specific, stylistic, and idiosyncratic to the probability of a design and the demarcation of meaning is found in a certain kind of activity rather than in a specialized medium.

This distinction between architecture and design, and the consequent shift in both social and aesthetic sensibilities, bypasses the persistent contradiction in contemporary architecture between its elitist and repressive condition and its obvious origins in social content.

Ideally, it may be possible to avoid this contradiction by restoring to people the full responsibility for their surroundings and for their shared identity. Design can then assume its architectural condition by virtue of its granting existence to an architectural concept in the heads of people, where it really happens, and where it belongs in the first place.

Thus two levels of design are set out. The first deals with the structuring of design resources, and the second with the communication of design.

On the first level, the *Memos* map out patterns of resources which are available for the architecture of an Air Force Memorial. Any subsequent reinforcement of these patterns by the selection – i.e., design – of one or several of these patterns constitutes an act of design intervention, and a deliberate political, social, and aesthetic act. For example, the selection – design – of the Memorial in the form of building is readily seen to constitute a repressive act, given limited resources, the size of the country, and the range of possibilities available, such as the reinforcing of a cross-country Memorial network by the installation of old aircraft or video equipment in centres of population, or the opening of old airports near several cities as instant Memorials where Air Force veterans could meet in the abandoned hangars. Rather than invest resources in capital expenditure on an isolated building set in a corner of the country, the money could be invested in real services such as housing, and the return used to maintain a network of facilities that can bring the "building" to the people.

The second level of design then belongs to all of us. The *Memos* describe the resources for the personal design of a Memorial which is so general and particular, simple and complex, as to encompass any experience that may be included in its architecture. The resulting continual variation of the external form of the Memorial reinforces the internal structure of personal experience.

Memo 1: On Location as a Network. The network locates Memorial constructs at any given point in time. It identifies and links specific zones where design opportunities exist or may exist. These zones may be found at an airport, or at the location of other similar experiential linkages. These locations are fixed neither in place nor time since there are no "real" physical boundaries to the Memorial's beginning or end to its actual location. A Memorial may disclose itself in several places simultaneously: a construct in Vancouver may be a Memorial at 8:00 a.m., and at the same instant another construct in Montreal may become a Memorial for someone else. Meaning is found in "real-time" and in subsequent immobilization of space.

24.1 Map of Air Canada flight routes linking principal cities.

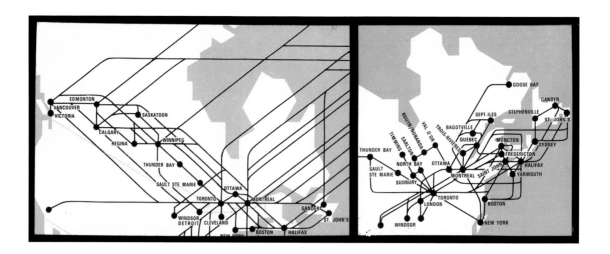

Memo 2: On Real-Time Topologies. Linkages throughout the network are established by reference to an existing physical matrix associated with flight. Airports locate points of contact between air flight and the ground readily accessible both physically and conceptually. The on-ground topology of the airport is determined by the configuration of in-flight air space: the lowering of buildings, warning lights on all projecting constructions, the flattening of the terrain, and a distant view of the horizon across a vast, flat, windswept clearing. The original function of the airfield suggests the possible function of the airfield as a Memorial. As Robert Smithson once suggested, in dealing with the simulacrum of the "object," the runway transforms itself into an enormous slab hovering over the expanse of the field, and on the scale of this slab, isolated aircrafts appear as scattered buildings. Further perceptual mapping could extend the identification of fine-grained design opportunities: Micro-Memos on Micro-Memorials.

24.2 Flight path zones of an aircraft guidance system.

Memo 9: On a Topology of In-Place History. The externalization of architecture includes a morphology of destruction – building-in-meaning – in reverse: the ruins of aircraft buildings and cities form a record of an architecture created by the Air Force. It is found and maintained in actual, in-place remains as some archaeologic deposit. In the case of a bombed-out building, or a destroyed aircraft, the "son et lumière" of the ruins would include a list of casualties, personal histories, families and friends, as well as the sounds of destruction, and remains of bodies left in place in order to personalize the experience.

ABOVE | 24.3 The remains of a French aircraft after the fall of Dien Bien Phu, 1954.

BELOW | 24.4 The collapsed structure of a seaplane hangar of prefabricated concrete elements built at Orbetello, Italy, 1939–41 by Pier Luigi Nervi, and completed by a Lancaster bomber in 1943.

Memo 4: On the Simulated Experience as the Actual Experience. Flight simulators with the addition of taped visuals and sound on the history of air flight and military aviation used as Micro-Memorials located across country. The experience of Lindbergh's flight is recreated by being closed in behind a vibrating engine for 33½ hours looking out at a passing ocean through a periscope. The experience of bombing in a Junker over Guernica, in a B-29 over Hiroshima, or in a B-52 over Laos, includes close-up zoom views of the victims, sounds of their cries, and a free napalm burn on the palm as a souvenir of the "Souvenir" for each visitor. Finally, developments in extraterrestrial flight, such as deep space probes have resulted in telemetered flight systems in which the astronaut-pilots are located in a capsule on earth which simulates an actual in-flight vehicle which it controls and which in turn provides the remote operator "real-time" information on the progress of the flight.

LEFT | 24.5 Forty-eight-hour vacuum chamber simulation of the flight of a Gemini Capsule.

CENTRE | 24.6 Interior of a simulator with a visualization system using Todd-AO 70-mm film of an actual approach, landing, and take-off; the perspective of the film is modified according to the actions ordered by the commands of the simulator and according to the simulated phase of the flight.

RIGHT | 24.7 Flight simulator based on a six-degree movement system designed by LINK.

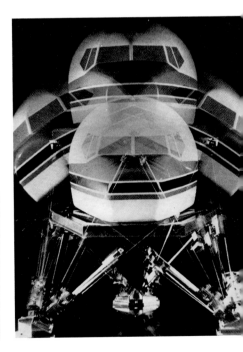

Memo 3: On Usage Preceding Meaning. The aircraft is used as a "building," and used isolated on the slab of a runway it appears as a "building." A visitor can enter the aircraft, pass through its fuselage, fit himself into the gunnery turret or into the cockpit. The moving stick, the switches and dials of the controls, along with taped sound, offer one man the opportunity of a Memorial to himself as a bomber pilot, and another man visions of himself on a bombing mission during the Second World War. As long as it can fly, the aircraft can bring this "Memorial Building" to several cities across the country and take people on Memorial Flights.

24.8 A B-29 open to visitors, parked off the end of a runway at Wright-Patterson Air Force Base, Ohio.

Memo 5: On Discrete Usages. As one becomes aware of the removal from the ground, motion through the air, and total dependence on a machine, communication discloses the relevant features of both "building" and "language."

24.9 Roll-O-Plane in Belmont Park, Montreal.

Memo 6: On Discrete Meaning.

24.10 A wind-up replica of an amusement park airplane ride; made in Japan.

Memo 7: On Instant Access. Video tapes on the history of air flight and military aviation available for instant distribution through any outlet. The tapes present actual scenes from the first flights to recent bombing raids including details of the lives of the people involved. Real images are transferred by the media into the realm of virtual events; history is simulated with the images of warfare. History and war become events locked into the media: important flights or air battles get prime viewing time, alternative outcomes are selected by instant audience rating, and "War is over if you want it" happens by simply pushing the *off* button.

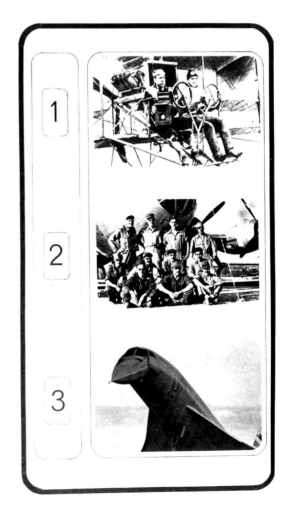

24.11 The media as virtual history. Multiple screen video monitor.

Memo 8: On Instant Access – The Media as Actual History. A real-time Memorial based on a "view that is constant and visual confirmation": a series of monitor channels giving a worldwide audience immediate access to actual events, such as bombing in Laos, via satellites and any home receiver. What is suggested is a rerouting of existing "intelligence" system so that the technology of military intelligence is tuned to keep the people intelligent.

THIS PAGE | 24.12 Radar device giving the pilot a "view that is constant and visual confirmation" on the position of the aircraft; developed by Texas Instruments.

FACING PAGE, ABOVE | 24.13 Melvin Charney, *Memo Series*, 1969–70. Installation at the Graduate School of Design, Harvard University, 1977. This early exhibition of the *Memo Series* is characterized by two levels of display, dividing large format images from the *Memo* texts, and a non-sequential ordering of the *Memo* texts.

FACING PAGE, BELOW | 24.14 Melvin Charney, *Memo Series*, 1969–70. Installation at the Musée d'art contemporain, Montreal, Canada, 1979. This subsequent exhibition standardizes the display of the *Memo Series* into a grid of 62 montages, 12" x 18" each, composed of black and white photographs, Xerox, drawings, and text on grid paper. It also introduced a new numbering of the *Memos*.

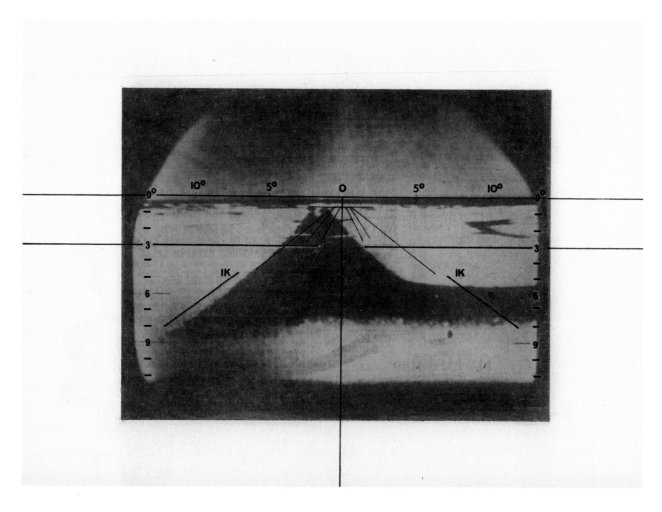

Two Other Versions of the *Memo Series*

Towards a Definition of Architecture in Quebec*

It is time to take stock of the situation of architecture in Quebec.

There is neither a historical framework nor a critical perspective within which to situate contemporary work and trends. Architectural activities happen in a sort of no man's land in Quebec, with only a few rare clues for reference points.

There are several reasons for this. Some are attributable to the more general problem of culture and the arts in Quebec, others to the social, political, and economic context. Architecture,

as it is traditionally understood, depends after all on buildings, and buildings depend on the resources available. But the principal causes for this situation are to be found in the state of architecture itself.

In a recent work entitled *Architecture contemporaine au Canada français* published by the Ministère des affaires culturelles du Québec in 1969, we are presented with a choice of thirty recent buildings. These demonstrate, according to the author of that text, the extent of contemporary architecture in Quebec. Not only is the selection limited and partial, it also puts forward the idea that the formal expression of these buildings is due to some outside influence as opposed to a national inspiration: "If one were to search for national sources of inspiration to understand contemporary architecture in Canada, the list would not be long."[1] In short, the assessment of contemporary architecture in Quebec is judged to be rather meagre and the sources of "national inspiration" practically non-existent.

This assertion is not an isolated act; the same appraisal is in large measure shared by

* This essay was first published in French as "Pour une définition de l'architecture au Québec," in *Architecture et urbanisme au Québec,* ed. Melvin Charney and Marcel Bélanger (Montreal: Les Presses de l'Université de Montréal, 1971), 9–42. The text presented here is based on a translation of this published French version by Nancy Dunton. Some additional editorial changes were informed by a typewritten English version of the text, which was found in Charney's archive as well as an English translation of a brief portion of the essay undertaken by Diana Agrest and published as "Towards a Definition of Quebec Architecture," in *Progressive Architecture* 53 (September 1972): 104–7. Translations of French-source texts are by the editor.

the cultural institutions of this country. For example, a widely circulated book such as *Building Canada: An Architectural History of Canadian Life*, published in 1966, restates the commonly held opinion that since the 1850s "in the French sections of [Quebec's] cities and in its countryside appeared a hideous assemblage of structures that belong to no conceivable architectural tradition whatever."[2]

To illustrate this observation, the author Alan Gowans shows a photograph of a 1920s house built in Saint-Canut.[3] What one sees in the photograph is a good example of a typical house found throughout Quebec. The house hides behind a stylized pediment, a simulacrum of neoclassical composition. A wood-frame structure (the standard construction system widely used in Quebec), its exterior cladding is made of mass-produced material; a gas pump adorns the foreground of the image like a totem to the new age of mass transport. Taken as a whole, the picture describes in very real terms the ingenuity of people and their capacity to adapt to the new conditions of architecture. The author, incapable of seeing this, resorts to ridicule.

If one turns to reality and looks at the villages, towns, and urban centres of the different regions of Quebec, one finds a built environment rich in form and in organization. This reality is expressive in and of itself. One finds elements of a genuine contemporary architecture as interesting and as real as one would find anywhere.

Here then are the two dimensions of architecture in Quebec: the first is architecture as an institutionalized system, limited by aesthetic prejudice and by an elitist and traditional ideology; the second is an authentic architecture born of real things and rooted in people's lives. At the very least, it can be said that institutionalized architecture in its present form has lost all meaning. The study which follows sketches out the contours of a new way of looking at architecture in Quebec and seeks to locate the sources of recent trends.

25.1 House and store in Saint-Canut, Quebec. Reproduced from Alan Gowans , *Looking at Architecture in Canada*.

The task is not an easy one. One has to trace the cultural identity of architecture as a changing system of ideas then link it to the changing identity of the Quebec people and their place in North America.

Because architecture is a reflection of the state of physical things, concrete examples best illustrate the situation in which architecture finds itself. Two examples demonstate this clearly.

First, the house of an architect, built at the beginning of the 1960s in the Laurentians, north of Montreal. This house was not only included but emphasized in the publication *Architecture contemporaine au Canada français*:[4] it's the only house illustrated and described in detail in the chapter on houses; it even appears on the cover. The house is carefully composed on a biaxial plan. Each part is controlled and forms part of a formal design plan. Its style – a sort of neo-Palladian – can be linked to the houses of Walter Gropius and Marcel Breuer built in New England in the 1940s and 1950s, and related to the tastes of the Museum of Modern Art in New York, modified and formalized by its curator of architecture Philip Johnson. At the end of the 1950s, this architectural language can readily be

ABOVE | 25.2 The house of an architect, principal facade: neoclassical adaptation of an aesthetic myth.

BELOW | 25.3 The house of an unknown person, principal facade: the real world.

found in the villas that many American architects were building for their rich clients. One of the best examples is the house of I.M. Pei – another house built by an architect for himself.

The interest of this kind of architecture lies in its judicious composition of each space and the relationship of that space to the rest of the house. Yet, in the Trudeau house the composition gets lost in ambiguity, lost in a confusion between the importance of living spaces relative to service spaces, the whole wrapped in a traditional package. The crossing of the axis is found at the intersection of two narrow service corridors, and the main living spaces are dispersed and separated one from the other by secondary corridors. One could simply write off this house as bad architecture, were it not for the obvious care and wilful effort found in the design, an effort that recalls the ambiguity of other well-known contemporary buildings such as the Quebec Pavilion at Expo 67 or the Grand Théâtre de Québec.

This ambiguity is heightened in the house's interior by a clutter of objects that inhabit the space: the impulsive touches of bright red, the smooth surfaces of the handmade *objets d'art* that make up a fetishistic *mise en scène* that stands in for human presence. The real world is carefully masked. Hand-crafted wooden surfaces carefully imitate machined finishes. The only way to get to the house is by car, but every sign of the presence of a car has been carefully camouflaged. The axes of the house are extended into the landscape by terraced lawns and field-stone-paved paths. The site is detached from its environment and modified so as to be integrated into the geometry of the composition. The house seems to be in temporal and spatial limbo, frozen in the mind of its creator. In a similar vein, the American critic Edmund Wilson comments on the fiction of Anne Hébert, who "take[s] us into the *maison seigneurales* ... And we are partly in a realm of dream ... These old line French Canadians in their cultural enclave on the North American continent do not always quite know where they are."[5]

The second house is located in the same area as the first. It dates from almost exactly the same time and uses the same kind of wood-frame construction. But there the resemblance stops. This house is truly integrated into the world which surrounds it. It is obviously not included in the publication on *Architecture contemporaine au Canada français*; it was found on the side of the road. A classic 1950s Detroit model Chevrolet is parked in front of the house.

The axis of the driveway follows the line of least resistance as traced by a car exiting the road at an average speed of forty miles an hour.

This house is built entirely of standardized, readily available materials. Those "natural" materials used as cladding are synthetic, the products of a highly complex industrial manufacturing process. Prefinished, they require little or no maintenance: corrugated galvanized metal roof, imitation slate shingles made of bitumen and gravel, dyed, pre-cut wood, pre-fabricated aluminum doors and windows. The aesthetic significance of the exterior cladding merits a detailed semantic analysis: a 3/8" thickness of bitumen imitates a 2" thickness of concrete "stone" which in turn imitates a natural stone cladding typically used in single-family houses in the American midwest. Aluminum doors lean up against one side of the building like interchangeable parts. A wooden pole sticks up above the roofline for electric and phone wires; a chimney supports the TV antenna. The presence of people is obvious: a clothesline flies the flags of daily combat. It is very much part of its setting; clearing and excavation of the surrounding terrain were kept to a minimum. The house is specific to its occupants and to its place, even if there are identical houses throughout Quebec.

Here we have two houses, both of which are examples of architecture. To determine what constitutes architecture requires an approach with no hierarchy in mind, no preconceived desire to find a monument, no classification – an approach that would consider both these houses as important historical events.

The first house revives the past by cloaking itself in a modern vocabulary. It is revealed as formal and isolated, recalling the language of aesthetic myth. There is in architecture of the house a tentative attempt to adapt to a new world, but the house cannot free itself from the past, fettered as it is to traditional barriers that have lost meaning, and ultimately to uncertainty, which asserts itself as an obsessive and authoritarian formalism. As an object classified to be architecture by the cultural establishment, the first house reflects the bias of architecture as an institutionalized, traditional system, whereas the second house is anonymous or, at best, "popular."

Looked at in another way, the existence of the first house depends upon the ownership of surplus resources and the ability to hire people who will build it and maintain its artifactual existence: the wood finishes have to be hand polished, the scrub bush has to be kept from returning to the manicured lawns. The second house clearly reflects the condition of those who have to struggle to house themselves with a minimum of resources. The formal idioms of this second house are much more common in Quebec. Recognizing this house as architecture takes traditional architecture out of its narrow confines in a search for a logic of the present.

The idea here is that the source of contemporary architecture in Quebec is to be found in popular architecture and in a way of building that has defined the relationship between people and the built form that they inhabit.

The historian Ramsay Traquair, in his book *The Old Architecture of Quebec,* notes that "Old Quebec is at its best in the cottage, the manor and the parish church. There were the work of the people, unassisted by academic architects and passed entirely unnoticed at the time of their creation."[6] What has to be done then is to retrace the evolution of the "work of the people" up until the 1960s.

The "work of the people" can be found in descriptions of the earliest structures in Quebec. Gérard Morisset, historian and former director of the Musée de Québec, describes it as follows: "One has but to examine our past architecture … where stone and wood are combined with the precise experimental knowledge of the properties of each material … a simple plan, rational and adapted to what human society

holds … it's truly the spirit of the Romanesque style that one detects in these naked walls."[7] What Morisset meant, as summarized by Alan Gowans, was that the architecture of New France "not merely looked medieval, it *was* an integral expression of the medieval tradition in Western architecture."[8]

What does "an integral expression of the medieval tradition" mean in the context of Quebec architecture? A tradition refers to an attitude towards building, an attitude rooted in an innate response to the need for the organization of physical space and conditioned by the resources available. The term "medieval" is an invention of the historian who, according to Panofsky, "cannot help dividing his material into 'periods.'"[9] This is, in effect, the attitude towards building during the medieval period of history that gave rise to the significant architecture of that era. But its expression, more communal than personal, is rooted in popular architecture. It is born of the experience of the site and the hands of the workers – the artisan, the labourer, and the builder.[10] This attitude towards building extends from the western Mediterranean to the North Sea; it could be said to have both preceded and continued after the medieval period. It is evident in pre-feudal architecture and persists into the twentieth century in certain remote regions of Western Europe as well as Quebec. In Quebec, as Traquair points out, this building tradition was "isolated for so long that it struck strong roots of its own."[11] The ferment of its expression can be seen in the "variety and contrariety of Romanesque which ranges from the planar simplicity of the Hirsau school and the severe structuralism of Normandy and England to the rich proto-classicism of southern France and Italy."[12] In Quebec, this tradition is evident in everything from the crude houses of the first settlers to the wave of neoclassicism that arrived from England in the eighteenth century and is the source of a good number of nineteenth-century proto-modern buildings.

Gowans recognizes three characteristics of this tradition. They are somewhat superficial and often repeated in studies on medieval architecture, but they suffice here to demonstrate the relationship to the equally superficial polemics of certain works on modern architecture. First, he points out "an additive principle in composition" of the buildings, meaning an organization of form that is both open and cumulative; second, the "frank expression of structure"; and finally, the "natural expression of materials."[13] These characteristics are found in the pioneer experience of early Quebec settlement and the period of isolation which followed, tempered by a "functional simplification and egalitarian standardization."[14] Terms such as these played an important role in forming the ideology of the modernist movement in architecture which developed in Europe at the beginning of this century.

In Quebec, it is this tradition that is brought to bear on the new problems of physical organization which appear at the end of the nineteenth century. One can follow this thread of continuity from the example of a primitive settler's house of the seventeenth century in Laprairie,

LEFT | 25.4 Maison Hector Brossard built at the end of the seventeenth century in Laprairie.

RIGHT | 25.5 Du Petit-Champlain Street in Quebec City, around 1890.

through to the eighteenth-century houses on Petit-Champlain Street in Quebec City, and the nineteenth-century commercial building in Montreal, prototype of the future glass-clad office building now such a familiar part of the urban landscape.* All these buildings have a persistent quality of rudimentary beauty. Looking at them now, they almost seem like facts of nature rather than objects of architecture.

To clarify these general observations, it is useful to look at some concrete examples. In 1912, Grain Elevator No. 2 was built in the port of Montreal by the Chicago firm

* Editor's note: In the English manuscript found in Charney's archive, the author used the Manoir Mauvide-Genest, Ile d'Orléans, as the first example and the Séminaire de Québec as the second example.

25.6 415–419 Des Récollets Street, Montreal.

John S. Metcalf Co. It was a terminal elevator in a system of grain transportation equipped for the latest methods for transferring grain from trains to ocean-going ships. The internal system of grain movement in the elevator was totally mechanized. The linear handling systems required a honeycomb configuration inside the vertical drums of the silos, equipped on top and bottom with conveyor belts linked by bucket lifts and extending out to the ships' berths by means of telescoping arms and mobile towers. The dominant impression was that of a simple, volu-minous cluster of concrete silos, bloated storage tubes at the end of a system in movement.[15]

The elevator was built by local labour using the most advanced techniques of steel and concrete construction available, which had been developed by Metcalf and other engineering and construction firms over a period of forty years. Experiments in the design of silos and eleva-tors, the names of important inventors like Max Toltz, different patented construction systems like Metcalf's (the square steel silo diagon-ally reinforced that closely resembles current three-dimensional structures), the mobile forms of poured concrete construction: all this was published in specialized books and periodicals of the era. For example, the 1911 publication of *The Design of Walls, Bins and Grain Elevators*[16] was its eleventh edition. The book gives a detailed description of the Montreal grain elevators and of research done on reinforced concrete silos erected in Montreal before the end of the last century. A photograph of Grain Elevator No. 2 under construction clearly shows its steel and concrete components and the electric conduits running along the surface of the equipment. Marché Bonsecours is visible in the background; built only a half-century before the elevator, it is separated from it conceptually by the irreversible conditions of a new age.

A photograph of the same elevator, taken a few weeks earlier when the extension of the left-hand section of the silos was not yet complete, was used by Le Corbusier in his important work *Vers une architecture* in 1923.* It appears in the

* Editor's note: The image used by Le Corbusier is the same one that Walter Gropius published in his essay "Die Entwicklung moderner Industriebaukunst" in *Die Kunst in Industrie und Handel. Jahrbuch der deustchen Werkbundes 1913* (Jena: Eugen Diederichs, 1913), n.p. Charney's source might have been *Old and New Montreal* (Montreal: International Press Syndicate, 1913), n.p. See the intro-duction by Jean-Louis Cohen in Le Corbusier, *Toward an Architecture*, trans. John Goodman (Los Angeles: Getty Research Institute, ca. 2007), 8.

section "Three Reminders to Architects – First Reminder: Volume," on the page opposite his famous definition: "Architecture is the masterly, correct and magnificent play of masses brought together in light."[17] In the image used in *Vers une architecture*, Marché Bonsecours has been carefully removed. The volume of the grain elevator is isolated and has no scale. Separated from its surroundings, it appears to be sitting on the edge of a vast plain in a mythological America. The deification of the machine is further emphasized by the lack of identification of either the builder or the location.* Moreover, the fact that the left section is incomplete means that the central section reads as perfectly symmetrical. It is clear that the silo is included as an example of heroic dimension. In the text which accompanies the photograph, Le Corbusier links the grain elevators to other monuments like the Temple at Luxor as similar elementary geometric volumes – a Platonic vision of the perfect cylin-

* Editor's note: The caption in *Vers une architecture* mentions that Elevator No. 2 was situated in the United States.

LEFT | 25.7 Port of Montreal, silos and Grain Elevator No. 2, 1912.

RIGHT | 25.8 Grain Elevator No. 2, 1912. Reproduced from Le Corbusier, *Vers une architecture*, 1923.

der and the perfect cube, direct from Cézanne via cubism.

The interest in the grain elevators is first and foremost formal. They hold out the promise of a new heroic architecture that has yet to emerge. They are not studied as functional machines or as organizational systems. Fundamentally, Le Corbusier looks at them as someone else would have looked at Marché Bonsecours; in both cases a certain proto-classicism is hidden behind the formal exterior appearance. The reader certainly feels on familiar ground when, in a later essay in the book, Greek temples at Paestum and the Parthenon appear. The formal image of the silos and the grain elevators had a considerable influence on the development of modern architecture. This influence was assimilated, stylized, and propagated by Bruno Taut and others as part of the "international style."* As a formal style, modern architecture was easy to accept and readily exportable, requiring little change in the existing conception of architecture as a cultural system.

It was the elements of this style that came to Quebec later in the 1930s, imported and supported by a small architectural intelligentsia. The architect Marcel Parizeau admired the grain elevators on his return from France in 1933.[18] Their smooth concrete surfaces certainly played a role in the creation of the typical Outremont bourgeois house like the Larocque house built in 1937 (see Fig. 32.6), but the grain elevators had little or no impact on its fundamental design. Even though certain Montreal architects worked in the offices of the builders and engineers responsible for the grain elevators, the structures had very little influence on the practice of architecture. It was only thirty years later that the conditions necessary for change emerged. Prior to that point, the elevators were at best identified with an aesthetic ideal rather than with the underlying conditions of a modern attitude which could have been found *sur place*.

To understand the evolution of an authentic modern architecture in Quebec in the latter half of the nineteenth century and the first half of the twentieth, one has to look to the streets. The changes which happened during this period happened outside of academic and official architecture. Not only is the literature about what was recognized as works of architecture practically non-existent, the very definition of architecture – and this was true even recently – was very narrow, so much so that there is almost no documentation of this period apart from certain rare studies. An interesting exception is the study of the evolution of Montreal housing by the geographer Raymond Tanghé.†

What one would look for in the streets were forerunners of some of the major themes of the twentieth century. These examples can be divided into two categories. The first deals with the structure of physical organization. One can list in this first category the rural settlement patterns that influenced the urban development that followed. The most common form was linear and cumulative, extending the village with its cluster of church buildings along a river, along a road, along a *rang* from which would emanate the narrow-fronted long lots dividing the land from the edge of the river to the edge of the forest. There are other examples in the dominant form of the street and in the collective form of housing settlement.

The second category includes examples that respond in a new way to new problems, examples that are principally found in Montreal. They are specific responses to particular problems posed by urgent physical needs – the equipment necessary for the rapid growth of Montreal as the commercial and industrial centre of Quebec and eastern Canada. These examples consist essentially of commercial and industrial structures like the grain elevators, housing for a growing population of workers emigrating from rural areas, and the structure of the expanding city itself.

The rapid growth in the last half of the twentieth century was the first large-scale expansion of Montreal. Urbanization tended to follow the orthogonal grid of streets established by the long, narrow lots with some of the roads and *rangs* becoming the principal arteries. Housing filled these streets with the brick facades of stacked flats two and three storeys high. A relatively high density – 200 people per acre – developed. The street was extended to the far end of the lots by passing through a first row of

* Editor's note: Bruno Taut, *Modern Architecture* (London: The Studio, 1929).

† Editor's note: Raymond Tanghé, *Géographie humaine de Montréal* (Montreal: Librairie d'Action canadienne-française, 1928).

flats via a *porte-cochère* to a second row of flats inside. The density was mitigated by a fabric of courtyards and common spaces. The brick cladding of the walls, the wood construction, the flat "Montreal roof" suitable for drainage, the very basic interiors all formed a functional expression that was both utilitarian and human and a direct consequence of the Quebec tradition.[19]

The loft building with its column-free floor space appeared at the same time as secondary industry. There are many excellent examples of this building type in Montreal: an open plan allows for different layouts, large windows throughout, an uncompromising example of utility. (See Fig. 25.6.) Standardized fenestration and wood-frame construction, as well as the use of cast-iron facades found in many of these examples demonstrate the introduction of serial production and the organization of buildings as a series of components. For example, a Trois-Rivières factory was producing the Siegwert system of precast reinforced concrete parts as of 1910.

The heroic scale of industrial buildings at the start of the twentieth century and the use of new construction techniques can be seen in buildings such as the Canada Cement Company's plant in Pointe-aux-Trembles. As in the case of silos and the grain elevators, the large-scale mass of the enclosing volumes is articulated by the diagonals of the conveyors, by the thin webs of steel framing, and by the lines of rails. This is the raw material for an image of an urban form of the future as seen in the work of the constructivists, for example, or the work of the futurist Sant' Elia. The Armstrong Whitworth plant in Longueuil is another excellent example, as is the unloading facility for Dominion Coal, with its battery of mobile and telescoping cranes.

Two important buildings of this period are to be found on Saint-Denis Street and on St Lawrence Boulevard at the corner of Sherbrooke Street, both built of reinforced concrete at the beginning of this century. The concrete

25.9 Mass housing in Montreal at the end of the nineteenth century. To make the conceptual link with the development of modern architecture in Europe, historians have tried to trace the evolution of functional architecture – the simple brick-walled structures – in North America. This tradition produced a large part of Montreal housing at the end of the nineteenth century.

structure, the slender, arched girders, and the sinuously cantilevered balconies illustrate a conscious effort to use the strength of a new material in the design of a building and to articulate an authentic expression of this plastic and composite material typical of avant-garde materials introduced later in the century.

These examples portray real solutions to architectural problems which many of the works of the modern movement seem to engage only superficially. As Colin Rowe remarked about Chicago architecture of the same period, "The architecture was there, it didn't have to be."[20] However, the presence of these buildings had no effect on the official and institutionalized establishment architecture of Quebec. Its commitment was elsewhere, completely preoccupied

by supplying the new merchant class with all the trappings appropriate to its new-found wealth. The content of this new work would only become evident much later, after a transformation of the identity of architecture and of the architect.

In Quebec, this transformation of architecture and of the architect can be divided into four phases. Each of these phases has a certain unity and is intrinsically analogous to a phase of social and political transformation of the country. Each phase overlaps with the development of the next, some elements persisting, while a general change happens in the substance of mainstream architecture.

The first phase corresponds to the original popular tradition with its sense of collective form born of construction experience and its predisposition to the proto-classical. It is well substantiated that the history of this early tradition is the basis for the history of architecture in Quebec. As an attitude towards physical

LEFT | 25.10 Multi-family housing, reinforced concrete structure, Saint-Denis Street, Montreal.

RIGHT | 25.11 Building at 2 Sherbrooke Street West, Montreal. The multi-functional layout, the regrouping of housing, commercial, and industrial activities, an elevator, and construction entirely of reinforced concrete characterize a building that is important in the modern architecture of Quebec.

organization of a place, this tradition persisted well into the twentieth century and is at the core of an authentic response to the need for architecture to evolve in Quebec.

The second phase began in the eighteenth century with the first attempts to shape an autonomous architectural experience separate from that of construction in itself, as evidenced in the use of the baroque style by the Jesuits for their churches. This phase is marked by a first schism between popular architecture, on the one hand, and an elitist architecture dominated by a succession of stylistic fashions, on the other. Iconographic constraints were imposed on building forms according to an aesthetic myth promulgated by a cultural elite. One has only to look at the neo-Gothic fetishism of Église Notre-Dame built in 1829 – a Carpenter's Gothic executed in stone, or the miniature pantheon of the 1846 Bank of Montreal, or even the grotesque classical motifs of the Montreal Museum of Fine Arts – an example of pure and unadulterated reactionary style.

This last example illustrates a second split that happens towards the end of the nineteenth century between a building's function and its image. New functions imposed changes in use, which, inevitably, imposed a new way of designing. However, despite this trend towards change, there are very few images to refer to. This is particularly true in the Montreal suburbs built at the beginning of the twentieth century, like the new city of Maisonneuve. The need for new kinds of urban equipment, such as laboratories to analyse water or milk, was translated into the familiar forms of public buildings like the City Hall, the Post Office, the public baths – veritable pastiches of neoclassic elements – and a public market, Marché Maisonneuve, of the purest French Victorian.

Those buildings that didn't figure as part of the stylistic consensus of the elite were relegated to the category of "popular architecture," of questionable and secondary significance. The profession of architecture was seen in this situation as both a discipline and an art – but it was also limited to the use to which the elite chose to put it and by the profession which identified with that elite. Architecture, as defined by the conditions of this second phase, was therefore distanced from the lives of the majority of Québécois by three different factors: it was conceived in the image of an elite, it was surrounded by a predominantly anglophone culture, and it was situated in a country implicitly provincial in its thinking. As Quebec was a relatively poor country with a practically non-existent elite, the majority of important buildings in this phase were built in the tradition of popular architecture. This tradition continued to serve to support the stylistic preoccupations of official architecture "without affecting the continuity of the tradition at all."[21] It was the strength of this popular tradition that gave architecture whatever substance it possessed.

In this phase, modern architecture was simply the latest and most recent in a list of styles. Morriset talks about "the Modern style... the prerogative of a small group of architects and connoisseurs," giving as examples the Université de Montréal by Ernest Cormier (1925) and the Larocque house in Outremont by Marcel Parizeau (1937). In both cases, the semblance of clarity in the modern style is betrayed by confused planning and by poor integration of the building to its site. Morisset seems to struggle with this apparent contradiction. On the one hand, the iconography of modernism presents an image that speaks boldly of a new, rational way of life: a university that will be a centre for learning and will breathe new life into the closed existence of the Quebec people, a home for family life benefiting from the advantages of the latest technology. On the other hand, the images lie to us. Spring has not come. The university is, in fact, a monolithic block isolated like a fortified castle. The house is typical of the bourgeois houses of Outremont. However,

Morisset recognizes the potential for authenticity of modern architecture when he says, about this house and other similarly "modern" houses, that "they have some of the qualities of our houses of the past."[22] He could have found the link between the two all around him, but, ironically, popular architecture was simply outside of his frame of reference. The "houses of the past," popular as they may have been, were acceptable as long as they were separated by the distance of time and aesthetics. This same attitude is evident in other historians such as Gowans and Traquair.

The eclectic modernist style lived on in adaptations of the work of Le Corbusier and others; undoubtedly more up-to-date with the latest trends thanks to mass communications but essentially disconnected from the human realities of Québécois life.

The third phase starts with the Quiet Revolution at the beginning of the 1960s, whose liberating effects revealed a new phase of national consciousness and a spirit of self-reliance. Some architects started to think about the question of their own identity and of its expression in their work. From that point on, there was no model to follow; they had only to look for an architecture that was appropriate to their immediate conditions and historical situation. The work that follows is sure of itself and has an imposing and essentially North American presence, in marked contrast to that built by architects of the previous century who struggled in a no man's land of borrowed images. Despite its cultural and linguistic originality, it is ironic to note that the strength of the Québécois nationalist expression lies in the depth of its American roots, as in the work of the poets Raoul Duguay or Camille Laverdière and of the singer Robert Charlebois, for example.

One sees in this architecture the landscape and spirit of the first settlers and voyageurs who opened up the North American continent and the "on the road" mystique in which so much of American life is rooted. The sources of this architecture are the same as those which produced the rich heritage of popular architecture elsewhere in North America. In Quebec, these trends are expressed in the rough gesture of anti-urban architecture, nourished by the local landscape. This insistence on naturalism is seen in the use of heavy, rough-cut timber and of walls of rough fieldstone – the walls of the recent Radio-Canada building seem to be an attempt to reconstruct the cliffs of the Plains of Abraham. It is as if architecture were in search of a mythology through which it could relive the history of the country.

In this third phase, the work of the architect Roger D'Astous is particularly significant. At the beginning of his career, he follows the path to Taliesin and to the work of Frank Lloyd Wright. His early work is particularly Wrightian in its motifs, relying heavily on certain well-known idiosyncrasies. His houses and churches constitute a sort of folkloric architecture, built by a folk hero who chopped down the trees, sawed the planks of wood, and cut the stone for his own buildings. In his work, he developed an expression founded in the specific conditions of the project, to which he gives epic, mythological dimension. For example, his houses – contrary to the Trudeau house illustrated earlier – find their strength in the landscape. As in Wright's work, there is an attempt to integrate them into the landscape or even to make them landscapes in their own right. With the Église Notre-Dame-des-Champs in Repentigny, he is fully in the vein of Bruce Goff. His 1967 design for the Château Champlain hotel (see Fig. 15.7), done in collaboration with Pothier, marks the height of D'Astous's career. The expression of the building is utterly urban, integrated into its milieu, while clearly affirming its presence. This is not the case for its immediate neighbour, Place du Canada, designed at the same time by the Toronto office of John Parkin, with its empty and anonymous expression, an insignificant copy of those

LEFT | 25.12 Église Notre-Dame-des-Champs, Repentigny, Roger D'Astous, architect, 1963.

RIGHT | 25.13 Église Notre-Dame-de-Fatima, Jonquière, Paul-Marie Côté and Léonce Desgagné, architects, 1963.

American office buildings so beloved by Canadian businessmen.

The search for an expression of identity is evident in the forms of such expressionistic buildings, forms which appear as if sculpted out of raw material by some folk architect and which so offended English-Canadian architectural sensibilities. The work of Paul-Marie Côté in the Chicoutimi region is particularly remarkable and important. The Église Notre-Dame-de-Fatima in Jonquière, the work of Paul-Marie Côté and Léonce Desgagné, a tall concrete cone whose top has been sliced off, looks like an immense Indian teepee set up in the hinterlands of Quebec. Here, again, the experience is a return to the archetypes of the national psyche in response to a need to assimilate the landscape. It could be said that the exaggerated gesture of these buildings is a deliberate attempt to counteract the overwhelming void of the landscape. Edmund Wilson speaks about this impression: "We have by this time in the United States very largely lost the sense of void. But one is aware of it again in Canada – looking out, for example, from the Ile d'Orléans in the St. Lawrence just above Quebec. From a high cliff, the wide smooth river and its flat opposite bank are of a magnitude quite dumbfounding ... such a prospect seems annulling to human assertion."[23]

However, the exaggerated forms of a lot of this work – a particular example is the Caisse Populaire in Saint-Henri by Henri Brillon – are overwhelmed by the aggressiveness of their creation. This last example appears to be some kind of sentimental decoration, a pastiche of the spirit of popular architecture. In the case of Brillon and others, this architecture is an expression of their frustration with a mode of expression which is hesitant, groping, and which

25.14 Caisse populaire Desjardins quartier St-Henri, Henri Brillon architect, 1965.

is contradicted by the very raison d'être of architecture. This highly personal expression may have meaning to Brillon, but the real question is whether it has meaning to others.

This important phase of Quebec architecture must be situated in the context of a national culture in evolution. Frantz Fanon, in his book *The Wretched of the Earth*,[24] talks about the transformation of conscience in an emerging national culture: "The demand for a national culture, the affirmation of the existence of such a culture represent a special battlefield ... giving rise to serious ambiguities ... the artist who has decided to illustrate the truths of the nation turns paradoxically ... toward the past and away from actual events. Enlightened circles are in ecstasies with this 'newer inner truth' which is so well-expressed; but we have the right to ask if this truth is in fact a reality, and if it is not already outworn and, denied, called into ques-

tion by the epoch through which the people are treading out their path toward history."

Even if the work of Quebec architects in this third phase externalizes the expression of a national conscience, it is cut off from the realities of urbanization and mass housing, realities which affect the lives of most people. This expression remains trapped in its nineteenth-century origins with meaning for only a small part of the population. The "Quiet Revolution" as André Langevin and others have remarked, was "that of the Quebec bourgeoisie," born as a class of executives, government officials, and technicians, of which architects are a part, cut off from the life of most people, as subsequent events in Quebec have shown.*

The fourth phase of this evolution of Quebec architecture is very recent and experimental. It represents a shift towards an identity with community and is related to a profound change in the conception of architecture itself. The recent emergence in Quebec of a collective identity tends to expose the ambiguous nature of architecture itself. On the one hand the architect sees that his work should be addressed to people in whose name it is created, while on the other hand he sees that it is not possible to free architecture, as it is presently conceived, from its elitist and repressive origins.

The recent transformation in architecture can best be understood by tracing the evolution of housing. Housing – the creation of the places of everyday life – is central to architecture. The emergence of the problem of mass housing is a turning point in modern architecture and a critical theme of contemporary architecture.

Even though the common image of housing in Quebec is that of the isolated habitant farmhouse in its rural setting, the use of this form "argues the previous existence of towns with

* Editor's note: André Langevin, "La révolution tranquille est celle de la bourgeoisie," *Maclean* 4, no. 6 (June 1964).

streets."[25] The town as an artifact, the street, and the public square shape the configuration of the individual house. For example, Quebec's Civil Code clearly defines *mitoyenneté,* the shared wall that links individual houses and the line that divides community and privacy.

The characteristic collective form of housing developed further in the expanding nineteenth-century towns and cities, particularly Montreal. The organization of dense housing around interior courtyards and on an orthogonal street grid emanated from the original settlement patterns. The mass of the population was thus accommodated in a communal structure of housing that was born separate from establishment architecture and was created by ordinary people making ordinary things. Evidence of this collective sense can be seen in the physical organization of the blocks of worker housing in east end Montreal near Papineau and Ontario streets whose form is reminiscent of Fourier's Phalanstère. It is also attested to by the persistent phenomenon of the tenant: while 60 per cent of the population of the average Canadian city may own their own houses, the opposite is true in most Quebec centres. In Montreal, renters account for more than 80 per cent of the population.

The phenomenon of the tenant exists for many reasons, not the least of which are socio-economic. Because people tend to define housing as a community object, these conditions are part of the relationship between people and their patterns of living; they define an ecology of housing. Housing reflects a way of life. The physical structure of housing, at its best, supports the activities that make up that way of life.

During the 1950s, mass housing in Quebec became a real problem for the architectural establishment. The National Housing Act of 1953 gave the government the means to subsidize the construction of low-income housing, as if such a distinct type exists. An example of such housing is the Habitations Jeanne-Mance, located in the heart of Montreal. Several tall towers stand as isolated islands on a bulldozed lawn; they float in a demolished area of the inner city like some displaced apparition from the London County Council, as inadequate as most foreign aid to underdeveloped countries. Not only do these buildings ignore the local ecology, but they are ultimately imperialistic in their very conception. The Habitations Jeanne-Mance are socially and culturally imperialistic to the extent that the architecture imposed on housing signifies a diminution of the sovereignty of a lesser group: the people who inhabit them.

The existing ecology of the quarter was simply destroyed. People were crowded together in towers completely controlled by the state. Housing of this type – and it is familiar to everyone – responds only partially to people's needs. Even fifteen years later, many housing projects in Montreal, such as the proposed Milton-Park housing project, exploit the ecology of the community in the same way, in the name of "private enterprise," while Habitat 67 does it in the name of a personal vision of the shape of things to come.

In trying to deal with mass housing, architecture remains enclosed in its historical and institutional mould. Architecture tends more towards being the expression of an *idea* of habitation and of a particular object rather than an organization of facts relating to the habitability of a place, facts as simple as the need for a block or a neighbourhood restaurant.

One must draw the parallel between the problematic institutionalization of housing in architecture and the equally problematic institutionalization of socio-economic policies with respect to housing. For example, government policy in Quebec encourages home ownership and construction of single-family dwellings in the suburbs instead of promoting construction of community housing, rehabilitation, co-ownership, and rent control. These priorities are a part of a policy of social and economic acculturation, which, although not explicitly formulated as such, nevertheless achieves the same results.

The Îlots St-Martin housing project designed by the architect Jean Ouellet and commissioned by the Service de l'Habitation of the City of Montreal in 1968, represents a remarkable evolution of sensibilities in relation to the projects mentioned above. Even if it fails from several points of view, its failures are the failures of our time. The indigenous architecture of the neighbourhood was explicitly accepted as relevant, and an attempt was made to respect, understand, and integrate the architectural language of the existing housing. The existing shells of some of the old houses were used. Some motifs such as roof profiles were repeated in the new construction, and the general sense of scale was maintained. However, in order to create the plan of a housing "project," the grid of existing streets was suppressed, and consequently so was any semblance of community coherence. As an architectural product, the cluster of houses was transformed into an object in the form of a housing "project." Before, it was the background to people's lives. Now it has moved to the foreground, denying the same life those people led, as can be witnessed in the rapid deterioration of buildings. Architecture has a long way to go.

Like everywhere else, architecture in Quebec is in a position where it must encompass a diversified field of activities which intervene in the relationship between people and their environment or in the physical structure of the environment itself. These activities also intervene in the development and distribution of resources in society. Consequently, there is a growing recognition that the intervention of architecture is, of necessity, a political act. Each product of architecture tends to be prescriptive in its design; that design tends to be based implicitly on a social and technical model (and either limited or liberated by it) before answering to the needs of society.

In Quebec, as elsewhere, a growing number of concerned architects are engaged in a democratization and growing diversification of their activities; they can be found working with the government, with community organizations, with citizen groups, with industry, and in advocacy planning. Nonetheless, there exists an enormous gap between recognizing the social dimension of architecture and putting it into practice, even if this gap is not always evident. In fact, even when driven by the desire to socialize architecture and to create places in the name of the people, or to defend their interests within existing limitations, design, and planning – processes that produce a building or a plan – these activities still tend to ignore people's needs and experience, thus contradicting that original intention.

Underlying the need for a change in the conception of architecture, one must recognize the shift that has recently emerged in our understanding of man-made systems. This shift is found in the differentiation between "the process of information and the process of energy."[26] One can see, for example, that the organizational system of the physical environment constitutes a *language* of interaction between people and things. In Quebec, we are conscious of the central role of the meaning of street and square in the organization of towns and cities. The problem now lies in developing a valid and relevant understanding of that meaning and the capacity to translate that understanding into coherent physical form: to translate the language of the street or square into a new context, as seen in the enclosed pedestrian system of the "underground" portion of downtown Montreal, in the interior of a new university campus, or in a new neighbourhood.

The understanding of architecture as based solely on the expression of buildings traps it in a limited vision. In downtown Montreal, an element as large as Place Bonaventure is caught in the ambiguity of its architectural rhetoric in that it tries resolutely to make out of its bulk a "building" in the traditional sense, that is to say a singular and isolated object, when its real meaning is as an extension of the city itself, linked to other urban poles.

The use of a thing precedes its meaning. In the case of Place Bonaventure, as with many other buildings in the downtown core, such as Place Ville-Marie, its use as a multi-functional and pluralistic extension of the city is trapped in an obsolete formalism. The meaning resides in the interior of this "public building," which has become the exterior of a public architecture. The conception of this "building" itself as a singular element is only the legal definition of real estate boundaries as interpreted by a developer, and not necessarily a unit of formal expression within a larger urban ensemble.

The physical environment is, in effect, a system of control which can be alienating or empowering. The elaboration of the physical environment is therefore related to controlling that which controls. If architecture is considered to be the elaboration of a physical environment responsive to the needs and expression of people, then it can only be responsive insofar as it is part of their means of understanding and controlling their own destiny.

This means that there are at least two levels of action possible in architecture. The first is at the level of the creation of physical resources (energy) necessary to construct the different places society requires. The second is at the level of expression (information) of individuals or groups using those resources. However, the actions of those working in architecture are almost entirely limited to the second level and are often false representations – an individual of a privileged class creates a thing that resembles a cultural object in the form of a building and presents it as an expression of society as a whole. The Grand Théâtre de Québec is erected in the form of a cultural palace when what is required is a network of cultural facilities accessible to all. We build a Palais de Justice in Montreal as

25.15 The centre of Montreal circa 1967 showing Place du Canada and Place Bonaventure still under construction.

an affirmation of political authority, instead of building a system of justice equitable for all as a network of places using existing facilities, and investing the resources instead in constructive social activities. We still build housing projects in the form of ghettos for the poor, isolated from the rest of society as if afflicted with an illness and kept in quarantine with no means of escape. In 1971, we build an expressway over the Îlots St-Martin and the people have no means of stopping it.

The future of architecture in Quebec, or anywhere for that matter, depends on the resolution of these questions. Technically, we can build almost anything. Solutions lie in a social and cultural evolution where architecture becomes part of the struggle of people to control their own lives. Even the problems of the construction industry are not due principally to the lack of technical knowledge but are caused by a lack of responsiveness in the industry to society's needs.

In Quebec, as elsewhere, all relevant architecture questions the state of architecture itself. And the answers can't be found in any of the usual places. Inevitably, the social condition of the architect as individual in relation to other people is evident. This means that the liberation of the architect depends on the political and social liberation of both the individual and the community. And in Quebec, this means that it depends also on the assertion of a renewed and original Quebec identity.

Unfortunately, the cultural hegemony of traditional architecture still persists. But now, at least, it is more and more of an anachronism than a viable reality.

NOTES

1 Claude Beaulieu, *Architecture contemporaine au Canada français,* Coll. Art, vie et sciences au Canada français (Quebec: Ministère des affaires culturelles, 1969).

2 Alan Gowans, *Building Canada: An Architectural History of Canadian Life* (Toronto: Oxford University Press, 1966), 64.

3 Ibid., figure 74.

4 Beaulieu, *Architecture contemporaine*, 36.

5 Edmund Wilson, *O Canada, An American's Notes on Canadian Culture* (New York: Farrar, Strauss and Giroux, 1965), 123–4.

6 Ramsay Traquair, *The Old Architecture of Quebec* (Toronto: Macmillan Co. of Canada, 1947), 93.

7 Gérard Morisset, *L'architecture en Nouvelle-France* (Quebec: "Coll. Champlain," 1949), 15.

8 Gowans, *Building Canada*, 15.

9 Erwin Panofsky, *Gothic Architecture and Scholasticism* (New York: Meridian Books Edition, 1957), 1.

10 It is interesting to note the analogous theme studied by Michael Polanyi, which supports in large measure the success of the later work about the idea of "tacit knowledge" which is acquired in practice and cannot be expressed otherwise.

11 Traquair, *Old Architecture of Quebec*, 55.

12 Panofsky, *Gothic Architecture*, 3.

13 Gowans, *Building Canada*, 16–17.

14 Ibid., 2.

15 For a detailed interpretation of Montreal's silos and grain elevators, see Melvin Charney, "Grain Elevators Revisted," chapter 18, 169–78, in this volume.

16 Milo Ketchum, *The Design of Walls, Bins and Grain Elevators* (New York: Engineering News Publishers, 1911).

17 Le Corbusier, *Toward an Architecture*, introduction by Jean-Louis Cohen, trans. John Goodman (Los Angeles: Getty Research Institute, ca. 2007), 102.

18 Marie-Alain Couturier, *Marcel Parizeau* (Montréal, l'Arbre, "Art vivant," 1945).

19 See Sigfried Giedeon, *Space, Time and Architecture* (Cambridge: Harvard University Press, 1954), 353–9.

20 Colin Rowe, "Chicago Frame," *Architectural Design* 40 (December 1970): 641–7.

21 Gowans, *Building Canada*, 16.

22 Morisset, *L'architecture en Nouvelle-France*, 118.

23 Wilson, *O Canada*, 57.

24 Frantz Fanon, *The Wretched of the Earth* (New York: Grove Press, 1968), 209–25.

25 Traquair, *Old Architecture of Quebec*, 52.

26 Geoffrey Vickers, *Value Systems and Social Processes* (London: Tavistock, 1968), 169.

Low-Income Housing into the 70s with Sewer Pipes and Subsidized Speculation*

While expenditure on low-income housing has increased during the past decade, deprivation in housing has become more and more evident to people.

Some of the endemic problems in housing are clouded by the persistence of a narrow conception of technology; others are obscured by fundamental contradictions in distribution and production.

Instant Sewer-Pipe Housing

Both instances can be cited as a spontaneous, popular development of a "soft" use of hardware for housing. The pipes provide instant, mobile, factory-produced, cross-ventilated space cells, easily maintained by regular flush-outs. And not only is the living space encapsulized in a "secondary use technology," but the very means of livelihood of some of the inhabitants is found in recycling the garbage of their society.

* From *Architectural Design* 43 (January 1972): 7–8.

In other words, in housing, people at the bottom of the social heap are by the very circumstances of their lives out in the frontlines of technology. As "victims" of society, they are virtually forced to live in the essence of its most advanced technology; they are the involuntary objects of the latest, benign solutions. Be they refugees in Calcutta sheltered in concrete sewer pipes, or workers in the U.S. housed in prepackaged mobile homes. In the U.S., by the end of 1969, the production of mobile homes dominated the low-cost housing market, representing 48 per cent of all housing units, and 94 per cent of all housing under $15,000.

That the problem of adequate housing is difficult to resolve, then, is not entirely due to the lack of available technology, nor to the resistance of people at the receiving end, but rather to other reasons which prevent available technology from being used effectively.

The experience of the last decade has shown us that technological innovation in low-income housing – limited to the transfer of "know-how" only to the production, to the form of housing,

CLOCKWISE FROM TOP LEFT

26.1 Sewer pipe housing in the Merak Park district of Jakarta. Sewer pipes, imported from France several years ago, and never installed, are used as the sleeping quarters in an open lot enclosed by a barbed wire. Some of the people who live here collect tin cans or used paper for sale; others gather brick from building sites and pound them into a fine dust for resale to construction concerns who turn the powder back into bricks.

26.2 A sewer pipe suburb – the Salt Lake refugee camp on the edge of Calcutta Airport.

26.3 East Pakistani refugees find a makeshift home in concrete pipes at a camp in Calcutta. "Garbage housing" may be a catchy title for an essay, but instant sewer pipe housing is where things are at, along with the misery of the people that goes with it. In all fairness, Yona Friedman must be cited as having first proposed pipe housing to ease a shortage in Israel, but no one wanted to live in pipes in the "promised land."

or to mechanisms of behavioural control in housing – affects, at best, the improved packaging of poverty, stabilizing housing while the poor remain locked into their condition.

It is now more evident that effective modifications depend on institutional innovation in the process of producing houses committed to the redistribution of resources and the control of resources in society. And as long as this is glossed over, low-income housing programs, no matter how efficient, simply remain ineffective.

Operation Breakthrough

Failure in low-income housing is not restricted to countries such as India and Indonesia. The processes of housing the "underdeveloped" sectors of the North American population operate with similar results.

In the U.S., in 1968, the enactment of the Omnibus Housing Act was, in the words of President Johnson, "the Magna Carta of housing." The Nixon administration inherited the law a few months after it was passed.

The emphasis of the law was on production. The theory was that if enough houses were built, a greater supply at a cheaper price would be

26.4 Sign at Klein Mobile Homes on Dort Highway in Flint, Michigan during the 1970s strike in the nearby General Motors plant. The real mobility of a mobile home is found in its low downpayment and trade-in liquidity. This sign however attracted few customers during the strike.

available to all. The law called for the construction of 26 million units over a ten-year period, including 6 million subsidized units for low- and moderate-income groups.

By the end of 1970, the number of subsidized unit-starts increased from 100,000 in 1967 to 470,000, out of a total of 1.16 million housing-starts. Much of this housing was built under the provisions of Section 235 of the 1968 Act, under which people of limited means could buy homes, with the government paying up to one per cent of the interest cost on each buyer's mortgage.

At the same time, in order to innovate house building, Operation Breakthrough was begun in 1969. The operation of Breakthrough is well known. Although the program is lagging, it did create an interest in housing in the industrial sector through subsidies to firms. Construction of the first prototype units was started in May 1971, by ITT Levitt Inc., who is, ironically, the nation's largest housebuilder and a subsidiary of a large and wealthy multinational corporation, hardly in need of a subsidy.

However, construction remains the most inflation-prone sector of the economy. The disproportionate rising cost of housing, irrespective of production methods, is such that any type of housing would have to be subsidized in order to bring it within the reach of a growing number of people who now find themselves in the low-income housing category. The housing produced under Section 235 during the last two years provides a closer measure than "Breakthrough" of where things are at.

Much of the housing built under 235 is in trouble. Housebuilders rushed to cash in on the enormous market that they could tap through subsidy programs; the slogan for builders during 1970 was "stay alive with 235." What has disturbed housing officials was that the builders were served handsomely by the subsidies – profits were high and risks minimal – while consumers were at the short end of the arrangement.

26.5 New houses on Staten Island, New York. Recent housing at the edge of what is regarded as the last frontier for new development within the city limits of New York. As one city official put it: "On Staten Island we have seen little houses marching down towards the shore like locusts ... back to back on sterile streets." Obviously, he has not had the message from Robert Venturi, nor learned from Levittown. Note the structural similarities in the organization of suburban housing in figures 26.3 and 26.5.

The Banking and Currency Committee of the Congress held extensive hearings in 1971, and found rows of small houses resembling a "company town or Mississippi plantation." It turned up evidence of shoddy construction, overpricing, and little regard for the availability of community facilities. In many instances, the thirty-year guaranteed mortgages with high interest rates would long outlive the houses they cover.

The problems, however, go much deeper. The Federal Housing Administration which oversees subsidy commitments is, by long tradition, oriented to market interest rather than to any considerations of housing needs or social priorities. It operates a state-subsidized market run according to private priorities, including "Operation Breakthrough."

These conditions are not unique to the U.S. Canada is very adept at borrowing U.S. failures. In the last two years, the housebuilding industry in Canada demonstrated the limitations of its capabilities when called upon by the government, through the agency of the Central Mortgage and Housing Corporation, to produce low-income housing under a special subsidy program.

The failure of the 1970 Special $200 Million Low-Cost Innovative Housing Programme did not reach the front pages of newspapers as did the guerilla activities of the Front de Libération du Québec in Quebec. But the widespread politicization of the large number of families across the country who could not afford any of the so-called low-income housing, or were caught in an ownership trap of expensive and inadequate housing, may have as serious a long-term and widespread effect on the future of the country as the more visible terrorist actions.

The response of the industry to the government's initiatives – low-interest money, 90 per cent financing of projects, easing of codes – was to produce the same kind of housing it produced over the last decade, only making it cheaper by such innovations as the use of poorly serviced marginal suburban sites isolated from community facilities, poor construction, and lower space standards. Risks were minimal to the builders – CMHC guaranteed the sale of the units in several cases – and profits were high. The per-square-foot cost was higher than similar housing on the market, and monthly payments of buyers were at 30 to 50 per cent of their incomes, if "low-income" goals of the Programme were respected.

In the words of the government, the Special Programme set a "new course ... for involvement

with the private market." This involvement resulted in the financing of the ongoing operations of the larger builder-developers who had abdicated low-income housing in the 1950s when they found that there was no easy money to be made without subsidies. The Programme not only caught the industry with its inadequate reflexes well exposed, but the government was found to be right up there with them, totally oriented to the needs of private builders at the expense of the low-income sector.

At the time of this writing, a similar program for low-income housing has been announced for 1971–72.

The rhetoric of these low-income housing programs is improving from year to year. But the programs remain meaningless as long as they only toy with the mechanisms of the distribution of housing. The control of housing distribution should serve both to bring housing to those who most need it, and to rationalize markets for the builders – the minimum requirements for effective social policy.

26.6 Multi-unit expediency – court housing built in 1970 on the outskirts of Ottawa, Canada. Given the squeeze of higher costs for serviced land, the typical builders of single-family-detached houses were able to effect a jump from 4 to 18 units per acre, while capitalizing on their high degree of on-site mechanization and coordination of sub-trades. The main problem according to these builders was the lack of appropriate models to follow in the organization of the housing.

Montréal

plus
ou moins?

plus
or minus?

27

Montreal ... More or Less[*]

This exhibition is about Montreal and the people who live in it. It attempts to focus on the physical qualities of Montreal, and make visible, through images and information, the meaning of the city in the minds of most of its people.

The understanding that each one of us has of the physical presence of this city is blurred and diffused by what can only be called the realities of living in Montreal.

These realities can perhaps be described with numbers. There are 2,720,413 people in the Montreal region at present. It is the urban centre of Quebec, and the largest urban centre in Canada, followed, in size, by Toronto with a population of 2,609,638 and Vancouver with 1,071,081.

Furthermore, Montreal has the highest overall population density of any city in Canada at 9,300 people per square mile; Toronto has 8,200 and Vancouver 6,000. It has a high density in the centre of the city, 26,000 people per square mile, which unlike that of other cities, has been

increasing in recent years. It also has fewer cars per capita of total population than other comparable cities; Montreal 0.24, Toronto 0.34, and Vancouver 0.34.

But these numbers only hint at the quality of a place different from any other city in Canada. They can hardly suggest the presence of a city unique in North America.

The character of this city is evident in our day-to-day experience of it.

Unlike most cities in North America, the place still works for some of its inhabitants. They live here by choice, and with pride. It has a dense, thriving urban and cosmopolitan centre. Its streets are alive with people. People crowd the streets at the first warmth of spring. In winter, public streets are found inside "buildings," and in the Metro. This is in contrast to the decaying cores and police reconstructions found at the heart of most other cities in this continent. The fabric of Montreal still retains traces of an urban tradition which most of these other cities never possessed in the first place; they began as small settlements that later became overgrown villages that merged into sprawling suburban

[*] From *Montreal Plus or Minus* (Montreal: Montreal Museum of Fine Arts, 1972).

megalopolis, betraying a general mistrust of city life – conditions alien to the origins of Montreal.

But things are changing. Montreal is now at a turning point in the history of its development.

Again statistics may suggest some underlying causes, such as a report by the Quebec Union of Municipalities on Montreal's unemployment index. In the period from 1961 to 1970, Montreal had a 21.3 increase in jobs, while Toronto's increase was 35.1. This poor performance happened despite the frenetic activity associated with Expo 67, and the rhetoric of the civic administration. It happened during a decade in which Toronto has been consolidating its role as the economic centre of Eastern Canada. The population of Toronto is now expected to exceed Montreal's by the end of 1974.

For most people in Montreal, this change is perceived in the day-to-day alteration of the city. The minimal, basic conditions which made life somewhat better than tolerable – the semblance of a decent way of earning a living, dignified parks, and clean air – can no longer be taken for granted.

The blight which has invaded so many other cities, deadening their streets, has now attacked Montreal. To many of us who live here, it seems as if the city is being used by some irrational force, reflected in the way we feel about our lives.

We all have our personal examples: it is seen in the debris of empty lots of a once-thriving Faubourg de la Mélasse along Lagauchetière Street – one of the city's oldest and most picturesque – destroyed to make way for the TV studios and offices of the Canadian Broadcasting Corporation. The new building uses only part of the site, and appears as an unpenetrable stone fortress needlessly protecting a glistening office tower.

It is seen in the construction of the Trans-Canada Expressway through the centre of the city, destroying it in its path. Given present levels of air pollution, the building of this roadway can only be looked at in terms of genocide.

It is also seen in such small, but significant, signs as the deterioration of a neighbourhood one passes everyday on the way to work; the disappearance of a familiar house; the growing gaps between buildings filled with abandoned automobiles; the building of wide, empty, and senseless boulevards; the construction of a viaduct over Mile-End above pathetic houses crumbling in a street where one spent one's childhood; the recent disappearance of Octave Crémazie's statue from its old resting place in Carré Saint-Louis, and its reappearance at a plastic suburban shopping centre, under the concrete pillars of an elevated highway.

Consider the city's housing. Montreal is unique in that it is a city of tenants. Over 70 per cent of the people of this city rent their homes. The reverse is true of Toronto and other typical North American cities. Even though many of the reasons for this condition are obviously social and economic, the fact is that the population of this city has evolved a fluid relationship with a thing called a house, moving often, usually on the first of May, while they retain a sense of belonging to and identification with the city. A sense of propriety used to be found in the large body of dense and livable housing built in the late nineteenth century and early twentieth century to the east and north of the centre of the city. This housing is now rapidly deteriorating. The houses have long outlived their value as a market commodity for the absentee landlords.

But people still live there. And they care. Their homes are important to them. By the city's own account, there are at present over 100,000 units of sound, low-cost housing in need of renovation. Yet, Montreal does not have a working rehabilitation program. Rather than promote rehabilitation, multi-family housing, and social forms of housing, government programs have actively encouraged the growth of the suburbs, single-family homes, and individual ownership, counterproductive to conditions in Montreal. Such policies force people out into the suburbs and into a dependency on the TV and auto-mobile for survival, and often an unpleasant job, needed to keep up monthly payments.

Montreal still has a good chance to do something about its future. For some, its assets are found in the fact that Montreal still remains an important financial and industrial centre; six of Canada's twenty largest banks, insurance companies, and financial institutions have their head offices in Montreal, as have twenty-nine of Canada's largest corporations. For others, the value of this city is found in the unique physical qualities that are still strong enough to be built upon and to be redefined in the growth of the urban region. This redefinition may be possible because of the mood of the city in which social options considered heretical in other parts of Canada can be developed here. For example, the Director of Planning for the Montreal Urban Community recently suggested that "One policy decision that could be taken … would be to build housing and turn it over to its occupants, free of charge, under some form of condominium (with the city) … it would give people a greater measure of dignity." Not only would it give them dignity, but it may also give them a stake in the future of a city they care about.

In other words, to realize the potential of Montreal implies a shift in thinking about the planning and management of this city. This shift has been considered to be largely a technical issue. Considerations of the environment, however, cannot be isolated from the people they affect. The physical development of the city cannot be separated from social and cultural issues.

Planning used to consist of relatively small additions to or subtractions from the slowly growing fabric of Montreal. The time element has now been compressed, and the scale of undertakings greatly increased. Projects are large. They are more critical than before. Decisions are no longer easy; they directly affect a great number of people. What matters is who is doing the planning and for whom; city planning has too frequently turned out to be window dressing for the strategies of the powerful. Each intervention has clearly become political in that we now recognize that it involves someone's idea of what Montreal is and what it ought to become. Yet, no mechanisms exist for public involvement or public accountability.

Even though the planning and management of the future city can no longer be comfortably carried on as some enterprise removed from the people, various levels of government were reluctant to participate in this exhibition.

A conscious sense of relatedness among sectors of the population, institutions, and physical form is important in an understanding of the potential of the city. For planners, it is called "integrative planning," the comprehensive planning for the rational use of related parts of the city. In other words, "integrative planning" means that the systems of the city are to be consciously tuned to collective needs of the people, rather than to the exploitation of isolated parts. It says that a "beautiful" city can only be meaningful if we can create "beautiful" lives for its people.

The real subject of the exhibition is the relationship between the physical presence of the city and people's lives. The early destruction of Indian culture and the destruction of housing for the building of a superhighway in 1972, the "housing crises" and the profusion of high-rise apartments, violence and culture, are all interconnected in Montreal.

The material of this exhibition readily shows the ties between physical and social phenomena in this city. The numerous contributors participating in the exhibition expressed this concern in their submissions. Their work sets up this thematic preoccupation, unifying the individual contributions.

The theme is found in the words "Montréal, c'est nous autres." The emphasis is on a public and communal city. On the city that is found

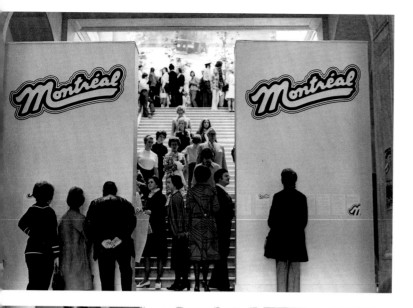

in the streets, in the parks, in the signs, in the graffiti, in the water we drink, and in the lives we lead.

The exhibition tries to look at what is seen in the city and how these things are understood. The perception of things, such as letter boxes, trees, buildings, signs, and taverns, may be different than the reality of the actual object. These differences speak of contradictions in the way people perceive their lives, each other, and their surroundings. For example, the windows along Sainte-Catherine present both a facade of fashion and the dilemma of the lives of men and women in a consumer society. The facades of Saint-Jacques Street, a "Wall Street" of sorts in the minds of Montrealers, no longer house many of the important financial institutions which have moved off either to Toronto or into the invisible quarters of anonymous glass and concrete retreats.

This sense of interaction is also extended to the form of the exhibition itself, and to art as a means of communication. The use of different media, three-dimensional walk-in tableaux, neo-realism paintings ordered by telephone, and multiple images which the visitor to the exhibit can remove from the walls and take home with him, attempt to push art beyond its restrictive, formal limits.

A large part of the material of the exhibition draws upon the popular, visual idioms of Montreal. This may make it legible to a larger segment of the population than a Museum of Fine Arts usually reaches. But, in doing so, one has also to be aware that there is a danger of mystifying the expression of the common everyday language of the city by presenting it in a repressive context.

The least that we can ask of an exhibition on the City of Montreal is that it gives us some

27.2, 27.3, and 27.4 Opening of Montreal Plus or Minus? 11 June 1972, at the Montreal Museum of Fine Arts.

critical account of our condition. The least we can ask of a cultural institution in this city is the possibility and encouragement to illuminate those bits of reality which accurately reflect the condition of its people.

There are many plans and projects which should have been included in this show, but were not. The plans for the 1976 Olympic installations; the exact position of the Eastern extension of the Trans-Canada Expressway; the plans for Saint-Sulpice lands in the centre of the city; the development of office buildings at the Windsor Station site; the plans for federal offices on the site of Montreal's Chinatown. All this is kept secret, through the complicity of "experts" who tend to remain quiet as long as they get the work. It is as if one is living in some company town where the employees need not be informed of their own condition.

The projects that are publicly available may be interesting, but they are usually either utopian or irrelevant insofar as they distract from the real issue and the real potential for the development of the city.

What we are looking for is the basis for realizable utopias.

We are looking for those conditions in a Montreal to which all plans and projects are accountable.

These are found in the processes of the city itself, starting with available resources, with what exists, and the immediate lives of the people. The message here is that the sense of the city – its future and its past – becomes "visible" for its people only when they can relate their lives to its destiny.

Thus, the exhibition tries to say that the future of the city is found not only in urban growth, in technological innovations, or in the exercise of planning and design talents, but in the social and cultural evolution of Montreal. It is clear from the exhibition that this evolution depends upon the position of Montreal as the predominantly French-speaking urban centre of a Quebec which is redefining its relationship with the rest of Canada.

This exhibition is the first of its kind on the city. There is too much to say. Much has to be examined and stated publicly about the past and future of this city. It is hoped that this exhibition will be the beginning of a further examination of Montreal's urban consciousness.

28

Learning from the Wire Services*

Built objects assume monumental attributes either because of their implication in some heroic event, or because of their display of a system of references positing their heroic content. In either case, monumentality is the result of a contextual displacement, isolating the iconic presence of built objects.

The practice of architecture functions predominantly in the latter system of attribution. Before the modern movement, the monumental intentions of architectural production had their place in the scheme of things. In the modern period, the fact remains that the end-products of architectural practice inevitably tend to reproduce a system of cryptic references that draw attention to the heroic content of built objects, regardless of intentions to do otherwise, and regardless of the generally held belief that the need for monuments has disappeared.

The idea of the Monument Series is to investigate the content of monuments generated by events, outside the confines of cultural practice. It is based on the image of social and political

upheavals – the usual run of improbable crises and catastrophes – reproduced in the "news" media. The media bring forth from the background of common things images of our built surroundings caught up in the accident of events and assign to these built fragments a sense of power. And insofar as these projected bits are cast in the forefront of our shared consciousness, in proportion to the significance of a particular event, they modify our understanding of the significance of the built surroundings and redeem a sense of history.

The Series that I presented in an exhibition at the Section ARC of the Musée d'Art Moderne de la Ville de Paris was derived from a survey of images transmitted by the wire services between October 1970, and March 1973. These images were arranged in a linear, open-ended archive; some of the images were decomposed to bracket their content.

In effect, the Series attempts to trace the iconic space of architectural experience within the stream of everyday consciousness. Several themes are suggested. Unlike the idealized state of cultural practice which thrives on images

* From *Architectural Design* (April 1976): 201–6.

28.1 Melvin Charney, *Monument 30: Monument to the Dormitory Barracks*, 1973.

of finished buildings complete in themselves, event-generated monuments engage segments and clusters of buildings all in a state of flux. Many of the images fix the form existence of a built artifact either in a state of construction or destruction, exposing the layers of the assembly and the human effort and pain involved in producing and sustaining that assembly: viz. the broken concrete slabs of bombed-out buildings hanging by the threads of steel reinforcement; a stark cluster of unfinished silos in the northern tundra where seven workmen fell to their death because of faulty scaffoldings; the burnt-out masonry shells of a town in Kansas etching the fragility of its human infill; or the hollow shell of the presidential palace in Santiago. Unlike the benign optimism that dominates cultural practice, these monuments objectify the physical evidence of violence. They expose human oppression locked into the control of physical form,

along with the desperation of countermeasure; viz. the white cubicles of a sterilization centre in India; a helicopter gunship hovering above the concrete grid of a mid-town motel in New Orleans, the scene of a police shoot-out; or the scrap housing built by a Cambodian family on the road to Angkor.

What emerges is a trajectory of pathological points of inference, connecting people and built things, externalizing the front lines of experiential encounters. Each crisis engenders a breakdown in practice and a return to the essential meaning of all building for people. And it all happens somewhere out there, away from the cultural capitals of the world.

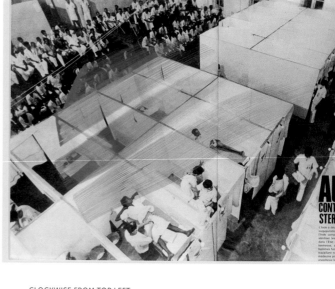

CLOCKWISE FROM TOP LEFT

28.2 The remains of buildings after a fire during a riot in Kansas City. The infill of human occupation was burnt off from the crude, cell-like containers sustaining the rudimentary substance of the town.

28.3 The improvised cells of a sterilization centre in Enkulam, Kerala. Back-to-back rows of compact white containers reduce the space of a large hall and reproduce the depersonalized and minimal enclosures symbolic of the reductive practice of population control.

28.4 A concrete stair tower and the grid of rooms of a midtown motel in New Orleans serve as a mini-fortress. Six hundred policemen and a Marine gunship developed in the battlefield in Vietnam were used to flush out a black war veteran who had infiltrated the protected enclave.

Closer to home, the most noticeable images reproduce monuments to the appropriation of resources or to the displacement of marginal sectors of the population. The disproportionate faces of bank presidents and corporation chairmen are seen to loom alongside fabrications of *their* buildings; possession, machismo, and power are translated into the tightly organized and cohesive models that can be grasped and fondled by their owners – the final form of the building no more than an exaggeration of this initial scale. Marginal sectors of the population – the old and the poor – are also experienced in close physical contact with buildings. But in

28.5   The debris of a Tent City after state troopers put down an uprising in Attica prison, New York: blankets, towels, and sticks of furniture were used by the inmates to transform a prison courtyard into a fragile, instant city – a veritable return to Adam's House in Paradise, assuring their human condition and their resistance – but one that hardly afforded them the protection they needed against the brutal assault that ensued.

28.6   Scrap housing erected by a Cambodian family on the road to Angkor. Poverty isolated the meaning of each piece of material in the assembly. Survival is imbued with a sense of humanity – look at the entrance. This house suggests that the significant architecture of the latter part of the twentieth century is found in the confrontation between advanced technologies and the rudimentary drive for survival on the most private levels of human adaptation. The physical evidence of this new world seems remote from the lumpy ruins of Angkor which Le Corbusier sketched earlier this century.

28.7   Canada's tallest building is put in place by Bank of Montreal's president in Toronto, appropriating a piece of the downtown. Since the end of the 1960s, Toronto has established itself as Canada's financial capital and its downtown core has experienced the highest building rate in North America. Rival banks vied with each other in the construction of towers, as in some latter-day San Gimignano. And each tower represented a move in an economic power play concentrating capital that cast the rest of the country into a hitherland of economic dependence.

La Presse, 7 Sept 73

Montréal.

M. D.W. Morison, vice-président de la Banque Royale, jette un coup d'œil entre deux tours de la maquette du nouveau siège de l'institution en Ontario. Cet immeuble de $100 millions sera érigé à l'intersection des rues Bay et Wellington, à Toronto, et les travaux seront terminés en 1976.

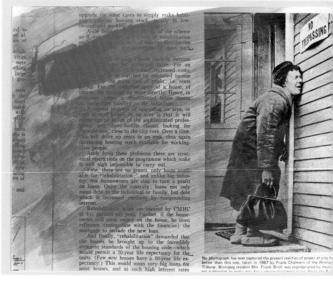

No photograph has ever captured the present realities of power as city hall... better than this one, taken in 1967 by Frank Chalmers of the Winnipeg Tribune. Winnipeg resident Mrs. Frank Birch was expropriated by municipal authorities to make way for a luxury apartment plan. When the city...

118 PAGES   MONTREAL, MARCH 24, 1973   FINAL   PRICE: 25¢

shoremen paid
000 to resign

Justice in North getting new look

This elderly woman is one of many who spend their days and nights locked up at Maison de Repos Laval

Slum-like home for aged run
without necessary permits

CLOCKWISE FROM TOP LEFT

28.8   Not to be outdone by rivals, one of the vice-presidents of the Royal Bank of Canada is seen holding a model of his new head office building for downtown Toronto.

28.9   A doorway frames the realities of power in municipal government. Despite the expropriation of their home, the Birch family of Winnipeg refused to move. The city then obtained a court order evicting them and police took possession of the house.

28.10   A window framing an elderly woman, one of many who spend their days and nights locked up in a slum-like home for the aged located on the outskirts of Montreal. Government intervention controls the population who are at the end of their life cycle, isolating the old in ghettos, programming their timely death.

their case, it is only with those parts of buildings that one is normally in direct physical contact with, such as doors and windows, except that these people are usually found to be closed out by doors and enclosed behind windows.

Finally, *Paris Match, Epoca,* and the *Daily News* emerge as the alter ego of *Architecture Aujourd'hui, Domus,* and *Architectural Forum.*

29

Housing in Canada: A Dead-End Choice[*]

Under the surface of Canadian housing policies is a Machiavellian web of political intrigue. With a get-rich-quick scheme for ruthlessly selling off resources to the multinationals, the country's leaders are caught up in a pointless attempt to keep up with the high consumption of the Joneses. To make these plans more palatable, cultural traditions of self-reliance and local-level co-operation are being viciously repressed. Housing has become the political instrument for entrenching consumer values. Increasingly, housing is being served up to the nation as a consumer goodie, and access to it in any other form denied.

What conclusions can one draw from housing in Canada? Figures on housing issued in 1975 show that ten new housing units per thousand population were started. This number compares favourably with production levels in other Western countries – e.g., 5.3 in the U.S. during the same period. And not only is there high output, but people are paying less for their accommodations; in 1974, Canadians spent about 16 per

cent of their disposable income on housing, whereas in 1962, this ratio was 18.6. There is also less crowding in existing dwellings: a "crowding index" shows that people had thinned out from 0.64 per room in 1971, to 0.61 per room in 1974. But perhaps most instructive is the fact that the output of new housing shows a 20,000-units surplus above the 210,000 units needed each year to take care of new family formations, the immigrants, and the existing houses that are demolished.

Yet, despite a surplus of new units, the prevailing mood in the country is that there is a crisis in housing. People know that they cannot find suitable housing at prices they can afford. Even a cursory review of the statistics furnished by government show that apprehensions are well founded.

Housing programs are measured only in numbers of new units; most of these units – 85 per cent in Quebec – are single-family houses out on the urban fringe. Government assistance is largely restricted to the purchase of a new, single-family home; over half the families in the country have to allocate a minimum of 45 per

[*] From *Architectural Design* (April 1976): 201–6.

29.1 Indigenous housing destroyed. Montreal's soundly constructed traditional housing form with its wood planked frame with continuous plank infill and its snow-catching and insulating roof is being deliberately destroyed by the government.

cent of their earnings to afford a house available under these programs. Nothing or little is mentioned about the housing needs of people, assistance to co-operatives, the maintenance or the rehabilitation of existing stock; a national survey of rental units does not include buildings that have six units or less, even though such buildings provide the bulk of low-cost accommodation in Montreal – Canada's largest city.

There is nothing new about the fact that housing is a political tool, nor is it news that in a country with a market economy, housing programs are exploited to maintain the market function. But the fact that in 1975, the right of

people to housing in a wealthy, developed country is caught up in a cycle of overproduction and crises mirrors the superfluity and deprivation in the worldwide distribution of resources, and suggests that it may be instructive to examine the modes of production in a developed country that promote deprivation.

In an attempt to examine these modes, two instances of housing in Canada are compared. The first is found in the *quartiers populaires*, the working-class tenement neighbourhoods built in Montreal during its initial period of urbanization, between the 1870s and 1920s.

The second instance is the new housing built in Quebec in the 1970s. Again, worker housing is examined. Again we find the raw accommodation of a paid labour class. Both instances are located in the Canadian province of Quebec. But here all resemblance to the *quartiers populaires* ends.

29.2 Housing as a consumer appliance. Entrepreneur-building advertisement for government subsidized mass-produced single-family homes.

Quebec was locked into a colonial limbo for over two hundred years – cut off from modernity. It emerged in the 1960s, an enclave of six million French-speaking people in Anglo-America, anxious to find a place in history. A "quiet revolution" plunged it into the formal imitation of modernity without transforming the substance of colonial structures. This happened at a time of an increasing worldwide demand for natural resources. And the subsequent opening up of hitherto untapped reserves of raw materials and energy in the vast northern region of Nouveau Québec tied the state into the web of the multinational, resource-based corporations.

Foreign control is a Canadian problem, but in Quebec it has assumed the proportions of a colonial crisis. Due to outside control – thanks to a federal government structure and the geopolitics of multinationals – the managerial elite of Quebec can only offer the hollow gestures of self-government without its content.

The *Quartiers Populaires*: Collective Traditions and Conflict

The urbanization of Quebec was largely caused by the expansion of greater Montreal when it became the industrial capital of the newly confederated Dominion of Canada. During this period, in Quebec an expedient, climatic shell was developed by craftsmen working for speculative builders. It consisted of a roughcut, wood plank frame 3-inches thick with a continuous plank infill equally 3-inches thick, covered by an air space, and enclosed in a brick veneer; the traditional roof slope of the *maison québécoise* was reversed and tilted inwards to a central drain – instead of the dangerous cascades of ice, the accumulation of snow on this "Montreal roof" served as insulation along with the layers of air trapped beneath the outer membrane. This shell represents an important breakthrough – a more efficient envelope and one that was easier to assemble than traditional building – the first truly indigenous construction to emerge out of the experience of this continent. (See Fig. 29.1.)

What emerged was a rudimentary system of accommodation providing no more than minimum shelter. Cramped interiors lacking in adequate sanitary facilities were common here as in other industrial ghettos.

Political conditions at the time were equally primitive. Québécois workers were not only locked into a factory system largely in the hands of English-speaking interests, but were also subjected to the control of the Church that pursued the role of protector of French Catholic culture against assimilation while collaborating with the English elite to maintain its hegemony.

The urban immigrants occupied what was available. Their contribution to the culture of urban housing in Quebec took place in neighbourhoods where over 85 per cent of their inhabitants were tenants.

The radical political base of these *quartiers*, which sprang up in the 1880s, still persists in the 1970s. In 1969, a coalition of Comités d'Action Populaire, each rooted in a *quartier*, formed a common front called FRAP. By the fall of 1970, the Front d'action politique (FRAP) emerged as the only serious contester of the entrenched

municipal power structure; housing and high unemployment were its main issues. But elections in Quebec are usually held in a state of crisis, and the October 1970 municipal election set a new high in violence. Following a political kidnapping, FRAP was linked to a guerilla action, and machine-gun emplacements took over polling stations. When the hysteria subsided, it became clear that FRAP was no more than a loosely knit minority locked into the workers' districts, with little financial resources and no access to the media.

By the 1970s, the *quartiers populaires* formed a ring around the inner city of a burgeoning urban region where more than half the population of Quebec resides. They still provide the bulk of low-cost family accommodations in Montreal, and constitute 44 per cent of all housing within the city. They still accommodate the poor; in 1971, the average income in some districts was $4,776, which is slightly above the poverty line, and half the national average. A typical profile of one of these *quartiers*, Plateau Mont-Royal, shows a population of 90,000, of which 93 per cent are salaried workers and 90 per cent are tenants.

In 1972, by the municipal government's own account, there are in these *quartiers* over 120,000 units of sound low-cost housing in need of repair – 30 per cent of the total stock in the city. Demolition is rampant. In a 10-year period to 1975, the rate of demolition accelerated from 1,600 units to 2,500 units per annum: 65 per

FACING PAGE | 29.3 Neighbourly, tiered porches are traditional in the flats of Plateau Mont-Royal.

RIGHT, ABOVE | 29.4 Rising militancy of small people: tenants refuse to move from housing scheduled for demolition.

RIGHT, CENTRE | 29.5 Systematic destruction: collapse of a building that was still occupied after government contractors had demolished adjacent sites.

RIGHT, BELOW | 29.6 Burn-outs are now a common sight. This one claimed the lives of six trapped children.

cent of the housing destroyed was sound, low-cost accommodation – *most of the demolition is deliberately carried out by government*. In the same period, the rate of abandonment has increased to 1,300 units per year. Fires are rampant.

An Office municipal d'habitation created in the 1960s has introduced one of the best housing codes in North America; however, if applied, its regulations condemn most of the remaining housing to further demolition. In the same period, 80 per cent of the new housing built in the city has one bedroom or less.

Until 1972, public housing was the only government program serving families in the bottom third of the income scale. Not only was very little money put into it (less than 0.05 per cent of all housing financed directly or indirectly through the government sponsored NHA), but a directive on the housing that was built suggested that it should "incorporate … a number of traits making it socially less desirable … higher density … limitations of room sizes … cement brick partitions … use of uniform colours … not too convenient locations," etc. The poor were to be punished. In 1975, the 5,000 families living in the city's public housing see themselves "caught in cages with no real say about running their affairs."

The *Villes Champignons*: Consumer Housing

Since the beginning of the 1970s, there has been a second period of urbanization of Quebec, which has given rise to a growing number of *villes champignons* – the mushroom cites that sprouted on the urban fringe beyond Montreal. In the *villes champignons* the confrontation between people and government shows changing relationships of control.

Consider co-op housing. The growth of the cooperative movement in Quebec combined the frugality of an uprising middle class with Christian communality, so that by the 1970s over 65 per cent of the French-Canadian popu-

lation belong to one form of co-op or another. In 1968, a Fédération des coopératives d'habitation du Québec, Coop Habitat was created out of a merger of numerous local associations. Despite federal government restriction on loans to co-operative housing, Coop Habitat managed in a period of two years to put up 1,600 units of new housing of better-than-average quality, and at 25 per cent lower than market prices. Coop Habitat introduced no more than an efficient middle-class alternative to housing that was not subversive but rigidly conformist. Yet, in 1970, an allocation of $24 million of federal loans destined to the co-op was cut off, and an equivalent sum was allocated to entrepreneurs-builders in the form of subsidized loans. The co-op was broken financially and dismantled.

In 1970, 94 per cent of all housing built in Canada was subsidized either directly or indirectly through government programs. At the first hint of a recession and a failing economy, federal government subsidies were shamelessly pumped into the private sector in the guise of a "Special Innovative Low-Cost Housing Programme" (see *AD* 1/72).* Quebec received the largest portion of these funds; and 76 per cent went into the Montreal region. Here, local entrepreneurs-builders with pipelines into government got off-the-shelf projects approved that included such innovative features as the use of marginal land that would normally be unacceptable for housing, shoddy buildings produced cheaply at the expense of the consumer maintenance. (See Fig. 29.2.) The only thing innovative about the program was its profits.

Housing as a Consumer Appliance

While government programs were tampering with ineffective policies to reduce the cost of

---

* Editor's note: Charney is referring to his essay "Low Income Housing into the 70s with Sewer Pipes and Subsidized Speculation," chapter 26 of this book.

housing, entrepreneurs-builders introduced techniques that kept the proportional cost of the labour component in house building stable for over a decade. The production for single-family housing was rationalized by assembling the house out of two pre-finished containers fabricated in factories and shipped to the site, using production techniques developed in the fabrication of worker camps for resources sites in the North. Profits, however, in this type of housing, depend on serviced land. And to obtain cheap, serviced land, the *villes champignons* were pushed further out onto the urban fringe, trading off the fast profits of builders against the high costs of maintaining municipal services and transportation. While the minister responsible for housing made speeches on the need to control urban growth, government programs pushed builders to spread out and to concentrate land in the hands of a few large companies. The expansion of the Montreal region into prime agricultural land can be directly co-related to the fact that by 1975 Quebec was dependent on the importation of food – via multinationals.

Resources and the Multinationals

Urban growth is directly related to regional development. Two episodes in the forest industry show that the only successful action to develop regional employment was the result of militant, grass-roots action.

In Quebec, over one-half of the productive forest land, an area equal to that of England, is ceded to private paper companies. Ninety

ABOVE AND CENTRE | 29.7 and 29.8 Mass-produced housing modules. Initially designed for opening up the resource-rich north and now packed for the consumer market.

BELOW | 29.9 Containerized housing at Manic 5, a hydro-electric installation developed to sell power to the U.S. eastern seaboard.

per cent of this production is controlled by seven companies, the largest of which is Canadian International Paper, CIP, owned by US International Paper, based in New York. In 1971, CIP decided to close a pulp mill at Temiscaming, in north-west Quebec, throwing hundreds of people out of work and destroying a long-established community of 3,000. Workers led by a French-speaking Cree Indian, and the people of the town organized a co-operative, Tembec, to acquire the mill. It took fourteen months of militant action to embarrass the government to assist the co-operative to meet the payments exacted by CIP. Tembec not only operated profitably from the restart, but within a year began to modernize equipment, improve working conditions, and expand into the production of dissolved pulp. The town survived.

In the same year that the workers of Tembec were struggling to keep their jobs, the Quebec government concluded a deal with ITT (of Chilean fame) for the exploitation of the remaining 30 per cent of its forest reserve, an area three times the size of Ireland, located on the Gulf of St Lawrence, north of the town of Seven Islands. ITT "was considering Brazil, but they came to Quebec because of advantages we offered them ... I rejoice to see our natural resources for which we have no use, profit humanity" declaimed a Quebec representative.

Profit humanity! ITT brought in very little capital; the Quebec government provided interest-free loans. Concessions to the company included reduced royalties, the building of access roads, free reforestation, preferred rates for electric power, housing for workers, and a treatment plan for effluence. All under a forty-year contract that ITT could cancel at any time without penalty. ITT was to construct the world's largest mill, near Seven Islands, to produce dissolved pulp for its synthetic fibre plants in Western Europe. Few jobs were created while a number of forestry co-ops and small mills in the area were forced to close; the native population of Montagnais Indians was simply ignored.

Militant Action

The growth of Quebec's involvement with multinationals parallels its increasing resistance to alternatives in the management of the resources.

In 1972, when a common front of labour organized a general strike to press for basic demands, such as a minimum wage of $100 per week for all workers – the poverty line for a family of three – what might have been an exercise in collective bargaining turned into a violent confrontation. Repressive legislation ordered the workers back, and union leaders were jailed. In Seven Islands – the archetypal *ville champignon* – an attempt by police to break up a protest on the eve of the jailing sparked across Quebec one of the greatest displays of worker revolts in Canada.

The town of Seven Islands, located on the north shore of the gulf of St Lawrence, some 500 miles north-east of Montreal, is the gateway to the eastern part of Nouveau Québec. By 1972, Seven Islands was the second-largest exporter of iron ore in the world, and first port in Canada according to tonnage; 80 per cent of the ore was exported to the U.S. by companies all of which are controlled entirely by or in partnership with U.S. interests. A boom town, salaries are high, pattern of spending depicts the web of neo-colonial dependencies: most workers are employed by Iron Ore Co.; Iron Ore is owned in part by the US Hanna Mining Corp.; Hanna Mining Corp. furnishes ore to National Steel (owned in part by Hanna), the major supplier of steel to Chrysler Corporation (owned 9 per cent by Hanna), and Chrysler in turn sells over 45,000 automobiles annually to car-crazy Quebec. In Seven Islands, cars are numerous. Streets are wide, but most of them end in sandy ruts after a short distance. There is nowhere to go. Fatal accidents are common.

29.10 Seven Islands – a typical *ville champignon*. Mushroom town gateway to vast iron ore deposits. In 1972 it had the highest salaries in Canada, along with wide streets that went nowhere. It was the flash-point of a general strike that engulfed Quebec in the largest demonstration of worker solidarity in the province's history.

During the Common Front in 1972, the workers took over the town. Within two days, the uprising was broken by the usual incidents – the killing of a worker, the infusion of police, a demonstration by housewives clamouring for the reopening of the supermarkets, and a threat of lock-outs by the executives of Iron Ore – shades of Chile. It also ended with a demand by the union for one last concession from the government: the right to acquire some land near the homes of Iron Ore executives to set up a land bank for low-cost housing.

The turning point was the James Bay project, 600 miles north-west of Montreal. The basic proposition was to create two power complexes – the world's largest capacity – drawing on a watershed equivalent in area to the size of France. The project was aimed at the energy-hungry U.S. eastern seaboard, and involved U.S. interest and capital.

Work began in 1973 on the LG2 station, the largest of the La Grande Basin part of the complex. Ten months later, an argument over union jurisdiction and the appearance of police in army gear erupted in the destruction of the town and

the closing of the project. It exposed working conditions that are primitive – over twelve-hour shifts, seven days a week for months on end; lives aggravated by the cold, isolation, confinement, and boredom; and a prison-like segregation of the sexes enforced by law.

The campaign is waged against people. Worker morale is low. A system of migrant labour is now successfully instituted in the country. The plans for the project ignored the Native population of Cree and Inuit: they were simply to be flooded out.

The comparison of the two instances of housing produced fifty years apart shows that government intervention has advanced systematically to eliminate all forms of alternative housing other than those which can be developed in partnership with entrepreneurs-builders. It outlines a half-century of policies by government to support the operations of big business at the expense of people. Recently, these policies involve the operations of multinationals. The *villes champignons* are evidence that housing has been refined as one of the instruments now used to maintain a relatively cheap, but well-

LEFT | 29.11 Housing as a mobile consumer appliance. A not uncommon home for a well-fed but subordinate people turned into a migrant labour force in their own country and pushed up against the front end of the consumer cycle.

RIGHT | 29.12 Asbestos slag heaps for backyards in the Thetford Mines means asbestosis and certain death for the inhabitants. A U.S.-based multinational exports 70 per cent of the world's asbestos from Quebec mines.

fed labour force which has the means and the taste for the consumption of the middle-class, high-income goods, including the purchase of an expensive family appliance called a home.

In the earlier *quartiers populaires*, housing was developed out of a climatic shell that rationalized the use of energy; in the *villes champignons*, housing is modelled on high-energy forms of consumption that push Quebec further into the cycle of hydroelectric development and foreign capital. In the earlier *quartiers populaires*, as in recent squatter settlements, a collective ecology of settlement emerged out of the political ferment of people seeking to make their lives

bearable with whatever means were available: in the *villes champignons*, consumer packaging of housing is robbing people of the symbols of their collective identity.

Appearances depict a cruelty of the imagination. People are not able to translate the anxieties of wasted lives and wasted resources into positive action. Cruelty is enacted in many ways, including the legislation of idealized social programs, such as housing, without the democratic institutions or resources necessary to make them work; it is exercised in the undertaking of alternative housing predicated on failure insofar as they ignore fundamental issues: it is promoted by the staging of conferences, such as Habitat, when rhetoric can only distort the potential of a country to come to terms with its riches in a deprived world.

30

Other Monuments: Four Works, 1970–1976[*]

In accepting an invitation to write on architecture for *Vanguard,* I hesitated. Much of what I do falls outside the purview of common practice. In order to explain my work, I virtually have to create a suitable vocabulary. Not because what I do or say is complicated, on the contrary, but because so little is being said or done about architecture in this country. What is said is either so bogged down in formalism, or caught up in the hype of the profession's white-wash of the market place, that it is simply difficult to assimilate other ideas. I have to invent, not write, and to decipher, not describe, the meaning of the built things. As the title suggests, the architecture that I do is preoccupied with monuments. The building of shelter is not merely a biological contingency, but involves the cultural transformation of utilitarian needs. A built gesture produces something that was not there before. As such, it cannot but idealize (make heroic) to some degree all those relationships that allow it to be conceived and materialized. But as Vitruvius would have it, monumental buildings reproduce the *necessary* forms of primitive construction in permanent and noble materials. And even though this attitude changed by the end of the eighteenth century, and it has been a long time since architects were paid by rulers to build noble temples and palaces, architecture still reflects its origins: the heroic content of building is reserved for the strategic embellishment of the lives of those who control the purse strings if not the privileges in society, and who desire the ultimate privilege: to see themselves privileged in their own eyes. The idea of the monument is still promoted as some atavistic emblem of class structure that dominates the practice if not the spirit of architecture.

In other words, my understanding of architecture is that it involves the substance of human discourse in the production and use of built things.

What follows are notes prepared on the occasion of an exhibition of four works done between 1970 and 1976, to be shown at Harvard University, 3 to 30 March.

[*] From *Vanguard* 6, no. 2 (March 1977): 3–8.

Memo Series

Early in 1969, the Canadian press published an invitation to architects to participate in a competition for the design of an Air Force Memorial. This memorial was to be a commemorative, a museum of air flight, and a place for meetings of Air Force veterans.

The program of the competition called for the submission of a series of drawings that describe a building. A site plan was given; the building was to be located in Trenton, Ontario.

This program is typical of the usual set of instructions that circumscribe the conception of architecture. It assumes that you can postulate a memorial by producing the image of a construction that reproduces references to formal values in building.

To the extent that we know that when we build, we denote the meaning of form by representing parts of a building, and that this system of representation also introduces references which situate the *aura* of the building beyond its surface appearance, it can be argued that the idiom of a commemorative museum is hardly as narrow as the program prescribed. The evident necessity of memory, as well as of form, suggests that prior to the imposition of a program, an examination could be made of the raw material in our experiential baggage – the simulacra of memory and their meaning to people – whereby we can decipher the language of architecture.

The very idea of a museum and the notion of commemorative acknowledge that human memory is embodied in the physical traces of people. The history of air flight, the long period of trial and error in the production and reproduction of the artifacts constructed for flight, has deposited the traces of a specific culture buried in our cerebral representation of things themselves. The structure of these built traces links the meaning, if not the memory of air flight to the form of these artifacts, and hence to their figuration.

Rather than play with the anonymous syntax of built form, I began to document the evidence of things and places that are known to materialize the traces of air flight.

This inventory began with the paraphernalia of air flight in my immediate surroundings. The noise of overhead aircraft recalled air battles that were raging in Vietnam at the time this piece was being done. Incidents in the news media, such as an item on people attracted to the site of an air crash, evoked the twisted ribs of the aircraft and the broken ribs of victims thrown together in some anthropomorphic stew that reached into our collective gamble with the flying machine. The disposition of hangars at an old airport in Montreal – the heroic, classic profile of articulated sheds – standing in a flat landscape against a distant rise of mountains recalled the temples in Paestum, the *envoi* of the Paestum temples by Henri Labrouste, drawn when he was a student in Paris at the École des Beaux-Arts, and the images of these temples at Paestum reproduced a century later by his admirer, Le Corbusier, in his essays on the machine aesthetic and aircraft in *Vers une architecture*.

The entries in this inventory were recorded in the form of *Memos*, as if I could register a series of memorandums on a memorial, and send them to the people responsible for its implementation. Each *Memo* described a piece of evidence and its subsequent bracketing into constituent elements. These elements presented idiomatic propositions – constructs – on the composition of the Memorial.

Briefly, the *Memos* included constructs on:

- The location of the commemorative/ museum, as found in a map of Air Canada flight routes linking principal cities. (See Fig. 24.1.) The terminal dots on the map indicated zones where an on-the-ground configuration of flight is found, and the lines between the dots traced the paths of flight across the vast hinterland where the sight of an overhead aircraft suggests a museum that programmed flights of old aircraft – simulating, for example, bombing runs, to work off the aggression of the Veterans of Foreign Wars. The map suggested a museum fixed in neither place nor time: the memorial may disclose itself in several places simultaneously.

- The topology of a real-time memorial, as found in the flight zones of an airport. (See Fig. 24.2.) Airports describe referential codes that situate the geometry of air flight in an on-the-ground configuration readily accessible both physically and conceptually. The configuration of in-flight space can be read in the lower buildings, the insistent flashing of red lights on projecting structures, the flattening of the terrain, and the distant view of a horizon across a vast, flat, windswept clearing: the idiom of a commemorative.

- The usage of built things preceding their meaning, as found in a B-29 parked off the end of a runway at Wright-Patterson Air Force Base, Ohio, and open to visitors. (See Fig. 24.8.) Isolated on the slab of the runway, the aircraft appears as a building. The visitor can enter this building, pass through its fuselage, fit himself into the cockpit where a moving stick, taped visuals and recorded sounds offer one man a commemoration to the bomber pilots of the Second World War, and to another, to the victims of war. And as long as it can fly, the aircraft can bring this commemorative/museum to cities across the country, and take people on memorial flights.

- The simulated experience as actual experience, as found in link trainers and recent flight stimulators (see Fig. 24.7), which suggests micro-monuments to be located across the country. Taped visual and sound can be used to recreate historical events,

such as Lindbergh's flight, to be relived by visitors who are closed in for 33½ hours behind a vibrating engine, fed stale sandwiches, and restricted to a periscope view of the passing ocean; or the flight of a B-52 over Laos that includes close-ups of destroyed villages, and a free napalm burn on the palm of the hand as a souvenir of the Souvenir.

- The typology of in-place history as seen in the remains of a French aircraft after the fall of Dien Bien Phu (see Fig. 24.3), the remains of an Air Canada, Montreal-Toronto flight that crashed in an abandoned field near Sainte-Thérèse, Quebec, or the remains of a sea-plane hangar at Orbetello, Italy, built by Pier Luigi Nervi, 1939–41, and completed by a Lancaster bomber in 1943 (see Fig. 24.4). This morphology of destruction – building-in-meaning in reverse – depicts the veritable architecture of air force, and suggests that actual, in-place remains be maintained as archaeological sites.

- Other *Memos* include constructs on the discrete meaning and usage of artifacts, as seen in an amusement park airplane ride where one first learned that flight involved a declaration of faith in the machine (see Fig. 24.9); or in a wind up replica of an amusement park air ride as a mantle-piece monument to this faith (see Fig. 24.10): both disclose relevant features of a building. And, finally, constructs on the media as virtual and as actual history, citing evidence of air flight as a media event, or the use of in-flight monitors developed by air force intelligence to give instant access to actual events used via home TV to keep people intelligent ... and so on.

This procedure of recording these constructs tended to be divergent and inclusive. Their proliferation reinforced propositions that brought to light relationships which would have otherwise remained inaccessible. The subsequent broadening of the meaning of a "building" paved the way for an idiom which acknowledged the contextual signification of the propositions.

Two operations were indicated: the first mapped out a pattern of constructs, and the second suggested their implementation – the externalization of the commemorative/museum by the selection clearly constituted a deliberate act, political, social, and aesthetic, that reinforced one set of patterns as opposed to another. For example, the selection of a commemorative/museum in the form of an isolated building that represented only the institutional values of architecture can readily be seen to be one of the most restrictive if not repressive designs, given the size of the country and the obvious range of possibilities. A cross-country commemorative/museum can be readily created by the installation of old aircraft in centres of population, or the use of old airports near several cities where exhibits and meetings of veterans could be accommodated in abandoned hangars – buildings which exude the memorial odours of air flight. And rather than invest capital on a building, the money could be put to social services, such as housing, and the return used to maintain a network of facilities that bring the museum to the people.

Following the submissions to the competition, the jury selected a pyramid-like building for the museum. Two years later, the plans for construction were cancelled because of insufficient funds.

Two of the issues raised in the *Memo Series* dominated my subsequent work. The first had to do with the prevailing concept of the monument in architecture. In examining recent history, I found that regardless of the intentions of the modern tradition to do away with the monument, as in decoration, its major buildings do nevertheless present the physicality of an object that is clearly monumental. It was obvious that monumentality had more to do with the meaning of built form than the attitude of the modern

tradition would lead one to believe. Every built gesture seemed, in effect, to assume a monumental connotation.

The second has to do with the reproduction of daily life in cultural practice – i.e., the reproduction of a monumental connotation – and the systematic institutionalization in architecture of references whereby the significance of built things is kept out of reach of the personal experience of most people. This suppression was contrasted by the number of *Memos* that originated with events that involve people and built things, as found in the mass media. These images projected into the forefront of our consciousness built fragments that assumed a larger-than-life significance: the sheer scale of numbers of viewers assigned to these built fragments a sense of power. The images presented a rupture of daily existence – a crash or a bombing – that disrupted the lives of people, exposed the relationships between people, and modified our understanding of these relationships. After the event, we are simply not the same.

Dictionnaire d'architecture: Learning from the Wire Services

In 1973, at the exhibition Canada-Trajectoires, shown at the Musée d'Art moderne de la Ville de Paris, I presented a work called *Quelques monuments nationaux* – some national monuments.

The title of this work refers to the traditional preoccupation of the architectural profession in France with monuments. Until 1968, the École des Beaux-Arts system which was founded during the reign of Louis XIV, and hardened during the nineteenth century, conferred a Prix de Rome on its outstanding acolyte. It gave him the title of Chief Architect of National Monuments, and a sinecure which assured him prestigious commissions from the state, as long as he toed the line in power.

The *National Monuments* that I presented, however, had more to do with the representation of everyday built form than with the institutionalization of form in the name of entrenched power. These monuments were derived from a survey of images of events that involved people and built things, and the classification of these images identified categories of inferences that demarcated the legibility of built things: architecture.

Several themes emerged in this rather tentative experiment. Unlike the institutionalized practice of architecture that thrives on idealized images of finished buildings, complete in themselves, event-generated images engage segments and clusters of built things in a state of flux. Many of the images freeze a building either in a state of construction or destruction, as if someone were parsing the layers of the physical assembly into a syntax of human effort and pain. Visualize:

- the broken concrete slabs of bombed out buildings hanging by the threads of steel reinforcing, in Vietnam;
- a stark cluster of unfinished silos where seven workmen fell to their death because of a lack of even the minimum safety measures, in northern Quebec;
- the concrete grid of a midtown motel in New Orleans where six hundred policemen and a Marine gunship perfected in Vietnam were needed to flush out an army of one black war veteran who had infiltrated the protective enclave;
- or the hollow shell of the presidential palace in Santiago, purged of its substance.

These images evoke monuments that denote violence and terror, so unlike the benign optimism that dominates architectural practice. Moreover, this violence is seen to be implicit in the organization of built form. Visualize:

- instant towns of concrete sewer pipe housing used to shelter refugees from Bangla-

desh, near Calcutta airport. The disposition of the pipes – stacked units of low-rise, high-density accommodation arranged in avenues and streets – reproduces the essential structure of the town from the fragile and transitory human infill. (See Fig. 26.2.)

The durability of the essential structure of built form can be observed as separate from the event itself, as if it had some autonomous logic of its own. But the images also show that the reproduction of this logic as the autonomous figuration of form, isolated from and neutralizing its context, can only signify violence. Visualize:

- an audience seated before the spectacle of men enclosed in the improvised cells of a sterilization center in Embulam, Kerala, India; back-to-back rows of white containers reproduce, within the space of a large hall, the reductive space of the imperial institution of medicine. (See Fig. 28.3.)

Ironically, it is in the images of violence where the urge of people to express metaphorically a human and heroic content in building is seen. Visualize:

- scrap housing erected by a Cambodian family on the road to Ankor (see Fig. 28.6); poverty has isolated the meaning of each piece of material, and survival imbued the assembly with a formal presence;
- the debris of Freedom City after state troops put down an uprising of inmates in Attica prison, upstate New York; blankets, towels, and the sticks and planks of furniture were used to transform a prison courtyard into a fragile, instant city which affirmed the collective resistance of the inmates, but hardly afforded them protection against the brutal assault that ensued. (See Fig. 28.5.)

Both these images suggest that architecture in our century is to be found in the confrontation between the forces of imperial power and the rudimentary drive for survival by people caught in this squeeze.

These images closer to home depict the significance of built form in the exercise of political power. Meaning in building is related either to those who manipulate power, or to those who are manipulated by the exercise of this power. Visualize:

- the face of Henry Ford II between the towers of Renaissance Center, described as the most expensive urban redevelopment project ever constructed in America, to be built on the Detroit river as an enclave for the rich in a decaying city;
- Mayor Beame of New York at a presentation of a cluster of new towers destined for lower Manhattan;
- the vice-president of the Bank of Montreal presenting an office tower, Canada's tallest, to be built in downtown Toronto, the year when Toronto's core experiences the highest building rate in North America (see Fig. 28.7);
- not to be outdone, one of the VIPs of the Royal Bank of Canada is seen clinging to his new head office, destined for downtown Toronto (see Fig. 28.8);
- or the chairman of National Steel Corporation showing a $1-billion new integrated works plant, as some general with toy soldiers ...

The meaning of these images is painfully evident: built form materializes the mania of a system that realizes itself in the irrational appropriation of resources. The figures of the bankers and corporation chairmen present disproportionate fabrications of *their* buildings, as if these are boardroom trophies acquired in a game of possession, and sculpted to resemble tightly organized and finished buildings in a size that can be fondled by their progenitors. The final dimensions of the building being no more than an exaggeration of this initial, generic scale.

Meaning in building is directly related to the physical appropriation of scale. Marginal sectors of the population – the unemployed, the old, and the poor: the predominant mass of the people – are also seen in these images to be in direct physical contact with built things. But they are in contact with only those parts of buildings that facilitate their daily routine, such as doors, windows, sinks, and urinals. And, unlike us in our familiar use of these devices, they are usually seen to be closed out by doors, enclosed by windows, or, as a victim of a gangland shooting, caught with their head in a urinal.

It is obvious that these images depict a pathology. And as in all pathologies, it is not only familiar conditions that are brought to light. Whether these images portray an event, or create an event out of an ordinary scene by portraying it in the mass media, they expose the cutting edge of new formations that are difficult to assimilate within the prevailing canons of discourse.

This is particularly evident in the predominance of images that show unnamed and anonymous people situated in transient, non-differentiated spaces, such as corridors, waiting rooms, lobbies, motel-like hostels, etc. Indifference and lassitude are evident both in the figures of the people and in the figuration of their surroundings: lines of people waiting at employment counters, waiting in hospital corridors, or waiting in school corridors ... The meaning of the corridor as the embodiment of a street, or of the waiting room and the lobby as a place of meeting at a conjuncture of streets, the physical substance of collective metaphors, are effaced, along with the identity of people. If conscious design has created this no man's land, then there must exist a form of practice that institutionalizes the reproduction of this effacement. How then do we go about dispensing with the lives of people?

The institutionalization of this practice of denial which effaces and makes natural the practice of the effacement is seen in the images of some practitioners trained in the art of configurating anonymous form: architects. They are seen to produce built things that do not seem to refer to another context than to a self-referential code of abstract physical markings that neutralize the legibility of relationships between people.

The *Dictionnaire d'architecture* presents the contours of a dialectic landscape. It suggests that within this dialectic, cultural practice manipulates the legibility of form, rendering only a part of the landscape visible.

The next question is self-evident: can architecture deny in practice the seemingly inevitable denial of people that is built into our surroundings?

The *Dictionnaire* also suggests that an answer may be found in the specificity of practice in a familiar context.

What is most striking in the corner of North America where I live is that cultural institutions maintain that contemporary architecture has no roots in this place; a view that is supported from the outside. Whereas I can see from my window an example of housing that emerged as a building type out of the industrialization which transformed the modes of production in the late nineteenth century, and that the body of this building displays an obvious formal and social content, I cannot determine the significance of this building in terms of cultural references. It is as if it didn't exist. The neglect of its fabric, the abandonment and demolition of similar buildings elsewhere in the city, verify the fact that I live in a corner of the world where culture works to support the systematic destruction of those traces of the past which do not socially affirm current practice.

Une histoire d'architecture – Le trésor de Trois-Rivières

I began this work by collecting evidence of anonymous, popular architecture, dating from the first period of the industrialization of Quebec: 1870s–1920s.

This material included fragments from demolished buildings, as the shards of a past civilization; postcard views dating from the turn of the century, showing churches, barns, factories, and parish halls as icons set in the classic geometry of thin, wood-frame construction; old photographs of new towns built near factories, showing an accumulation of shed-like houses, each set against a facade that aligned a street; newspaper clippings showing one of these facades as the remains of a house, following a windstorm; a Walker Evans photo of a house in the southern United States – a facade on a non-existent street; the main street of Rawdon, Quebec; a photo of the remains of the main street of a 1930s Hollywood set for a western – two lines of facades in some 3-D billboard; an illustration of a house in Saint-Canut, Quebec, presented in Alan Gowans's *Building Canada* as the only example of degenerate architecture in a selection of over 200 photographs; a quotation by Colin Rowe, from "Chicago Frame" (1970), that modern architecture which was *there* in proto-modern American buildings became an architecture in-a-state-of-becoming in subsequent modern architecture … all an accumulation of evidence that was added to and subtracted from during a period of five years.

Two basic themes emerged. The first had to do with a typology of housing in the worker neighbourhoods of Montreal; and the second – the subject of this work – was on a more rural and isolated idiom of housing than the first, but one which nevertheless displayed closer affinities than the first to a similar expression elsewhere on this continent.

This theme depicted a particular departure in building history. With the introduction of

30.1 Photograph of part of a wall in Melvin Charney's studio during the realization of *The Treasure of Trois-Rivières*.

sawmills and the standardization of materials, the massive wood frames of traditional construction gave way to a simple and sturdy method of stick buildings that not only provided a new means of shelter at a time when vast tracts of this country were being opened up, but also furnished a convenient tableau whereby people could express themselves in built form. The subsequent idiom gave rise to the first materialization of a North American – as well as Québécois – architecture, growing out of the experience of this continent.

In Quebec, the cultural isolation of people sharpened its resolution. Not only do these buildings clearly articulate a residue of collective images that mirror Western history, but they do so with heroic tints and Amerindian echoes.

One particular image stands out: a rather small house located in a nineteenth-century worker's quarter of Trois-Rivières, built in the shadow of a massive pulp mill. Although in a relatively good condition, this house was destroyed in 1974 as a result of a federal program of urban renewal.* The site is now bare. A few forlorn houses are the remnants of a once lively *quartier*.

The formal content of this building is striking. A simple geometric volume reproduces the essential structure of a classic temple. (See Fig. 30.2.) This volume is set against the flat plane of a thin facade on the line of the street. The profile and openings of this facade are cut in such a way that it recalls a portico found in Meso-American architecture – a monument to the passage from the street to the house. Moreover, the window and door frame in the facade draws out a heavy

cross: an exquisite figuration that reaches deep into the expression of built form.

In contrast to the expression of its forms, the house exudes equally obvious signs of the marginal existence of its builders and inhabitants. Regardless of the scale of its references, the house is small, its materials are meagre.

This house was an uneasy discovery. Its classic forms suggest both the temple and sarcophagus. (See Fig. 30.3.) This contradiction permeates its scale, as if the figure of the house were both there and not there, at the same time. At the confluence of three rivers – the meeting of a trinity – some French-speaking Québécois whose livelihoods were caught up in a factory run by Anglo capital, and whose redemption

* Editor's note: The house was not demolished and is located at 1085 Sainte-Geneviève Street, Trois-Rivières. (See Fig. 23.2.)

30.2 "A Story ... The Treasure of Trois-Rivières," 1975.

30.3 "Chapter Two ... A Doric Monument in Trois-Rivières," 1977.

was refuted by the church, built the figure of a house of death, and lived in it as if to expurgate their fate.

Is this not architecture? Is not the ultimate idealization of our existence the libido at rest (death), and the perfect building the ultimate realization of *Adam's House in Paradise* (the tomb)? And if this architecture is refused its place in the consciousness of our culture, is it not because the culture denies the consciousness of its people?

In order to know this architecture I examined its site, photographed its surroundings, documented its history, and reproduced the original building in a set of drawings. I found these drawings, however, were too abstract, too remote, and that the only way to actually *know* the architecture would be to reproduce a full-size wood figure of the building itself.

The act of physically assembling this building ritualized the figuration that gave it meaning. What emerged was a totem: a built effigy that reproduced the original documentation (see Fig. 30.4) as if it were the program of a building. This act reversed Vitruvius's dictum – it presented a monumental construction that reproduced the *necessary* forms of permanent and noble buildings in primitive materials; and it turned around the modern tradition noted by Colin Rowe – it put back meaning into the thing itself, rather than proposing its meaning in a project.

In other words, the piece showed architecture to be part of an ever-developing discourse closer to the language and understanding of people than our cultural institutions would have it.

This place was exhibited in *Québec 75,* and was shown in several museums across Canada. Generally, most critics were disturbed that a work on "architecture" was included in a show on "art." But more revealing than this rather usual reaction of those who have little to defend other than prevailing formalist beliefs, was the argument by a critic in Quebec that this piece was not "Québécois art," even though the idiom of this work was obviously drawn out of the specificity of Québécois history. What interested me was the fact that I had presented the ideas in this piece a few years ago in a published lecture that I was invited to give on the arts in Quebec, and the reaction of the same critic was more than laudatory. In other words, you can talk about the democratization of art/architecture, but don't expect to bring it into the museum and have it certified.

Une histoire d'architecture presented collective values built into our surroundings. As such it commented on the use of art as an instrument that serves to alienate us from the formal meaning of our immediate surroundings. In Montreal, for example, the reaction by critical institutions to this work is related to the fact that people are unable to see that their city has become an open-pit urban mine and its resources have been sold off to foreign speculators.

30.4 "A Story ... The Treasure of Trois-Rivières," 1975.

Corridart

The streets in Montreal are different. They not only convey people from one place to another, as in other North American cities, but, until recently, some of the streets were made to be urban rooms. The facades were lined up as walls. Every dwelling had a front door that gave onto the street through an elaborate system of pictur-esque stairs. Cornices, porticoed entrances, and trimmed window openings elaborated further the physical markings of a shared space. These markings reflected a bond between people and their city which reached past the baroque notion of the street into the significance of the street in the collective consciousness of people.

And of all the streets in Montreal, Sherbrooke Street was very special. In the early nineteenth century, the original section of the street was situated on the top of an escarpment that separated the upper from the lower town. This division gave body to the social layering that has marked the history of this city. To the east, the remains of commodious homes of old-line French-Canadian families can still be seen to float over a worker's slum – as if they did not know where they were. To the west, Sherbrooke Street followed the foot on Mount Royal. Here the dominant English class established their residences and institutions; at McGill University, one can still see hard, parsimonious, stone buildings set in a manor-like disposition against the rugged slopes of Mount Royal, as in an idealized nineteenth-century tableau. The prestige of this part of Sherbrooke Street flourished and grew in the first hundred years after Canadian Confederation, 1867, when Montreal emerged as the financial and industrial centre of a burgeoning nation. With its broad thoroughfare, its wide promenade, and a panoply of wealthy homes and institutions, Sherbrooke assumed the character of the processional street of the city. Kings, queens, and the effigies of Santa Claus and of St John the Baptist, the patron saint of Quebec, were paraded here. Sherbrooke Street was Montreal.

Since the early 1960s, the character of the street has changed. In recent years, unbridled speculation and irresponsible government, the removal of wide sidewalks and trees, and the demolition of important buildings have reduced it to a vehicular thoroughfare with few vestiges of its past.

In 1976, on the occasion of the staging of the Olympic Games in Montreal, Sherbrooke was again cast into the role of a prestigious thoroughfare, now linking the city centre to the site of the main Olympic installations. The Organizing Committee of the Olympics, under the sponsorship of the Quebec government, undertook a program of cultural events that included an exhibition of art, called Corridart, to be presented on Sherbrooke Street.

I was asked to examine the potential use of the street for an exhibition, and then to design what was to be, in effect, a five-mile-long museum-in-the-street.

Again, the work proceeded from a detailed inventory that described and deciphered the morpho-history of the street, along with a survey of possibilities inscribed in its configuration. Given the nature of the street, I conceived the exhibition as a double-edged show. First, it was to present the fabric of the street itself as an exhibit of its various meanings, and, second, to show works of art inserted into its fabric as a comment upon its meaning. Both steps were intended to transform the street into a museum that exhibited its collective significance, and to suggest the possibility of a new role for Sherbrooke: a street whose prestige may now be derived from a place that belongs to all the people in this city.

Corridart passed through three distinct urban zones. In the west, it traversed the city centre and the remains of a significant slice of nineteenth-century Canadian architecture, the established art museum and art market. Here the exhibition attempted to illuminate what is in place: a private cachet of art and architecture. Further to the east, Corridart was defined by the oldest part of the street that still retains an original sense-of-place; here one can find rows of terraced, stone houses that are still occupied as dwellings; the École des Beaux-Arts and the old École d'Architecture de Montréal; the site of a gallery where the momentous *Refus global* was signed; and side streets filled with a history of studios and cafés where ideas were thrashed out and art was produced. This was the principal zone in which the works of art were concentrated. From this zone to the main Olympic site, the street passed through the mindless strip development that has taken over this part of the city since the 1940s – the drive-ins and instant flash cut a swath through Canadian Mortgage and Housing Corporation postwar slums and articulate a show of their own.

In varying degrees in the various zones, the material of the exhibition traced the archaeology of the street. A photo documentation unearthed images of the past; evidence of events that affected and were affected by the street was displayed; portraits of residents were shown, along with the legend of artists that could be found behind its facades. This documentation was mounted on a system of pipe scaffolding that set the images flat against the street in a disposition that mirrored the local idiom of billboard-like buildings with a front of prestigious stone and sidewalls relegated to brick. The scaffolding reached behind the baroque staging of the street: it was of a type used to prop up movie sets. Its dumb ordinariness reached behind superficial embellishment, a framework of pipes that signified nothing other than what it was. The scaffolding was held in place by concrete counterweights that were cast to resemble the remnants of ruined Doric columns. (See Fig. 31.5.) These ruins lined the sidewalk as the remains of an ancient city, and as a sign of the destructive hubris of autocrats. The colours of the City Parks Department, whose budget was cut for several years because of Olympic spending, were used to designate the exhibition. Finally, a hand with a pointing finger, a common didactic image that indicates direction, was reproduced in plastic and mounted on the scaffolding to guide people in this museum-in-the-street.

The migration of art from the museums and galleries to the street was not easy. Contemporary art is spawned in the neutral places of museums which isolate the art object and aestheticize it. Nevertheless, most of the participating artists took their cues from the context of the street. Briefly, some of the work included: numerous performances presented on two stages set into the configuration of buildings; a line of trees that define the street was redrawn with swatches of colour woven into its branches; a two-mile line of colour effaced the line of the curb so as to enlarge, figuratively, the space allocated to pedestrians; photographic images mirroring the perspective of the street presented an essay on perception; existing buildings were represented as monuments to the corporality of the street; a stone maze drew people into an isolated park; a café was inserted into a corner parking lot to reclaim it as a place where people could meet; along with the usual paraphernalia of street art such as wall posters, banners, and kites. In effect, a quilt of projects that tried to transform the street into a collective artwork.

The street is a harsher place than a gallery. Art in the street is exposed to the vicissitudes of weather, vandalism, and political interference.

The weather gave us no more than the usual predictable problems. There was far less vandalism than expected. The public, in general, was curious and protective. However, one week after the opening of the exhibition, the mayor of the city, Jean Drapeau, had it demolished in a spectacular night-time blitzkrieg, reminiscent of Germany in the 1930s. A flotilla of cranes and trucks laboured under the glare of floodlights to destroy the work.

The Bourassa government ordered Drapeau to put it back in place. The order was simply ignored, as was the outcry of the news media, the Civil Liberties Union, the association of architects, the association of artists, etc. The habitual abuse of power inures autocrats to disregard even the semblance of democracy.

It took three days to remove the larger pieces. The agony of their destruction was carefully detailed in the news media, and watched over by the artists themselves.

On one of the main intersections of Sherbrooke Street, in the principal zone of Corridart, is a vacant piece of land which was cleared of terraced housing in the early 1960s by the provincial and municipal governments for some institutional project long forgotten. On this site I erected a full-size reconstruction of the facades of two typical Montreal greystone buildings which are still standing on the street, on an opposite corner – *Les maisons de la rue Sherbrooke*. Rough plywood and reclaimed lumber were wired to a frame of pipe scaffolding, similar to the display of the documentation. As a document, these facades defined the scale and substance of the street. The hollow window openings of the facades (either a ruin or a building in the midst of construction) framed the high-rise office towers in the centre of Montreal. (See Pl. 29.) They reclaimed a layer of the city. The mirror image of the facades on opposite corners aligned the intersection of the streets on an axis which demarcated the square-like signification of the intersection in the urban structure of the city, a reflection that related this "square" to similar squares, such as the Piazza del Popolo in Rome, and the Place de la Concorde in Paris, for example, in order to designate a monument to the singular existence of such an urban space in North America.

Prior to the opening of the exhibition, photographs of this piece appeared in the media, and it became a symbol of Corridart. As a result, its deliberate dismembering symbolized the rape of the city. (See Pl. 31.)

Drapeau's attitude is best revealed when he is quoted as saying, some years prior to Corridart: "The ugliness of slums in which people live doesn't matter if we can make them stand in wide-eyed admiration of works of art they don't understand." He was making explicit a practice which is implicitly institutionalized in the art system in this country. Drapeau's action may constrain art, but it doesn't hinder it. "True censorship, the ultimate censorship, does not consist in banning (in suppression) but in unduly retaining, stifling, getting bogged down, in taking for nourishment the word of others"

(Barthes).* In the case of Corridart, the art community was upset, of course, by the violence of the mayor's gesture. For one thing, it was too obvious and too crude in its tactics. However, while the destruction was denounced as fascist, few people spoke up on the significance of the exhibition itself.

Despite the constraints of its situation, Corridart did succeed in staging one of the first large-scale public exhibitions in the streets of a city. It did manage to show some urban archaeology and contextual art on a monumental scale. In a subsequent inquiry into the staging of the Olympic Games, Corridart emerged as the only event which disturbed the otherwise impenetrable serenity of those responsible for this extravaganza.

Therein lies the significance of its situation. It says that art in the street is meaningful insofar as it signifies that culture is created by people who move together with others in a common purpose, and that this purpose is defined by the need of people to change the conditions of their lives. The rest is history.

What began in 1970 with the *Memo Series*, which deciphered contextual metaphors including some drawn from events in the news media to compose a museum, evolved by 1976 into Corridart, a museum which built contextual metaphors into the public domain. Because of the circumstance of the work these buildings appeared in the news media as events in their own right: a symmetry which verifies the evident *necessity* of architecture.

* Editor's note: Roland Barthes, *Sade, Fourier, Loyola*, translated by Richard Miller (New York: Farrar, Strauss and Giroux, 1976), 126. The actual sentence is: "Yet, true censorship, the ultimate censorship, does not consist in banning (in abridgement, in suppression, in deprivation), but in unduly fostering, in maintaining, retaining, stifling, getting bogged down in (intellectual, novelistic, erotic) stereotypes, in taking for nourishment only the received words of others, the repetitious matter of common opinion."

*LES MAISONS DE LA RUE SHERBROOKE**

The intention of this work was to draw on a ruined city site and to focus its urban form: a configuration of houses at the intersection of two main streets.

There are essentially two ways of approaching the idea of a house. The first draws on the notion of an elemental shelter in nature; that is, it involves a model which is rooted in the idealization of the house as an Arcadian pavilion and as a tableau for individualized expression. The second approach is through the house as an element of collective human settlement; that is, through the art of building cities. This latter approach is the more problematic of the two, since it goes against the grain of modernist tradition, which largely denied urban form and figuration.

In Montreal, until recently, the physical definition of a street described a configuration which subsumed the form of individual buildings. And of all the streets in this city, Sherbrooke Street was very special. It was the major artery and processional thoroughfare at the time Montreal became an important metropolitan centre. By 1976, despite a decline in the fortunes of the street, it still maintains an appearance of urban civility.

At one of the main intersections of Sherbrooke Street is a vacant piece of land. It was cleared in the early 1960s for an institutional project which was subsequently built elsewhere. On this site I constructed two full-size facades similar to two nineteenth-century greystone townhouses which typify the street, and which are still standing on an opposite corner of the intersection.

Rough plywood and reclaimed lumber were wired to ordinary pipe scaffolding in a billboard-like configuration. This rigging recalled the articulation of stone facades supported by ordinary brick walls which are found elsewhere on the street; it also echoed its initial baroque staging. However, in contrast to nearby buildings, the hollow openings and the exposed underpinnings of the installation presented either the ruin of

* Excerpted from Melvin Charney, *Oeuvres 1970–1979* (Montreal: Musée d'art contemporain, 1979), 42–8.

a building or a building under construction. In either case, it described something more physical than a drawing on paper and less material than a finished building.

The mirror image of facades on opposite corners of the intersection aligned the axis of the intersection and directed it to an early nineteenth-century cathedral and to an eighteenth-century square in the core of the city. The replication of facades created a gate-like configuration. It denoted the syntax of a city square, and related the figuration of this square to the structure of similar squares in the history of city building, such as the Piazza del Popolo in Rome or Place de la Concorde in Paris.

December 1977

Éléments communs: les maisons de la rue Sherbrooke

Melvin Charney

Un élément essentiel de la rue est la façade qui l'enferme. Les façades de deux maisons de la rue Sherbrooke sont ici reconstruites afin de rendre à la rue ses dimensions et de souligner la destruction de bâtiments qui pouvaient encore être utilisés. Cette reconstruction n'est pas seulement un document sur la rue mais le contexte historique dans lequel il est fait le transforme en monument. Un temple est créé. Il rappelle le décor d'un drame urbain.

An essential element of the street is the façades that enclose it. The façades of two houses on Sherbrooke street are here reconstructed in order to restore to the street its scale, and to present evidence of useful buildings that are being destroyed in this city. This reconstruction not only documents the street, but the historical context that surrounds this document transforms it into a monument. A temple is produced. It recalls the décor of an urban drama.

COMMUN.

Il rappelle aussi les bâtiments existants de l'autre côté de la rue, créant une place dans la rue qui en rappelle d'autres plus célèbres dans l'histoire, comme la "Place du Peuple" à Rome, et laisse voir ainsi le contenu humain d'une ville qui se doit d'appartenir à tous.

It also recalls an existing building on the opposite side of the street, creating a place on the street that recalls, in turn, other similar places in history, such as the "Place of the People" in Rome, mirroring thus the human content of a city that ought to belong to all.

INTRO.

Les contrepoids de béton maintiennent en place les structures de tuyaux. Ces contrepoids prennent la forme de ruines de colonnes gréco-romaines: comme s'ils étaient les vestiges d'une "politique de grandeur" qui a détruit tant de villes dans le passé et qui pèse toujours sur Montréal.

Concrete counterweights hold the pipe structures in place. They are cast in the form of ruined Greco-Roman columns: as if they are the remains of a ruinous "politique de grandeur" that destroyed other cities in the past and that still weights on this city.

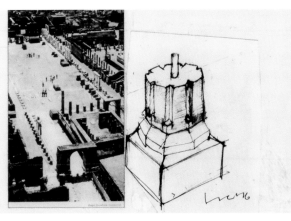

Pl. 24   Series of three montages which were presented next to the construction.

Pl. 25 (FACING PAGE, ABOVE), 26 (FACING PAGE, BELOW), 27 (ABOVE)
The site altered.

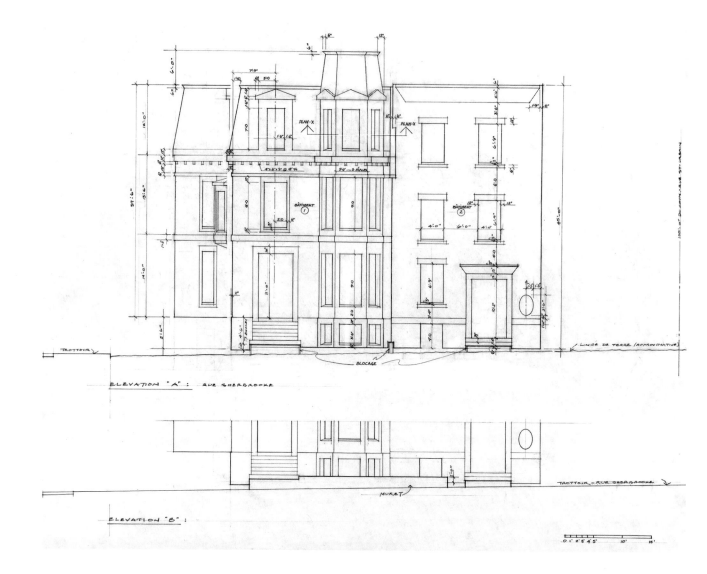

ELEVATION "A" : RUE SHERBROOKE

ELEVATION "B" :

Pl. 28 Elevation, 1976.

Pl. 29 The construction, 1976.

FACING PAGE | Pl. 30 Construction, close-up, 1976.

ABOVE | Pl. 31 One week after the installation of *Les maisons de la rue Sherbrooke*, municipal authorities of the City of Montreal ordered it to be destroyed. A flotilla of cranes and trucks were moved in during the night of 13 July 1976, and demolition began under the glare of floodlights.

RIGHT | Pl. 32 Cover of the brochure of the master program of the Art History Department at Université du Québec à Montréal

31

Corridart: Art as Urban Activism*

Just before midnight on 13 July 1976, municipal workers, guarded by police and on orders from the mayor's office of the City of Montreal, moved along Sherbrooke Street demolishing a Corridart five-mile-long museum-in-the-street exhibition which explored the neglect and destruction of street life in the city. Despite widespread protests from civil rights organizations, unions, architects and artists' associations, and Quebec's minister of cultural affairs, the systematic destruction continued until Corridart was obliterated beyond repair. Four days later, on the opening of the Games of the 21st Olympiad, nothing remained of what was supposed to be the core of the Olympic's Arts and Culture program.

The Organizing Committee of the 1976 Olympic Games (COJO) had conceived of an Arts and Culture program largely oriented to crowd-pleasing events. Culture was to be used to soften public hostility to the staging of the costly Games, which were seen by the public to be part of a determined and disturbing dis-

regard for people in Montreal, and Quebec. Yet, ironically, only $400,000 was set aside, out of a total budget of $2 billion, for what was to have been one of the few public events of the Olympics – a corridor of art objects on a main street of Montreal. However, since any incident on the streets of Montreal tends to attract people, and since very few Montrealers could afford the price of admission to the Olympic events, Corridart would have been for most people the only tangible festivity which they could witness first-hand. It was for this reason that I accepted to design what was to become, in effect, a collective happening.

Given the limited budget, the grandiose scale of strategic embellishment that was envisaged by COJO, and the cultural and political constraints imposed by the Olympic program, I conceived Corridart to be a double-edged show. It was first to be an exhibition of the street itself, using as much of its existing material as possible; and second, an exhibition of artworks, selected by open submission, and inserted into the interstices of the street in order to heighten its meaning to people.

* From *Architectural Design* (July–August 1977): 201–6.

The streets in Montreal are different from elsewhere in North America in that many were made to be common urban rooms where people gathered. The physical traces of the streets define a bond between people and the city as a collective, public artifact which subsumes individual buildings. And of all the streets in Montreal, Sherbrooke Street is very special. It flourished in the first hundred years of the Canadian confederation, 1867–1967, when Montreal was the centre of a burgeoning nation. In the west the street follows the foot of Mount Royal that commands the city. Here the dominant English classes established their residences and their institutions; one can still see hard, parsimonious, greystone buildings cast in a manor-like disposition against the rugged slopes of Mount Royal (tailored by F.L. Olmsted), as if in an idealized nineteenth-century tableau. To the east Sherbrooke Street follows an escarpment, where the remains of the commodious homes of the old-line French-Canadian families and their Church-dominated institutions can be seen to float above workers' slums, bathing them in benign spirituality. Sherbrooke Street drew a common thread of class and privilege through the two cultural solitudes that composed Montreal. It thus assumed the character of the processional street of the city, and was made to echo a baroque impulse that gave body to the street in the first instance.

The main thrust of Corridart, therefore, was on the signification of the street. The container of the exhibition – the street – was to be contained within the larger meaning of the street in its urban context. Each element was to draw on the familiar language of the street, accessible to and understood by people. Traces of the civility of Sherbrooke Street were to be re-presented. But the representation was to attempt to depict its baggage of status and power in a changing role: a street whose significance now derives from a place that belongs to all people of this city.

31.1 A typical Corridart assembly. This points to a sidestreet where community groups had demonstrated to save local housing from demolition by the city. The photos on the scaffolding record the buildings and the actions taken.

At varying intervals along the street a series of documentations were mounted. The documents unearthed images of buildings and scenes that have disappeared; evidence of events that affected or were affected by the street were displayed; portraits of some of its residents were shown, along with details of their lives; processions were depicted (see Fig. 31.2), and

monuments (see Fig. 31.3) were explained. These documents were mounted on a system of pipe scaffolding and set in a disposition similar to the local idiom of billboard-like stone facades that are supported by ordinary brick walls. Moreover, the pipe-frame system was of a type used in Italian film sets, a play on baroque staging. The pipe-frames were anchored by concrete

31.7 *La croix du Mont-Royal sur Sherbrooke* by Pierre Ayot and Denis Forcier.

counterweights that were cast in the form of ruined Doric colums, as if they were the remains of some under-layer of history and a reminder of the destructive hubris of autocratic rulers. Colours were borrowed from municipal departments, such as the city parks, whose budgets had been illegally channelled into Olympic spending. Finally, the common image of a hand with a pointing finger that indicates direction was cast in red plastic and mounted on the pipe supports to guide people along this museum-in-the-street.

Corridart traversed three distinct urban zones. In the city centre the documentation only illuminated what was in place: it made public a private cachet of art and privilege. The principal zone of Corridart was located in the oldest part of the street, which was also once part of its *Quartier Latin*; here, in neglected corners, the artworks were concentrated, along with a density of documents. From this zone to the main Olympic site the mindless development which overtook the street in the late 1940s was allowed to articulate a show of its own, with the help of the documents.

Most of the participating artists also took the cue from the context of the street. Swatches of colour were woven into the city trees to suggest an anthropomorphic configuration; performances of street theatre were organized on stages that were set into theatrical-like configurations of buildings; a two-mile-long line of colour effaced the line of the curb, drawing it into the street and so extending the sidewalks; a photo-mosaic mirrored the linear perspective of the street in an essay of urban perception; telephone booths were inserted to keep the public in contact with the artists as well as written messages on conditions of life in Quebec: in effect a quilt of projects attempted to transform the street into a collective artwork.

31.8 A location map of the Corridart exhibition showing approximately half of its five-mile route from the city centre to the Olympic Games site. The numbers indicate locations of historic sites, the letters refer to the locations of artists' installations.

At one of the main intersections of the street is the principal zone of Corridart; on a vacant lot which was cleared of housing by the government for some institutional project now long forgotten, I erected a full-scale re-presentation of the facades of two typical Montreal greystone buildings dating from the nineteenth century, and still standing on an opposite corner. (See Pl. 26.) Rough plywood and reclaimed lumber were wired to pipe scaffolding in a manner similar to the display of documents elsewhere in the street – as if it were a physical documentation of a monument to the corporeal substance of the street. The hollow window openings of the facades framed the high-rise office towers of the city centre in the immediate background; their unfinished look resembled either a ruin or a building under construction. Their mirror image of buildings on opposite corners aligned the street on an axis which demarcated the square-like significance of the intersection of two streets in the urban tissue of Montreal. It also related this "square" to similar squares in the history of city building, such as the Piazza del Popolo in Rome, or the Place de la Concorde

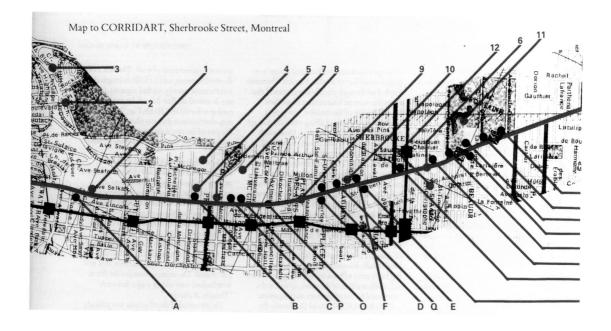

Map to CORRIDART, Sherbrooke Street, Montreal

in Paris, and to the fact that the city of Montreal has been systematically destroying a significant number of squares inherited from the eighteenth and nineteenth centuries.

Prior to the opening of Corridart the media picked up on the image of these facades, and it became a symbol of the exhibition. As a result, its deliberate demolition was also carefully recorded in the media, and its dismembering became a symbol of the destructive forces at work in this city. The nature of these forces and the reasons for the destruction of Corridart are best revealed when the mayor of the city was quoted as saying at the time of Montreal's Expo 67: "The ugliness of slums in which people live doesn't matter if we can make them stand in wide-eyed admiration of works of art they don't understand." Corridart was understood. Its destruction was a form of overt censorship that upset many people. But in effect, the mayor's actions made explicit a practice which is implicit in the institutions of the country. Canada has been hard at work effacing its history for the past hundred years, so that even a straightforward representation of life (history) is taken to be a radical if not a threatening departure; witness, for example, the trauma of Anglo-Canada caused by Quebec's desire to reclaim a slice of its history.

The *New York Times*, 17 July 1976, quoted "informed sources in the city government" who said that "the Mayor and his colleagues on the Executive Council were really bothered by one series of photographs. It showed graceful, sometimes historic old Montreal homes that had been razed to make room for featureless high-rise structures, under the city's expansion programme. These pictures, it was said, were taken to be such an intolerable political statement that the whole thing had to go." The *Times,* however, neglected to explain that the only expanding program of the administration during the past decade has been the encouragement of unbridled speculation (Montreal has yet to state some

31.9 Dismantling Corridart.

coherent development objectives, or to submit one plan to public scrutiny or referendum), the demolition of inner-city housing,* and the running of the city into a financial ditch during which time the mayor and his cohorts scattered the stardust of a *politique de grandeur* in the eyes of its citizens: Expo 67 and Olympics 76. The mayor is so inured to the abuse of power that he was indignant at the widespread criticism of the violent destruction of Corridart.

During a subsequent government inquiry into Olympic costs, Corridart emerged as the only indicant of the 76 Olympics which seriously disturbed the otherwise impenetrable serenity of those responsible for the $2 billion debacle. Therein lies the significance of Corridart. It affirms the strength of a well-aimed, figurative gesture in architecture as a means whereby we can come to terms with the way people understand the conditions of their lives. After all, autocrats still fear the power of an image.

* Editor's note: Charney refers here to his essay "Housing in Canada: A Dead-End Choice," chapter 29 of this book.

32

Modern Movements in French-Canadian Architecture*

The interesting thing about modern architecture in French Canada is its apparent absence – even the place as such has to be located: French Canada is Quebec.

Yet, Quebec is present. It is an industrial, resource-rich corner of North America, with a population over six million, and with a relatively high standard of living. Politically, it is in the throes of a vigorous independence movement. Any drive for autonomy stimulates all areas of expression, including architecture. That is, there has been substantial building activity in Quebec during the past decade, and some of it obviously warrants critical comment, if not recognition. The fact that this does not happen suggests that it may not be architecture in Quebec that is amiss, but rather that the cultural processes of institutions in Canada block out significant movements.

All cultural systems impose distinctions. In America, the tendency of immigrant people to deny history gave way in subsequent generations to an affirmation of the specificity of their experience on this continent. It gave their experience a cultural expression, i.e., a history. This happened in the United States between 1850 and 1950.

The history forced upon Quebec was quite different: the British conquest of French North America in 1759 cut off the settlers from their origins and locked them into the cold half of the continent. The grip of British colonialism hardened in 1776 with the arrival of the United Empire Loyalists, who found the republican experiment of the United States too heady for the royalist blood. French-Canada was further insulated by a Catholic Church which remained untouched by the revolutions of the eighteenth and nineteenth centuries, and which, until the early 1960s, played on nationalist sentiments to maintain its hegemony over the lives of people.

* From *Process Architecture* 5 (March 1978): 15–25; reprinted in *Documents in Canadian Architecture*, ed. Geoffrey Simmins (Peterborough, ON: Broadview Press, 1992), 267–81. Editor's note: Charney's title refers explicitly to Charles Jencks's *Modern Movements in Modern Architecture* (Harmondsworth: Penguin, 1973).

Finally, the massive immigration of the majority of people from the countryside to urban centres, at the beginning of this century, left behind a traditional elite which remained in power and untouched by the changes of industrial society.

Thus an accident in the history of North America, colonialism, the threat of assimilation, industrialization, and the ensuing struggle of a marginal people to define their existence imbued all forms of expression to appear either as an open affirmation or denial of cultural boundaries. This cultural compression meant that the codes whereby built form was expressed were taken to be an integral element of the way people come to terms with the articulation of their lives – which is what architecture is about in the first instance.

In other words, a review of modern movements in Quebec has to focus on the contribution of people outside the mainstream of history. Their contribution originates in a proclivity to resist dominant values. It is therefore an excellent occasion, however brief, to examine the evolution of modern movements in the way people project in built form a struggle for cultural affirmation.

The Heroic Period

In a special issue of *Architectural Design* in 1965, Peter and Alison Smithson defined the "Heroic Period of Modern Architecture" as a series of buildings which appeared in Europe between 1915 and 1929 when "a new idea of architecture came into being." "This period," they wrote, "is the rock upon which we stand." They found nothing heroic in America.

The Smithsons' view represents a generally held opinion that modern architecture germinated in the ateliers of European practitioners. This opinion obviously reflects on an interpretation of history which accepts as given a metropolitan view of culture, and a "great man"

conception of historical process. It confuses invention with institutionalization, as Colin Rowe and Manfredo Tafuri have pointed out.

A proliferation of built evidence can be cited to demonstrate that the cutting edge of invention emerged out of the efforts of many people in several countries to come to terms with the means and relationships of industrial society which transformed the body and the figure of building. Modern architecture as an idea in building can be shown to precede modern architecture as an idea: both influenced, and were influenced by, the stylistic interpretation of these transformations called modern architecture.

In Quebec, the roots of modern movements may be traced to the resistance (*méfiance*) of people to the nascent apparatus of the modern, centralized state. In the late seventeenth century, a minister of Louis XIV, Colbert, who created the Académie Royale d'Architecture – it later became the influential École des Beaux-Arts which spawned architecture as a cultural system as we know it today – was also responsible for ordering the intendant of New France to settle the colonists in planned towns to be created about a central square. (See Fig. 33.1.) The settlers refused to comply – only six of these towns were built. Instead, they persisted in arranging their landholdings in thin strips, perpendicular to access routes, in a pattern known as *rangs*, unique in North America. The linear and extensible geometry of these *rangs* was suitable to the expansive terrain of this new continent; it redefined a generic system in the rural occupation of space. Above all, it provided some degree of loosening of the neo-feudal ties which bound the social fabric of New France.

The generative organization of these *rangs* underlies the conception of the grain elevators constructed between the 1860s and 1920s. The heroic scale of these grain-handling machines recalled proto-classic forms in modern materials.

Thus, illustrations of these elevators, including some in the port of Montreal, were lifted out of engineering manuals and published by Walter Gropius in the *Deutscher Werkbund* journals prior to 1915, and later Le Corbusier in *L'esprit nouveau*. What they positioned was an iconography and a syntax of a functionalist idiom. The information necessary to situate these machines as evidence of a change in the instrumentalization of built form, other than in the rhetoric of form, was avoided. That is, the grain elevators as facts were presented as the symbol of a desire for fact, i.e. a desire for meaning in architecture. Similarly, the introduction of sawmills and the standardization of materials transformed the massive frames of traditional construction into a rationalized, simple, and sturdy method of stick building at a time when factory towns were expanding and vast tracts of this continent were being opened up to settlement. This system of building was universal; it engendered various building types, regardless of style, and provided

an accessible tableau wherein people could express themselves in built form. The subsequent idiom gave rise to a copybook *Sachlichkeit* which became commonplace in late nineteenth- and early twentieth-century America. (See Fig. 32.1.) It was the first materialization of an authentic North American architecture to grow out of the experience of their continent. Later, Sigfried Giedion was to claim this idiom in the name of modern architecture. In Quebec, the isolation of people sharpened the resolution of this idiom. The commonplace here gave way to local themes that mirrored the cultural baggage of Western architecture, as well as an obvious delight in, and an expression of physical pleasure in building. (See Fig. 32.2.)

The heroic thrust of this movement was affirmed in the urban *quartiers populaires,* the worker neighbourhoods that emerged in Quebec between the 1870s and 1920s. Two distinct steps took place in the evolution of an urban architecture. The first, as in the case of the *rangs,* was the introduction of more generic relationships in organization of form than there were in existing methods of town building. As in much of industrial innovation, known methods were put together in a new way. An orthogonal street

LEFT | 32.1 Rawdon, Quebec, from an old postcard.

RIGHT | 32.2 House in Duparquet, Abitibi.

grid followed the alignment of these *rangs*, attesting to the continuity in Quebec of a building that can be traced from Etruscan origins to the Roman cardo, to the medieval tradition, which produced the Zahringer new towns of the eleventh century, and to the nineteenth-century typology of the City. And within this grid, a new building shell was introduced: it was forged out of a marriage of crude plank construction with a sophisticated layering of materials that incorporated pockets of air for insulation; it reversed the traditional concept of the massive wall, and signified a revolutionary breakthrough in the material concept of building in a climate where shelter is critical. (See Fig. 29.1.)

The second step was the differentiation of an urban typology. The initial forms of these *quartiers* provided no more than a rudimentary system of terraced flats. Cramped interiors and inadequate sanitary facilities were common here, as in other industrial ghettos. Political conditions of the time were equally primitive. Most of the inhabitants were unskilled French-speaking workers in an industry controlled largely by minority anglophile interests; they were subjected to the tight-knit parish structure imposed on the *quartiers* by a Church which riled against capitalism while maintaining a reactionary bastion against the inroads of unions. The subsequent physical transformation of these *quartiers* evolved in speculative, tenant housing by builders who emerged from the ranks of the urban immigrants. It resulted in a series of modifications that caused particular sets of physical instructions to prevail. The planar brick facades were pulled back from the street. Balconies, stairs, window projections, and entrances were made to articulate an array of direct, physical exchanges between each flat and the street. (See Fig. 29.6.) The street grid became *avenues, rues,* and *ruelles,* each with a specific connotation. And the density of the whole was increased further by a system of court houses which evolved out of converted stables and sheds. These physical

traces concretized social links built on common needs and extended the flats into larger social units, which went against the grain of the Church and the factory system.

This architecture was thrashed out by people using available means to humanize living conditions in the wake of industrial expansion. Its vocabulary became the language of urban Quebec. It described, figuratively, the possession of the industrial *quartiers* by its inhabitants. The architect-workers who produced it were a half-century ahead of their elite in coming to terms with industrial society.

The Institutionalization of Modern Movements and the Quiet Revolution

A second phase in the perspective of modern movements in Quebec surfaced with the rise of an urban middle class. These self-made men translated the national aspirations of French Canada into a movement for a national state. Their architecture followed their drive for self-management: each stage was marked by an appropriation of modern symbols to which they aspired.

By 1900, a new class of successful shopkeepers, factory owners, landlords, and builders established themselves in the urban centres of Quebec. They followed class instincts along the well-chartered course to the suburbs. In 1900, the new town of Maisonneuve was founded to the east of the centre of Montreal. Its architecture picked up on the thread of the utopian tradition of the idealized villa which can be traced from the Palladian country houses of sixteenth-century Venetian merchants, to the architecture of merchants ensconced in the suburbs of Chicago. Two hundred years after Colbert, Maisonneuve was laid out according to a strict, though naive, interpretation of French Beaux-Arts principles. The axes of the town were drawn along tree-lined boulevards, and vistas were focused by civic monument, which

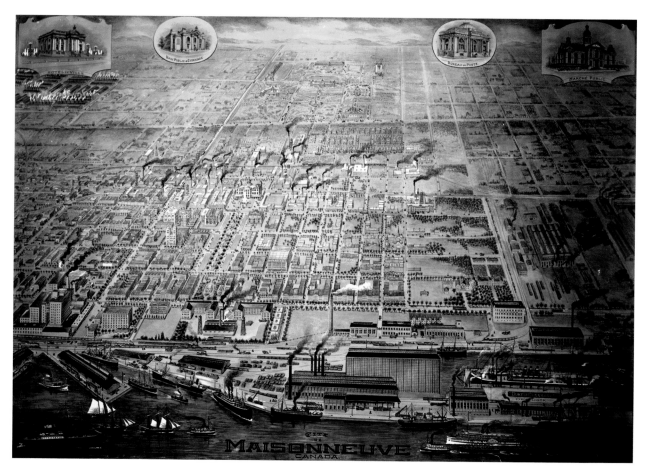

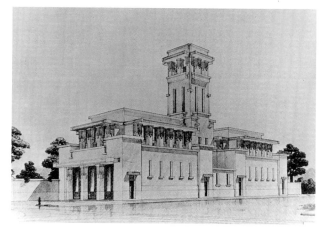

ABOVE | 32.3 A view of Maisonneuve, along with vignettes of its public buildings, ca. 1910.

BELOW, LEFT | 32.4 City of Maisonneuve, former city hall, 1916.

BELOW, RIGHT | 32.5 City of Maisonneuve, former fire station, 1914. Marius Dufresne, architect.

followed the structures of Durand's codes for the edification of such establishments: neoclassic for the city hall and the baths, French renaissance for the town market, and Petit-Trianon for the town builder. To the side of one of the main axes, a police and fire station was completed in 1914. Unlike the other municipal buildings, it is a copy of the Unity Temple designed by Frank Lloyd Wright in a suburb of Chicago and built virtually in the same year. The idiom of the building was instantly contemporary in form. Even though it looked more like nearby warehouses and factories than the other Beaux-Arts exercises, its figuration was derived from similar relationships in the manipulation of built form: the modern was just another style in the articulation of authority, unrelated functionally to the use of the building.

During the first half of this century the few architects who exercised the tenets of the modern movement were part of a small, urban, intellectual elite. They followed French and American sources in their work rather than the English and Scandinavian influences that marked the architecture of their colleagues in English Canada. The case of Marcel Parizeau is particularly instructive: in the late 1930s he designed a house in the international style in a comfortable neighbourhood of Montreal. While the general plan was based on a traditional nineteenth-century scheme, its exterior was clad in functional motives. Parizeau had studied in France, where he had discovered a modern idiom derived, ironically, from sources in Montreal. He then returned to Montreal and applied its mannerism to a villa of a well-to-do burgher, as if to bestow upon him the figure of industrial Quebec.

Parizeau's work prefigured the thrust of the later *Révolution tranquille,* the so-called Quiet Revolution of 1960–70, in which Quebec was rapidly modernized by a new generation which brought its government in line with the needs of a modern industrial state.

32.6 Beaudry-Leman House, Outremont, 1936. Marcel Parizeau, architect.

A house designed by the architect Charles Trudeau, in the Laurentian mountains north of Montreal, illustrates well this turning point. (See Fig. 25.1.) It is totally composed in the language of a mimetic, formal idiom. Its manner was derived from the style of neo-Palladian villas, which were promoted by the Museum of Modern Art of New York in the late 1950s, a style originally derived from the American work of Gropius, with whom Trudeau studied, and ultimately from the American tradition of stick building common in Quebec. The composition of the house is, however, unresolved. Its axes float above, rather than relate to, the surrounding landscape. And its cultural references are deliberately restricted to the ideology of a universal style.

A compulsive and formal idiom, irresolution, the disengagement of the building from its physical context, and its isolation from the culture which nourishes it are characteristics typical of the mainstream of modern architecture produced in Canada at this time. These buildings remain, at best, a repository of *idées reçues:* the work may look good, but it is culturally weak. The practice of a relevant architecture would seem to require some collective trauma to shake culture out of its comfortable stupor and into the hands of history.

This happened in Quebec. The obvious necessity of architects to define their work in terms of the historic conjuncture of the Quiet Revolution pushed them against this architectural void. As elsewhere in Canada, the ideology of architecture maintained that modern work had no roots in this country, and the recognition of authentic sources of expression involved attitudes which neither class interests nor the existing relationships of practice (client, capital, consumers) would allow.

There were two ways out: the first was an attempt to create an indigenous vocabulary by delving into modes of self-expression. It can be seen in the work of Roger d'Astous, who after a sojourn with Frank Lloyd Wright, returns to Montreal in the early 1960s and embarks

on a series of residences and churches drawn along the lines of Bruce Goff and Herb Green. (See Fig. 25.9.) It is also seen in the buildings of Paul-Marie Côté: his bold gestures set in the semi-tundra of the Saguenay region of northern Quebec recall Niemeyer's Brazilia on the fringe of the Matto Grosso. (See Fig. 25.10.) The emphasis of this movement is on individual creativity, as if to exercise the ability of architects to express themselves, and on a replay of the themes of modern architecture, as if to catch up with history. Forms were scaled, metaphorically, to the expanse of the American landscape and, symbolically, to an after-image of footloose Canadian *voyageurs* who opened up this continent, as if the only thing to build are way-stations in a vast landscape – a primal phase in the maturation of American architecture. The strength of this movement is found in its expressionism. Its intuitive forms were taken to be the antithesis of a growing bureaucratization overtaking Quebec in its drive for modernization. Its visceral metaphors exposed the bias of the dominant Anglo-Canadian taste. It was labelled, disparagingly, "sculptural." What was meant was that it offended repressed values and the ideology of a universal style. Its weaknesses are those of self-indulgence: the movement burns out quickly as a flare on the scene of an accident.

32.7 Sports centre, Université Laval, Quebec City, 1969–71. Gauthier, Guité, Roy, architects.

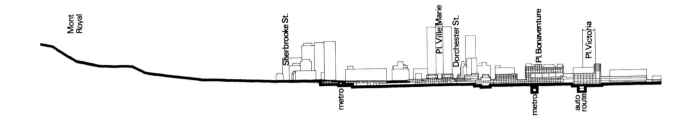

32.8 A section showing Montreal's new underground network drawn by Melvin Charney.

The second tendency of the Quiet Revolution, the more dominant of the two, was prompted by a newly trained technocratic elite, which included architects. They adopted, at first, the dominant genre of architecture in Canada. An initial overwrought formalism, such as that of the Quebec Pavilion at Expo 67 in Montreal and the Trudeau house mentioned above, was eased in the subsequent design of a proliferation of schools, universities, and government buildings – the apparatus of the Quiet Revolution. Later, the best of this work, such as the Sports Centre at the Université Laval by Jean-Marie Roy, shows the development of an abstract figuration of geometric forms, relating this work to that of the contemporary "Plasticiens" movement in painting in Quebec, and thus to an authentic, modern, avant-garde expression which distinguishes architecture in Quebec from that in the rest of Canada.

Finally, this period achieved an indigenous modern idiom. As modern architecture, however, its mindless avant-gardism and anonymous, universal style tended to deny possibilities in the architecture of Quebec other than those defined by the needs of a managerial class seeking its place in history, and of a market economy to which it remained committed.

This period also witnessed the development in Montreal of an integrated urban core. Individual superblocks designed by well-known architects such as I.M. Pei (Place Ville-Marie), Luigi Nervi and Luigi Moretti (Place Victoria), and Mies van der Rohe (Westmount Square), were linked by a subterranean pedestrian network to a newly constructed Metro system. (See Figs. 25.15 and 33.12.) This well-known network is the result of expedient accommodations to existing conditions. It produced a series of overground passages set below the podiums of new buildings – a private domain which, in effect, reproduced the market function of the street without its public content.

Perhaps the most important of these buildings is Place Bonaventure, a superblock designed by the Montreal firm of Raymond Affleck. This modern, multi-functional urban complex is plugged into the transportation hub of the city and boasts an extensive pedestrian network, but its tight vistas are turned in on themselves and enclosed in a heavy concrete behemoth which ironically turns it back to the city and destroys it. A less well-known, though more integrated and successful version of this new urban type, Place Alexis-Nihon, emerged out of the architectural subculture of the city.*

By the mid-1970s, Montreal may be one of the few cities of its size in North America to maintain a vital urban core, but the concentration

* Editor's note: For a description of Place Alexis-Nihon, largely inspired by Charney, see Reyner Banham, *Megastructure: Urban Futures of the Recent Past* (London: Thames and Hudson, 1976), 127.

of highly capitalized buildings was achieved at the expense of the destruction of the *quartiers populaires* and led to the sell-out of any building of consequence to itinerant foreign capital and to absentee landlords. The conditions which produced this initial development have turned the city into a speculator's paradise without effective guidelines to control urban growth, and now threaten to destroy the initial achievement.

Recent Departures

By the 1970s, the technocrats of the Quiet Revolution began to believe their own scenarios. They gave in to self-induced illusions of grandeur and proceeded to launch a series of schemes such as the James Bay Hydroelectric Project (planned to be the world's largest installation) and the staging of the extravagant 1976 Olympic Games in Montreal. These proved to be their undoing.

In architecture, the last gasp of the Quiet Revolution, and, hopefully, the beginning of a third and new phase was marked by the build-ing of Complexe Desjardins. The most recent superblock, Complexe Desjardins was conceived to rival Place Ville-Marie as the focus of the centre of Montreal and to shift the centre to the east, closer to the historic, French-Canadian core of the city. While the former building was conceived and financed by New York interests with the backing of the Anglo-Canadian banking establishment, Complexe Desjardins was scrupulously developed as a French-Canadian undertaking. It was backed by a local credit union, which was founded at the turn of the century in church basements, and which, by the 1970s, is one of Quebec's most important financial institutions: what began with the implantation of a new relationship in society was translated into a system capable of reproducing the society itself. Complexe Desjardins dominates the skyline of Montreal. Its four towers, varying in height between forty and twelve storeys, reproduce the profile of a city. The building demonstrates that its architects were not only capable of producing an efficient urban complex, but also that they

COMPLEXE DESJARDINS

32.9 Complexe Desjardins, model.

could be more successful than their counterparts in the west in relating this complex to the fabric of the city. Montreal is a city of squares, and the plan of the Complexe was conceived about an enclosed *galleria* at the scale of a square, accessible to and oriented by a public perspective of the city.

A cycle in the evolution of Quebec is now complete. Within months of the opening of Complexe Desjardins in 1976, the people of Quebec elected a government clearly committed to political autonomy. The option for self-government is now real. It exposes an existing polarization of practice between a technocratic, centralizing, and ultimately conservative tendency, which has for its key word "hierarchy," and a humanitarian drive, with its key word "equality" – a polarity which aligns tendencies in architecture with those in other industrial countries.

The thrust of a technocratic architecture emerged out of the Quiet Revolution. An anonymous figuration of modern idioms has acquired, by default, its own bureaucratic context and typology to which people have given

LEFT | 32.10 Services de santé du Québec, 2525 Laurier Boulevard, Quebec City, 1971. La Roche, Ritchot, Déry, Robitaille, architects.

RIGHT | 32.11 City of Montreal, municipal housing.

meaning. These buildings are as good and as bad as similar institutional edifices produced in other countries by a similar cast of managerial men, modified here by a latent intuitive expressionism: some corners remain unresolved, or an edge of kitsch is introduced to soften the whole with a subversive touch. The possibilities and limitations of technocratic architecture are well illustrated by the work of the Office municipal d'habitation de Montréal. Some architects in its employ tried over a decade to introduce innovative schemes involving the participation of people in the amelioration of their *quartiers*. More recently, they introduced urban configurations to the form and scale of public housing so as to insert them into the vacant lots of inner-city *quartiers*, and into the shells of rehabilitated houses, and to restore existing neighbourhoods. These endeavours, however, are short lived and kept marginal to the total production of housing by a city administration which remains tied politically to regressive interests.

In contrast, a second and significant track of current architecture is found in the fusion of the diverse elements of counterpractice which first emerged in the 1960s. Like the co-operative movement, which has now assumed an important role in the development of Quebec, the roots of this movement issue from a long history of communalism nurtured in the isolation of Quebec. Its origins are also found in a history of resistance to Canadian federal government programs in housing, which singularly channelled funds into single-family suburban housing, and into the use of housing to support a market economy. These groups argued for a form of habitat specifically aimed at socializing relationships between people.

Of necessity, the work produced by this movement is scattered, small in scale, and, therefore, less visible than the traditional mainstream of architecture. For example, a group of architects with the Comité logement Centre-Sud, work-

ing in one of the most ravaged of the *quartiers* of Montreal, rebuilt ten units of housing in an existing block of flats. The building as such cannot be seen, for it was carefully made to form part of the continuum of the neighbourhood.

Another example is found in the work of a group of architects that is part of a tenants organization living in government-built and -subsidized housing. Their redesign of this bleak welfare ghetto added to it the physical attributes of a neighbourhood, drawing consciously on a common vocabulary of identifiable elements. Physical preservation here does not mean social conservation. In both cases, design was practised with the people who live in the housing and was part of their collective acquisition of its ownership – a gesture which aligned these groups with the thrust of the Quebec government to reclaim its jurisdiction in housing and to shift priorities to co-operatives.

Between these two polarities, recent, unplanned-for, and expedient adaptations still generate an important cutting edge in the ferment of architecture in Quebec. A radical contextualism can be seen in the use of existing urban forms. The new campus of the Université

32.12 Université du Québec à Montréal, model of the campus, ca. 1976. Dimitri Dimakopoulos and Jodoin, Lamarre, Pratte, architects.

du Québec à Montréal was more or less forced to incorporate parts of historic buildings into its design.* The hurried enactment of a recent bylaw in the City of Montreal froze the demolition of some buildings and has left behind a series of facades which maintain the figure of the street and the form of the city. In Quebec City, one of the main shopping streets in a run-down *quartier* was covered over by a transparent roof, creating a new version of a nineteenth-century urban *passage* out of existing buildings. Here the enclosed street retained its public content both physically and legally – its rich pastiche of styles, metaphors, and idioms are regulated by the syntax of the city and are caught in vibrant, but crude, collage architecture.

In other words, the marginality of Quebec remains its source of strength. The significance of new movements in the architecture is found in the radical use of existing codes to redefine a typology of building types, and to articulate the possibilities of an alternate discourse to traditional practices.

* Editor's note: Project designed by Dimitri Dimakopoulos.

Finally, it should be noted that this is taking place in a corner of North America suffering all the symptoms of advanced consumerism: in housing, the production of suburban units has advanced to a point where the fabrication of codes has virtually been automated as a function of the marketplace – the most recent style playing, shamelessly, on traditional Québécois themes. It is also taking place on one of the few remaining geographic frontiers: the opening up of Quebec's north to the exploitation of its resources has resulted in a vernacular of prefabricated cities, built out of the same, but stripped-down, units used in the suburbs further south, and organized in urban forms reduced to the bare essentials of computer-like circuitry. It presents a country with a history of dissent, struggling to come to terms with advanced industrialization in the latter part of the twentieth century – a potentially exciting mix.

33

The Montrealness of Montreal: Formations and Formalities in Urban Architecture*

A cycle in architecture would now seem to be complete. An interest in the specificity of urban form, the idea of building in sympathy with and in relation to the specific context of an urban site, and the acceptance of past typologies of the city as given forms of contemporary building, are returning centre stage. A discourse prevalent at the beginning of this century, prior to the advent of the modern movement – compositional devices, monumental attributes, the narration of cultural memory – has reappeared as some echo filling a void. This interest in the form of the historic city arrives, however, at a time when the physical bulk of cities in which most people live exists only since the 1950s, as though coherent practices in regard to historic forms can only be articulated once the physical evidence of these forms has been reduced to

mere abstract outlines, to ruins of their former selves. Nevertheless, be it nostalgia or a fashionable delight in the picturesque, the packaging of history as advanced consumerism, strategies in the face of capitalist transformations of the city, or an outburst of conservatism, the return to a preoccupation with the form of the city indicates a shift in the spectrum of analogies whereby models of the city are conceptualized. A mechanical, biologic analogy (organism, growth, tissue, heart, arteries) may be seen to be displaced by a semiologic analogy (vocabulary, signification, syntax, narration). It also suggests a structural displacement in the understanding of architecture as a societal practice, since semiology is based on the assumption that there exists shared referential links to which human artifacts convey meaning, and these links, be they biologic or established by habits of schooled recognition, are socially bound: society makes every use a sign of itself.

Montreal is a North American city. Yet, as John Reps noted, "the older sections of Montreal preserve the results of an early age of town planning ... almost unique [on this] continent."[1]

* From *Architectural Review* 167, no. 999 (May 1980): 299–302; translated into French by Nicholas Roquet as "Montréal Formes et figures en architecture urbaine," in *Ville, Métaphore, Projet – Architecture urbaine à Montréal, 1980–1990*, ed. Georges Adamczyck (Montreal: Éditions du Méridien, 1992), 17–30.

Founded by the French in the early seventeenth century, it fell into the hands of the British in 1759. The isolation of one culture within the other, and the ensuing resistance of one to the other, intensified the articulation of built form, pushing at cultural boundaries, particularly at urban – i.e., collective – forms of the city. Differences were asserted, but so were underlying currents of architecture which cut across the expansion of European empires, and the articulation of a North American experience, sharpened by an accident in the history of this continent. The essential structure of Montreal is found in the plan of the initial French settlement. This plan can be seen to be an instance, one of many in the Americas, where the organisation of a town was adapted from devices found at the roots of classic planning which appear throughout history, particularly in the creation of new urban centres. The device itself was less of a "model" than a series of reproducible relationships based on an undifferentiated grid. The grid subsumed the potential structure of a town: a tacit representation of "knowledge" of town organization. In Montreal, the essential elements consisted of an orthogonal street grid, elongated on an east-west thoroughfare; a specific house type defined by party walls; and the street and the square as defined spatial entities.

A similar structure can be seen in the organization of the Zahringer new towns, settled in the eleventh century.[2] The historic cores of the Zahringer towns (Bern, Freiburg) still flourish today, as does that of Montreal. The dynamic in both cases may be found in an "open" relationship between the town and the surrounding countryside: the continuity of the town structure in a system of rural land division.[3] Beyond Montreal, a system of *rangs* – long, narrow lots perpendicular to access roads – reproduced a rural configuration of the city grid, unique in North America. French authorities under Colbert made an attempt to organize the settlers in a normalized system of landholding set about

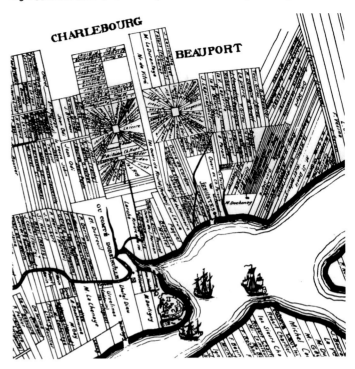

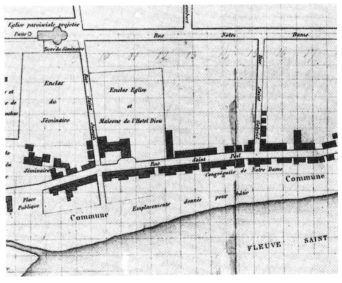

ABOVE | 33.1 In the 1670s the Intendant of New France, Jean Talon, tried to settle the colonists in a disposition of radial lots set about a symmetrical town square. The extensible system of long lots, the *rangs*, prevailed.

BELOW | 33.2 The first aligment of Montreal's streets in a drawing of 1672. The rudiments of an orthogonal grid, and a tight alignment of buildings defined by and defining the street, plot the main elements of the city.

Figs. 33.3, 33.4, and 33.5 | The predominance of an
urban, greystone, terraced architecture

a central square, emblematic of authority; the English tried to institute similar towns in Upper Canada.[4] The *rangs*, however, prevailed. Its extensible grid embodied a potential for the reformation of the old social order, the resistance of the settlers and the seeds of rational forms of settlement to emerge out of the American experience.

The plans of numerous American cities were also derived from the linear grid. But the difference in Montreal is found in the sustained development of an urban architecture based on the predominance of the street as a physical entity which subsumed individual buildings. Herein lies one of its strongest features. The city evolved about a distribution of public "interiors," unlike the pattern of American cities which was dominated by individual buildings set in city-like patterns, as characterized by Thomas Jefferson's expressed mistrust of terraced houses in Philadelphia.[5]

The British conquest in 1759 cut off the original French settlement of Montreal from its origins. The arrival of American royalists further isolated the French. Scottish and Irish immigrations followed. Montreal became an English city with French-Canadian inhabitants. Yet, the original urban articulation of the city found its echo in methods of town building emanating from the British Isles, so that even though few structures remain from the French regime, a "French" tradition persists. It can be seen in a photograph of 1851 which shows an alignment of

ABOVE | 33.3 The street alignment of a house type defined by party walls, and an austere, provincial, greystone articulation, as seen in 1851.

CENTRE | 33.4 Prince of Wales Terrace, Sherbrooke Street, 1865.

BELOW | 33.5 Late nineteenth-century flats in a *quartier populaire*; a strong physical articulation of the common wall of the street.

terraced stone houses, as in a French town. It is seen in the Prince of Wales Terrace, a speculative venture built in 1860, one of the finest terraces in the English tradition in North America – destroyed in the 1960s by McGill University to make way for a business school. It can also be seen in the rows of flats in factory neighbourhoods dating from the late nineteenth century. They show an austere, proto-classic, and greystone architecture of terraced buildings defined by and defining the street. Rough, inexpensive masonry was used to build party walls and lanes, differentiating the form of the city in the replacement of materials.

In the late nineteenth century, Montreal emerged as the financial and industrial metropolis of Canada. At the same time, the status of French Canada was further reduced from that of a founding nation to that of a province – Quebec – clamouring for equal rights. Montreal grew as an English city with French-Canadian inhabitants, floating – an island in a river – on the edge of French Quebec.

The metropolitan city presents us with two essential layers drawn along class as well as cultural lines. The first was built out of and fitted into the greystone tradition as the strategic embellishments of metropolitan civility modelled on, or directly imported from, nineteenth-century world capitals. The distinctive greystone architecture flourished, its initial austerity somewhat mollified, but still marked by a parsimonious view of architecture and a mistrust of self-expression.[6]

Again individual buildings, though interesting in themselves (such as McKim, Mead and White's Bank of Montreal Building on Place d'Armes or the Redpath Museum, McGill University, both excellent examples of Beaux-Arts mannerism which dominated architectural taste), are less distinguished than urban constructions. Typical is the transformation of the mountain in the centre of the city into an urban park by Frederick Law Olmsted, 1874–76. Olmsted's work can be traced from his visit to Parc des Buttes Chaumont in Paris with its man-made hill of cement rising precipitously out of an artificial lake as some "natural ruin," resembling the interior of Boullée's Musée de la Nature, to the later artificial wilderness, "a sylvan monument," which Olmsted created on a run-down site in New York City. In Montreal, he argued for a park as a work of art in the city: nature could not be left alone, it had to be forced where necessary to achieve "poetic charms of scenery."[7] The existing primordial stone cliffs were incorporated into a picturesque composition of a mountain rising, precipitously, out of the centre of a city. The wilderness was composed into a representation of itself, a harbinger of the mechanical reproduction of urban artifacts for public consumption.

The urban constructions in Montreal were in fact skilful and opportune transformations of neglected areas within the city. Major squares were created in this way. Victoria Square began as a haymarket. With expansion, commercial establishments gravitated about the open space. The formal figure of a square was then implanted in the space – the statue of a monarch, an alignment of walkways, rows of tailored trees, and a carpet of grass – and this was followed by a reconstruction of the enclosure of buildings, formalizing its "ground." The square was then drawn into a sequence of streets and squares, focusing a north-south axis. By the 1920s, commercial activity shifted, trees were cut, and part of the square lopped off for a streetcar right-of-way. By the 1960s, Victoria Square was reduced to the grass apron of an office tower – Place Victoria – which not only usurped its name, but also its public function.

Expedient adaptation, followed by opportune insertions and the subsequent reproduction of the insertions as a formal urban type, characterize the city. For example, the innovation of pedestrian networks in the 1960s was again less a case of a deliberate plan than of the deliberate use of existing opportunities: the open space of

ABOVE | 33.6 Victoria Square, 1873; Mount Royal in the background.

RIGHT | 33.7 St James' Street, the late nineteenth-century financial centre of Canada, as seen in the mid-1960s with the tower of Place Victoria in the background.

an excavation created by a train tunnel, as the site of Place Ville-Marie, and the slope of the land falling away from the building's podium as a continuous lower-level precinct protected from the harsh winter climate of the city.

The counterpart of the metropolitan monuments of the late nineteenth century city – its second layer – is to be found in the extensive *quartiers populaires* which house the human material of Montreal's industrial expansion, the *émigrés* coming mainly from rural and small-town Quebec. The structure of these *quartiers* was based on a more generic form of physical organization than current practices: the re-urbanization of the rural *rangs* and the

innovation of a unique building system forged out of crude plank construction and a sophisticated layering of materials which incorporated pockets of air and snow for insulation – a reversal of traditional massive wall construction and a revolutionary breakthrough in the material conception of building in a climate where shelter is particularly critical. (See Fig. 29.1.)

The architecture of the *quartier* emerged out of this rudimentary shell and in speculative, tenant housing. It was the result not so much of a process of selection of one element as opposed to another, as of a series of modifications causing particular sets of physical instructions to prevail. Facades were gradually pulled back

Figs. 33.8, 33.9, 33.10, 33.11 | The *quartiers populaires*

CLOCKWISE FROM TOP RIGHT

33.8 The initial formation of the *quartiers* via the reurbanization of the rural *rangs* into a grid of streets and blocks.

33.9 The initial ingredients of brick-veneered flats, set against the street. The first of May, a worker's day in the rest of the world, was moving day in the *quartiers* of Montreal, celebrated by a parade of paltry possessions, as seen here in the early 1930s.

33.10 Evolution of the urban architecture of the *quartiers* with the extension of each flat into the street, creating the figuration of a unique social zone, appropriating the space of the street.

33.11 The Arcadian transformation of the streets of the *quartier* into linear gardens.

from the street to make way for a dense zone of entrances, staircases, and balconies, fitted with a band of trees as in some urbanized park – a zone which related each dwelling directly to the street. The grid was differentiated into *avenues, rues,* and *ruelles,* each with a specific use and form. At the intersection of streets the corners of buildings were truncated, setting apart the outline of a square. Entire blocks were composed as singular buildings, while each dwelling maintained a direct access to the street. And the density of flats was increased further with the conversion of stables and sheds in the interior of the blocks, where the street was drawn via a *porte cochère* into a system of court housing.

The architecture was thrashed out by people who had no choice but to use available means to humanize living conditions in the wake of rapid industrialization. It cemented collective links built on common needs and extended the individual flats into larger social units. It became the urban architecture of Quebec, an authentic urban architecture; the "knowledge" of its inhabitants to appropriate in an empirical way the city for collective life.

By the 1960s, Montreal expanded to include over 50 per cent of the population of Quebec. It became an urban region which engulfed the nineteenth-century metropolis in an ever-expanding suburban fringe which was heavily subsidized by the Canadian government to the detriment of all other forms of housing, particularly the extensive housing stock of the inner-city *quartiers.* The core of the city was ripe for development, and while the Canadian financial interests moved off to Toronto, foreign interest moved into Montreal to capitalize on a virtually laisser-faire attitude reminiscent of the sell-out of Quebec's natural resources in previous decades. What emerged, nevertheless, was an integrated urban core. The units of transformation were large-scale superblocks, designed by architects such as I.M. Pei (Place Ville-Marie), Luigi Nervi and Luigi Moretti (Place Victoria), and

Mies van der Rohe (Westmount Square). These superblocks were connected by an enclosed pedestrian network, in a series of north-south axes, linked by a newly constructed Metro system. The new superblocks became the "places" (squares) of the city and their corridors became "streets," replacing the exterior public city with a private interior area geared to the marketplace.

Perhaps the most interesting of these buildings is Place Bonaventure. Unlike the earlier superblocks with their arrangement of office towers set on a podium of shopping malls, similar to such developments in other cities, this building has a distinctive low volume reproducing a city block, as though its "podium" was moved out of the underground. The interior of Place Bonaventure, however, remains a series of confusing corridors turned in on themselves and buried in a concrete behemoth with raw blank walls backed up against adjacent streets, destroying the city. A less well-known, though more integrated and successful, version of this new urban type, Place Alexis-Nihon, combines towers and a low block, shops which open to the street, and an interior focused by a central, sky-lit volume: innovations to emerge out of the commercial subculture of the city.

During this period, Quebec passed through a "quiet revolution" in which French Canadians rapidly modernized their society. Montreal became essentially a Québécois city with an English-speaking minority. The second and most recent development of the core of the city emerged out of this change. Typical is the construction of Complexe Desjardins, intended to rival Place Ville-Marie as the focus of Montreal, and to shift the centre of the city closer to its French-Canadian origins. While the former building was conceived and financed by New York interests, with the participation of the Anglo-Canadian banking establishment centred in Toronto, Complexe Desjardins was scrupulously developed as a French-Canadian undertaking backed up by a local credit union

founded at the turn of the century in church basements and which by the 1970s was one of Quebec's most important financial institutions. The Complexe bears witness to architects who were not only capable of producing a multi-functional urban superblock, but also could be more successful than their counterparts to the west in creating an urban context. The plan was conceived about an enclosed volume reproducing the configuration of a nineteenth-century city square, adjacent to a main thoroughfare. Large glazed porticos on two ends focus the "thoroughfare" on an exterior perspective drawn from a recent cultural centre to the seventeenth-century core of the city, creating in this way a north-south axis similar to those found in earlier periods of the city and along which further large-scale insertions are presently under construction. What is also revealing is the profile of the Complexe as a fragment of the core. A series of four towers varying in height between twelve and forty storeys

LEFT | 33.12 Initial suppression of the street below podiums, destroying the urban articulation of the city; Westmount Square, Mies van der Rohe, 1965.

LEFT | 33.13 The simulation of public, urban formations inside a typical superblock; the interior "square" and "boulevard" of Complexe Desjardins.

reproduce the profile of the city itself, as if all of Quebec had arrived figuratively, if not actually, at embracing its urban condition, and was at the threshold of recreating a "national" city, Montreal, in its image. In 1976, within months of the opening of the Complexe, a government committed to political autonomy was elected in Quebec.

During two decades, 1960–80, the public open space of the centre of Montreal was extensively internalized in a sequence of buildings which demonstrate a progressive re-objectification of its public function. The initial superblocks

LEFT | 33.14 The introduction of existing fragments – a square and a steeple – into the fragments of the superblock; a north-west corner of the Université du Quebec.

RIGHT | 33.15 Existing fragments as urban symbols. Facades of typical greystone terraced buildings, preserved by law and awaiting the insertion of a building.

reproduced the interiors of suburban shopping malls, cut off from the street. Within these malls, as in late twentieth-century *passages,* signs of the city – entrances, streets, squares, etc. – were systematically abstracted in the transformation of public urban space into a commodity. The introduction of urban-like internal volumes and an urban focus to the outside city began to appear with a shift from private to public and para-public development. The most recent addition to the core, the campus of the Université du Québec à Montréal, has introduced into the formation of the superblock fragments of existing buildings which previously occupied the site. In contraposition to the new blank walls of the massive building, these fragments appear

as nervous, sculptural intrusions, supercharged with connotations. The introduction of textural urban figuration and typologies is soon to follow.

The expansion of the core has also involved the systematic destruction of nineteenth-century buildings. The leading edge of destruction, the counterpart of the new inner city, is seen in the extensive ruins of the peripheral *quartier populaire.* Here also a coherent practice emerged during the past two decades, but it is one founded on the preservation of the architecture of these neighbourhoods, and rooted in communalism nurtured in the historic isolation of Quebec. The dominant mode is either the restoration of existing buildings, or the insertion of new flats into existing shells, restoring as well a gentrified patina of innocent proletariat existence which has joined the rural myth in the pantheon of idealized visions of Québécois existence.

Even the rather regressive Office municipal d'Habitation of the city has developed forms of public housing which reproduce elements of the traditional units of the *quartiers.* In 1978, on a typical greystone terraced street near the

Université du Québec, nineteenth-century facades were carefully dismantled and reconstructed as the facade of a modern structure. The new building cannot be seen as separate from the historic street.

[Two cities now thrive, one within the other. Outside, the remains of an aging, traditional city, charged with signification: the bearer of urban figures, the "interior" of the urban consciousness of people. (See Fig. 34.14.) This traditional city is, however, in a constant state of disrepair and dismantlement, as if it can sustain no more than the crumbling traces of neglect and disinvestment. It also remains in a state of exile for five months of the year, banished to subsist in the snow and wind of a harsh climate. While inside the bulky, blind superblocks of a new, primitive city, people flounder in the abstraction of streets and squares, lost in the hermetic remains of urban traces that are, at best, shadows of their former selves: "ruins before they have begun to crumble." Here, however, in the "ruins" of a street-wise, urban culture, one is undeniably warm and dry.]*

Be it the introduction of an urban configuration in inner-city superblocks, or the strong identification with the urban architecture of the *quartiers*, public symbols of the city are seen to be alive and well in the cultural affirmation, if not the social articulation, of people. The resolution of these references in architecture is caught, however, between the total reproduction of large-scale urban interventions, with its tendency to automate and normalize sign systems, and the replication of things-as-they-are, emanating from small–scale interventions in the *quartiers*.

[Montreal is one of those cities where a sense of destiny is vividly ingrained in its physical urban demeanour.]

* Editor's note: paragraphs between square brackets were added in 1992.

NOTES

1 John Reps, *The Making of Urban America* (Princeton, NJ: Princeton University Press, 1965), 71.
2 Paul Hofer in *The Zahringer New Towns*, exhibition catalogue (Zurich: Swiss Federal Institute of Technology Zurich, 1966).
3 Fernand Braudel, *Civilisation matérielle et capitalisme* (Paris: Armand Colin, 1967).
4 John van Nostrand, "Roads and Planning: The Settlement of Ontario's Pickering Township, 1789–1975," *City Magazine* (December 1977).
5 Vincent Scully, *American Architecture and Urbanism* (New York: Frederick A. Praeger, 1969), 83.
6 Edmund Wilson, *O Canada: An American's Notes on Canadian Culture* (New York: Farrar, Strauss and Giroux, 1965). He describes an influence that "has notoriously worked in Canada to discourage the practice of the arts" (39).
7 S.B. Sutton, ed., *Civilizing American Cities: A Selection of Frederick Law Olmsted Writings on City Landscape* (Cambridge, MA: MIT Press, 1971).

34

To Whom It May Concern: On Contemporary Architecture in Quebec*

Since the mid-1960s, our understanding of contemporary architecture has changed considerably. The premises of modernism have been revised. The history of modern architecture has been rewritten.

Our thinking has become more articulated in the face of the implacable specificity of a language of architecture as formal representation of place, a thinking developed in the social dimension of all forms of cultural practice.

What started at the end of the 1950s as a premonition that a relationship exists between buildings and their environment was affirmed in the mid-1960s by a physical and spatial "contextualism" of all contemporary architectural conception. This contextual approach later expanded to include the urban, temporal, and symbolic qualities of architecture. *Contextualism* was transformed into *rationalism* as the autonomy of a *language* proper to

architecture was recognized. *Rationalism* became a certain kind of *realism* by virtue of the introduction of the ideas of lexicon and of a typology of place. Finally, the discourse on contemporary architecture is now characterized by this acceptance of an existing typology of historic forms and places as given forms – if sometimes analogical – of contemporary buildings. A formal imaginary has taken hold. A careful reading of the theories from Alberti to Venturi and Tafuri, the techniques of architectural composition, the iconography of signs, the figurative preoccupations, the monumental attributes of public buildings, and a narration of memory are part of this discourse like so many echoes of the polemics heard before the beginning of the [twentieth] century and reverberating since in the void of modernism.

It remains to be seen whether architecture has gone beyond the point of rupture with the tradition of modernism, a so-called postmodernist genre, or whether it is, yet again, in one of those cyclical returns to the past that have happened before in the inevitable transformation of modern cultural relations.

* "À qui de droit: au sujet de l'architecture contemporaine au Québec," *ARQ – Architecture Québec* (January–February 1982): 12–23. Translated by Nancy Dunton; revised by Louis Martin.

One must conclude, however, that there has been a change in the way that built form is conceived. If we take the city as an example, we see that the mechanical-biological model of the "functional city" (urban growth, urban fabric, heart of the city, arteries of circulation) has given way to a structural-linguistic model (typology of place, vocabulary of signs, syntactic connections, organizational structure, narration, etc.). Everything visible has been semiotized. Architecture no longer has to call into question a *langue* or a *parole* in creation but rather has to make obvious what is *said* and for whom it is *said*. On the one hand, we find those who use conventional and popular codes as points of reference in a reality that they represent in their work, a reality situated nonetheless in a formal and historic reading of architecture. On the other hand, there are those who reject the existing conventional codes in the name of the specificity of a collective memory of historical form hidden behind modernism and in particular the archetypal and urban forms of the historic city as an essential of all rationality in architecture.

This change in the conception of built form has equally meant that there has been a structural change in our understanding of the social dimension of architecture. The analogy of a *language* – the contribution of signs – is founded on the idea that there exists referential links to which each human act gives a sense. And these links, biologically rooted or evolved through use, are socially determined: each human act in a social context becomes but a sign of itself.

These transformations in architecture don't escape anyone's notice. In 1980, there are no more innocents, with the exception of those who are divorced from history or who lack the means to understand their own historical situation.

It remains now to measure how these transformations in architectural thinking and creation have affected Quebec's architectural production over the last twenty years. If one bases one's judgment on the Prix d'excellence awarded by the Ordre des architectes du Québec over the last few years – apart from two interesting houses – most of the buildings reveal a hesitation about where contemporary architecture is now. It's as if history stopped ten years ago. It is true that the same thing has happened elsewhere in Canada. At best, one sees there a certain desire to give abstract configurations a certain contextual, semantic, and urban sense. In Montreal, for example, the great central void of Complexe Desjardins is an important step towards the articulation of an interior public space and towards the discovery of an urbanity, but it still needs to create the shape of an urban place within the place. Or consider the example of the Palais des congrès, which, in covering the trench of an expressway, could have repaired the fabric of the city. Of this desired contribution to the city, the building is instead nothing but an immense ship after an emergency landing. It is the last of the megastructures that adorn Montreal and which serve only to institutionalize the destruction of the city: one has only to look at the rest of Saint-Antoine Street or de la Gauchetière Street on the borders of this Palais.

The words used by certain architects clearly show that they know that something has happened but they're not sure what it was all about. The illusions that date from the end of the 1960s are still expressed with a frustration both apocalyptic and typically modern: "The architect is a species on the road to extinction" (*Le Devoir*, 5 December 1981), while elsewhere there are signs of a renewed interest in architecture. There is a growing interest in the cultural dimension of architecture as opposed to the business of architecture: numerous exhibitions, animated discussions, more publications, bookstores that specialize in architecture, open competitions etc.

It has to be understood, however, that during the 1960s in Quebec, there were architects – Paul-Marie Côté, Roger D'Astous, and Henri Brillon, among others – who generated an authentic avant-garde movement. This movement was distinguished by its attempt to create symbolic forms, abstract and sculptural gestures that are sometimes naive but plastically expressive of a people in their landscape. This desire to manifest symbolically an awareness of the country – whether in the Saguenay or in Montreal – was an important step in the affirmation of a Quebec architecture. This was the first truly avant-garde movement in Canada born, like that of the *Automatistes* and the *Plasticiens,* out of the particular cultural circumstances of the era. However, in 1980, it is as if the "Quiet Revolution" had exhausted many architects. If the cultural *semanticization* of symbols is still to be done, the urban context still needs to be articulated into a landscape proper to architecture.

The history of Quebec shows that, in previous periods, there has been a gap between the ruling architectural practice here and the advancement of architectural thinking and practice elsewhere. However, real-life experience in Quebec has shown that one finds the roots, and even the existence, of these advanced practices here. All of which means that architecture in Quebec is alive and well but, once again, it is to be found outside of that produced by most architectural offices and government services. The distinction has to be made between what is contemporary practice and what is still inexplicably contemporary – that which will soon be put into practice.

So, in the great museum that is Quebec, there are traces of a *postmodern* discourse – if you want to put an easy label on it – that is beginning to find its way into the conscience, if not the practice, of architects. What one is looking for is the presence of a formal imaginary.

Here are some points of reference, starting with a different look at familiar things and continuing with praise for the rich and colourful – if not secret – life of Quebec buildings. This is also an attempt to reconcile the desire to do something with that which exists, of the knowledge and the pleasure of an architectural gaze.

Most of these photographs were chosen by students in architecture at the Université de Montréal – many of whom are now young architects – in response to the question: "Could you identify some examples of built forms in Quebec that you find significant of contemporary architecture?"

A call to memory ...

Why not start with a reminder to remember?
Here's a very *ordinary* house built in 1951 by
the owner and his brothers according to a
plan done by his father-in-law. Smooth surfaces and the most basic design. It recalls
what Gérard Morisset wrote in *L'architecture
en Nouvelle-France* about the links between the
modernism of Marcel Parizeau and the *architecture d'autrefois*.* These connections evidently
run deep and wide in the knowledge of built
form. It is not a question of recreating the past
but rather of understanding it and situating it
relative to the present.

34.1 House at 17210 Côte Saint-Pierre, Saint-Janvier

The essential image of the house ...

One could also start with a portrait of the architect from the 1960s to the 1980s, a young boy on
a stage set: the pediment on axis of a *maison-
palais* which opens to the exterior via the steps
of a theatrical staircase. This image cannot
help but be fixed in his memory of built form
and show up in his work, in his architecture. A
true house in paradise.† Memory also links it
to an image of Palladio's Villa Rotonda – other
pediments on axis of a *maison-palais* that opens
out to the exterior ... Essentially, it is not the
memory that matters as much as a recollection of
the collective self through built forms.

34.2 House in Sainte-Agathe, Quebec

* Editor's note: Gérard Morisset, *L'architecture en Nouvelle-
France* (Quebec "Coll. Champlain," 1949), 15. Charney is
referring to the thesis he developed in "Towards a Definition
of Quebec Architecture," reprinted here as chapter 25.

† Editor's note: A reference to Joseph Rykwert, *On Adam's
House in Paradise: The Idea of the Primitive Hut in
Architectural History* (New York: Museum of Modern Art;
distributed by New York Graphic Society, Greenwich, CT
[ca. 1972]).

Recalling the unrecognized ...

The formal qualities of this type of house (construction of industrial materials that represent the essence of modern architecture) and the circumstances that produced it, as well as its place in the collective imagination, make this an authentic monument of both Quebec and North American architecture. The recognition of this typology known as *rational* in contemporary parlance only confirms the power of architecture in the culture of Quebec.

ABOVE | 34.3 House on Route 309 to Mont Laurier, Quebec.

BELOW | 34.4 House on avenue des Sables, in the area of Rawdon, Quebec.

Knowledge of the ordinary ...

The German architect Erich Mendelsohn came to the United States in the 1920s and found a modern architecture in the alleys of New York and Chicago, an architecture that can equally be found in alleys here.* A perspective that evokes a seventeenth-century stage set makes us enter a structured sequence where each element is carefully placed in an architecture that only affirms the signs of its own existence: here is the idea of the modern, paper brick facing and all.

34.5 House at 2823–25 Ontario Street East, Montreal.

The madness of knowledge ...

Imagine having built a facade where each element (a door that opens, a vertical window, a glazed window, an axis ...) is equally expressed in a completely contradictory way (a walled-up door, a horizontal window, a blocked-up window, an axis off-axis ...). Think of Le Corbusier's Ronchamp – a heavy roof with no visible support, bearing walls pierced at random ...

34.6 Garage transformed for light industry on Saint-Christophe Street, Montreal.

* Editor's note: Eric Mendelsohn, *Amerika* (Berlin, 1926), reprinted as *Amerika: Bilderbuche eines Architekten* (New York: Da Capo, 1976).

Urban knowledge ...

The setback of a building from and its engagement with the street as public space make evident the traces of urban structure, traces of knowledge of architecture in the landscape of collective memory. This is very different from the configuration of most modern buildings where neither a front nor a side is visible; everything floats in an ideal – but regressive – space.

34.7 (ABOVE) and 34.8 (BELOW) Unidentified buildings.

LEFT, ABOVE | 34.9 Cottage under construction, Domaine du Lac Carillon, Chatham, Quebec.

LEFT, BELOW | 34.10 Coop Saint-Polycarpe, Quebec.

RIGHT, ABOVE | 34.11 Building on Bishop Street, Montreal.

RIGHT, BELOW | 34.12 Church near La Sarre, Quebec.

The city of knowledge ...

In Montreal, there still exist two cities: that of *urban* knowledge, a city of *quartiers* and that of *architecture,* buried in that other city that is the metropolis. These two cities live one inside each other like Freud's analogy of the collective psyche, which he based on an image of Rome where all the buildings of every era existed together. It could be said that Montreal's libido, its life, exists still in the city of *urban knowledge* where ruins project its future.

ABOVE | 34.13 Prison on Parthenais Street and houses in the *quartier*, corner of Dufresne Street, Montreal.

BELOW | 34.14 Victoria Street at the corner of President-Kennedy Avenue seen from McGill College Avenue, Montreal.

Knowledge of ruins ...

"Yes, it looks like a city that has been bombed" (Montreal, August 1975). The destruction of *urban knowledge* by those who don't know how to act, except out of fear. Nevertheless, the memory of Saint-Norbert Street is still alive and, four years after its destruction, its past has become project – to reconstruct the street as a creation of a knowledge proper to architecture.

TOP LEFT | 34.15 Before 1975, Saint-Norbert Street, view towards the west.

TOP RIGHT | 34.16 Before 1975, Saint-Norbert Street, view towards the east.

BOTTOM LEFT | 34.17 After 1975, Saint-Norbert Street, view towards the west.

BOTTOM RIGHT | 34.18 After 1975, Saint-Norbert Street, view towards the east.

Traces ...

It's hard to tell which are the traces of what is to come and which are those of the past. They appear sometimes as nothing more than a stain on the side of a building ...

Lines ...

The archaeology of urban knowledge – which is to say of an architecture – has always served as the reference point for the invention of the new. In Montreal, we have started saving the facades of some buildings. The building behind the facade has been removed and another will soon appear. The old facade has become the start of something new.

ABOVE | 34.19 House on Lagauchetière Street, Montreal.

CENTRE | 34.20 House on Saint-Hubert Street, Montreal.

BELOW | 34.21 House on Sherbrooke Street, Montreal.

More ruins …

New construction, which is badly built or simply unfinished … a sort of disintegration is spreading.

From ruins to signs …

Are we as architects the last to understand that the milieu has been semioticized and *to say* something while saying nothing? Here are some houses that become *houses* by adding a schematic image. The *sign* of the house, the mansard roof, evokes memories of a Quebec both *innocent* and rural. The way these signs speak is exploited in home construction: *"Come and live in the paradise of Quebec."* Finally, all built form is only representation.

ABOVE | 34.22 Restaurant in Sherbrooke, Quebec.

CENTRE | 34.23 House near Montreal.

BELOW | 34.24 House in Sainte-Marjorique.

In the world of signs ...

Similarities obsess us. We can't get away from them. At the corner of one street: a *"city hall,"* a *"castle,"* a *"palace"* ...

ABOVE | 34.25 Corner of Pine Avenue and Drolet Street, Montreal.

BELOW | 34.26 Former Maisonneuve city hall at corner of Pie-IX and Ontario, Montreal.

The folly ...

Everyone searches to affirm himself in a metaphor of existence and to find himself in a *house in paradise.*

ABOVE | 34.27 Behind this body lives a rich car dealer of the Montreal region.

CENTRE | 34.28 House in Hampstead, Montreal.

BELOW | 34.29 Unidentified building.

And more follies ...

This is the imagination that makes architecture out of the existing ... One finds Lucien Kroll in the extension to a shed or the enthusiasm of Philip Johnson for a Peter Eisenman stair at the entry to a rooming house on Saint-Hubert Street.

ABOVE | 34.30 Shed in Montreal.

BELOW | 34.31 House on Saint-Hubert Street, Montreal.

Replicating the real ...

The real in the image of itself.

34.32 and 34.33 House in Saint-Sauveur, Quebec.

Forming or giving form to the real ...

There is one kind of outcome represented by
Les Habitations Jeanne-Mance in the 1950s and
Habitat 67 in the 1960s, arrogant and destructive
ideologies, an architecture without knowledge
and without attachment to the city, a ghetto
for social welfare in one case and for the rich in
the other, both heavily subsidized. An outcome
of another kind in architecture: the repair of
the urban fabric (new housing is situated in a
building giving onto two streets so as to take
back the original block as well as the urban
structure), the reintroduction of the figurative
shapes of an urban knowledge (contribution of
housing to street, open space in interior courtyard), the reintroduction of signs of a collectivity
(each unit has a front with a door which gives
directly onto the street as well as a back). This
is to redefine a different future. The whole was
conceived and built by a cooperative in a *quartier
populaire* beside an expressway.

34.34 Coopérative Louis-Cyr, Saint-Jacques Street, Montreal.

The other architecture ... the consequences of the signs ...

Mineshafts and a house in Rouyn-Noranda. Balconies on housing in Sherbrooke.

LEFT, ABOVE AND BELOW | 34.35 and 34.36 Mine and house in Rouyn-Noranda, Quebec.

RIGHT, ABOVE AND BELOW | 34.37 and 34.38 Balconies and housing in Sherbrooke, Quebec.

The primitive hut in paradise ...

Finally, to finish this discussion properly, a return to the essential.

From its origins, the fundamental nature of architecture has been evoked by images of small primitive huts, symbols of a return to the essential nature of man. Vitruvius shows some naked men at the edge of the forest in front of simple but geometric constructions. In the eighteenth century, with J.-F. Blondel, geometric order reappears in his reconstruction of a cabin in the form of a Greek temple. The search for a rational and neoclassical ideal returns to the scene in 1855 with M.A. Laugier: "The primitive hut ... is the model for all the splendors of architecture. It is through approaching the simplicity of this first model that essential mistakes are avoided and true perfection is achieved." Laugier's primitive hut is represented by four trees whose trunks are arranged like columns to form a perfect square, their boughs forming beams and their branches arranged to form a sloped roof. Here is the *natural* of the built form. Nature itself has become a construction of man. Laugier then moves on to the idea of the city laid out as an ideal garden – in contrast with the disarray of existing cities, the "forests." In twentieth-century suburbs, we're still living with the consequences of this thinking.

When compared with Laugier's hut, Viollet-le-Duc's 1860 "primitive hut" demonstrates a better understanding of true primitive construction, but here the model of the natural order is used as justification of the Gothic style he was promoting at the time in the École des Beaux-Arts in Paris. In the 1920s, Le Corbusier situated modern architecture in a natural order. He proposed the image of a primitive structure of a universal construction, this time in concrete: the Domino house.

Images of the "primitive hut" are equally present in the encyclopedia of built form in Quebec. However, historical circumstances are such that the significant structures are not those born out of the imagination of architectural discourse but rather of the most marginal conditions of daily life. The "primitive

FAR LEFT | 34.39 The building of the primitive hut, from *Vitruvius Teutsch*, Nuremberg, 1548.

CENTRE LEFT | 34.40 "The Primitive Hut" after Jacques-François Blondel, 1771–77.

CENTRE RIGHT | 34.41 "The Primitive Hut" from Marc-Antoine Laugier, *Essai sur l'architecture*, Paris, 1753.

FAR RIGHT | 34.42 "The First Building" from Eugène-Emmanuel Viollet-le-Duc, *Histoire de l'habitation humaine*, Paris, 1875.

 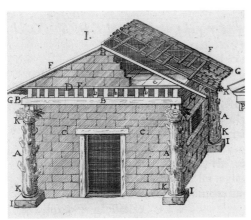  

huts" are truly that, at once both *primitive* and metaphorical.

Take the case of the "primitive hut" discovered on Logan, not far from the Parthenais prison in Montreal or of another in Laval or the Laurentians. They are all built as an assemblage of materials recovered from the detritus of contemporary life: rusted nails, old doors, cracked concrete blocks, wrecked buses etc. As other "primitive huts" in other periods of history have done, they serve as an essential model of architectural creation. They confirm the arrival of an architecture that is finding its place in the new order of things and aware of the images of images, the symbols of symbols, and the signs of signs. It is as if architecture started by the refusal of a refusal, by the desire to affirm that continuity between art and life.

ABOVE | 34.43 Rustic hut in Laval.

CENTRE | 34.44 Rustic hut on Logan Street, Montreal, near Parthenais prison.

BELOW | 34.45 Rustic hut in the Laurentians.

PART FIVE

The Image and Its Double

"The Image and Its Double" presents a selection of four essays published between 1982 and 1989. At the height of postmodernism, Charney revisited some great narratives of Western architectural tradition and reformulated his dialectical reading of architecture by contrasting temples and sheds. This period was also marked by the deconstruction of the architectural sign, a critical trend in which Charney participated that shows how architectural images are never innocent or transparent as they can deceptively mask the ruthlessness and violence of power. The CCA garden is the emblematic project of this section. This open-air museum consists of a group of monuments that are an amalgam of local and international, popular and learned, past and modern images. The garden may be interpreted as an attempt to represent metaphorically the dialectical substance of architecture.

35

The Image and Its Double

LOUIS MARTIN

During the 1980s, Charney scrutinized the intersection of the real and the metaphorical (or symbolic) in the multiple image suggested by the "architecture of signs." This new formulation of the dialectic of architecture added another layer to those he had proposed previously.

Layers

Built for Chicago's Museum of Contemporary Art in 1982, *A Chicago Construction* put "meaning back into the thing itself" with words and images in the manner Charney had done for *The Treasure of Trois-Rivières*. But rather than looking at a piece of popular architecture, this work examined the latent meanings inscribed in the modernist facade of the museum's building.

Although the modernist style was "said to signify nothing other than itself," Charney saw in the street facade evocations of three buildings.[1] On first impression, the building looked like the entrance of the emergency clinic of a hospital. But with its quasi-symmetrical composition and heavy corners the museum's facade suggested

the classic palaces of the Renaissance used as podiums for twentieth-century skyscrapers. Consequently, the building seemed incomplete and haunted by the spectre of a yet-to-come tower. Charney imagined the facade of that tower as a perfectly square grid, the figural device modern architects used to cover the actual horizontal grid of the steel frame. Finally, the spectre of typical Chicago pitched-roof workers' wooden houses was evoked in the bridge-like truss that spanned the facade. Charney drew these figures onto a photograph; the resulting image was built in plywood to materialize the layers that inhabited the place's architectural unconscious. Charney explained: "Together, the pieces become part of a larger tableau. The tableau does not so much restore what is buried in the sedimentation of the place, as to try to come to terms with its existence. A distinct iconography takes over. One 'building' draws away from the other. And whereas the first building is used to contain works of art, the construction has no other 'use' than that of being itself."[2]

A Chicago Construction made concrete a sophisticated narrative about the latent meanings of the place and suggested that the memory of the site could not be repressed in a deliberately amnesic composition.

Figura

When asked to conceive the setting of the exhibition Les villas de Pline at the Montreal Museum of Fine Arts, Charney reflected on the mechanisms of architectural representation at the heart of the pre-modernist tradition. (See Figs. 3.7 and 3.8.)

The pretext of the show was a recent *concours d'émulation* organized by the Institut Français d'Architecture (IFA), which proposed to reconstitute the "Laurentine villa" described by wealthy Roman Pliny the Younger in a famous letter written around the first century A.D. The exhibition was organized in two parts: the first showed examples of the reconstitutions of Pliny's two villas, the Laurentine and the Tuscan, from the Renaissance to the nineteenth century, and the other showed the drawings done by the post-modernist architects who participated in IFA's competition.

The peculiarity of this archaeological exercise rested on the fact that there existed no remains of Pliny's villas. While ancient models were derived from the study of Roman ruins, the reconstitutions of Pliny's villas rested only on the affinities between antique images and the surviving texts. Charney noticed: "Each [image and text] reinterpreted the other, seeking out appropriate sources, and assimilating an increasing knowledge of Roman and then of Greek sites as well as changing attitudes to antiquity, given the imperatives of the time."[3]

The first part of his text described how, over three centuries, this exercise developed into a real tradition of restitution in which "the reconstruction of what the antique villa may have been tended to emulate and idealize existing buildings, creating the natural history and contributing to the self-reflexive codification of an autonomous and 'true' architecture."[4] In other words, the process of restitution projected an idealized present onto the past: the invention of the Roman villa provided a norm, i.e. an architecture, by which modern buildings could be judged. But by the nineteenth century the process of emulation gave way to one of replication: the École des Beaux-Arts systematized composition, which was then reduced to the combination of a repertory of forms according to neoclassical principles; tradition was thus locked into convention. Charney concluded:

> Herein lies the interest of the exhibition: it presents us with the traces of a slice of the history – with a beginning and end – of formative processes which over a period of three centuries established a body of architecture drawn out of an ancient lineage. The archaeology it presents is not that of the Roman house, nor of the evolution of the villa as a type, but of a sustained tradition of interpretive drawings which served to internalize the figura of what we understand to be architecture and in which "significance," if it were forthcoming, could be recognized.[5]

It is not abusive to suggest that Charney's own architectural production was an extension of that tradition of interpretative drawings. Yet, works like *The Treasure of Trois-Rivières* and *A Chicago Construction*, in their search for meaning, inverted and even negated architecture's urge to establish a norm.

On the other hand, Charney judged the post-modern drawings insignificant. They revealed the futility of reviving a dead tradition symbolized "by the column" that only the Third Reich tried to resuscitate in the twentieth century. "In a 'fallen' and later time," he wrote, "we see only empty signs and hollow gestures."[6] Among the postmoderns, only Léon Krier showed that, beyond the vestiges of the classical tradition, fundamental themes were there as constant references. Krier deconstructed and reconstructed Pliny's villa. His fragmentation of the nineteenth-century grand Beaux-Arts compositions into small units relating to each other "in a dialectic subsumed by the order of a town" assumed "a didactic, if not moral stand."[7]

Charney saw an analogous dialectic in the plan of Maisonneuve, one of Montreal's *quartiers populaires*. The insertion of a major order of avenues and boulevards into the minor order of the street grid of Maisonneuve was "evidence of a fundamental order that [gave] form to the city as an urban construct: the figure of a city within the city."[8] Montreal's *quartiers populaires*, he argued, were built according to the *habitus* of city building by which houses structured the collective domain of streets. This "classic" urban tradition was the exact counterpart of the "classic" monumental tradition embodied by Pliny's villas. This dialectic was also visible in the anonymous architecture of the *quartiers populaires*:

At the front doors of numerous tenements in these Montreal quartiers, entrances are made to appear as "classic" temples inserted into the flatness of the facade, perpendicular to the street. These vestiges ritualize a passage into dark interiors. They also externalize a surrogate *figura* of the urban tenement as a dwelling and, hence, as a temple: on streets aligned with trees all you see is a line of "treasuries" along a sacred way. Everyone wants to dwell in the sacred precincts where nature is no longer a threat to one's existence: is this not the essential *figura* of architecture, verified not only by the temple-like reconstructions of Pliny's villas, but also by the "longue durée" of the monumental transformations by most people of the lowly sheds they inhabit?[9]

With the amalgam of the figure of the temple developed by the architectural tradition and the "primitive huts" of the industrial age, distant and new origins seemed to merge in multi-layered images charged with meaning.

Deception

As mentioned above, the postmodern moment was characterized by a rising interest in "the presence of the past." For Charney, the postmodernist return to history was problematic because it did not put in question "a practice so obviously tied in to institutionalized power."[10] He wrote in 1984: "It is as if the 'innocence' of history were now being advanced in place of the 'innocence' of pragmatic functionalism of the modernist decades."[11] But history was far from being innocent and architecture was far from being a transparent means of representation.

To illustrate his point, he compared two modernist projects found in the vicinity of Houston, Texas. The first was a housing development made of a series of drab industrial blocks, which he described as a "ghetto in the form of a concentration camp lodged in the heart of the city."[12] This architectural figure, which represented "nothing more and nothing less than institutional gesticulations of societal order – i.e., its historic condition," epitomized the fact that the history of housing had been "moulded by the form and development of prisons and concentration camps."[13] The second project, a design of Philip Johnson, was a glass corporate office tower in the shape of a 1920s masonry skyscraper. Seen from one angle, the surface of the building was transparent and revealed its skeleton, but seen from another angle the glass skin reflected the light of the sun and became as opaque as masonry. The trouble with this formalist play was that it restrained the viewer to surface appearances. Its architecture's historical references trivialized and even contradicted history. By a deliberate ruse, the building did not reveal its historic condition. This example showed that the reintroduction of figural content in recent architecture was accompanied by a new dialectic of sensibilities opposing a critical discourse of revelation and an insidious exploitation of figures. He explained:

Herein lie the outlines of a drama. It is found not so much in the fact that figural content of architecture as a representational system has been consciously reintroduced into practice in recent years (as if figurative content was expunged from modern architecture), but in the underlying train of sensibilities which this consciousness represents – a predisposition to unearth a strata of references, correspondences, and allusions to figural constructs with a potential to diagram equally evocative references, correspondences, and allusions whereby built objects may be conceived – and in the tendency to act upon these sensibilities in the actual creation of buildings. This troubling "discourse of revelation" lays bare the possibility to expose that what is accepted as natural is in fact historically constituted and thus subject to change. Thus we witness a genuine resistance to the reopening of the channels of representation, as well as an insidious exploitation of representational devices to belie the very significations promulgated in the name of history.[14]

Charney's critique of the innocent conception of history was consonant with Roland Barthes's disclosure of everyday myth as a delusory device which presented an ideological discourse under the guise of benign, natural common sense.[15] His "discourse of revelation" was also in tune with a sensibility that K. Michael Hays later described in terms of a post-1968 critical architectural theory which conceived culture not "as something that one both belongs to *and* possessed" but as something that must be "constantly constructed, deconstructed, and reconstructed through more self-conscious theoretical procedures."[16] Yet, Charney's persistent anti-formalist stance appears retrospectively to be what distinguishes him from contemporaries like Colin Rowe, Peter Eisenman, Robert Venturi, or Aldo Rossi and brings him closer to Manfredo Tafuri's ideological criticism.[17]

Charney registered that significant changes had transformed architectural sensibilities since the 1960s. "The exposure of the historic specificity of architecture as a system of representation" had not only served "to resuscitate a more militant alignment of its cultural boundaries," it had also "exposed the ambiguities of those who struggle within its boundaries."[18] With the concurrent loss of social illusions, the semiotic paradigm had given rise to a renewed formalism animated by "the very desire to evoke the autonomous life of architectural forms." This tendency drew one back to "the archetypal structure of all buildings," to "the internal strata of built objects," to crystal clear formal principles which could be found in the press, in Nantucket and in Paestum. But for Charney, "the actual representation of these principles in built form [could] only be lodged in some societal flux which carries with it a valence which simply cannot be willed away or subtracted from its meaning."[19] In other words, architectural meaning was not dissociable from life. As he argued in a comparison of an anonymous Montreal house and a house designed by Peter Eisenman, a figure found in popular architecture was always more significant than the same figure presented in the specialized context of architecture.

Intrinsically related to the rediscovery of "architecture as a system of representation" was the popularization of the idea that architectural meaning emerged from a sense of place, which was conceived in terms of collective memory (Rossi), of contextual visual coherence (Rowe), or of a pervading spirit of the place conceived as a substitute to the modernist spirit of the time (Norberg-Schulz). In his criticism of the "incipient 'innocence' which pervaded" practice, Charney formulated a unique and original outlook. He wrote: "There is no such thing as a 'Place' other than the sum total of the representations of that place. There are, therefore, no 'innocent' sites. There have never been neutral voids to be filled by buildings, other than the destructive imposition of a strategic emptiness. Nor can I relate to such notions as *genius loci* which seems to grapple with the phenomena of constructed presences in a pre-contextual, if not in anti-urban terms."[20]

Visibly, Charney's conception of place was founded on the correspondences and analogies which his temporary site-specific constructions intended to materialize. Meaning was constructed by the inherent logic of a narrative that blended images and words. And meaning acquired depth by a process of layering: "Layers of correspondences and association focused the formalization of these pieces, each with an overlay of content derived in particular from their limited existence – these pieces were destined to be destroyed."[21]

As seen above, Charney's constructions of the 1970s represented fragments of a repressed urban culture, symbols of a people's innate knowledge of architecture. In making visible the "signs of recognition," the collective symbols of the city erased by institutionalized power, his activism constituted a positive, quasi-utopian form of action. When, in 1980, he discovered the remains of a factory bombed during the Second World War near Frankfurt, Germany, he found a void haunted by the spectre of a dead camp. It struck his mind that the figure of the archetypal dead camp of Auschwitz-Birkenau represented a farm. He wrote: "This farm facade was part of an elaborate deception devised by the authors of the death machines of the 'Final Solution' to hide their terrible secret from its victims and from the world. People were said to be 'relocated' and not deported; Auschwitz was a camp for farm labour; on arrival people were sent to the 'showers,' that is, the gas chambers; and so on."[22]

With this image in mind, he conceived the series entitled "Better if they think they are going to a farm …" for the Kassel Documenta. His drawings superimposed this deceptive farm facade on pictures of some of the sites which were selected by the organizers of the Documenta to erect art installations. The juxtaposition of the death camp facade and the typical modern architecture of the postwar German reconstruction generated troubling and painful realizations for an architecture that was rediscovering figuration. So he concluded: "If in architecture there is now a conscious movement to emphasize a figural content which is said to have come to terms with history and to have lifted the veil of the modernist amnesia of our recent past, then the resolution of this movement, as others, revolves about the significance of the work. Given the potential of this discourse, it ought to confront at least the incipient fascism inherent in the manipulation of surrogate realities which blind us to our condition."[23]

Contrasting with his previous work, the Kassel series made visible the "ciphers of deception," the manipulative side of architectural oppression by institutionalized power. Far from innocent, architecture's figurative content served to mislead and hide death. The ghost of the death camp appeared as tragic evidence of architecture's historical bad conscience. In denouncing architecture's complicity with power, the series was an exercise in exorcism much different from the 1970s urban activism.

Once again Charney was in touch with the sensibilities of the period. His critique participated in a collective discovery: that of the disenchantment of the architectural sign which predated its deconstruction in the 1980s. With his cemetery at Modena, Aldo Rossi was said to have reintroduced the tragic character in architecture; with House X, Peter Eisenman explored the repressed unconscious of architecture by a process of decomposition; and in parallel John Hejduk developed narratives and imagery for an unprecedented architecture of pessimism. Yet, in contrast to his contemporaries, Charney, who had denounced the authoritarianism of formalism since the 1960s, exceeded the poetics of architecture and revealed with his parables the fundamentally political role of architectural representation.

Amalgam

The notions unearthed by Charney's "troubling discourse of revelation" merged in the realization of the garden of the Canadian Centre for Architecture (CCA) inaugurated in 1989. In many ways, CCA's garden constituted a synthesis of his ideas.

Locked between two ramps connecting the city to the Trans-Canada Highway and a large six-lane boulevard, the site was no more than a piece of rubbish produced by urban renewal. In spite of its isolation, the empty lot, situated at the edge of an escarpment, offered a spectacular, panoramic view of the city.

Charney put meaning back into that "place" by means of an elaborate narrative about urbanity, history, and memory; the site acquired its garden meaning through a chain of associations linking urban figures drawn from both Montreal and Western architectural tradition. He explained how meaning was already there on the site: "The site exists as an urban fact. It embodies concrete traces of human passage rooted in history and memory, layer upon layer. The layers of history have neither a past nor a future; they are simply there to be dragged up as a measure of the place, a map of its ongoing transformation. The layers of memory, however, are ever-present. They cut deep, transcend place and time, and summon forth typologies of an ideal city and models of rural idylls and Arcadian forest edge."[24]

The new garden broke deliberately with the landscape tradition established by F.L. Olmsted,

in which a piece of nature in rupture with the city created a pastoral scene. In contrast, the CCA garden was conceived as an urban scenography realized with two basic strategies. The first was the layering of type figures (an arcade, an esplanade, a meadow, an orchard, etc.) which filled the site with "traces" evocative of previous patterns of rural and urban occupation and of the conventional imagery of urban gardens. The second strategy consisted of a multiplication of mirror images which duplicated and re-presented the immediate surroundings of the site in a kaleidoscopic *mise en abyme*.

The inaugurating gesture consisted in producing a mirror image of the museum on the other side of the boulevard. This operation had visibly Lacanian overtones for Charney, who explained: "The mirror image blurs the distinction between subject and object and registers a measure of narcissism inherent in the monumental form of the city – the necessary anthropocentrism of urbanity, of the collective 'self' of people reflected in the body of the city, if such still exists."[25]

Mirror images also introduced a displacement of meaning from one object to another. For instance, the reconstruction of the museum image took the form of a literal ruin which acted as an arcade protecting the garden's esplanade from the street. Facing the actual museum, the garden was conceived as an allegorical open-air museum exhibiting a series of didactic images installed on two rows of columns. These images linked the surrounding city to the museum's content by means of "self-reflexive dualities," which created meaning with allegorical narratives. Charney explained the process:

An allegory is a narrative, a commentary of one text read through another, an extended metaphor. The narrative presented by the columns is intended to capture and objectify an architectural discourse derived from distinctive buildings, as befits a museum of architecture. As elsewhere in the garden, the columns were made to establish self-reflexive dualities. A first line of columns was set up as the direct counterpoint to and reflection of actual parts of the city, while a second line was set up as a counterpoint to and reflection of the first series of columns, echoing the first as the first echoes the architecture of the city.[26]

Charney's allegorical narratives established a dialogue between the memory of the site and the history of architecture. Cast in concrete and copper, each narrative was reified in the juxtaposition of artifacts drawn from the panorama of the surrounding *quartier populaire* and images drawn from the Western architectural tradition preserved in the CCA. Thus, a grain elevator was transformed into an ideal classical temple, a Montreal triplex sliced a traditional *maison québécoise*, a classical pediment was supported by a tilted constructivist tower, and so on. It is hard to know if these self-reflexive dualities were meant to express a confrontation, a collision, or a reconciliation of the dialectics of architecture. But each allegorical column proposed an uneasy collage, which produced a kind of alchemical reaction in which the meaning of each image produced a new and unstable evocative amalgam of ideas.

The garden was not conceived as a commemorative monument but as a device "to expose the place in the present, as a singular fragment of the city, and as an ongoing process of transformation whose most recent embodiment is that of a garden."[27] And, just as the origin of architecture was found in the mythical primitive hut, the foundation of any garden was found in the lost Garden of Eden. The CCA garden evoked this sense of loss of a distant paradise transformed into architecture by history: "A garden by its very nature tends to evoke old, stereotypical images of a lost Arcadia. This garden is situated on an expressway that is no more than a place of lost urbanity, a lost city. And if Paradise is a garden at one end of time and a city at the other, somewhere outside the world, as the underpinnings of tradition would have it, then either all is lost or we are now outside history in a world in which new relationships can be forged only out of an amalgam of elusive metaphors, be they a garden or a city."[28]

With its complex plays of reflections and metaphorical dualities, the garden was a piece of pure architectural representation in which architecture stripped of its functional content communicated its essence as both mirror and reification of human existence.

The Image behind the Image

Like other major architects/critics of his generation such as Colin Rowe, Peter Eisenman, or John Hejduk, Melvin Charney's work represents a sophisticated extension of Le Corbusier's didactic lesson encapsulated in his famous slogan "eyes which do not see." Over thirty years, he evolved an original dialectical reading of architecture which developed from at least three sources: the embryonic opposition of the classical pleasing image and the brutalist perturbing image proposed by Reyner Banham, Louis Kahn's dialectics of architecture and design, and pop art's uncovering of the mythological and archetypal realities of pop imagery.

For Charney, architecture never was an aesthetic or a formal problem. As such, he searched to surpass the Corbusian paradigm. Beyond the emotions stirred by the image, there were principles which explained the genesis of forms. These principles were not uniquely the rational formal principles of composition exposed by Le Corbusier or the search of a shock effect of the brutalist image imagined by Banham. In Charney's trajectory, beginnings, process, social content, innate knowledge, cultural resistance, reification, myth, memory, meaning, place, representation succeeded each other, were metamorphosed and layered to constitute a reading machine meant to circumscribe a collective architectural unconscious, the image behind the image.

Just like Le Corbusier, Banham relied on empathy, a nineteenth-century psychological concept made popular by Wilhelm Worringer in his famous work *Abstraction and Empathy: Essay in the Psychology of Style* published in 1908. This model, however, reduced the meaning of the image to an emotion. Triggered by his discovery of Michael Polanyi's concept of tacit knowledge, Charney upgraded so to speak the purist-brutalist model. The phenomenon of architecture was no longer the product of an individual genius but an innate, if unconscious, faculty, common to everyone, which gave their meaning to collective built forms such as cities. Like Robert Venturi and Denise Scott Brown, Charney's interest in pop environments led him to consider architecture as a system of signs. But rather than conceiving the built environment as a system of communication, Charney, in a way analogous but distinct from Aldo Rossi, saw in popular architecture a repository of experience, a reified memory of the heroic struggle for a place realized by people often deprived of their legitimate means of subsistence and cultural expression by a repressive technocracy. At the moment architectural culture repudiated utopia, the founding notion of the historical avant-garde, he affirmed architecture's fundamental political role. Charney's criticism of power was undoubtedly inspired by the work of Michel Foucault, who exposed the repressive mechanisms of power in works like *The Archeology of Knowledge*, *The Order of Things*, *The Order of Discourse*, and *Discipline and Punish*. Yet, Charney did not limit architecture to the status of a repressive apparatus, as he believed that it could also be a means of liberation when it was appropriated by people. In addition, rather than considering architectural figures as heraldic and decorative devices, he

saw in architectural images traces of a language rooted in the collective unconscious. In the manner of the Freudian analyst who studies the language of dreams, his projects revealed the mythical content of the architectural unconscious in careful readings which made visible the layers constituting the everyday images and places that we see inattentively. Finally, Charney conceived architecture as a system of representation which created the ideal image – the architectural *figura* – of a place by a Lacanian process of constant replication which revealed architecture's inherent narcissism.

Throughout his meditations, Charney metamorphosed constantly the dialectics of architecture. His psychoanalytical model drew architecture out of the semiological duality opposing the syntactic (Eisenman) and the semantic (Venturi) sides of the sign. For him, architecture could be understood as a dialectic between the reification of a mythical narrative and the *mise en abyme* of this reification by its replication as an architectural image. In our disenchanted world in which empty signs and manipulative gestures are the norm and convey a sense of loss, Charney creates meaning in blending images and language together and seems to indicate that architecture could still make carpets fly.

NOTES

1 Chapter 36, 372.
2 Ibid., 379.
3 Chapter 37, 381.
4 Ibid.
5 Ibid., 384.
6 Ibid., 385.
7 Ibid., 386.
8 Ibid.
9 Ibid., 387.
10 Chapter 38, 390.
11 Ibid.
12 Ibid., 388.

13 Ibid., 390. The reference to Michel Foucault's
    Discipline and Punish is here quite explicit.

14 Ibid.

15 Roland Barthes, *Mythologies* (Paris: Éditions
    du Seuil, 1957); translated by Annette Lavers
    (London: Paladin, 1972).

16 K. Michael Hays, ed., *Architecture Theory since
    1968* (Cambridge, MA: MIT Press, 1998), x.

17 Tafuri had introduced Barthes's criticism of myth
    in architecture in the fifth chapter of his book
    Teorie e Storia dell'Architettura in 1967. The book
    was published in English translation in 1980.
    See Manfredo Tafuri, *Theories and History of
    Architecture* (New York: Harper and Row, 1980).

18 Chapter 38, 391.

19 Ibid.

20 Ibid.

21 Ibid., 392.

22 Ibid., 393–4.

23 Ibid., 395.

24 "A Garden for the Canadian Centre for
    Architecture," 397.

25 Ibid., 401.

26 Ibid., 402.

27 Ibid., 405.

28 Ibid.

36

A Chicago Construction*

The work begins with a construction on a city site.

The city in question is Chicago. The site is on a street which is part of a street grid typical of North American cities. And typical of a city site, there is an existing building upon it: the point of departure of the construction.

On the Existing Building

Within the existing building there are the remains of three other buildings. From without, we are presented a bridge-like metal truss which spans between two solid corners of different height; it is all of two storeys, and set between the front of the former bakery building and the sidewalk. Below the metal truss are stairs and a ramp, leading to the inside of the building. The appearance of this entrance – it does after all "look like" something – suggests the emergency clinic of a hospital: perhaps the wounded and the sick enter here for rehabilitation. This facade

was executed in a style which even though it was said to signify nothing other than itself, as the modernists would have it, was expected somehow to exude the look of "technology": stripped-down structural exhibitionism, smooth surfaces, and taut details. Beneath the stylistics, further suggestions appear. The diminutive size of the facade belies a grandiose composition: the heavy corners evoke the lateral bracing of large-scale masonry construction. This vision is enhanced by the grey, stone-like aluminum panels of the cladding, each undercut by deep reveals. If the corners elicit the classic palaces of Renaissance Italy, they also suggest the Renaissance palace-like base of early twentieth-century office towers. The spectre of the tall office tower is further drawn out by the position and scale of the bridge-like truss which is usually used to strengthen buildings of more than thirty storeys. Given the context of the high-rise and speculative real-estate economy of Chicago where the existing building is located, its low volume is a function of the unbuilt and therefore unexploited air-rights above it. This economic reality appears as a building in a state of partial

* From Mary-Jane Jacob, *Melvin Charney* (Chicago: Museum of Contemporary Art, 1982).

completion or ruin: we are presented with no more than the fragments of a tower.

The construction then assumes the form of a tower: a tall box-like shaft stands out from the street.

On a Tower-like Structure

The presence of a tower in Chicago focuses our attention on other tall buildings near the site of the construction, and hence on the tall commercial buildings of the Chicago School at the turn of the century. What is of concern here is not so much the development of the skyscraper as a building type, but of a system of representation of the type in our imagination. "For although the steel frame did make occasional undisguised appearances elsewhere, it was in Chicago that its formal results were most rapidly elucidated."[1] These formal results can be seen in the distinction between the expression of the structural frame as structure, and as a structural grid; that is, between the expression of the structural frame of a tall building as a fact, and the representation of this fact as a figural device. This distinction is seen in the Second Leiter Building (1889–90) by William L. Jenney, in which the horizontal and rectangular openings of the steel frame are contained as some minor order within a larger square grid superimposed on the facade. The square grid dominates the facade of the Luxfer Prism Skyscraper project (1895) of Frank Lloyd Wright. However, Henry-Russell Hitchcock saw it as a "mature type of horizontal screen-wall design toward which three previous Adler and Sullivan buildings were leading the way."[2] A later Adler and Sullivan building, the Schlesinger and Mayer Store (1899), or the

ABOVE | 36.1 Booth, Hansen, and Associates, Chicago, Museum of Contemporary Art, Chicago, 1978.

BELOW | 36.2 Melvin Charney, *The Building as a Tower,* 1981.

Boston Store (1915) by Holabird and Roche, reveal the horizontal grid as the fully formalized and mature expression of the Chicago frame. Whereas the horizontal grid represents the frame as a type, the square grid presents the idealization of the frame as a symbol. By 1920, in the work of the German painter George Grosz, buildings are depicted as square grids emblematic of the metaphysics of the industrial landscape; it is interesting to note the influence of the Italian metaphysical painters on Grosz and on the emergent *Neue Sachlichkeit* movement central to the evolving modern ethos and to the work of Mies van der Rohe. By the 1970s the square grid had assumed the existence of a disembodied icon, a representation of a representation, as seen in the work of Sol LeWitt.

The construction draws a frame out of the tower. A square grid is delineated both by the geometry of the existing building and by the representation of the ideal type.

On the Structural Frame

The elements of a structural frame are structural. A frame is in effect a stress distribution grid composed of struts, each of which contains in itself a structural grid. Be they the flanges and webs of steel sections, or reinforcing rods embedded in concrete: a structure structures a structure.

A structural grid is set within the grid of the structural frame, which, in turn, is set within a grid of streets – and so on.

On Containment within the Grid

If the two major themes of Mies van der Rohe's early work in Europe, the structural frame and the composition of intersecting planes, reveal the influence of the Chicago School – the first spawned by the tall commercial buildings of the Loop, and the second by the residential work of Frank Lloyd Wright – in Mies's later work in Chicago both the tall office tower and the residence are absorbed within the neutral grid of a transparent space and enclosed within a schematic, skeletal structure. Be it the Lake Shore Drive apartments (1951), or a 1950s suburban house in Elmhurst, Illinois, which is no more than a grounded horizontal slice of the high-rise grid of an apartment block, all signs of dwelling are imprisoned in the grid.

On Reinstating the Appearance of Appearances

It is evident from the existing building that the conventions derived from Mies have assumed a multitude of associations. The surreptitious appearance of historic and popular signs is also evident. The outline of a two-storey, pitched roof, and gable-end wood-frame house, typical of the worker neighbourhoods of Chicago in the 1920s, can be seen to appear full-size between the diagonals of the bridge-like truss and the glazing mullions adjacent to the main entrance. The spectre of other houses is also seen in the other diagonals of the truss.

Houses are then made to appear in the construction, along with other house-like forms, such as an entrance composed of the gable-end of a house cut into split pediments, as in the Tempio Malatestiano of Alberti. Actual houses are made to stand within the frame of a tall structure and in place of the sublimated house. An actual entrance is made to replace the outlines of an entrance.

The suggestion of the Tempio Malatestiano of Alberti also refers to the fact that (a) Alberti was asked to transform the exterior of an existing building; (b) he proceeded to do so in such a way as to reduce "the importance of the pre-existing organism which would have been incorporated into the new as a mere incidental episode;"[3] (c) he picked up on the forms of nearby ruins;

LEFT | 36.6 Mies van der Rohe, House, Elmhurst, Illinois, 1954.

RIGHT | 36.7 Working-class housing, North Side, Chicago, 1934.

primacy of the street in the initial conception of the buildings. It is as if the displacement of the émigré to America also displaced the urban models which he brought along in his cultural baggage. The wide-open spaces of the new continent, and the Arcadian pavilion as the dominant unit of expression of American building, reduced the street to the suggestion of frontal planes. Passage through the frontal planes calls forth the numerous entrances found in the city – gateways, arches, neoclassic and Gothic aedicules cut into or out of facades as sculpted orifices evoking the mausoleums of rites of passage.

The construction picks up on the frontality of the street. It also calls forth an entrance as an aedicule set within a larger structure – a sacral "house" of sorts, similar to but standing apart from the profane houses of the street.

On Wood-Frame Construction

The reappearance of the wood-frame houses takes us back to wood-frame construction and to the introduction in North America in the mid-nineteenth century of a system of stick building known as the "balloon frame," which replaced traditional heavy timber construction by a system of standardized, lightweight, and machine-cut struts, and which is said to have made its first appearance in Chicago.

and (d) only part of the facade and two side walls were constructed.

On the Frontality of a Construction on a City Site

The houses call forth a street of houses. The so-called "fake fronts" of typical late nineteenth-century worker neighbourhoods in Chicago can be taken as the tangible evidence of the

ABOVE | 36.8 L.B. Alberti, Tempio Malatestiano, Rimini, 1468.

RIGHT | 36.9 Traditional frame (1847) and balloon frame (1873). (Traditional frame from William H. Ranlett, *The Architect, A Series of Original Designs*, New York, 1847. Balloon frame from James H. Monckton, *The National Carpenter and Builder*, New York, 1873.)

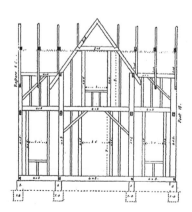

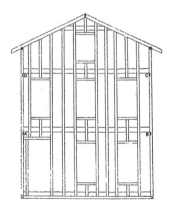

The construction picks up on stick building as it would upon some representative gesture depicting a way of building as a North American experience. And as in all frame construction, crassbraces are used to stiffen the structure against the wind. The line of the diagonal wood crossbracing picks up on the delineation of the diagonal struts of the bridgelike truss of the existing building. But whereas the diagonal struts of the existing building are ornamental – rightly so, given its stylistic predisposition – they are made in the construction to revert to their original structural state.

In the traditional view of building, monumental building was said to reproduce the necessary forms of primitive construction in permanent and noble materials. In this exercise, the guise of permanent and noble materials and the semblances of form in the existing building are reproduced in a "primitive"construction and out of used materials, but as "necessary" forms.

On Necessary Forms

The assembly of constructed devices – fragments of a tower, a frame structure, a structural grid, and sections of houses, crossbraced to stand in the wind – presents an object that is more physical than a drawing, yet less substantial than a finished building. Inside and outside are seen simultaneously, a simultaneity of view that has been said to have been one of the attractions of ruins in the eighteenth century and at the roots of the later cubo-machine aesthetic.[4]

The transparency of intersecting exterior and interior planes also draws on a meeting of two historic threads: (a) the resolution of the Prairie house in a composition of planes as seen in the work of Frank Lloyd Wright, which was published in Berlin in 1911 and which influenced De Stijl; and (b) the planar compositions of cubism in the work of Malevich and suprematism, cubo-futurist constructions such as that of Tatlin's *Corner Relief* (1915), which via De Stijl

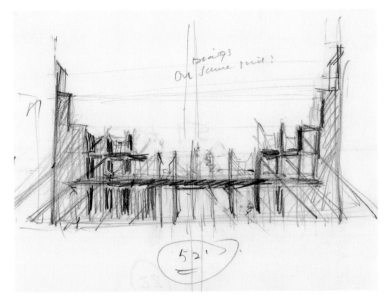

ABOVE | 36.10 Melvin Charney, *A Chicago Construction No. 4*, 1981.

BELOW | 36.11 Ruins of the Tribune Building after the Chicago Fire, 1873

and van Doesburg, and van Doesburg's influence on the Bauhaus, arrived later in Chicago along with the Bauhaus and modernism.

The braced interior voids and propped-up walls in the construction also recall a faded stereopticon view of the ruins of the Tribune Building in the aftermath of the Chicago fire. The exposed interior planes of the construction pick up on the traces of tinted plaster as seen on the exposed walls of partially demolished

36.12 Melvin Charney, *A Chicago Construction No. 6*, 1981.

rows of houses, typical of most inner cities of North America.

But, more to the point, the transfer of the public function of the street into private interiors of large-scale developments which is being advanced throughout American cities – such as the shops of Michigan Avenue which are now to be found inside Water Tower Place – has served to subvert our grasp of outside and inside. Inside, the representation of the street is reduced to diagrams of its former self: "ruins before they have crumbled."[5] While outside, buildings are allowed to decay and become no more than metaphors of their former selves. As ruins, they evoke the existence of built things: shades of meaning which cannot be forgotten.

Shades of inference which cannot be forgotten are gathered up in the construction. The pieces are built, layer upon layer, into and out of the existing building. They appear full-size and in a one-to-one relationship with their actual position to each other – a frame, a wall, a door, etc.

are placed where they ought to be. Together, the pieces become part of a larger tableau. The tableau does not so much restore what is buried in the sedimentation of the place, as try to come to terms with its existence. A distinct iconography takes over. One "building" draws away from the other. And whereas the first building is used to contain works of art, the construction has no other "use" than that of being itself.

NOTES

1   Colin Rowe, "Chicago Frame," *Architectural Design* 40 (December 1970): 641.
2   Henry-Russell Hitchcock, *In the Nature of Materials, 1887–1941: The Buildings of Frank Lloyd Wright* (New York: Duell, Sloan, and Pearce, 1942), 14.
3   Leonardo Benevolo, *The Architecture of the Renaissance*, trans. Judith Landry (London: Routledge and Kegan Paul, 1973), vol. 1: 106.
4   Peter Collins, *Changing Ideals in Modern Architecture, 1750–1950* (London: Faber and Faber, 1965). See chapter 2.
5   Walter Benjamin, "Paris: Capital of the Nineteenth Century," *Perspecta, The Yale Architectural Journal* 12 (March 1969), 172.

36.13   Melvin Charney, *A Chicago Construction*, Installation at the Museum of Contemporary Art, Chicago, 1982.

37

Of Temples and Sheds*

Why bother with the ruins of an obscure past? What can the reconstruction of a wealthy Roman's country estate contribute to any cogent debate about the condition of contemporary architecture? And why revive a *concours d'ému-lation* of an antique monument following the curriculum of the École des Beaux-Arts, an insti-tution which has long given up the ghost as the

repository of the classical tradition? There has to be some sense in this rather absurd enterprise.

Several notions about architecture would have to be clarified in order to approach such arcane material. Otherwise, the exhibition may be trivialized by misreading it as a discourse on the disposition of the villa as the retreat of the privileged class, be it in early Renaissance Fiesole or nineteenth-century Montreal.[1] Or, at worst, it may be dissipated as a series of attractive images to be appropriated in the current fashion of cari-caturing built devices lifted gratuitously from history and proffered in the name of "postmod-ern" sensibility.

The fascination with Pliny's villas may lie in the fact that their physical remains have never been found. There is no evidence of their exist-ence other than in the letters Pliny addressed to friends in which he described in vivid terms and with precise detail a way of life in, and the physical characteristics of, his country estates outside of Rome. Fourteen hundred years later, a renewed interest in antiquity and the reread-ing of Vitruvius drew attention to these letters. It was also a time when the emergence of a

* From: *ARQ – Architecture Québec* (October 1983): 11–15. Editor's note: This essay was written as a commentary on the exhibition La villa de Pline et les éléments classiques dans l'architecture à Montréal, presented at the Montreal Museum of Fine Arts at the end of 1983. The exhibition showed contemporary projects presented at the Institut Français d'Architecture in Paris and a section organized by the Canadian Centre for Architecture on the presence of the classical tradition in Montreal architecture. On this occasion, Charney created *Pliny on My Mind*, an installation which acted as an entrance to the exhibition (see Figs. 3.7 and 3.8). On the exhibition, see Pascale Beaudet, "La villa comme archétype architectural," *Vie des arts* 28, no. 113 (1983–84): 74. On the projects, see *La Laurentine et l'invention de la villa romaine* (Paris: Institut Français d'Architecture, 1982), and Pierre de la Ruffinière du Prey, *The Villas of Pliny from Antiquity to Posterity* (Chicago: University of Chicago Press, 1994).

powerful merchant class and the growth of cities spawned an architecture of villas. A "vita rustica" gave way to a "villa rustica," the architectural postulates of which were advanced by Alberti, Palladio, and Scamozzi, following the interpretation of antique models.[2]

The antique models were derived from reconstructions based on the study of Roman ruins. Pliny's villas could only be derived from literary references and from analogies and affinities latent in antique images which were assumed to agree with the texts. One exercise proceeded from another. Each reinterpreted the other, seeking out appropriate sources, and assimilating an increasing knowledge of Roman and then of Greek sites as well as changing attitudes to antiquity, given the imperatives of the time.

Thus, three centuries of reconstructions of Pliny's villas, each work "echoing, mirroring, alluding to previous works in the tradition,"[3] contributed to the establishment of a body of architecture which, by the eighteenth century, flourished as the "true style" sustained by an ingrained, formally consistent, and self-contained process – *habitus*[4] – of reasoning the physical formation of buildings, the rightness of which was upheld by remains of antiquity, the "orders," if not by "nature" itself.

The actual process of recreating the physical entity of the antique villa also mirrored the process with which an architect would instrumentalize the design of a villa for current habitation. In both cases, a project (projection), analogous archaeologic sources, and similar representational devices were invoked. Hence, the reconstruction of what the antique villa may have been tended to emulate and idealize existing buildings, creating the natural history and contributing to the self-reflexive codification of an autonomous and "true" architecture.

Thus, formulation of Pliny's villas arrived at by the eighteenth century represented at once the invention of the "Roman House" and the invention of a model, of a class that is

37.1 A villa in Arcadia set against the skeletal ruins of a city: idyllic illusion and the spectre of death haunt architecture. A photographer on a street in Warsaw, Poland, circa 1947.

exemplary – i.e., architecture – against which the composition of modern buildings could be measured. Needless to say, when the remains of Roman houses were discovered at Herculaneum and Pompeii in the mid-eighteenth century, the unearthed vestiges were indeed disappointing.[5] The important finds revealed large-scale wall paintings which depicted Roman country villas that clearly could not be accommodated within the precepts of classicism.

Robert Castell's restitution of the Laurentian villa, published in London in 1728, presents an

elaborate country estate with a central building not unlike seventeenth-century estates found in the English countryside, set upon a flat plain between mountains and the sea following Pliny's letter.[6] Within the confines of the estate there is an extensive garden rendered more "natural" than its natural surroundings. Artificial hills, irregular streams, forest walks, hermetic temples in a grove, effigies on ritualistic sites, Arcadian pleasure lions, all bound in this zoo of antique delights. Its saturation with things "natural," an inventory of things named and categorized, out-lines the emulation of a natural history and the proclivities of an aesthetic rationalization of the irrational order of nature. The villa abounds with representations of things mirroring themselves: landscapes of the landscape and villas within the villa. These representations can be seen to link the past with an order of architecture liberated from classical rationality that was to emerge in the nineteenth century and influence archi-tecture ever since. The figure of the garden as an "artificial rural solitude" can be traced back to descriptions of Roman villas[7] and forward to later parks, such as Regent's Park, London, Parc des Buttes Chaumont, Paris, and Mount Royal Park, Montreal, as the green lungs of nineteenth-century urban centres. A villa set in a grove within the villa reappears in the pictur-esque classicism of nineteenth-century Arcadian distractions be it the Grange in Toronto, or

Temple Grove, the McCord residence on the southern flank of Mount Royal in Montreal.

In the nineteenth century, the wide dissemination of "neo" classicism was concurrent with the institutionalization of architecture as a system of practice. Following Durand, so rational a style was rendered eminently reproducible and adaptable. It provided the incipient architect, whatever his skill, a measure of agreement about what was deemed exemplary, if not "best." It became the stock and trade of an *architecture officielle* which furnished public monuments for the burgeoning capitals of modern states. More emulations of Pliny's villas were committed to paper during this century than ever before.[8]

The significance of emulations during this period may be exemplified by Karl Friedrich Schinkel's restitution of Pliny's Laurentian villa in the 1830s at the time he was working on several country residences and on a palace for the King of Greece to be sited on the Acropolis (where "he managed to make the Parthenon look like a garden ornament").[9] The restitution obviously provided him with a point of reference and an occasion for the salutary exercise of evoking the sources of the "best" of all architecture. Schinkel's emulation, however, resembled more a traditional version of a reconstruction of Pliny's villa in "romantic" terms – a *Formendichter* at work, so "poetical and picturesque his composition"[10] than any felicitous reconstruction of an antique villa following the extensive archaeological evidence available at the time.

The practice of restitution of antique buildings had its place in the nineteenth-century curriculum of the École des Beaux-Arts. So rational an architecture was also one which was eminently teachable. And as composition was systematized

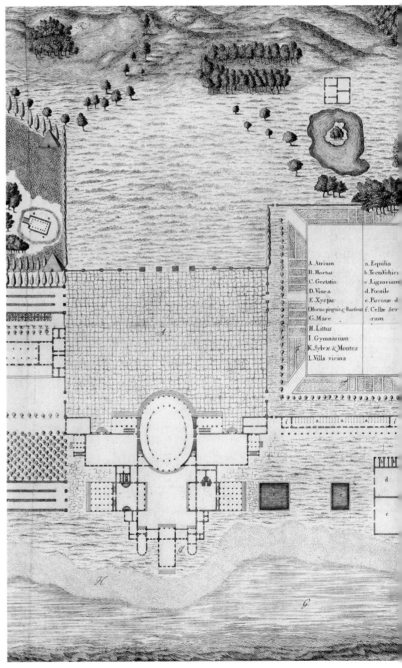

37.4 Robert Castell, Pliny's *Laurentian Villa Facing the Sea*, 1728.

37.5 Robert Castell, Pliny, *Plan of the Laurentian Villa*, 1728.

ABOVE | 37.6 *Temple rustique, Ermenonville,* engraving by Merigot *fils,* 1788.

BELOW | 37.7 Temple Grove, Montreal, ca. 1875.

in the repertory of forms and in the combinatorial syntax of neoclassicism, so tradition was locked into past convention. The process of restitution gave way to one of replication. The return to "sources" was limited to the copying of a prescribed repository of historic effigies, denying the very tradition of architecture that the École claimed to uphold.

So it was with most of the nineteenth-century restitutions of Pliny's villas: moribund replications lacking the essential re-enactment of the architectural condition. Significant transformations lay outside their purview. Perhaps the last word should be left to Léon Krier, who was to participate in the 1982 revival of a *concours d'émulation:* "l'architecture est avant tout une affaire d'ordre et de beauté; à mon avis, les Beaux-Arts ne se souciaient d'aucun de ces éléments."[11]

Herein lies the interest of the exhibition: it presents us with the traces of a slice of the history – with a beginning and end – of formative processes which over a period of three centuries established a body of architecture drawn out of an ancient lineage. The archaeology it presents is not that of the Roman house, nor of the evolution of the villa as a type, but of a sustained tradition of interpretive drawings which served to internalize the *figura* of what we understand to be architecture and in which "significance," if it were forthcoming, could be recognized.

Herein also lies the dilemma of the exhibition: it pretends that a classic "literacy" in architecture persists in the latter part of the twentieth century.

A second part of the exhibition presents drawings that were prepared in response to yet another *concours d'émulation* of the Laurentian villa following Pliny's letter, organized at the Institut Français d'Architecture in 1981–82.

In the 1980s, postmodernism has sent architects scurrying back to vestiges of the past. But it is somewhat presumptuous to assume their familiarity with the classic codes, the archaeological erudition, and the conceptual skills based

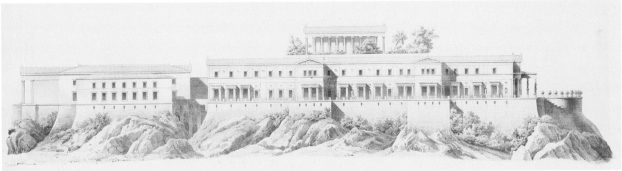

on the "orders" required by an emulation. The results of the emulation show that an attempt was made by some of the participants to resuscitate necessary figurative devices and appropriate sources, and in some cases even to attempt a contemporary interpretation of the program. However, except for Léon Krier's exceptional drawings, the results are insignificant. Krier presents us with decorous and knowledgeable formulations which he has been working on for several years, in a *mise en scène* drawn from painterly sources.[12]

In general, the exercise appears as some ill-defined homage to a past whose authority is still prevalent. "C'était un jeu en effet."[13] It was no more than a game of codes in which, as hap-

ABOVE | 37.8 Karl Friedrich Schinkel, *Reconstruction of Pliny's Laurentian villa*, 1841.

BELOW | 37.9 The end of history: the Parthenon, restitutions of Pliny's Laurentian villa, and F. Gilly's project for a monument to Frederick the Great, 1797, contribute to Karl Friedrich Schinkel's project for Castle Orianda, designed in 1838, on a promontory by the sea.

pens in other simulations which have become part of life in the latter part of the twentieth century, a scenario was confused with reality. In a "fallen" and later time we see only empty signs and hollow gestures. "We have seen the collapse of hierarchies and of radical changes in the value-systems which relate personal creations with death ... mutations (which) have brought an end to classic literacy."[14] The mindlessness of the revived emulation may well be illustrated by the anecdote whereby its authors introduce the catalogue. It tells of a text published in 1942 by the architect Henry van de Velde, in which he dramatizes in the form of a play the mortal passage of a character called "The Column" from its first physical presence centre stage, so to speak, to its eventual demise in the hands of *Fantaisie*.[15] Imagine worrying about the "passing" of the long-dead figure of the column in the midst of the barbarity of the Second World War. The Third Reich was after all interested in the resuscitation of "classic" columns! How is it possible to plead for "order" and "meaning" when the events of this century have put into question the very nature of tradition and of history?

These events have also taught us to look beyond tradition and, therefore, beyond the vestiges of classicism at fundamental themes which are there as constant reference.

Léon Krier's *émulation* is a case in point. Unlike the traditional restitutions of Pliny's villa, beginning with Scamozzi in 1615, which conceived of the villa in the form of a single block organized about major and minor axes and atria, Krier proposed the villa as a sequence of individuated buildings. Each building confronts the other and relates to the other in a dialectic subsumed by the order of a town. This deconstruction and reconstruction of the villa assumes, as *émulations* were intended to, a didactic, if not a moral, stand.

It is difficult for morality and reality to come into contact; imaginary causes and imagined effects intervene. Nevertheless, several lessons can be traced through Krier's work. Given the modern, turgid landscape of vast and undifferentiated buildings, Krier's project suggests that there are limits to what we can grasp to be a unit of expression in architecture, and that the large blocks be broken up into distinctive buildings each clearly differentiated from the other in a hierarchy of parts; this, in keeping with neo-classic architecture, which emphasized the contrast between the various masses of a building and of a group of buildings.

Krier then establishes relationships between these parts in a dialectic of urban devices – the essential form of the city. The parallel lines of planar trees, a building on axis, and a less prominent building to the side on a sub-axis, apparent in the villa, pick up on tenets of urban order which can be found in nineteenth-century Beaux-Arts urban constructs, an example of which can be seen in the Hochelaga-Maisonneuve *quartier* of Montreal. (See Fig. 32.3.) Here we have a "major order" inserted into the "minor order" of a street grid and flats – an alignment of trees along the axis of a boulevard, a city hall and baths set off on a secondary axis. It is not so much that Pliny's villa can be discovered lurking in the structure of this *quartier,* as evidence of a fundamental order that gives form to the city as an urban construct: the figure of a city within the city.

Beyond the "major order," the fabric of the city itself can also be drawn out of its historical condition. The orthogonal street grid of the *quartier* lies at the roots of classic urban structures. It is less of a model than a series of relationships which subsume the potential urban form of a town.[16] And beyond the *quartier,* a system of rural land division, known as *rangs,* unique in North America, is no more than an extension of this antique grid.

This ordinary *quartier* brings forth further continuities underlying the classic tradition. The utilitarian, brick-faced architecture of multiple dwellings situated within the interstices of the grid presents us with a way of building dwellings which is the classic counterpart of the "classic" tradition of Roman houses similar to Pliny's villa, as Axël Boëthius has pointed out.[17]

Until recently, this *habitus* of city building persisted with amazing consistency. From the

Roman insula, to the strip house of medieval towns, to the tenements of the late nineteenth-century industrial cities, such as the *quartiers* of Montreal, this fundamental way of building sustained an architecture of dwellings which, in turn, structured the streets, the *carrefours,* and hence the squares, ordering the public existence of people.

At the front doors of numerous tenements in these Montreal *quartiers,* entrances are made to appear as "classic" temples inserted into the flatness of the facade, perpendicular to the street. These vestiges ritualize a passage into dark interiors. They also externalize a surrogate *figura* of the urban tenement as a dwelling and, hence, as a temple: on streets aligned with trees all you see is a line of "treasuries" along a sacred way. Everyone wants to dwell in the sacred precincts where nature is no longer a threat to one's existence: is this not the essential *figura* of architecture, verified not only by the temple-like reconstructions of Pliny's villas, but also by the *"longue durée"* of the monumental transformations by most people of the lowly sheds they inhabit?

These entrances were usually built out of wood, and represent, as Blondel's eighteenth-century schemes of primitive huts, the wood antecedents of the stone construction of the classic temples. And within the tenements, the structural walls are filled with the rubble of previous constructions as was done in Roman times – a city, after all, is a continuous *chantier.* The system of constructing these walls, plank upon plank, unique to Montreal, draws us further into antecedents ... to constructs which embody underlying themes in the "real" life of forms which are imprinted, hopefully, with our sense of self.

Hence, to the dusty ruins of antique temples and lowly sheds: the tedious search, of necessity, for meaning.

NOTES

1 In the preface to the catalogue of the original presentation of this exhibition, Maurice Culot and Pierre Pinon clearly caution the reader: the description of Pliny's villa "n'est pas à confondre avec celle d'une seconde résidence quelque peu enflée sur la Côte d'Azur" in the Eastern townships or in the Hamptons; in *La Laurentine et l'invention de la villa romaine (*Paris, 1982), 8.

2 See Richard Bentmann and Michael Müller, *La villa: architecture de domination* (Brussels, 1975).

3 See George Steiner on the rise and demise of classic literacy in Western culture: *In Bluebeard's Castle (*London, 1971), 78.

4 *Habitus:* "un système de dispositions durables et transposables qui, intégrant toutes les expériences passées, fonctionne à chaque moment comme une matrice de perceptions, d'appréciations et d'actions." Pierre Bourdieu, *Esquisse d'une théorie de la pratique* (Geneva, 1972), 178–9.

5 Hugh Honour, *Neo-Classicism (*London, 1977), 45–6.

6 *La Laurentine,* 110–11.

7 Axël Boëthius, *Etruscan and Early Roman Architecture* (London, 1970), 194–5.

8 Fifteen out of the twenty-two exemplary projects cited in the *La Laurentine* date from this period (68–9).

9 David Watkin, "Karl Friedrich Schinkel," *Architectural Design* 19, nos. 8–9 (1979): 62.

10 An appellation applied to him by his countryman Seidel in 1831, from Hugh Honour, *Romanticism* (New York, 1979): 151.

11 "Architecture is for me, first of all, a question of meaning and beauty; to my mind the Beaux-Arts was concerned with neither." Léon Krier, "Au nom de la loi et du désordre" in "The Beaux-Arts," *Architectural Design* 48, nos. 11–12 (London, 1978): 86.

12 Compare for example the Krier drawing on page 161 of *La Laurentine* with the "Vue générale du Laurentine" by Jules-Frédéric Bouchet, executed in 1852, on page 136.

13 *La Laurentine,* 217. "It was only a game after all."

14 See Steiner, *In Bluebeard's Castle,* 77–85.

15 *La Laurentine,* 7.

16 See "The Montrealness of Montreal," chapter 33 in this volume.

17 Axël Boëthius, *The Golden House of Nero* (Ann Arbour, 1960), chapter 4.

38

Signs of Recognition, Ciphers of Deception*

This story begins and ends with images of the concentration camps.

One morning in February, on a drive into Houston, Texas, I found two buildings which stood apart from the unfolding panorama of the city. The first appeared, momentarily, below a turn of an elevated six-lane expressway, downtown, by the bayou. One virtually fell in upon a tableau of neglected 1940s public housing. The vision of repeated industrial blocks, drab materials, and a dusty, trodden terrain contrived to call forth the ghetto in the form of a concentration camp lodged in the heart of the city.

Ironically, the apparition of the concentration camp emerged from the remains of one of the better examples of social housing built at the same time as the barbaric German death camps. Yet, the debris of displaced lives and the spectre of a machine created to efface the existence of people seemed to seep through the walls of this housing, regardless of what I knew about its intended use.

The second building was seen from a distance. It lingered on the horizon for some time as a thin line hovering above the haze of the city. On approach, the line became a dark obelisk rising tall above a flat landscape of low buildings and wide streets of an outlying area of Houston. Closer yet, the smooth, glass surfaces of the obelisk suggested the outline of a stepped-back and pyramid-topped 1920s skyscraper, similar to skyscrapers found in Montreal (the Royal Bank building of McKim, Mead and White)† or in Chicago (the Board of Trade building on La Salle Street) or, more usually, in New York.

The actual physical presence of the tower – the Transco Tower, by Philip Johnson, completed in 1983 – seemed to change with the incidence and intensity of light which fell on its surfaces. From one angle its glass sheathing was virtually transparent, revealing a structural skeleton behind a curtain wall, as modernist buildings were made to depict. From another angle, the reflected light of the sun hardened the glass surfaces into

* From *Parachute* 36 (October 1983): 11–15.

† Editor's note: The building was designed by New York architectural firm York and Sawyer.

38.1 George Grosz, *The Diabolo Player*, 1920.

opaque masonry shapes depicting the 1920s sky-scraper. One image was concealed and revealed by the other in a cat-and-mouse dialectic.

The play of images focused one's attention on the surface of the building. Both its exterior (its urban situation) and its interior (a workplace engaging hundreds of people) were relegated behind the projection of a "presence" which appeared as some holograph of a "classic" sky-scraper taken out of a 1930s picture book (*The Boys Own Book of Great Buildings*) and projected, full-size, above the dusty sagebrush and sun-drenched parking lots of a Texas town. This "presence" also enveloped a hard-sell piece of real-estate promotion which projected, in fact, the economics of high-density downtown land

38.1 George Grosz, *The Diabolo Player*, 1920.

use as some disembodied piece of Manhattan real estate floated out on the prairie.

Thus, in the first vignette – "public housing" – time and neglect peeled away an ideological veneer from the surface of the object, showing it to be no more than what it is: an architectural figure, a diagrammatic formation, and, hence, a construct which represents nothing more and nothing less than institutional gesticulations of societal order – i.e., its historic condition. And if, as Lewis Namier, the British historian, pointed out, "the social history of nations is largely moulded by the form and development of their armed forces,"* the social history of housing has been similarly moulded by the form and development of prisons and concentration camps (viz. Drancy, Phalanstère, etc.).

In the second vignette, the Transco Tower, figural devices were introduced to envelop the building in a presence which suggests the formal strata of the building as a type. But rather than reveal its historic condition, the figural devices restrain the viewer to surface appearances by creating seemingly oppositional images which feign to reflect the world more urgently than is ordinarily experienced. It is as if the presence of the building had degenerated into its own surface by the creation of a deliberate ruse.

Herein lie the outlines of a drama. It is found not so much in the fact that figural content of architecture as a representational system has been consciously reintroduced into practice in recent years (as if figurative content was expunged from modern architecture), but in the underlying train of sensibilities which this consciousness represents – a predisposition to unearth a stratum of references, correspondences, and allusions to figural constructs with a potential to diagram equally evocative references, correspondences, and allusions whereby built objects may be conceived – and in the tendency to act upon these sensibilities in the actual creation of buildings. This troubling "discourse of revelation" lays bare the possibility to expose that what is accepted as natural is in fact historically constituted and thus subject to change. Thus we witness a genuine resistance to the reopening of the channels of representation, as well as an insidious exploitation of representational devices to belie the very significations promulgated in the name of history. It is as if the "innocence" of history were now being advanced in place of the "innocence" of pragmatic functionalism of the modernist decades.

* Editor's note: Sir Lewis Namier, *England during the Age of the American Revolution* (London: Macmillan, 1961), 7.

What is one to do with this incipient "innocence" which pervades a practice so obviously tied in to institutionalized power in any society?

An entrance to a run-down rooming house which I found on a street in Montreal was seen to be enclosed in an aedicule in which the stair leading up to the front door was mirrored in the form of a similar stair set at right angles to the first, but in the roof of the aedicule. The presence of the stair was represented by a reverse image of the stair poised as it were as a fragment of Jacob's ladder leading angels to the entrance of heaven. The same device used several years later by a New York architect in the design of a house in Connecticut registered less the significance of

38.2 Entrance to a rooming house, Saint-Hubert Street, Montreal.

38.3 Peter Eisenman, *House VI*, detail of stairs. Cornwall, Connecticut.

this gesture than the specialized context within which it was posited. The gesture interprets the tacit impulse within architecture to present the meaning of a form by representing it in the guise of a "deterritorialized" (in Guattari's term) figure – the symbolic order of the stair in its pre-significant state. However, the meaning of the architect's stair was also overlaid by and dependent upon a distinction between what does and what does not constitute the specific boundaries of architecture as a cultural "machine," and the stair found in the street, the *objet trouvé*, remained obviously more striking if not less pretentious than the same device institutionalized within architectural discourse. Thus are we bound by our modern condition.

In other words, the systematic contextualization of architectural sensibilities since the 1960s has cut deep. The consequent exposure of the historic specificity of architecture as a system of representation has served to resuscitate a more militant alignment of its cultural boundaries. But this has in turn exposed the ambiguities of those who struggle within its boundaries, because the very desire to evoke the autonomous life of architectural forms drew one back to the archetypal structure of all buildings. There is no turning back.

Social illusions have also been cut away. While the internal strata of built objects may readily be observed to possess an autonomous life of their own – to glow with the crystalline clarity of a "Principle of Form," be they found illustrated in the *Police Gazette*, on the shores of Nantucket or in Paestum – the actual representation of these principles in built form can only be lodged in some societal flux which carries with it a valence which simply cannot be willed away or subtracted from its meaning.

There is no such thing as a "Place" other than the sum total of the representations of that place. There are, therefore, no "innocent" sites. There have never been neutral voids to be filled by buildings, other than the destructive imposition of a strategic emptiness. Nor can I relate to such notions as *genius loci* which seems to grapple with the phenomena of constructed presences in a pre-contextual, if not in anti-urban terms.

In Montreal, in 1976, at the intersection of two main streets, there was a large empty lot from which buildings were removed for an institutional project which was later built elsewhere. One of the two streets was the main street of the city and traversed the present city centre, while the other descended into its ancient core and terminated at an 1820s cathedral situated on one of the oldest squares of North America. The historic stratum of the site was such that its specificity as an urban construct was virtually self-evident. It revolved around the nascent structure of an urban meeting place – a Square – created by the intersection of two streets. It delved into urban figures via the alignment of a gate-like axis connecting it to the inner city and to another square and to an important civic focal point, the cathedral: strata which picked up on the essential figure of a square as found underlying the Place de la Concorde in Paris or Piazza del Popolo in Rome. Correspondences and analogies fathomed further dimensions of formal description as found in the frontality of the facades of buildings aligned along the street as in the setting of a *lieu du spectacle* which can be traced through the street facades of American frontier towns such as Duparquet or Trois-Rivières, Quebec, or Utopia, Texas, to a formative impulse underlying the baroque, to Alberti's prescription for city streets, to the frontality of chalcolithic house urns dating from 3400 B.C. and found in a museum in Jerusalem, and so on.

The subsequent construction on the site simply gave body to its resplendent riches. I did not attempt in this piece to "foreground" the context of the site, as to sort out and consolidate its levels of representation. Local figural components were given a "hermeneutic motion," so to speak.

The content of this lays in the formation of a square and in the particular situation of the axis of this square in relation to an adjacent axis of an underground and privatized city for which Montreal is well known – the "ruins" of this new city were externalized in the "ruins" of the construction. The contents of the piece also arose from the medium of a veritable "earthwork" which displaced the urban strata; from the techniques of film set construction which invoked fragments of urban scenography; from its scale in the public arena; from the creation of a work with a limited lifespan; from its being part of a ritual – the cultural embellishment of the city on the occasion of the staging of the 21st Olympiad; from its

relationship to art history as an antecedent to similar pieces constructed several years later at the Venice Biennale; and, finally, from the violent reaction to its construction and its subsequent destruction by the mayor of the city who ordered it to be demolished one week after it was put into place.

While I could build out from the rich urban strata of a site in Montreal, I found that in similar sites in Toronto, in 1982, and in Kingston, in 1983, I had to build-in the initial presence of a site in order to draw upon it. Not only are there fewer urban traces outside Quebec, given the history of North America, but the few traces and references that do exist have been blurred by a distrust of history and a mistrust of collective urban form. In both these cities, I had to put a site back into the site by building out the presence of the site; the actual built surroundings of the site were represented in built form on the site. I then drew processional axes from one vantage point to another, drawing people along a ritual disposition through a "découpage" of its constituent parts.

In Toronto, the site faced a church, and the axis picked up on its aisle, extending it from street to lane, from a spire to a shed as from the religious institution to a mausoleum-like kernel of "Adam's House." One followed this liturgical progression on the way in; but it became a bombed Vietnamese village on the way out. In Kingston, the axis progressed from an interior walkway and out along a railway trestle which ended up as a sight-line leading people through the rebuilt layers of the site. In both pieces, these processional ways moved beyond the site, passing on to the horizon as if across the continent as in some ritual passage through a place in an eternal state of becoming.

Layers of correspondences and association focused the formalization of these pieces, each with an overlay of content derived in particular from their limited existence – these pieces were destined to be destroyed.

Every construction embodies the traces of its own destruction. One building is made to replace another. One construction sifts through and consolidates the strata of previous construction. Abandoned images are given a new life and meaning only to recede into the silence of time.

In 1980, on a road outside Frankfurt, I came across the ruins of a bombed factory which had been overlooked in the general clean-up of the German economic miracle of the 1950s and 1960s. Rusted girders stuck out from the rubble of brick walls. Within the ruins, adjacent to a still-standing massive brick chimney, were the remains of large furnaces with rusted doors askew … Again, the spectre of a death camp. How could it be otherwise? The correspondences were most direct. The mind slid into the layers of recall and into the ovens of a hideous death machine created by people to systematically exterminate others. A figure of the camp self-constructed: the familiar, stereotypic image of the railway lines and the main entrance gate of Auschwitz-Birkenau. Ironically, this image which now represents the archetypal death camp was originally constructed to represent the entrance to a farm with the actual camp hidden behind this facade. "Better if they think they are going to a farm," the SS architects proposed.

The representation of the camp as a farm was not gratuitous. The chain of references is such that it recalls the rise of fascism within the Pan-Germanic Nationalist movement in Austria in the 1880s under the aegis of Georg von Schönerer, who was the first to elevate anti-Semitism into a modern political force.[1] In keeping with his belief in the redemption of the *Volk* through a return to the soil, he acquired an estate in lower Austria and became the Knight of Rosenau. This Knight influenced Karl Lueger, who was the mayor of Freud's Vienna of 1900, and the first public official to be elected to office on an anti-Semitic platform. Lueger, in turn was admired by Hitler. More important, however, beyond this chain of associations, is the fact

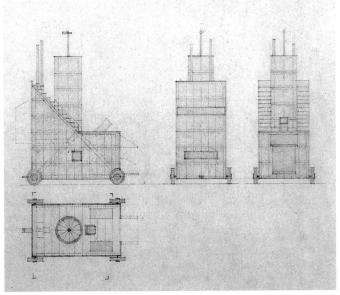

ABOVE | 38.4 Crematorium ovens, Auschwitz.

BELOW | 38.5 John Hejduk, detail of *Berlin Masque*, 1983.

that this farm facade was part of an elaborate deception devised by the authors of the death machines of the "Final Solution" to hide their terrible secret from its victims and from the world. People were said to be "relocated" and not deported; Auschwitz was a camp for farm labour;

on arrival people were sent to the "showers," that is, the gas chambers; and so on.

With this image in mind I began to work on a proposal I was asked to submit for a construction to be built in Kassel on the occasion of Documenta 7. The piece was to be built on one of several sites for the Documenta Urbana exhibition, which was intended to draw part of the Documenta show out of the confines of the museum and into the life of the city, as well as to suggest the development of its neglected areas. I worked on several sites, the second of which was the Bahnhofplatz. Kassel was an important railroad centre during the Second World War, and it was heavily bombed by the Allies. The area around the Bahnhofplatz is now nothing more than a disparate collection of mindless

modernist buildings unrelated to anything other than a commitment to the collective amnesia of the "economic miracle" of the 1950s and 1960s, a setting so well depicted in Fassbinder films. The figure of a city square obviously emerged from the strata of the site. The square was to be enclosed on one side by the mute, glass walls of the new railway station, and on the other by a full-size construction of the now-familiar figure of a place of arrival by railway – one which is etched in the collective psyche – the well-known

38.6 Melvin Charney, *Better if they think they are going to a farm ... No. 2,* 1982. Project to be constructed on the Kurt-Schumacher, Strasse, Kassel, on the occasion of Documenta Urbana, Documenta 7, 1982.

farm facade with its rails running across the square from one station to another to the final station on the Mount of the Fridericianum. The evocation of this image was situated between the silence of modernism and the presence of similar facades which are now found to adorn suburban farms.

A second version of this piece was proposed on yet a third site, a typical postwar German street leading into the centre of town. On one side of the street there were three-storey walk-up flats symptomatic of postwar *Volk* architecture; on the other, the modernist office buildings which housed the economic miracle workers. Again the proposal engaged the figure of the farm entrance. It was to be constructed across the street, with the existing tramway tracks passing through it. It was to stand in the middle of the street as the gateway of a medieval wall which marked the entrance into the core German towns if not into the psyche of their inhabitants. It also picked up on the image of tramway lines which passed through the walls of the Jewish ghettos transporting people on their daily trips to the city centre through the zoos of the puppets condemned to death. And given the conditions of present-day life in Kassel, "Better (perhaps) if they think they are going to a farm ..." indeed!

In a series of recent drawings, I have moved through the entrance gateway and into Birkenau itself, "the worst of all the camps."[2] The first drawings replicated the structure of the camp as if seizing upon the narrative potential of architecture to reconstruct, ritually, an event, and thus evoke "the time of a resurrection (when) even the wicked will rise together with the saintly. Then they will die again, and will become ashes under the soles of the righteous."[3] Imagine, the place could actually be rebuilt as in an allegorical tale, only to be destroyed again.

I then worked and reworked the alignment of the huts which resembled the form of hundreds of other barracks and army camps, into

the essential figure of a "City." A perimeter, a gateway, streets, rows of dwellings replete with body racks, a parade ground (the perennial Champs de Mars), a monument to its collective existence (in this case, a Temple of the Ovens), and a City Square inhabited by dogs – fragments of a "City" lining the strata of Kassel, Frankfort, Stuttgart ... and haunting the Bauausstellungs of Berlin.

The presence of death is thus impugned. One is condemned to live with the horror of the slain, if not graced with an ability to expunge our capacity for destruction.

And if in architecture there is now a conscious movement to emphasize a figural content which is said to have come to terms with history and to have lifted the veil of the modernist amnesia of our recent past, then the resolution of this movement, as others, revolves about the significance of the work. Given the potential of this discourse, it ought to confront at least the incipient fascism inherent in the manipulation of surrogate realities which blind us to our condition.

Finally, what is one to make of the fact that a group of huts adjacent to the gas chambers in Birkenau was designated to be "Canada"? This name was given to the storehouses containing the various looted articles and the clothes, the hair and the teeth which were stripped from victims. Hence, a place of plenty, a land of promise, if not a cruelty of the imagination.

NOTES

1 See Carl E. Schorske, *Fin-de-Siècle Vienna* (New York: Alfred Knopf, 1980).
2 From Martin Gilbert, *Auschwifz and the Allies* (New York: Holt, Rinehart and Winston, 1981).
3 As recounted by Chaim Grade in "My Quarrel with Hersh Rasseyner," in *The Seven Little Lanes* (New York: Bergen-Belsen Memorial Press, 1972).

A GARDEN FOR THE CANADIAN CENTRE FOR ARCHITECTURE

How does one conceive of a public garden for an architectural museum and study centre, a garden situated on no more than a residual plot stranded between the entrance and exit ramps of an automobile expressway?

The site of the CCA garden presented the typical contradictions of twentieth-century urban life: a derelict piece of the city left over after an expressway was pushed through its older centre. By the time the expressway – the autoroute Ville-Marie – was built in the mid-1960s, the site had already been cleared of early nineteenth-century estates and late nineteenth-century townhouses which were demolished in a post-Second World War drive to modernize the infrastructure of the city, an effort that devastated the substance it was intended to renew, as if the pre-war emulation of European cities had given way to an emulation of their subsequent destruction.

The site of the garden is also typical of the location of important urban parks built since the eighteenth century, such as the parc des Buttes-Chaumont in Paris. These parks were created on residual terrain cast aside by transformations of the city. Obsolete fortifications and quarries, abandoned abattoirs, railway lines, and, later, expressways – all neglected and degraded areas caught between layers of the city – were made into ideal figures of verdure in attempts to redeem the reality of urban life.

The widening of Dorchester Street (now René-Lévesque Boulevard) into a boulevard in the 1950s and the subsequent construction of the autoroute Ville-Marie left few traces of the tight-knit urban structure of Montreal in the area of the site. Earth-fill and rubble were bulldozed to create a flat terrain in between two ramps of the expressway and over two traffic tunnels that pass under the site. The terrain now floats on the edge of an escarpment, a dislocated wasteland between streams of traffic set off against the horizon and the city below. (See Pl. 33.)

* From *The Canadian Centre for Architecture: Buildings and Gardens*, ed. Larry Richards (Montreal and Cambridge, MA: Canadian Centre for Architecture/MIT Press, 1989), 87–102.

The Garden in the City

The very idea of a garden confronted the marginal condition of the site and its relationship to the city. The site exists as an urban fact. It embodies concrete traces of human passage rooted in history and memory, layer upon layer. The layers of history have neither a past nor a future; they are simply there to be dragged up as a measure of the place, a map of its ongoing transformation. The layers of memory, however, are ever-present. They cut deep, transcend place and time, and summon forth typologies of an ideal city and models of rural idylls and Arcadian forest edge.

Even though the site was a ruin, its situation is magnificent. It is located on a major east-west thoroughfare and on a prominent escarpment that marks the edge of a plateau – both important features of the city. (See Pl. 34.) To the south, the escarpment overlooks the remains of nineteenth-century factories and working-class neighbourhoods, a panorama which opens out to the St Lawrence River and to the mountains beyond. The site thereby affords a direct encounter with the horizon and the landmass of the city, and along with the presence of Mount Royal to the north, above the CCA building, it also reveals a sense of Montreal as it was originally settled, between the river and the mountain.

Given the nature of the CCA as a public institution and the formal signification of the boulevard that passes between it and the site, the creation of a public garden complementary to and directly across from the CCA establishes a north-south focus and an event in the collective order of the city. That order is suggested by the block system, by the grid alignment of streets, by the party walls between buildings, and by the remains of the organization of earlier farms in the area, all of which follow the original cadastral system of land division. The few nineteenth-century greystone buildings, which survive in the vicinity of the site, are the remains of an urban architecture that distinguished the area at the turn of the century. The CCA was designed around the restoration of one such surviving building, the Shaughnessy House, constructed in 1874. The site is also adjacent to a residential neighbourhood, recently revived, but with little public open space for the community.

The CCA building was in itself an urban fact to consider. Its situation on a major boulevard, with its front and main entrance on a secondary street, suggested the configuration of a typical *hôtel particulier* as it evolved in Paris in the eighteenth and nineteenth centuries. Visualize the residence of an eighteenth-century grandee, now a public institution, with its main entrance on the narrow rue du faubourg Saint-Honoré and a portico leading from the street into a walled, paved courtyard. Within the courtyard is the principal facade of the building, a front door, and, inside, a sequence of public reception rooms which open onto gardens and onto the avenue des

Champs-Élysées at the back. Whereas the front of the *hôtel* is no more than a wall scaled to the enclosure of a secondary street, the back of the building appears as a series of pavilions set within the garden-like, monumental avenue, setting off a dialectic between front and back, between the figure of a house on a city street and the representation of a house in an Arcadian revision of an urban boulevard. So it is with the relationship between the CCA building and René-Lévesque Boulevard. The back of the building is its urban and monumental front: the garden was conceived accordingly.

The CCA garden thus had to respond to at least three programmatic categories: a garden that is a public and urban event related to major elements of the city; a garden related to the CCA as a study centre, archive, and museum of architecture; and a neighbourhood garden.

These gardens were established by invoking the site as an urban composition, and by invoking the formal specificity of garden architecture as a parallel text. The urban constituents of the site were then correlated to basic garden formations. In other words, the formal constituents of a garden were taken to be not so much the dialectic opposites of the constituents of a city, the persistent notion, expounded by Frederick Law Olmsted, of a city park as an innocent, rural retreat, a "lung" of verdure set in "the greatest possible contrast to the restraining" city, but as the transfiguration of the city itself.

Such a garden is not scenic but scenographic. Each constituent assumes a specific form: an esplanade was made to appear in the guise of an "esplanade," a boulevard was made to be a "boulevard." This was done with the understanding that the critical operation, which unravelled the "textual" composition of the site and of gardens, also exposed intelligible and paradigmatic figural formations. These type formations were then situated in a referential framework that challenged their representational capacity. This was done in two ways. Each constituent of the garden was set up as the direct counterpart of an existing element of the city that could be seen, or could be made to be "seen," from the site – for example, a "facade" is placed in the garden in relation to an existing facade on an opposite street. Each constituent was also countered in the garden by the placement of a second and analogous construct derived from the first – by the representation of the representation, so to speak – an arcade is represented by a second "arcade," for example. Each constituent of the garden is thereby tied directly to the surrounding city. And Montreal has a rich urban history which is well grounded in the tradition of city building, as well as a history of numerous formal gardens – fragments of a *paradis terrestre* – implanted in the walls of its initial settlement. (See Pl. 35.)

Central to the compositional propositions outlined above are the three essential visions of the CCA garden.

The "Urban Garden" is organized about two series of north-south axes drawn out of the structure of the city and superposed one on the other.

The first set, parallel to the axes of the CCA building, enjoins the two sides of the boulevard. One side of the boulevard is set up as the counterpart of the other by the placement in the garden of a mirror-like reconstruction of the Shaughnessy House in the form of an arcade. The two "houses" frame the boulevard and incorporate it into a larger composition that traverses the roadway and joins the CCA garden to the building in a monumental gesture. The terrain of the garden is sloped up from the boulevard, between the ramps of the expressway, so as to establish an esplanade and a belvedere on the edge of the escarpment. The rise of land enhances the escarpment, sets the landscape of the garden to the horizon, and creates a tilted-up facade whose general composition is readily perceptible to the passerby. The garden was conceived to be a place to look at, as well as a place to look out from.

The "Museum Garden" extends the museological function of the CCA outdoors, on an urban scale and accessible to the public at all times. In the manner of a building that reveals the history of building, the garden reveals the historicity of its existence. Layers of settlement, such as older forms of land division and plant material, were made to appear. The plan of the CCA building also appears; the reconstruction of the Shaughnessy House and the long *allée* of the garden esplanade correspond to the configuration of the CCA building with its long suite of exhibition galleries. Allegorical columns, situated on the esplanade, interpret the architectural signification of distinctive buildings in the surroundings, features of a city on display.

The "Neighbourhood Garden" is episodic, with defined places and objects to go to, along with bucolic delights such as a meadow and an orchard, convenient promenades, and ample seating.

The CCA garden was thereby composed of type figures – for example, an arcade, an esplanade, a meadow, an orchard – that are set about a series of shifting organizational axes and that cut across and sustain its diverse, programmatic requirements.

The North-South Axes

The location of Montreal, between a river to the south and a mountain to the north, accentuates the distinction between attenuated east-west routes of access and limited north-south axes of urban activity found in the settlement of Canada. This distinction can be seen, for example, between Sherbrooke Street, which traverses the island of Montreal from east to west, and the Place des Arts / Complexe Desjardins axis which crosses the downtown core from north to south. A similar distinction can be made between the east-west run of René-Lévesque Boulevard and the autoroute Ville-Marie, and the orientation of the garden in relation to the CCA building and to the city.

Two sets of north-south axes traverse the CCA garden. The first set, already described, aligns the composition of the garden with that of the CCA building. The major axis of the building is picked up by the arcade. Minor axes are drawn out along the walkways of the garden. The main walkway prolongs the entrance axis of the building; the entrance sequence to the building – fence, park, door, hall, main stair, bay window, courtyard – extends in the garden along an *allée* of trees up to the esplanade and to a view of the horizon. However, while the tripartite composition of the CCA buildings is reflected in the garden, its symmetry is displaced, its centre shifted. The axial register between the mirror-like facades on either side of the boulevard is countered in the garden by a second register of opposites situated on either side of the axis of the main walkway: on one side, the arcade, a configuration that gives body to the interior of the garden, and on the other, the meadow, which represents the garden as an exterior, rural landscape.

Early nineteenth-century maps of Montreal show that the initial urbanization of the area of the garden proceeded from the east and the south of the site up to and along the escarpment. (See Pl. 36.) The alignment of the orthogonal lots – the cadastral subdivisions – to the south of the present-day boulevard is parallel to the run of streets emanating from the river and the lower town. The land to the north of the boulevard, however – the area that formerly made up the Sulpician Domain where the CCA building is situated – was settled at a later date along cadastral divisions that descended from and are perpendicular to Sherbrooke Street and to the mountain. This shift in the alignment of the underlying system of land division is located on the northern boundary of the site and is reflected in the garden in the shift between the two sets of organizational axes about which it was composed: the urban grid from the north is offset from, and superposed upon, a second grid rising from the south. One grid is made to undercut the other. (See Pl. 37.)

The second series of axial alignments is grounded in the garden by a series of "cadastral" walls and by the allegorical columns that pick up on parts of the city to the north and south of the site: to the north, the remains of the eighteenth-century Fort de la montagne and the pediment of the seminary of the Collège de Montréal on the site of the old fort; to the south, the factories, grain elevators, churches, and tenements. (See Pl. 38 and Pl. 39.)

The Shaughnessy House as an Arcade

The introduction of objects which represent existing objects – the introduction in the conception of the garden of recursive, self-reflexive devices – also introduces a register that scales the presence of one object with regard to the existence of another. This device introduces a degree of displacement of the meaning of one object in relation to another and, hence, to itself.

The reconstruction of the Shaughnessy House in the garden suggested its reappearance not as a "picturesque" or deliberate ruin, but as a building stripped of all functional overlay other than that of being "itself" in a garden, an abode in Arcadia. The "self" in the garden assumed the form of a *fabrique*, a building type inseparable from the art of gardening, an arcade in Arcadia. The Shaughnessy House was emptied of content and its envelope was sliced off in part at an appropriate height. (See Pl. 40.)

The similarity of the two buildings establishes a direct physical and visual link which centres the CCA building and the garden upon each other. Repetition sets up a duality, a reflection of one building in the other, a mirror image. The mirror image blurs the distinction between subject and object and registers a measure of narcissism inherent in the monumental form of the city – the necessary anthropocentrism of urbanity, of the collective "self" of people reflected in the body of the city, if such still exists. (See Pl. 39.)

The arcade also situates the interior of the garden, represented by a second arcade set within the first. The second arcade was also created by the reconstruction of a cut-off segment of the first. And while the first arcade is aligned with the set of axes emanating from the CCA building to the north, the second is related to the set of axes drawn up from the south. One arcade is thus enclosed by and offset from the other. The repetition of the two arcades sets up a duality reflecting the duality of the two buildings facing each other across the boulevard. A repetition is thereby set within a repetition, each attesting to the presence of the other.

The Cadastral Walls

Before 1950, des Seigneurs Street extended up the escarpment from the lower town and traversed the site. There were houses along Dorchester Street and along Edgehill, a private street that extended from Dorchester to the edge of the escarpment. Today, all that remains on the site of earlier buildings and streets are traces of the cadastral subdivisions, which still appear on legal surveys and can still be extrapolated from buildings in the area.

The cadastral grid has its roots in the classical system of land subdivision and in the planning of cities throughout history. It appears to be less a model than a primal structure of human settlement, a series of reproducible relationships that subsume the form of a city. One of the strengths of this system is the direct relationship between the structure of rural land and the structure of the city, seen in the plans of newly implanted Greek and Roman cities, and in the Zähringer new towns – Bern, Freiburg – created in the twelfth century. The cadastral system was also implanted in Montreal, where the continuity between the city grid and rural land divisions can be readily seen in the conversion of the rural *rangs* – the long and narrow orthogonal farm lots – into orthogonal city blocks, one a direct transposition of the other. (See Fig. 3.6.)

The layers of the cadastral grid, once located in the strata of the site, reappear in the garden as a series of walls, which emerge from the slope of the terrain, below the esplanade, as if the soil had eroded away to expose an ancient structure. These walls – cadastral walls – deform the slope of the terrain as some accidental slippage. They can be seen either as the remains of the party walls on the property lines between buildings that once existed on the site – the eighteen-inch-wide mitoyen wall prescribed by laws dating back to the fourteenth century in France – or as fieldstone walls that separated the early farm *rangs* which also existed on the site. Rural and urban strata overlap.

The Columns

Gardens ... should not be wanting of columns and obelisks.

Leon Battista Alberti in *De Re Aedificatori*

The placement of columns in the CCA garden was derived, as were other devices, from a reading of historical types. In the same way as the cadastral walls "reveal" an ancient structure of land division, so the placement of herms, statues that served to mark farms and boundaries in Greek and Roman times, is recovered by the position of allegorical columns on the esplanade and in relation to the cadastral grid of the garden. These columns also reveal the situation of allegorical, columnar figures, which lined garden walks, *allées*, avenues, and esplanades in later centuries. (See Pl. 41 to Pl. 44.)

An allegory is a narrative, a commentary of one text read through another, an extended metaphor. The narrative presented by the columns is intended to capture and objectify an architectural discourse derived from distinctive buildings, as befits a museum of architecture. As elsewhere in the garden, the columns were made to establish self-reflexive dualities. A first line of columns was set up as the direct counterpoint to and reflection of actual parts of the city, while a second line was set up as a counterpoint to and reflection of the first series of columns, echoing the first as the first echoes the architecture of the city.

The buildings which can be readily identified from the esplanade and which constitute a slice of significant architecture can be discerned in what remains of the late nineteenth- and early twentieth-century industrial *quartiers* of the lower town, below the escarpment. The essential elements of an industrial city are evident, even though most of the factories have been abandoned and large parts of these neighbourhoods were demolished during the wave of urban "renewal" that swept across Montreal in the 1960s and 1970s. The area directly south of the site, known as la petite Bourgogne, was particularly affected. Nevertheless, the surviving buildings reveal the transposition of a proto-classic vernacular brought over to North America by settlers into an indigenous, proto-modern typology that re-emerged later in the heroic period of the modern movement in Europe. It still reverberates in our grasp of built form.

The narrative begins at the column bases, which pick up on the tenement blocks typical of the industrial *quartiers* – the houses of people whose lives were crushed by the factory and the church. Commentary on the form of the house as a type and as an archetype is woven through the sequence of columns, a subtext to the overall narrative. These "houses" are built of wood and encased in copper in the manner of local religious statuary, and inserted into columns of concrete and steel.

The narrative sequence of the columns is arranged in rows from east to west, starting with the column closest to the edge of the esplanade. (See Pl. 45.)

ROW A

Column one takes the numerous chimney stacks which rise above the factories and houses of the lower city as its subject. The prominent chimney of the Northern Electric Building in Pointe Saint-Charles is reworked into a tall shaft that speaks of obelisks, a Ledoux cannon foundry, a cenotaph, and the smokestacks of the industrial era.

ROW B

Column three interprets the form of houses found in the *quartiers* below the esplanade. This column speaks of the urbanization of the *maison québécoise*, a type of house imported from western France by the first settlers, and of its rationalization into an equally traditional urban type, the tenement, related to Roman domestic architecture. This indigenous transformation is contrasted to the rationalization by Le Corbusier of houses in northwestern France similar to the *maison québécoise*, which gave rise to his Maison Domino.

Column four is about the legacy of modernism, a dancing "Domino." Le Corbusier's Maison Domino was drawn out of column three. The tenement was freed of enclosing walls so that De Stijl-like planes now slide in and out of its floors in a seemingly liberating gesture.

ROW C

Column six picks up on the numerous grain elevators in the lower city. It also recalls illustrations which appeared in tracts of the modern movement. Specifically, the column represents the elevator of a flour mill located on the Notre-Dame Street, directly south of the garden.

Column seven shows the grain elevators again, this time as a temple of rational architecture. This narrative reflects upon two complementary pages of Le Corbusier's *Vers une architecture*, one illustrating grain silos in Canada, the other the Parthenon in Athens.

ROW D

Column eight picks up on the twin-spired Sainte-Cunégonde church in the *quartier* immediately below the site. (See Pl. 47 and Pl. 48.) The form of the church is drawn back to the Gesu in Rome, to Neolithic horned gates and symbols of passage; the arms of the spires suggest an anthropomorphic reading of the ancient composition. The two domed mini-temples which presently top the Sainte-Cunégonde spires, somewhat closer to God than is the congregation below, are reinterpreted on the column in the form of a house – Adam's shack in Paradise – closer to the congregation than to God.

ROW E

Column ten treats the monumental presence of the tall cylinder of a shot tower, the remains of the Stelco steel mill on Notre-Dame Street, directly south of the site.

ROW F

Column eleven is situated on the western extremity of the esplanade, directly above the expressway, on the axis of du Fort Street and the facade of the seminary of the Collège de Montréal to the north. The expressway and the seminary are united in this column. A tubular steel structure that usually supports the directional signs for the expressway now supports a facade, another "sign," similar to the pediment of the seminary. One facade is posited as the representation of the other, as elsewhere in the garden. A steel strut extends above the column to hold up a straight back chair high above the expressway. And on the chair sits a house, the final house of the sequence of "dwellings" which began at the base of column one. This "house" is a sign of the city as a collective abode and of the essential content of a centre for architecture.

Plants

The composition of the plant material, its variety and configuration, emphasizes stratagems used in the conception of the garden: the "natural" was approached through its cultural representation. A "textual" invocation of the site and of gardens was used to unearth land and plant formations specific to the site and to correlate them to equivalent formations specific to garden architecture. Typologies were suggested; an attempt was made to distinguish indigenous species from varieties introduced into Montreal since its settlement in the seventeenth century.

Horticulture was thus generated by the formal composition of the garden. Each constituent contained a history of landform and plant material. Trees dominate. Given the nature of the site, the configuration of trees is essentially urban. There are no "woody clumps," but alignments and grids, consciously planted. Walkways are framed by rows of trees. Since the garden is located on the southern slopes of Mount Royal, considered one of the best apple-growing districts in the world in the nineteenth century (note the numerous orchards in the 1846 map of the area (see Pl. 36) and part of the site itself was once an apple orchard, a grid of apple trees is planted in the garden. Similarly, the planting along the cadastral walls reflects the shrubs and flowers – prickly raspberry bushes, wild roses, sumac – which grow spontaneously along the stone walls dividing farms, and which can still be found on the island of Montreal. The landscape of rural fields was incorporated into the meadow. And the boulevard between the garden and the CCA building was made to assume the appropriate form of a "boulevard," with a tree-lined median and sidewalks. The "appropriateness" of the planting of the boulevard, as with the other elements of the garden, is related to figural formations inherent in its existence as a type, formations readily found in Montreal.

Finally, the configuration of the planting was used to extend the boundaries of the garden to include the ramps of the expressway within its purview. Cars enter and leave the garden through a thicket of trees and shrubs as they enter and leave the city.

Thus the garden and the expressway are superposed. One is above, below, inside, and outside the other. A double presence is established. While the expressway cuts an indifferent east-west swath through the city, the garden is intertwined with the city, the mountain, and the river, north and south.

The garden transforms the site into a temporal medium. Plant materials introduce a dimension of time – the cycle of the seasons, decay and generation – while some of the formal elements recognize previous states of the site, and the columns suggest the transience of things. The purpose is not to celebrate the past, but to expose the place in the present, as a singular fragment of the city, and as an ongoing process of transformation whose most recent embodiment is that of a garden.

A garden by its very nature tends to evoke old, stereotypical images of a lost Arcadia. This garden is situated on an expressway that is no more than a place of lost urbanity, a lost city. And if Paradise is a garden at one end of time and a city at the other, somewhere outside the world, as the underpinnings of tradition would have it, then either all is lost or we are now outside history in a world in which new relationships can be forged only out of an amalgam of elusive metaphors, be they a garden or a city.

ABOVE | Pl. 33 Melvin Charney, *Panorama of the City from the CCA Garden,* 1987.

FACING PAGE, BELOW | Pl. 34 The site of the future CCA garden in 1986.

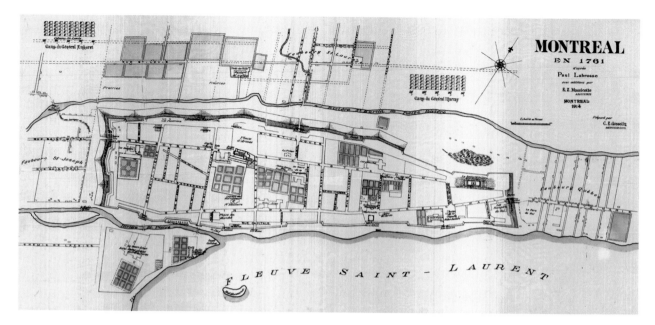

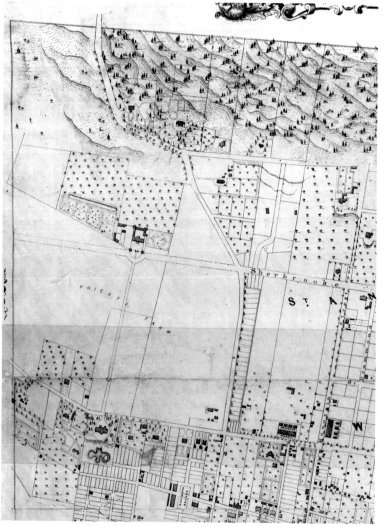

ABOVE | Pl. 35 *Montreal in 1761*. Cartographer: Paul Labrosse, revised in 1914 by E.Z. Massicotte. Bibliothèque nationale du Quebec, section des cartes. Note the extensive formal gardens attached to religious establishments within the walls of the original settlement.

LEFT | Pl. 36 *Topographical and Pictorial Map of the City of Montreal*, 1846. Cartographer: James Cane. National Archives of Canada (NMC 2053). This detail, the upper-left corner of the map, shows the initial urbanization of the site of the CCA garden, the location of Dorchester Street (now René-Lévesque Boulevard), the Priest's Farm, and numerous apple orchards.

FACING PAGE | Pl. 37 Melvin Charney, *The Canadian Centre for Architecture Garden: Urban Axes*, 1987. Coloured pencil and ink on vellum. Note, in red, des Seigneurs Street, which traversed the site, and buildings dating from the mid-nineteenth century.

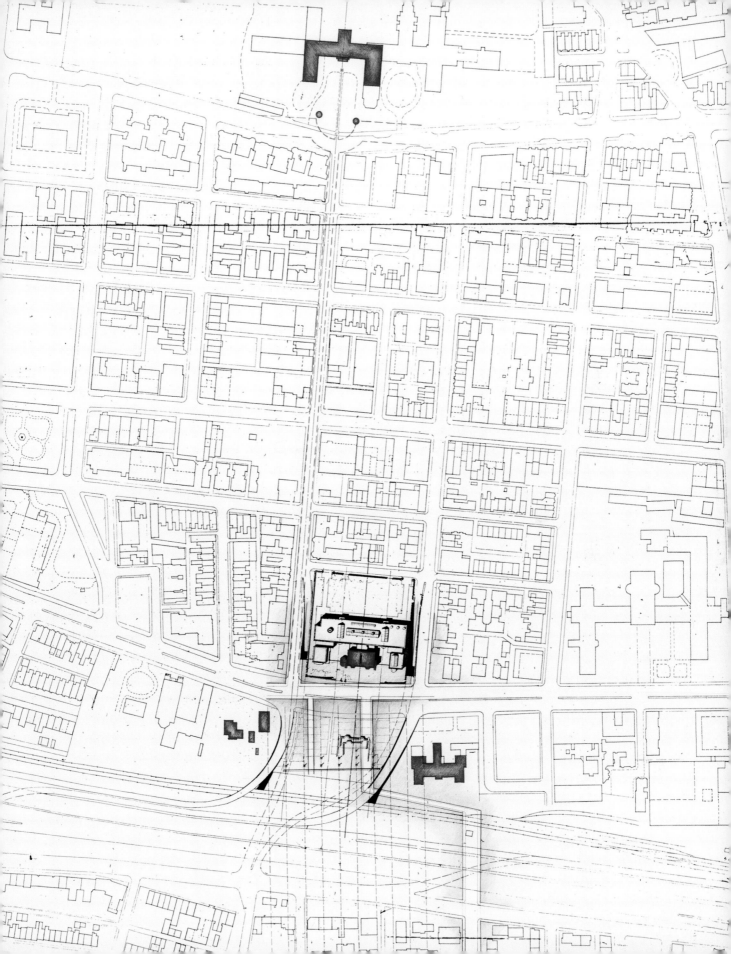

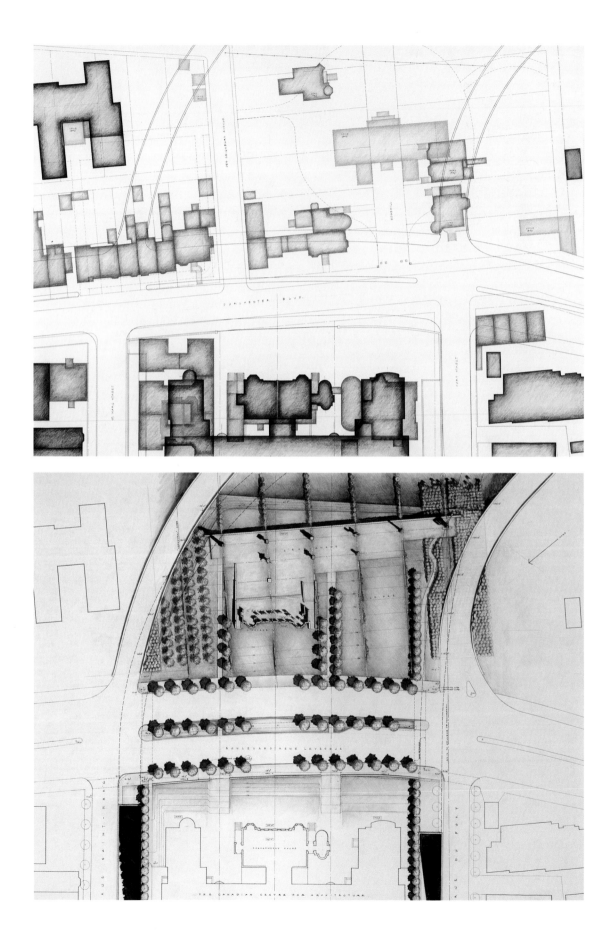

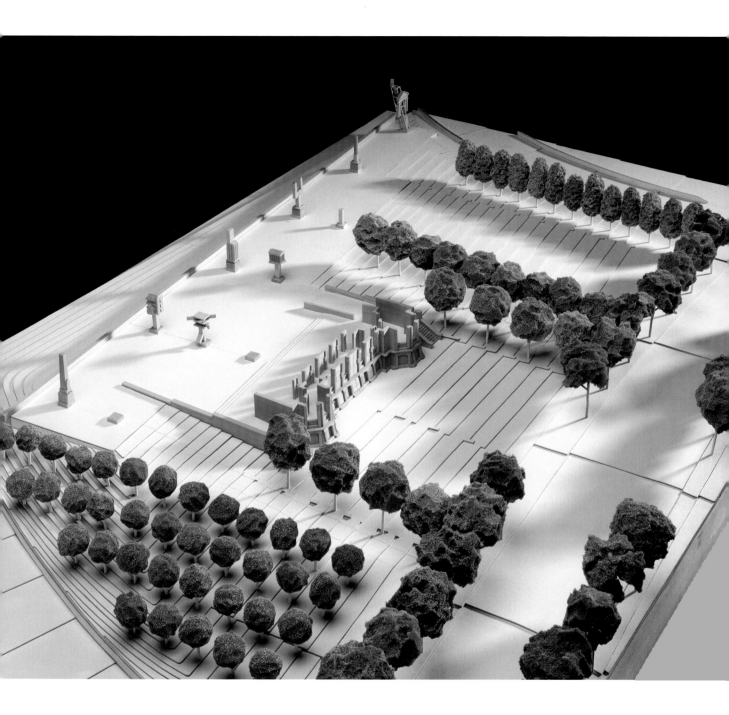

FACING PAGE, ABOVE | Pl. 38 Melvin Charney, *The Historical Layers of the CCA Garden Site between 1800 and 1950,* 1986.

FACING PAGE, BELOW | Pl. 39 Melvin Charney, *Plan of the CCA Garden,* 1988.

THIS PAGE | Pl. 40 A south-west view of the original study model of the CCA garden. Melvin Charney, 1987.

LEFT | Pl. 41 View north along the axis of du Fort Street to the pediment of the seminary of the Collège de Montreal, from the position of column no. 11 on the esplanade of the *CCA* garden in 1987.

BELOW | Pl. 42 Jean Antoine Watteau, *La Perspective,* ca. 1719. Watteau's painting reveals the pediment of Montmorency through the hundred-year-old trees of Le Nôtre's original layout, similar to that of the view of the seminary of the Collège de Montréal shown in plate 41.

RIGHT | Pl. 43 The Canefori in the sixteenth-century *giardino segreto* of the Casino, Palazzo Farnese, Caprarola.

BELOW | Pl. 44 The Emperor's Walk at Grimston, Yorkshire, landscaped by William Andrews Nesfield, nineteenth century.

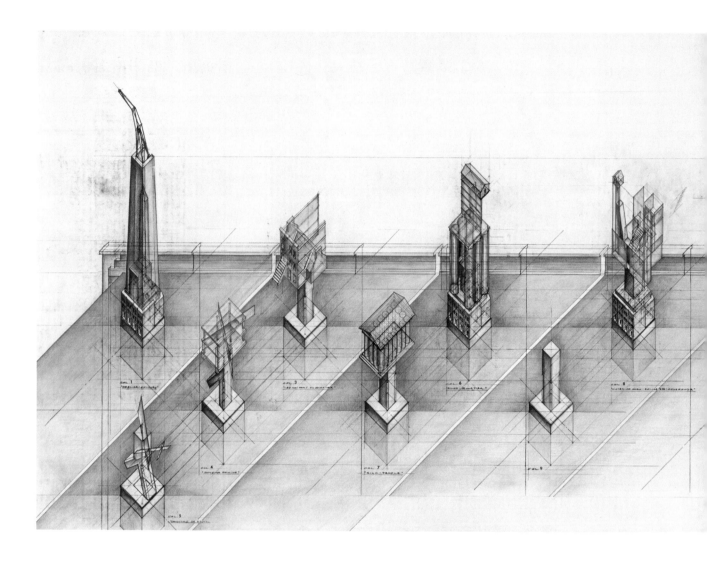

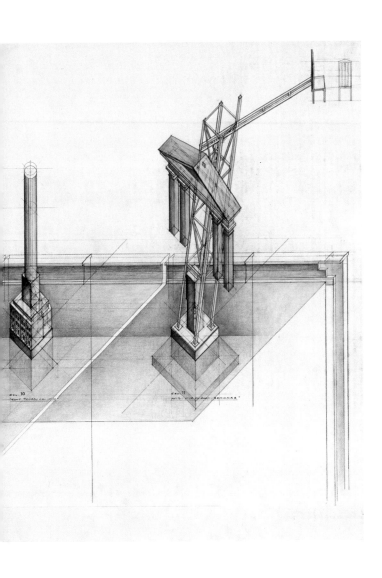

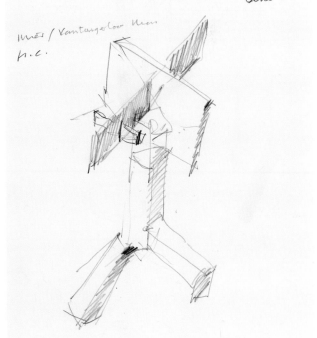

ABOVE | Pl. 45 Melvin Charney, *The Allegorical Columns*, 1988.

RIGHT | Pl. 46 Melvin Charney, *Column No. 5, Dancing De Stijl Study*, 1987.

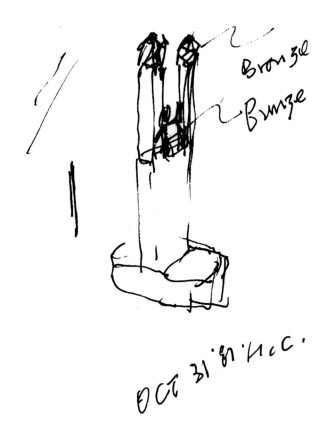

ABOVE | Pl. 47 Sainte-Cunégonde church from the west end of the esplanade, 1987.

LEFT | Pl. 48 Melvin Charney, *Study of Column No. 8,* 1987.

PART SIX

Postscripts

39.1 Melvin Charney with the Dalai Lama during the
inauguration of the Canadian Tribute to Human Rights,
Ottawa, 30 September 1990.

Explorer of Collective Memory[*]

Besides using a variety of media, Melvin Charney creates constructions in, on, or over existing buildings and sites. Yet far from masking the original space, his additions point up the multiple layers of images underlying these places. A kind of excavation at the centre of our collective memory, a displacement of strata that holds not a few surprises.

How do your drawings, constructions, and texts work together since you contend that writing is an integral part of your output?

The texts refer to ideas that can only be expressed in writing. It is clear to me that what we see is not what we say. So I work on several different levels – on different registers – at once. My texts, drawings, and constructions are operations in which you can find the same concerns superimposed on one another. Of course I favour the visual, but I cannot bring myself to pass up that whole that allows me to come to grips with what is essential.

I would add photography to the different domains that you have mentioned. Photography, either the images I produce or those I appropriate, is an important constituent of my work. It lies at the very source of my art. In fact, I only look at so-called "reality" through the photographic image. How can anyone today ignore the fact that photography has been a milestone for the twentieth century, and that it is through that medium that this century has validated its image of reality? What I look for is the image behind the *image*.

My latest work is more concerned with photography than before. It will be the subject of forthcoming exhibitions. For the past four years I have been working on a series of photographs of buildings embodying the international style of the twenties and thirties. I photograph these

* This interview by Catherine Millet took place in the Centre Georges-Pompidou, where the exhibition La Ville, art et architecture en Europe 1870–1993 was held from 10 February to 9 May 1994 and which included the work of Melvin Charney. First published in French as Catherine Millet, "Interview: Melvin Charney, explorateur de la mémoire collective," *Art Press* 202 (May 1995): 56–60. Translation provided by *Art Press*.

now-dilapidated structures as they are often found in some corner of a city where there is not enough room to move back from a building and capture it in one shot. Thus, I have to build up the image of a building. I superimpose the prints on top of one another and then draw directly on the surface of these montages. What comes clearly to light then is the profound breakdown of the ideology running through the years of modernism – it is seen in the rusting strands of steel bars pushing through cracked concrete like the tendons of an arm or a leg torn from someone's body.

The realm of the visible is made real by juxtaposition. Photography, drawings, constructions, and sculpture are positioned in relation to one another. I often build things in order to know what to draw, whereas in architecture you draw in order to build. If I prepare a drawing or model that is too complete, that would already be the artwork. You might say that one of the problems with architecture these days is due to the fact that scale models are too often transposed directly to an urban scale with no distinction made between the two scales.

So you don't make models?

I avoid them as much as possible. I am often obliged to create a model in the case of a so-called "public art" competition. What I try to do is submit several models of the same piece in order to relativize the scaling registers in the work – to invoke issues such as site/non-site – and not isolate the work within the artificial objectification of the competition. Of course that creates problems for me.

Shifting Layers of the Visible

I find that these parallel disciplines are likely to produce displacements in the Freudian sense of the term, if only because you haunt the area where the (dream) image passes into language.

That's right. The fear of someone in analysis is not having the right words to express his or her fears. My displacements spring from superimposing the various registers the work engages. Often we have to shift everything to get our bearings in the spate of images that is drowning us nowadays. These images are both limpid and meaningful, and opaque and empty. They cancel each other out. I am currently showing at the George Pompidou Centre a drawing done in 1986 after an engraving in the British Museum. The engraving is of a reinterpretation of Ezekiel's vision of Temple of Solomon in Jerusalem that dates from 1631 by Matthias Hafenreffer, a friend of Martin Luther. I redrew the engraving in order to position it with respect to its referential content. After all, the appropriation of this symbol of hope and renewal of the Jews was yet again a usurpation, banishing the Israelites from their Jerusalem once more. Three hundred years later, by shifting the "image" from the image I was able to discern in this appropriation of the Heavenly City a prefiguration of the twentieth century's Earthly City of death. The structure of the extermination camps created by Nazi Germany during the Second World War is clearly inscribed in the very logic of Hafenreffer's scheme.

In the case of *Les maisons de la rue Sherbrooke*, which dates from 1976, I displaced part of the "city" from within a city. I constructed the mirror image of two existing buildings on opposite street corners in order to centre the axis of the street and to focus it on a church and square in the old core of the city. The intention here was to reveal an urban mentality that is closely linked to the most familiar traces of collective will, traces still evident in certain cities. The insertion of this construction in its setting shifted various layers of the visible towards other more sedimentary strata underpinning the foundations of urban relationships.

This work raised issues of figuration. The opposite of representation does not seem to lie in abstraction, or non-figuration, but rather in what cruelly occurs when the plethora of signs within which we are submerged is such that they neutralize each other and nothing can be grasped. *Les maisons de la rue Sherbrooke* provoked a debate when it was demolished a few days after its completion on orders of the mayor of the city. Afterwards in Milan the radical left, for example, read *Les maisons* as a piece of social realism, a work of art that the people could appropriate. In Paris, a curator with monarchist sentiments saw in the replication of the facades the former Place Louis XV. Whereas for me, the mirroring of the facades visibly evoked the figure of collective narcissism which is inherent in numerous urban formations.

I subsequently used the idea of urban mirror formations in the conception of a garden and sculpture for the Canadian Centre for Architecture in Montreal in 1987. The garden is located opposite the building that houses the Centre, on the other side of a boulevard on an abandoned piece of terrain caught between the entrance and exit ramps of an automobile expressway, and on an escarpment that overlooks a working-class neighbourhood dating from the late nineteenth century. This neighbourhood was razed as a result of 1960s city planning, as if Montreal had declared a war on itself. On this no man's land floating above a wasted neighbourhood, I superimposed a series of "portraits" that were drawn from whatever could be seen in and around the site. Since there seemed to be nothing there, I recorded what was absent as much as what was present. A series of pieces that emulated significant buildings that can be seen and that I imagined could be seen from the site were inserted into a series of type garden formations, which were, in turn, inserted into a series of "portraits" of the same site in its rural state, and so on. In other words, I built up figures of a reality that could only be validated in the reflection of reality, in a mirror, and the site became nothing less than a mirror of itself. Visitors can see

in the garden stone walls and wild rose bushes similar to the typical stone walls and bushes that divide rural fields. These walls correspond to ancient divisions of land that were marked off by the placement of "Terms," or, rather, "Herms." In the garden, the busts of Hermes were made to assume the guise of other "portraits" of, for example, the twin belfries of Sulpician churches that visitors can make out in the distance and in which appears something of the horns of ancient Cretan cults ...

One of the garden's "Herms," the *Tribune*, is facing a street that leads to the ruins of a fort built in the early seventeenth century by Sulpicians. So you can see in the *Tribune* the pediment of the Sulpician Seminary built in the nineteenth century behind the old fort. In the summer, you can also see an evocation of a painting by Watteau in which the pediment of the château of Montmorency is seen to float in a garden one hundred years after it was laid out by Le Nôtre. The verdigris of the copper on the pediment of the *Tribune* picks up on both the statutes of saints that decorate the parapets of churches throughout Montreal, and the road sign that hangs above the entrance to the expressway adjacent to the garden. The whole piece is hanging from a tribune that suggests the one that El Lissitsky had designed for Lenin. You can indeed read the piece on several levels. It is like riding a magic carpet: you never wonder how the carpet can float in the air so long as the logic that is inherent in the story holds up. That is, so long as "image" and "language" blend with one another.

Everything Precisely Laid Out

Have you ever met with violent reactions from the public?

Never from the public, even in those cases when my artwork is placed outside the museum. What I have occasionally experienced is the vandalism of those in power, as in the censorship of *Les maisons de la rue Sherbrooke*.

I raised the question because of your project for Kassel in which you proposed to set up over a railway junction a facade recalling the entrance to concentration camps ... Although the project was not carried out, didn't it risk antagonizing the public?

You are referring to the piece I did in 1982 following an invitation from Kassel to create an installation to be set up in the town. I proposed to reconstruct on the existing Bahnhofplatz, that is, on the square before the railway station, the principal railroad entrance to Auschwitz-Birkenau. The idea was simple. It consisted of introducing a critical figure of a place of arrival by train in an existing place of arrival by train. In other words, I proposed to construct one Bahnhof in another Bahnhof; the facade of the inserted Bahnhof to be reflected in the glass facade of the existing Bahnhof, which was rebuilt after being destroyed during the war. The railway entrance to Auschwitz-Birkenau was designed by SS architects to resemble the entrance to a country estate – it was no more than an innocent building. Yet that innocence was part of the vicious lie conceived by the creators of the Final Solution to conceal their criminal death machine from the eyes of their victims, and to camouflage it before the eyes of the whole world: "Better if they think they are going to a farm."

The structure and function of the camps had been carefully worked out. We cannot hide the fact of their existence. And we cannot drown it in sentimentalism. I tried in my work to reconstruct the camps such as they were in order to understand them better. I redrew the plans. I located the access ramps and the watchtowers, the layout of the stable like barracks and the system of shelving for stacking sleeping bodies – those racks seemed to descend deep into the ground. Then there were the gas chambers,

the cremation ovens invented by the J.A. Topf engineering firm, and the chimney stacks, in a word, all the workings of that well-orchestrated machine whose twisted logic defies all understanding. What I found especially terrifying was the cold flawlessness of the gas chambers. Everything was laid out on a precise grid. Here is the condition of *Degré Zéro* of being, the zero degree of death. The camp's main railroad entrance is the other dimension to that zero degree: a device that blots out the system for blotting out life. It was important to me in the early 1980s to confront that conjuncture. I saw no danger of antagonizing the public, on the contrary.

Violating Visual Habits

Many of your drawings use axonometric projection and one of your first constructions, the one you did for PS1 in New York, was based upon the principle of axonometric elevation. Isn't axonometry a representational mode that brutalizes classical perspective and our habits of seeing the world? I think there's an analogy between that mode of representation and all your constructions which disrupt real space, and what these constructions produce in terms of meanings that disrupt consciousness.

I used axonometric projections in my work until the late seventies. Axonometry represents a modern conception of space that displaced classical perspective and subverted the visual field. Over the years it has also become a figurative convention, a contemporary brutalization of space, as you point out.

It is important to question the conventional figures of modern space. I have often taken issue with assumptions concerning our understanding of modern space. An installation I did in 1978 at the Art Gallery of Ontario began with an appropriation of a photo of a drawing by Malevich that I had come across in a newspaper. The museum was designed by one of Walter Gropius's students, the same Gropius who had evicted Van Doesburg from the Bauhaus while appropriating the ideas of de Stijl. The source of de Stijl can be traced to Malevich's Suprematism, and so on. So I built the Malevitch drawing by inserting one wall into another existing wall of the museum, so that the intersection of these two wall planes formed a Suprematist composition. In other words, I recomposed a stratum that was inherent in the site – a site whose presence is nothing more that a superimposition of various underlying fictions. I only did the axonometric drawings after taking down the piece, in order to record the event.

In 1979, PS1 in New York invited me to exhibit in Room 202, which was set aside for architects. Frank Gehry and Mario Gandelsonas had presented their work before me. The latter had repainted the room in "Matisse Red" to show his so-called "postmodernist" work to advantage. Like a number of others, he was repressing history in the name of history, and effacing the site in the name of architecture. I had to reposition myself then vis-à-vis history, as well as the existence of a place within the place. When all is said and done, Room 202 is no more nor less than a classroom, like those found all over America, and in which I spent years of my childhood, like many other children, staring out the windows up at the sky. I therefore replaced the "room" within the room by setting up several constructions one inside another, each being a projection of the other. I also had to make a drawing of these constructions according to conventions that allow one to record their material dimensions, hence the axonometric projection. What I installed afterwards was not a three-dimensional translation of that projection, but rather the materialization of the distortion that is inherent in the concept of axonometry. Displaced in this way, Room 202 filled Room 202 entirely, and visitors had to climb onto the installation to see it. The succession of the room's planes forced people to turn towards the windows of the existing room,

then towards the windows of the second room, and finally towards the windows of the third until their gaze was turned back to the inside of the original room. There was no longer any outside on the outside. Representations of the site were freed up to such an extent that the visitors could no longer make their way out of them.

The Totemic Space of Images

You usually make a close study of the places that you photograph. Then with print in hand, you begin to discover things you hadn't seen when you first viewed the site. Isn't your piece Un dictionnaire *meant to enable viewers to follow the same development, albeit more quickly?*

Exactly. *Un Dictionnaire* draws us into the totemic space of the most familiar photographic images. Since 1970, I have been obsessed with cutting out and classifying wire-service images showing people, buildings, and cities, torn from their day-to-day existence by some event and projected onto the front page of newspapers before the whole world's eyes. If the function of a monument is to be seen, then here is a record of places permeated with a certain aura, or at least singled out for a certain lapse of time by the media and by our collective memory.

Repetition – the various images of the same event, the inevitable cycle of natural catastrophes – reinforced the system of classification of these images. The system recorded their "general usage," that is, a dictionary. A dictionary is self-referential; words refer to other words. Similarly, the images of *Un dictionnaire* are defined with respect to one another – one image pushes at the visibility of another. Day-to-day events affecting human beings are brought to the fore in the very fabric of this piece. The world we see in press images is the very opposite of the world of architecture: people stuck in doorways, laid out in the street with their head in the gutter, and a CEO is seen embracing a model of

a skyscraper – you wonder why he is grinning …
As an artist, you cannot help but be concerned
with what seems to escape us.

*The colour wash you apply over your photographs
forces viewers to look at them very closely.*

… forces them to look at the materiality of
photographic images. The ephemerality of media
images is striking, and corresponds to the real
use of the photograph in the twentieth century –
flashes of lightning in the night that explode
the visible for an instant and then leave us in
even deeper darkness than before. I rephoto-
graphed these images to lend them a certain
visibility, then I reworked their surface, adding
a grey wash in order to reposition the surface of
these black-and-white images in relation to the
shadows out of which they rise – I efface them so
that they may be seen. The latest version of *Un
dictionnaire* comprises 232 plates.

In the recent *Parable* series, a colour overlay
forces the surface of these images even further
back – it pushes at what one sees in relation to
what one could see either on or beneath the surface of the image. I covered the surfaces with oil-
based pastels, then removed certain parts of the
colour layers to expose fragments of the underlying photos. Given that many of these photographs depict violent scenes, the *Parables* assume
an odd appearance of indifferent calm, which
vanishes as soon as you take a second look.

The *In Flight* series is made up of images of
airplanes that have crashed. The layers of pastel
that I have superimposed on the image this time
refer to the fictions that we have worked around
our instincts before the real danger of flying, and
the conventions conditioning our visual field –
like the tropes of Suprematism that were derived
from the idea of flight. With the end of our
century, have not those supports underpinning
our ability to grasp the visible come crashing
down as well?

40

In Conversation*

A City Differentiated, Montreal

YS *I am so pleased that we decided to meet in Montreal. From what I see of the city, I feel that your work and much of its energy is grounded in the sense of place and people that mark this corner of North America.*

MC Montreal, in January. A sense of impending crisis seems to infuse the city. Pedestrians carefully scrutinize everything as they slip-slide along icy sidewalks. [...] The three dominant cultural groups embodying the consciousness of Montreal – the Aboriginals, the French, and the English – have always been wary of one another, hardly tolerant of their compatriots' existence, yet peacefully disposed to one another in times of crises. And all of this is accentuated by a sense of displacement, an émigré's feelings of loss, as in most of the Americas, heightened here by a generalized sentiment of defeat dating from the end of the eighteenth century: the defeat of the French at the hands of the British; the subsequent defeat of the British by the Americans; the influx of Empire Loyalists who found the American Revolution too heady for their blue blood; the influx of Iroquois warriors and Hessian mercenaries who fought on the side of the British [...] And even though these events may have long been forgotten, people in Montreal seem to live on a cantilever weighted by the past, and in one of several cultural spheres. The main issue is language. You are what you speak. A display of the letters on a sign – PAIN – would send English-speaking Montrealers to a doctor, whereas their French-speaking counterparts would salivate at the very thought of a baguette. Most people in this city are aware, consciously or unconsciously, that the meaning of signs is directly related to shared language, ingrained habits, and cultural values. Signification is understood to be a human construct and subject to change, in part, by the will of the people.

* First published as "In Conversation: Yasmeen Siddiqui with Melvin Charney," in *The Painted Photographs of Melvin Charney: Between Observation and Intervention*, ed. Gabriela Rangel and Gwendolyn Owens (New York: Americas Society, 2009), 20–39. This interview took place in Montreal on 4 and 5 January 2008.

*YS Walking around different Montreal neigh-
bourhoods, I noticed that the housing is mostly
attached row houses, in an arrangement
resembling the long farms jutting out from the
banks of the St Lawrence River. I understand
that Montreal was initially founded by settlers
from France and re-founded, so to speak, in the
latter part of the nineteenth century by French
Canadians who migrated from rural farms to a
burgeoning industrial city. This is a usual story
for cities of the first industrial age in North America. In Montreal, however, streets appear to be
different than streets in other American cities.
What strikes me about your work is that it is
underpinned by a concept of urban form. How
did you arrive at this position?*

MC I grew up in a dense urban neighbourhood
where lives and clotheslines abutted in close
proximity. The notion of shared space seemed
self-evident. The accessible city extended beyond
my immediate neighbourhood via public spaces,
streets, and department stores – downtown
mercantile cathedrals [...] As a young person I
was somehow convinced that an understanding
of my immediate surroundings could serve me
well and, contrary to a standard education in
architecture, tried to ground my work in the
reality of a given context. I still cannot deal with
the idea that cities can be "created," *tabula rasa*,
as detached entities, seemingly out of the air
we breathe, and I am after a reasoned attitude
founded on first-hand observation as a way of
understanding a city.

My nascent years as an urban *flâneur* began
at age seven, following Saturday art classes at
the Montreal Museum of Fine Arts. I adored
wandering the streets of 1950s Montreal as if
I were on some mission of discovery. Later, I
would associate the character of city streets with
museums. [...] New York City was another one
of my haunts. Most of my family on both my
mother and father's sides had arrived in New
York City by the late 1920s, and we would visit

often. I learned to use the subway and began to
explore Manhattan and its museums [...]

In my early teens I began to photograph
Montreal in a somewhat more systematic way,
reversing figure and ground. Streets, the spaces
between buildings, steam shovels, and railway
engines drew my attention, as did the processes
and conventions of photography. What I had
stumbled upon at that time were fragments of
new urban formations emerging in the interstices of an evolving city – the transformation
of the urban structure of a metropolis into a
regional sprawl.

The underlying structure of Montreal can be
readily extrapolated from a plan of the initial
French settlement. It consisted then, and still
does now, of generative and reproducible basic
elements of classical cities found throughout
history. Key elements are a specific house type
with party walls, city blocks, streets, and squares
as defined entities, all set within an undifferentiated orthogonal grid. In Montreal, beginning
in the latter half of the nineteenth century,
the advent of industrialization and the influx
of immigrants, particularly from rural Quebec,
engendered a significant morphing of the
basic urban house type. The traditional, iconic
"*maison québécoise*" was radically transformed
into an innovative response to the new conditions of urban life: a homegrown, three-story
tenement, the "triplex," became the standard
in industrialized Montreal. Unlike elsewhere in
North America where lightweight stick building
was introduced, the new system reverted to a
heavyweight archaic encasement of three-inch-
thick planks, *madriers*, in use early in the history
of French settlement in North America. Nonetheless, with the advent of industrialization
the traditional wall was transformed: lumps of
stone were abandoned for a layered epidermis.
The archaic sloped roof, with its death-dealing
winter avalanches triggered by a knock on the
front door, had its slopes reversed, its planes
tilted to a central drain in a scheme that used

layers of snow and air as insulation yet in section resembled a Roman *impluvium*. Industrialization in French Canada invoked a sense of history, and people, in order to proceed, reverted to the same archaic techniques where they had left off in an evolutionary process prior to the British conquest.

The evolution of the working-class neighbourhoods of Montreal resulted in a unique "rust-belt" of North America. What emerged was a primitive but highly adaptable shell of an urban system loaded with information that subsumed a potentially collective structure. With use, and from construction to construction, the structural shell underwent further differentiation. For example, a zone of elements emerged between the housing and the street – an articulated *parvis* – making visible a transition from the inside of a house to the outside sidewalk. What emerged was a dense zone of staircases directly connecting the front door of each dwelling to the street, balconies, stoops, and entrances extending each flat out into an intermediate area giving body to an evolving dialectic between the individual dwelling unit (the family) and collective, hierarchic forces within society (the street, the block, the neighbourhood, the *paroisse*, etc.) A body of radically new urban formations assumed the guise of a familiar city.

YS *What you describe as occurring between buildings informs the physical and social character of Montreal. And while people are housed vertically, each dwelling asserts some autonomy by maintaining an entryway, a direct link to the street. The disposition of these residential areas along factories and industrial spaces appears in a number of your painted photographs. Could you explain your attraction to these places?*

MC My family lived in one of "these places." We adopted the habits of *quartier*-dwelling Montrealers and moved every three years or so from one flat to another in the same neighbourhood.

By the age of twelve, I could say that I grew up on the top floor of four different triplexes. Our sojourn in the second triplex, located on St-Laurent Boulevard, three doors south of St-Joseph Boulevard, is most vivid. On the ground floor there was a shop that produced and sold religious statuettes. Angels with gilded wings, miscellaneous saints – they seemed to specialize in a mini St Joseph – the Virgin Mary, and, of course, several versions of the Crucifix. One summer, after haunting their open door, I was invited in to assist with the removal of the plaster casts from the moulds: what auspicious beginnings for a contemporary artist!

I was, and still am, instinctively drawn to older, seedier parts of cities where layers of social pretension have long slipped away. The streets and buildings of the historic core of the city known as "Old Montreal," and large-scale industrial structures dating from the initial period of industrialization, interested me, as did experimentation with borrowed cameras. And of all the industrial structures, the grain elevators that lined the Port of Montreal were the most impressive. I began photographing grain elevators in the mid-1950s. Much to the distress of my father, I would board European grain ships as they passed through the locks of the Lachine Canal on their way up the St Lawrence River to Chicago or to one of the Great Lake ports and would hang out for several hours on the top deck or in the pilot's cabin. From the deck the grain elevators appear as towering clusters of geometric shapes pulled together by lengthy strips of conveyors standing on spindly legs. The conveyors were extended via mobile towers rolling on rails – "marine legs" – from which an arm-like bucket lifts and conduits reached into the holds of ships to unload or load grain.

Grain elevators are located at transfer points in a worldwide network that collects and distributes wheat and other cereals. They vary in size from the wooden structures used by farming communities to the automated steel machines at transoceanic terminals. Within each elevator the grain is kept in a state of movement via conveyors and bucket lifts, as it is prone to explode if stored for too long a period. The movement systems within the grain machines still suggest a reinterpretation of streets as "conduits" for people. In Montreal the primacy of the street as a public passageway was heightened over time by differentiations such as a change of materials to line the street with a more "noble" revetment, i.e., stone, as opposed to inexpensive brick reserved for back and side walls of buildings. In other words the "facade" of a grain elevator – the primary surfaces of interface between grain (people) and the conduits (streets) – are inside the machine. The outside was no more and no less than an accumulation of the volumes of each of the constituent elements – a functionalist ideal of international style modernism. [...]

The Collective Glue of a City, Outside-Inside

YS *There is an aspect of your intellectual development that strikes me as particularly intriguing and relevant here as we delve into the notion of inside and outside. As you know, the "Islamic city" is characterized by a determination to maintain a division between public and private space. But what remains confusing about the "Islamic city" is that the street, the public space, feels private. It is often difficult to distinguish the path from the place: monumental portals are sometimes used to indicate entrances to major public buildings (mosques, schools, markets), but for the most part entrances are discrete and can be easily overlooked. [...] Are these "cities" as paradoxical and confusing as they appear?*

MC Yes. The first essay that I published, "A Journal of Istanbul: Notes on Islamic Architecture," appeared in 1962 in an otherwise staid professional journal. It included a drawing of the plan of the sixteenth-century Ali Pasha bazaar in Edirne, Turkey, attributed to Sinan (an architect and engineer who, it is said, was responsible for every major building in the Ottoman Empire during a fifty-year period in the sixteenth century). The bazaar consists of a covered "street" set in three contiguous city blocks. Once the subsidiary buildings attached to its outside walls were completed, as they are today, the Sinan building was no longer visible except for several entry portals. Composed of vaulted masonry corners situated between the walls of a square room and the circular dome that is inscribed within the walls of the room, the portals emulated parts of the building that could only occur on the inside. Within this composition, aedicule-like repetitions of the initial corners play with scale and depth, marching one's eye out to infinity, dematerializing the portal. In other words, Sinan created a significant urban structure that could not be seen. There is simply no "building" there. One can surmise from this example that some of the key formations of urban architecture are often constructs that cannot be seen. And if, as Le Corbusier maintains in *Vers une architecture* (1923), in the chapter entitled "Three Reminders to Architects" – illustrated, incidentally, by images of grain elevators – "Architecture is the masterly, correct and magnificent play of masses brought together in light," then how can the streets and squares, the structure of public spaces between buildings, qualify as "architecture"? Neither Sinan's bazaar nor city squares such as Place des Vosges, Paris, can qualify as having "mass" and therefore are not architecture. I would argue that the form of the public spaces of a city constitutes its primary architecture – its collective glue, so to speak – and that individual buildings are there to sustain the form of communal presences thus engendered.

YS *Your readings of Le Corbusier's texts resound in the way you break apart buildings and float pieces of them across your photographs, tracing a trajectory. You perform a very explicitly critical, and often witty, analysis of modernism through the way you construct your painted photographs. How did you come to this way of interpreting and expressing your observations and comments?*

MC Following graduate studies at Yale, long conversations with Louis Kahn and James Stirling, and a sojourn in New York City, I was convinced that the only way to move beyond the current discourse that was bogged down in a late-modernist cant was to step back and reconstruct a working history from "origins," and origins, as Kahn maintained, are to be found in the in-between periods when nothing seems to be happening.

In the autumn of 1961, with Paris as a base, I set out to circumnavigate the Mediterranean basin. After fourteen months I found myself in the town of Edirne located a few kilometres inside the frontier of Turkey on the overland route from Thessalonica to Istanbul. Given the history of Edirne (it was the capital of Ottoman Turkey between 1365 and the capitulation of Constantinople in 1458), its strategic location, and its role as the setting of numerous battles, Edirne was still, in 1961, considered part of a "military zone." Turkish authorities were wary of foreigners with cameras and notebooks; as the 1960 Hachette *Guide Bleu* put it, "travelers are warned that, apart from rapid visits to places of interest, or a stop at a cafe or restaurant, they may neither stop, take photographs, use field glasses nor leave the main road." The main road, its pavement hacked up by tank treads, traversed an austere and pockmarked no man's land leading to the massive fortifications of Stambul.

Dating from the Byzantine period, the fortifications drew a solid barrier across the land. Outside the walls, the scattered and dusty tombstones of Muslim cemeteries seemed suspended in time; inside a busy street life flourished under a sky pierced by minarets – including the impres-sive minarets of Sinan's sixteenth-century Süleymaniye Mosque. Conceived at the same time as St Paul's Cathedral in London, the Süleymaniye Mosque resembles a cleaned-up emulation of the nearby Hagia Sophia. If the minarets that the Ottomans tacked onto the already thousand-year-old building of Hagia Sophia – the Church of Holy Wisdom in the capital of Orthodox Christianity – are removed, what would remain is an ungainly and buttressed accretion of lumps of masonry, the order of which emanates from somewhere inside the heap. The Neolithic origins of Hagia Sophia are evident. An egg-like domed interior that turns in onto itself, with screened and diffuse amniotic-like light entering from apertures overhead, resonate as a presence in one's psyche, as do other such uterine palaces as the Church of the Holy Sepulchre, Jerusalem. Inside the Church of the Holy Sepulchre, the figuration of space is defined by a religion that affronted death with a promise of resurrection – the "Mother Church" – and, insofar as built relationships still define comprehensible models of built form, the public, urban facade of Hagia Sophia is very much inside [...]

YS I have dedicated a period of my life to the study of this architecture, and this is the most perceptive and moving articulation I've had the pleasure to muse over. The way you describe the building's innards being turned outwards is precisely how this odd blurring of what is inside and outside transpires. I think you've hit upon the core of an architectural theory. As with your painted photographs and also a number of your public monuments, you show how an architectural form can be reconfigured. When you intervened with Les maisons de la rue Sherbrooke *(1976),* A Chicago Construction *(1982), and* A Toronto Construction *(1982), you filled empty lots with constructions that mirrored something nearby within eyeshot. What you highlight is one of the ways architectural memory can be activated and recollected.*

MC Let us pick up on sites and buildings and on "memory [that] can be activated and recollected," as you suggest. Yes, I am invoking "memory," but memory to me is a given, a normative articulation of thought, if not the intrinsic formulation of thought itself. [...]

Religious sites and buildings in the Mediterranean basin seem to emerge out of re-formations of existing places and constructs that have acquired a rooted, autonomous, and sacred existence of their own. A gamut of religious tropes are found: from a 3500 B.C. burial device found in a museum in Jerusalem, in which a human corpse was placed for burial – and, hence, rebirth – curled into a fetal position within two halves of a clay egg, as in some Chthonic cargo cult; to domed enclosures of collective eggs denoting potential resurrections; to the Temple Mount, Jerusalem, where, standing alone on a raised platform slightly tilted toward the sun, the sharp light etches an overwhelming sense of responsibility for one's actions, as if in a Camus novel. [...]

From appropriation to adaptation, transformation to imitation, the specificity of religious tropes evolved from building to building. In Syracuse, Sicily, a Greek temple, the Temple of Poseidon, was transformed into a Christian cathedral by reversing the inside-outside relationship between the building and the faithful who frequented it. The Greek temple once stood as a sacred vessel focusing the surrounding land formations into a representation of a God, picking up threads of persistent Chthonic rituals while people remained outside its precinct, whereas in the church people congregated in an otherworldly interior to partake in the ritual of a resurrection – rebirth – of their saviour. Attached to the front of the temple is a "building of entry," a passage through a mnemonic device – through the frontispiece of a volume on the lives of Christ and the saints – hagiographic instruction for an illiterate populace.

The Muslim appropriation of sacred buildings engendered other re-formations. In Cordoba, Spain, a church – originally derived from the columned temples of Egypt and Greece in which rows of columns describe an allegorical 'sacred grove' or 'Hall of Mysteries' – was converted into a mosque. These Halls of Mystery were eventually relegated to the crypt-like sombre halls that can be found in the lower levels of churches (as in San Miniato al Monte in Florence), as if they belonged to some buried past. Inside these "Halls," as in the church at Cordoba, a diffuse light bathed the rows of columns and drew the eye away along a multitude of darkened vanishing points; infinity was inside the church. With the transformation of the church into a mosque, a source of light was introduced at the apex of each row of columns, dissolving the interior. The building is at once both there and not there, an appropriation of an appropriation.

Inside the mosque of Hagia Sophia, again a re-appropriation of a borrowed building, an all-embracing light replaces the filtered, amniotic-like light in the suffocating belly of an all-embracing Mother Church. And rather than floating in the vagaries of a domed and dripping belly of the church – as in the Church of the Holy Sepulchre, Jerusalem – the interior as a mosque introduces an abstract otherworldliness defined by strong, direct light in which the space for people is contained between a flat plain of rugs and a low-hanging, horizontal filigree of wires, suspended lights, and calligraphic medallions. The materiality of mosques is rather tenuous, tentative, gestural, transitional, and certainly not urban in the classical sense of a city.

In Istanbul, 1911, Le Corbusier revealed in his sketchbooks an obsessive struggle to fit the exterior mass of Hagia Sophia into some kind of compositional framework. He drew it over and over again so that its masonry bulk would fit some canon of architecture. And so it was with the grain elevators. On the page facing his definition of architecture (noted above) is an illustration of *Grain Elevator No. 2* in the Port of Montreal, recently demolished. The illustration was based on a photograph of this elevator under construction, which was first published in 1908 in *Engineering News* (McGraw Hill, New York), and reprinted by Walter Gropius in the 1913 *Deutscher Werkbund* Yearbook. Le Corbusier altered the photograph by drawing over the unfinished structure so that it would assume the hard-edged composition of a symmetrical building. Within a few years, the analogy of the grain elevator had been transformed into a building type that qualified as having the "look" of modern architecture.

Inside–Outside, *Streetwork*

YS *Regarding this line between outside and inside, public and private, I was looking at a fascinating installation called* Streetwork *that you constructed in 1978 at the Art Gallery of Ontario, Toronto. You inserted a wall through the museum and continued it out into the street. The wall destabilized how we read inside and outside. You were challenging modern architecture's desire to efface the identity of an interior as being different from an exterior, the street – a question that repeatedly surfaces in your work. The AGO project in particular strikes a chord with me. You were doing something entirely different from what Gordon Matta-Clark was up to. And given that I work at Storefront, with its iconic facade designed by Steven Holl and Vito Acconci in 1994, and which attempts to tackle this same issue, I would love to better understand how you arrived at the concept.*

MC An outside-inside conundrum is turning out to be a central theme of our conversation. This distinction should also elucidate issues prevalent in the photo-paintings, from an appreciation of the surface of an image, the outside, to the extraction of an image from the inside – the interior – of an image. [...] I usually proceed from project to project in a flow of ideas that percolate up and evolve from one work to the next. Nevertheless, from time to time, and for various reasons, I may slip into a black hole that tends to dissipate my energy and absorb all thought. The AGO piece was snagged from the vortex of one such black hole that I, unwittingly, got caught up in. [...]

After working for several years on an ongoing project involving the front pages of newspapers – *Un dictionnaire* (1970–2001) – I was commissioned by Montreal's 1976 Olympic Games Committee to put together a 1.5-kilometre exhibition of art along one of the city's main thoroughfares leading to the Olympic Stadium. Five days after the opening of the exhibition, on the evening prior to the opening of the Olympic Games, the mayor of Montreal ordered municipal authorities to demolish the show. The drama made the front pages of major newspapers, nationally and internationally, including one photograph of the Olympic flag going up and another of *Les maisons* coming down. To cover for his abuse of power, the mayor claimed that we had violated municipal regulations, even though his flunkies sat in on every one of our meetings and issued the necessary city permits. Later, in court, the mayor would claim that he was obliged to protect the public from "blasphemy"!

The exhibition Corridart included the work of 150 artists, as well as a full-size construction-installation, *Les maisons de la rue Sherbrooke*, which I conceived for a critical intersection. The destruction of *Les maisons* marked the culmination of a cycle in my work. What began five years earlier, using images of events that appeared on the front pages of newspapers, seemed to come to an untimely conclusion with one of my artworks on the front pages of newspapers. As the victim of the political connivance of the mayor, I was systematically demonized as having provoked the incident, and it was difficult to work in the year following his aggression. Both artists and politicians juggle symbols. Unfortunately, politicians tend to alter the artist's attitude of "now you don't see it and now you do," into "now you see it and now you don't." And then in 1977, an invitation from the Art Gallery of Ontario, Toronto, to exhibit my work was a veritable clarion call [...]

At the time of the AGO call, I was preoccupied with questions about "figuration" in particular with *Les maisons de la rue Sherbrooke*. I was also musing about a dull, black-and-white photograph of a Kasimir Malevich painting, *Suprematisme Dynamique* (1916), which appeared in a newspaper along with a notice that 1978 marked the centenary of his birth. I began the AGO work with an examination of the paradigmatic trope that generated the "figure" of the museum and of the exhibition space allocated for the show. I then proceeded to paint two similar intersecting planes over both the photograph of Malevich's painting and the AGO gallery plan. I then constructed a wall across an existing wall so as to pick up on the composition of the intersecting planes in an attempt to distinguish the underlying trope of the modernist abstraction of architecture, such as that of the AGO, which has long been cut off from its sources. The existing museum building did not so much house the work – contain it – as combine with it. The form of the inserted wall changed according to its position in relation to the existing building: outside, in the street, the wall was made to assume the form of an "arcade"; inside it became a series of partitions, i.e., a void on the outside (access) became a volume on the inside (closure). The construction opened the envelope of the building so that intersecting planes were extracted from its presence. Instead of moving out to infinity in an idealistic, modernist haze, as the legacy of De Stijl would have it, the inter-

secting planes drew the body of the building into a *Streetwork*.

Another issue brought forth by *Streetwork* was the question of categorization: is it a work of art or architecture? The answer: both. Given that *Streetwork* was published simultaneously in art magazines (*Artforum*, New York) and in architecture journals (*AD*, London), it was considered to be art if seen in an art journal, ditto architecture. For me, this overlap of disciplines has been going on since *Memo Series* (1969–70). In order to get things done, one simply carries on with one's work regardless of institutional terms of reference that no longer relate to what is going on [...]

Art–Architecture, On *Memos*

YS *The way you live and the way you work linguistically and practically embody the notion of a "hybrid practice." You operate in two worlds, art and architecture, in that you make "art" and you work on public architectural projects. Somehow this has formed a meeting ground between the two disciplines [...] and re-formed you into an artist, an intellectual, and an academic as well as an architect. I'm curious to know how these categories operate in the way you conceive projects and understand your practice.*

MC It is difficult to categorize what I do. Even though my activities are not all that complex, the available words are too blunt, as if an ossification of nomenclature has taken place in the face of change. [...]

In an essay on Oxford teachers of philosophy and language that appeared in the *New Yorker* (1961), Ved Mehta comments on "questions like 'What is 'truth'?'" Oxford philosophers are liable to say, following the late Wittgenstein, "'Look at all the different ways the word 'true' is used in ordinary speech." So let's look at the content of "ordinary speech." In commentaries and reviews describing my work, curators, reviewers, and bureaucrats have to establish some kind of categorization. I am referred to as an artist, a photographer, and a sculptor, "*un peintre canadien*," who shows photo-based work, who works with oil pastel, and, of course, an architect and a landscape architect. In other words, the old framework of art production divided according to medium, with architecture as the "mother" of the arts, still holds sway. However, in the world I live in, the tendency is to focus on a sphere of endeavour where media is part of the content and "crossover" disciplines have become the norm.

In Paris in the early 1960s, I worked four days a week for an architect, Guillaume Gillet, whose church of Notre-Dame in Royan, France, completed in 1958, I noticed at an exhibition at the Museum of Modern Art in New York. The three remaining days of the week I would revert to my art. I found then, and still do now, that it is difficult to shift from one sphere to the other. I would begin by drawing anything in sight, a table, a chair, a water glass – *repose en paix* Morandi – but could not relate the social disposition of architecture to the general detachment of art. Each activity has its charm. As an architect I would compose my *oeuvre* and send out instructions to be executed – performed – by others, whereas in art, an object is said to pour out of the artist's fingers, a most gratifying experience. The institutional barriers that we thought would simply dissolve of their own accord in the 1970s are alive, well, and in place, and often enforced with a vengeance.

YS *Architectural installation can be a way for artists to refer, superficially, to cities and buildings. In the same way, architects dabbling in art tend to superimpose onto architectural renderings more engaging images than architecture can accommodate. Nevertheless, it is important that authentic practices that fall between disciplines*

be recognized. You bring to your art the expertise and experience of an architect. Could we talk through your work to discuss how you fused these two disciplines?

MC A discipline involves regulation, authority, and the application of a specific slice of knowledge, and if an innovative, "interdisciplinary" endeavour appears, it will emerge in the "doing" of a project [...]

In 1970, in response to a competition for the design of an Air Force Memorial and Museum, with a minimal budget, and on a residual piece of land at an air force base some 100 kilometres east of Toronto, it seemed to me more reasonable to base a "solution" on readily available sources derived from a world radically altered by technology – produced in part by air flight – rather than the look of a built container. A salient part of this process was the identification of "off-the-shelf" and in-use resources so that the monument-museum could become a network of parts that could bring a "building" to people across Canada. The resources were described in a series of memoranda, the *Memo Series*. Each *Memo* was conceived as a printed plate with texts, photographs, drawings, and instructions suitable to be shipped to the Department of Defence, the sponsors of the competition, for implementation.

The series initiated an ongoing process of pushing at the edges of what was possible and seemed limited only by one's ability to discern new phenomena. The final count: seventy-four finished plates (thirty-two of which are now in the collection of the National Gallery of Canada). Key plates include a found map of scheduled Air Canada flights locating the museum-memorial as a network of available facilities that people can visit simultaneously across the country; abandoned hangars and their reuse as instant network outposts; plots of land consecrated by the loss of people's lives, locating memorial sites such as that of a Liberator bomber that crashed north of Montreal in 1945. On another plate, an abandoned landing strip suggests the actual construction of a kilometre-long slab of concrete oriented towards the wind, with red lights set up at diminishing heights on top of surrounding buildings, like a memorial where one could simulate flying by dashing down the runway with arms outspread. [...] Often, sources originated in media photos of news events, some of which I would overlay with paint and oil pastel. [...]

The *Memo Series* began as part of my preoccupation with the idea of "tacit knowledge" (cf. Michael Polanyi) embedded in the material formations of fabricated things – knowledge beyond the threshold of what we are capable of naming. By 1970, I began to collect and classify newspaper pages with photographs showing buildings and cities caught up in various events. Certain images would appear over and over again regardless of the events they depicted, suggesting some kind of order in the display of each day's news. From time to time a news image would provoke a sense of urgency to draw out from the image certain elements. [...]

The Painted Photographs, *Un dictionnaire*

YS *For over thirty years, 1969–2004, you have been compiling an archive of over 1,400 newspaper pages with images of events that catalogue the many ways in which our constructed world is represented in the media. How does the stream of images emitted by the media affect our understanding of the constructed environment?*

MC Images emitted by the media tend to focus our attention on a particular building or city, and attribute a certain cachet of consequence to structures and places caught up in an instance of celebration or, more likely, disaster. The images depict a world in a state of distress, of flux. A crowded street protest, a house shoved off its foundations by water and wind, a building with its walls blown away all reveal inner supports. The layers of contrivance are stripped away. Relationships are uncovered, hidden connections exposed.

Recurring images suggest themes. The themes, in turn, propose a system of classification in which images can be grouped, roughly, in series according to what they disclose about the interaction between people and their constructed surroundings. Insofar as a series of images may constitute a coherent record of a discernible interaction, a record of common meaning, the classification assumes the character of a "dictionary," *Un dictionnaire*. A dictionary is self-referential; words are defined by other words. Similarly, the images of *Un dictionnaire* define one another, one image pushing at the visibility – the meaning – of another. A dictionary also traces the mutability of meaning. Emerging relationships are named, rendered visible – picking up on ideas of tacit knowledge where the *Memo Series* left off.

Seen together, the diverse images of calamities, disasters, and celebrations fuse into a single all-embracing reality. One's focus shifts from the singularity of an event to its place in a field of evolving relationships between people and built things. One is no longer certain whether buildings and cities are going up or coming down. What is certain is a sense of pervasive turmoil. Even the benign models of buildings and cities in the hands of their progenitors, *Series 20–29*, seem to evoke the struggle inherent in the accumulation of capital and social order required to marshal resources so that the models can be transformed into buildings.

The current version of *Un dictionnaire* consists of 428 plates organized in a sequence of forty-six series and nine themes. Each plate reproduces, photographically, a slice of a newspaper page. The initial series, *Series 0.1–0.9*, introduce the capacity of events to propel buildings and cities into our consciousness. *Series 1–9*, bombings, earthquakes, fires and floods lay bare the fragility of buildings and cities reduced to ruins and rubble. *Series 10–19* gather images showing surfaces of buildings and cities peeled away to reveal undifferentiated frames and grids, the structure of structures. *Series 20–29* concentrate on models of buildings and cities in the hands of people in power; the degree of control they exercise appears inversely related to the size of the models. *Series 30–39* highlight mechanisms of societal control where men in uniform target our gaze at mere details, the doors and windows that attract their feet and fists, so that one does not get the whole picture. *Series 40–49* allow a glimmer of a world of exclusion where people are in physical contact with their constructed surroundings but are trapped in the minutiae of their existence, often reduced to vague blurs suspended in a hiatus of time and place. *Series 50–59* and *Series 60–69* gather images of people thrashing about on the fringes of society where "sacred" and even "sublime" constructs appear in a cruel replay of deeply rooted human impulses, as if Adam is still struggling to rebuild a house in Paradise. *Series 70–79* presage a world where overpopulated cities cruise the face of the earth like so many Noah's Arks. Finally, *Series 100* presents a replay of all previous themes as seen in images of the destruction of the World Trade Centre, New York, in September 2001.

YS *Our world is saturated with images. How do you go about selecting those images that you include and those that you set aside or even discard? How do you select the most iconic images, the ones that best describe your intentions? The selection process would seem to be a central issue in your work, since most of your photo-paintings are based on, or derived from, your* Un dictionnaire *archive.*

MC Certain photo images seem to speak directly to my hands. Some murmur away that they need a line here, others lust for a stroke of colour

there, particularly matte prints or high-contrast photocopies that ache to receive the caress of some smooth graphite! Lines drawn on a photograph open the image, extracting the layers of an extended landscape enticing you to get in and walk around.

YS *At some point in your work you began to paint over photographs that you took yourself …*

MC In the 1970s I went through a concentrated period of photographing buildings in various regions of Quebec. What emerged are carefully wrought images conveying the formal, often heroic character of ordinary buildings. A few of these images led later to photo-paintings, for example *Parable No. 3 … La Prairie* (1990). This interest in the buildings of Quebec culminated with *Les maisons de la rue Sherbrooke* (1976), followed by a series entitled *Front Page Constructions* (1978–79) in which Suprematist figures and De Stijl planes are extracted from the front pages of the business sections of newspapers.

Two images from Trois-Rivières, Quebec, were crucial to my subsequent development of photo-paintings. The first image was appropriated from a 1974 government publication announcing federal funding for the "urban renewal" of a workers' *quartier* in Trois-Rivières, at a time when urban renewal meant urban removal. The image of a shabby house with a striking presence, its simple volume outlined a classical temple. The traditional orientation of a house on a street was turned ninety degrees, so that its *"mitoyen"* (party) wall was facing the street as a monumental frontal plane in a Baroque gesture; within this plane the frame of a door and a window cut out a Latin cross. This house embodied heroic evocations while exuding obvious signs of poverty. It was no more than a converted garage; the walls were thin, the materials meagre. The imminent demolition of the house accentuated the fragile existence of its inhabitants trapped in the shadow of a factory and in the grip of an authoritarian Church. At the confluence of a trinity of rivers, people built a house evoking both a temple and a tomb where they lived to expunge their fate.

If one is to go by reference books, this small house has no history. The first thing I did was to paint an image of the house on an illustration of a Greek temple with similar proportions in a book called *The World's Greatest Monuments*. Then, on a photograph of this house I superimposed a portrait of the house. This portrait then served as the basis for a third action, the reconstruction of a full-size version of the house recast as a sphinx to emphasize its enigmatic content.

The second Trois-Rivières image – the significance of which revealed itself slowly over a two-year period – was a 1975 photograph of three ordinary structures, each picking up on facets of contemporary archetypes: a wood-box building resembling an embodiment of Vitruvius's "primitive hut"; a wood tenement reeking of the urban history still haunting cities in Quebec; a cylindrical reservoir of a nearby factory invoking ideal geometry as a force of nature. The photo-paintings that ensued focused the metaphoric content of these currents.

The photo-paintings evolved. There was no turning back. What seemed to be a marginal "hinge" activity at first brought together two major concerns in my work: (1) a constant impulse to transform my surroundings into photographs – the necessary transposition of an existing local onto a set of manipulable images so that it could assume the characteristics of a "site," a place to build on – with (2) an equally constant desire to construct, to physically assemble materials on a given "site."

If in photo-painting, figure and ground are interchangeable, then the transposition of a figure of a place into a site to be built on becomes the ground for the figure of a construction-installation. In some cases, the photograph of a construction-installation became the "site" since many of the construction-installations were purposely temporary. Subsequent photographs of these temporary constructions would serve as the basis of painted images – the after-life, the reincarnation of temporary pieces – for instance, *Room 202, P.S.1* (1979.) A series of temporary and site-specific works followed, including *A Chicago Construction* (1982), *A Toronto Construction* (1982), and *A Kingston Construction* (1983), each composed of mirror-image portraits of their emplacements. This phase of work came to fruition with a 1992 commission for the inaugural exhibition of the Musée d'art contemporain de Montréal. The resulting artwork – *Parabole no 9 … ainsi soit-il: les usines ferment, les musées ouvrent* (1992) – consisted of two large-scale photo-paintings out of which stepped constructed 'site-specific' figures. As a young friend mentioned, "something broke out of the painting and walked across the room." By the 1980s, what began as superimposed drawings and paintings on images of "sites" became autonomous works in themselves. I began painting over photographs that I had been taking since the late 1960s, particularly those photographs that evoked ready-made counter-images that were just waiting to spring out of the emulsion of an enlarged print.

The primary source of images that dominated the photo-paintings, however, was the *Un dictionnaire* archive. The edgy tabloid news images involving aircraft from the *Memo Series* evolved into *In Flight* (1990–94), a series of pastel paintings on photographs of airplane crashes. *In Flight* responded to a questioning of the faith people had in technology, and hence the symbols whereby twentieth-century artists would signal their avant-garde status – for example, Suprematism with its airplanes in flight, Marcel Duchamp with his chessboard. In studies I had done while working on key photo-paintings in the early 1990s, Suprematism came to be denoted by the intersecting planes of the broken wings of crashed airplanes, Duchamp by a floating chess table – virtual parables. If *Un dictionnaire* elucidated meaning within a proliferation of news images, the *Parables* drew viewers into the totemic space of these images. The photographic surfaces became no more than transparent openings onto a world behind and before the camera. It is as if the surfaces of the photographs were activated, figural structures were detached, transformed, and superimposed onto the original surfaces to elucidate the content and the historical roots of the images. What become evident was an ongoing tension between contemporary idioms and past habits, between shifting "thresholds" of perception and the struggle to represent such elusive boundaries. [...]

YS *The way you build an image of a painted photograph, the way you strip it down and go back and forth, how you blow up a photograph then wash it with some paint and draw an axonometric, a plan or elevation, you construct a very convincing social space that distinguishes your work. [...] What does the grey paint that you add in an almost casual manner to newspaper photos bring to the work? What happens when the original newspaper page becomes obscured?*

MC Rather than obscuring the original, the painted layers highlight its substance. At first I presented (P.S. 1, New York, 1979) the photographic plates of *Un dictionnaire* without a grey overlay and discovered that people were more attentive to the images if the surface of the photograph was "placed" inside itself – a hint of obscurity proved to be a necessary incentive to encourage people to look for substance in an image. [...] The grey wash was partially transparent, the random edges of the roughly applied brushstrokes left parts of text uncovered. Time has rendered these odd bits of text intriguing – I now find myself trying to complete unfinished sentences. Many viewers assume that the pieces of text were strategically left visible as clues to the content of the work and/or the artist's intentions.

YS *What about people who seem to be involved with real buildings in real time? The body does make its appearances in Un dictionnaire but it is codified with emptiness, negation, and the "marginal other."*

MC It seems to me that all of *Un dictionnaire* is about people who are "involved with real buildings in real time." Moreover, human figures appear in virtually all of the plates, from people shifting through the debris of buildings, to people in power clasping mini-models of built reveries, to people in uniform aligned in a depiction of a uniform, public, urban open space. Let's look at *Series 44* as an example of people involved with real buildings. Here is a group of images focusing on people at the bottom of the social heap, the unprivileged in our societies for whom the built world has become a restrictive place of reduced space and confinement – *un monde concentrationnaire.* They inhabit a new world of corridors, "mean streets," where the marginal and the poor are obliged to wait, be it for a permit or for medical treatment, as if it was a punishment for their indigent condition.

Bodybuildings, Building BODIES

YS *There is a filmmaker, Dorothy Arzner, from the 1930s who made the film* Craig's Wife *about a house, or rather, a woman in a house. The house is not just a house, but also the film's protagonist. Over time Craig's wife (Harriet) becomes the house. She occupies it and rids it of the factors she detests – her husband, for instance. This film makes me think about Louise Bourgeois's commitments, and yours. There is a clear difference in the way you both convey and use architecture; nevertheless I sense a strong resonance between you two.*

MC I grew up on a diet of art journals that my father would recycle from his various acquaintances and I was at least aware of Louise Bourgeois's existence when, in the early 1980s, I found in a basement bin of art oddities in a New York City bookstore a catalogue of a show of her work at the Max Hutchinson Gallery. Reproduced in the catalogue were several prints of her *Femme maison* series (1947) that impressed me both in terms of her take on Freud and her manner of spontaneously sketching a fusion of animate and inanimate. I then came across a book published on the occasion of a 1995 exhibition of her drawings. From her *Femme maison* prints, to the drawing *Les voleuses de gratte-ciel* (1949) and to *The Accident* (1992), the resemblances to my work were evident even though the reasons why were obscure. Louise Bourgeois would draw a body as if it were a house, whereas I would draw buildings as if they were bodies.

The metamorphosis of buildings into body parts evolved slowly in sketches over a number of years. The abandonment of American cities began to make the news by the mid-1970s so that when a 1977 image of President Jimmy Carter walking on the rubble of a city block in the South Bronx appeared in the wire services it was simple to pick up the elements of a photo-painting (*Walking Stiffs ... Strutting through the Embers*, 1993). A row of abandoned buildings in the background of the image provided a key to the forms of the "building bodies," which led to the transformation of these figures into large-scale constructions in the 1992 Musée d'art contemporain de Montréal artwork. This preoccupation "building bodies" came to a head with a 1997 invitation to do a public artwork in Hérouville-St-Clair, France.

A satellite town on the periphery of Caen, Hérouville-St-Clair founded in the early 1960s, is an example of the 1920s tradition of German *Siedlungen* gone awry: a paradisiacal blend of buildings and gardens caught between bloated social intentions and weak material forms. There are no streets and no houses. People are set adrift on footpaths that lead them through a disparate mass of indistinguishable blocks floating in fields. Ironically there is no communal spatial substance in this city conceived in the name of social democracy.

The suggested location of the work was in a pivotal area called the "city centre." What city centre? Nothing was there; it was no more than a name printed on town maps and in public-relation brochures. These brochures also revealed several projects for the site. In 1988 a proposal originating in the mayor's office for a 100-metre "Tour Européenne" was composed of three dissimilar buildings sitting one on top of the other, to be designed by three different architects. Obviously, the *Tour* could not be built and was replaced by an equally improbable proposal for a commercial centre. The commercial centre, a low-level mall tucked in beneath a kite-like roof hovering over the site, was succeeded a few years later by the most recent of projects, an administration building by Jean Nouvel that was to be buried in mounds of earth – to be lowered into uterine-like tumuli. History was thus undone from skyscraper to cave, to the origins of all building.

My proposal for an intervention at Hérouville-St-Clair focused on the absence of the public urban content and on the transient materiality of the city. The human body is taken to be a fundamental register; the movement of the body is taken to be the basic spatial generator of urban form. In other words, the work's point of departure comes from the people who can be seen passing through or stopping to chat with each other in the interstitial no man's land between buildings. These figures are made to reappear, larger than life, as stainless steel constructs composed of pieces of buildings walking away from or toward a site: *Cities on the Run ... Tenements in Search of Streets* (1996–98) and *Cities on the Run ... Blocks in Search of a City* (1997–98). The figures are conceived to be displaced from one location to another. In Hérouville-St-Clair the presumption is that mobile figures placed in urban situations are to be catalysts of the catalyst. There is no specific location for the work. The pieces are moved at intervals from one site to another to designate the emplacement of a public urban structure and to invoke the expectation of its realization. Critical sites are identified by use, by their demonstration of the characteristics of a street or a square or an intersection. This city is now inhabited by large, shiny steel figures that can only be accommodated outside buildings and in public spaces. Here are the mobile *golems* that have emerged from the muddy tumuli to create life in the city.

YS *What occurs in both Louise Bourgeois's and your representations of architecture, what is most interesting to me, is what you take away, the way you extract aspects of the image to create room in a form that, in turn, creates potential, creates a sort of life force. [...]*

MC To create "a sort of life force. [...]" I take it that you are referring to what I mentioned yesterday about a droll epiphany that I underwent a number of years ago while accompanying a person close to me, a journalist on assignment to cover a meeting of representatives of a United Nations committee on Aboriginal rights, with Mohawk band councils and elders in their longhouse at Kahnawake, on the south shore of the St Lawrence River across from Montreal. During the long wait for the meeting to get under way, I was sitting with some Mohawk "Warriors" who were to perform the ceremonial component of the gathering. The meeting got under way in the late afternoon with drumbeats, chants, and dancing of the Warriors, while the women conducted business with the UN rep-

resentatives. What a division of labour! Those humans who are the veritable creators of life, who carry and gestate the species eggs, were busily negotiating important matters while their dandified counterparts – the artists, feathered warriors – emulated birthing rituals, ritualizing "creation" [...]

In other words, the emulation of relationships between people and their manufactured world can only but idealize it, or serve up a third-hand vision of reality. Moreover, the unravelling of this twisted cultural heap is complicated by the off-putting discourse of the specialist. Example: at a time when not only are ergonomic issues critical – we live physically in an ill-fitting world while the perception most people have of their bodies is drowning in a surfeit of images in an image-soaked world – the gurus of official cant are busily purging architecture of its anthropomorphic baggage. [...] So, along with the classified ads, I now seem to find pertinent images in the back pages of newspapers [...]

Visualize a newspaper page with a grid of sixty vignettes of female torsos encased in standardized name-brand bras, all on sale! The photo-painting that ensued was the first of a series entitled *One Fit Sizes All*. Through overlays of images, the series examined the total standardization of the built world we inhabit from J.N.L. Durand who set up in the early nineteenth century the compositional rules for all building, to the present with its potential for genetically modifying the human form via the morphing of the size, shape, and behaviour of the human species so that it will fit the spaces that technology is capable of providing, starting with critical components of human reproduction, the preening of the males [...]

On the back pages of local publications such as New York's *Village Voice*, Montreal's *Voir*, grids of calling cards advertise the denizens of the sex trade. Arranged under such headings as "Bodyworks" are photographs of seductive females, who are in fact 'she-males,' whatever that may be. *One Size Fits All No. 6: Bodybuildings: Guys & Grids* (2000–03) is a photo-painting with an overlay depicting structural grids enclosed within armour-like sections of skin that seem to have been peeled away from various body parts. The suggestion of buildings with body-like wrappings parallels the work of artists who intuitively return to the human figure as a primary reference, particularly at times when there is no dominant aesthetic. Another work, *One Size Fits All No. 3: Blobs on the Grid* (2000–02) looks at the current rash of "blob" architecture with its round, bulbous, and humanoid shapes. The strength of the "blobs" is intuitive; however, its discourse is weak. It represents itself as computer generated and without traces of anthropomorphic references, as if there could be no-*body* in the body of a building other than a suggestion of the dismembered cadaver of Classical Orders, or a hint of the emergence of new creatures that satisfy any "reproductive" urges of anyone in sight […]

A recent work, *Cities on the Move, The Swinging Burbs* (2003–06), is also painted on a grid of advertisements for "Bodywork She-males" looking for "action." The "action" they get is depicted in the painted overlays that attempt to show things as they are. A "She-male" sensuality is confronted by an equally seductive vision of a weekend visit to a local "burb." Recognizable media images of "the good life" that can be enjoyed outside on the periphery of urban centres – a country estate sheltered by trees, tailored lawns, a family, a husband, wife and children – linger in the thoughts of the *paterfamilias* whose imagination dances with the sensuality of it all. The actual greening of the male's existence is still conditioned by the *quartiers* of the city […] Are these stories I tell myself once the day's work is done? Stories weave words, mere props, the approximations of visual depictions.

I am now working with images borrowed from swinger magazines, published prior to the advent of Photoshop. The self-conscious narcissism apparent in these images is juxtaposed with the collective narcissism evident in the figures of urban spaces such as city squares – for example, the Piazza del Duomo in Milan – another long-time preoccupation of mine. I have also returned to the *Femme maison* prints and drawings of Louise Bourgeois – how she deals with the female body. If a house is a receptacle and female, how could one treat the male body in a similar manner? A breakthrough for me came following a remark made by a female acquaintance. "Imagine," she said, "he wanted to put his thing into me!" I imagined my *Running City* figures, the golems with eight-foot lengths of two-by-fours standing out from their bodies, signifying the eternal male drive to penetrate anything in sight in order to perpetuate the species. So here I am again backing into edgy phenomena […]

Melvin Charney

A SHORT BIOGRAPHY

Melvin Charney was born in Montreal on 28 August 1935, the eldest of three sons of Fanny and Hyman Charney.

His parents were both Eastern European Jews who settled in Montreal in 1929. His father was a builder, decorator, and woodworker, well known for the doors he crafted for Montreal churches and synagogues.

Charney attended the Jewish People's elementary school from 1941 to 1948. When he was eight years old, his parents signed him up for Saturday morning classes held at the Montreal Museum of Fine Arts (MMFA). There, the young boy learned to draw and paint with teachers that included Arthur Lismer, a member of the Group of Seven.[1]

From 1948 to 1952, he went to the Strathcona Academy, an English Protestant school situated in Outremont, then a predominantly French Catholic neighbourhood. During his high school years, Charney developed an interest in science and technology, which he pursued by cutting out articles from newspapers and magazines and assembling them in scrapbooks he kept all his life. This way, he became familiar with the work of Dr Robert Goddard, a pioneer of modern rocketry, the inventions of R. Buckminster Fuller, as well developments in atomic energy and space exploration.

Architectural Education

In 1952, Charney began studies in civil engineering at McGill University and opted for architecture two years later. He had to interrupt his studies in December 1954 after he broke a leg during a ski competition. He completed his first academic year in architecture during the summer of 1955 under the intense and inspiring tutelage of Stuart Wilson. A self-taught Scottish architect, Wilson was somewhat at odds with the director of the school, John Bland, who was known for the large mansions he built in Upper Westmount for wealthy clients. With Wilson, Charney looked closely at Montreal's working-class neighbourhoods and understood that architecture was not meant to decorate the lives of the rich.

At that time, the influence of Mies van der Rohe on the members of the faculty of McGill's School of Architecture was pervasive, but after visiting Crown Hall in Chicago shortly after its opening in April 1956, Charney found their teaching to be superficial. While his teachers at McGill talked of Mies as someone who presented the inherent logic of architecture, Charney thought that Mies was "a pure romantic." To make his point, he wrote a paper on Erich Mendelsohn in his history class in which he argued that Mendelsohn's vision of America was fascinating because he showed that grain elevators and the back of New York's buildings rather than their facades anticipated the industrial aesthetics of modern architecture. Charney received a bad grade for what was perceived as a provocation, an experience which reinforced the young architect's belief in the school's social prejudices.

In 1956, Charney met R. Buckminster Fuller when Fuller was invited to McGill to conduct a project involving the design of a geodesic dome which was erected at the training centre by the students. In his third year, he met Peter Collins, who had been hired by McGill to teach architectural history. A disciple of Auguste Perret, Collins had spent the academic year 1955–56 at Yale University on a Fulbright scholarship and worked on a history of concrete that was published in 1959.

In 1957, Charney won the Canadian Pittsburgh Industries Design Award and the A.F. Dunlop Travelling Scholarship. Charney attributed his plans to leave Quebec to the trying socio-economic conditions in Montreal during the Duplessis era. Collins suggested he apply to Yale's master's program in architecture and put him in contact with Christopher Tunnard, who taught there. In 1958, Charney won the William McCay Fellowship to study at Yale. After he received his diploma from McGill in the spring of 1959, he left Montreal with no intention of coming back.

In contrast to McGill's Victorian stiffness, Yale's elitist ambience was conducive to debates informed by the idea that art and architecture were parts of a thinking life. The central requirement of the one-and-a-half-year curriculum was the conception of three projects under the supervision of three different advisers: Philip Johnson, Louis I. Kahn, and John Johansen. With Johnson, Charney drew a housing project inspired by the ideas of Alison and Peter Smithson, whose works were part of an exhibition on Team X shown at the school at the time. With Kahn, he worked on the reconstruction of an entire city block in downtown New Haven. Although he believed his final project with Johansen was the most daring, Kahn was his real mentor. Charney considered that Kahn was the only one who had relevant ideas and he believed this state of affairs caused conflicts with the new dean, Paul Rudolph, and with Johnson as well, and led Kahn to leave Yale in 1960. Of Vincent Scully Jr, Charney remembered his existentialist, Camus-like accoutrements, and his fascinating lectures on American architecture which connected architecture with the great ideas of the era, notably with D.H. Lawrence's masterpiece *Studies in Classic American Literature*. In addition to the required seminars in architecture, Charney attended classes in the departments of arts and philosophy.

Travels

After his studies, Charney applied for a job at Walter Gropius's firm The Architects' Collaborative in Cambridge, Massachusetts. The atmosphere at the office was so awful that he left after only three hours of work; he subsequently referred to the office as "The Architects' Calamity." Thereafter, Kahn invited him to a review of his students' work in Philadelphia and introduced him to Robert Venturi, who was then undertaking the construction of his mother's house. As we know, Venturi's little house would become the founding symbol of American postmodernism. Charney settled in the region of New York City to work with John Johansen. Johansen's interesting commissions enabled him to explore new ways of working with the envelope of buildings, such as the innovative, prefabricated concrete-bearing elements of the facade of the U.S. Embassy in Dublin. Charney's task was to translate Johansen's small sketches into architectural plans, notably for the Dublin Embassy, the Taylor house, which was built in Westport, Connecticut, in 1966, and the Morris Mechanic Theater in Baltimore. If his experience with Johansen stimulated his interest in new technologies, Charney also cultivated a genuine interest in vernacular architecture going back to his studies at McGill with Stuart Wilson; this interest was reinforced by Kahn's belief that the seed for all things that must follow lies in authentic beginnings. Following Kahn's advice, Charney applied for a Canada Council Scholarship for a year's study of European architecture from the early Greek to the medieval period. He received the scholarship in 1960 and thus left Johansen's office after a year and a half.

Charney settled in Paris in 1961 and used his scholarship to travel to Italy, Sicily, Greece, and Turkey. The photographs, notes, and sketches he made during his travels led to several essays on vernacular building traditions which he submitted to the magazine *Landscape*, founded and edited by John B. Jackson. In Paris, he also worked for the architect Guillaume Gillet until 1962.

He returned to North American in 1963 when John Johansen offered him a job running his design studio. At the same time, he was offered a job at Columbia University, but a dispute involving the provost of the University, Jacques Barzun, an educated Frenchman, and the dean of architecture, Charles Colbert, a French Acadian from Louisiana, led to a one-year postponement of his contract. While in New York, he visited art galleries, wrote about the emerging American pop art movement, and began producing works of art of his own.

Back to Montreal

Charney returned to Montreal for family reasons in 1963 and found a job as a lecturer in design and construction at the new École d'architecture at the Université de Montréal. The École d'architecture had just been created after a major reform of the former École des Beaux-Arts de Montréal. Now fluent in French, he found the new school a dynamic environment in which to promulgate recent developments in environmental design. With his students, he explored the potential of using new materials, such as plastics and precast concrete, for construction; he also wrote extensively and published important essays on Montreal's grain elevators, the issue of prediction in environmental design, and the urban transformation of his home town, among other subjects.

After working for a few months with Montreal architect Victor Prus on the design of the future Bonaventure metro station, Charney opened his own studio in 1964. The same year, Charney's artwork was selected by jury to be shown in the spring exhibition at the Montreal Museum of Fine Arts. Concurrently, Stanford Anderson, a graduate from Columbia University recently hired by MIT, invited him to participate in the Association of Colleges and Schools of Architecture's teachers' conference at the Cranbrook Academy of Art in Michigan. Held during the summer of 1964, the event, co-organized by Henry Millon from MIT and Peter Collins from McGill, lasted a whole week, during which Charney met many personalities, including Colin Rowe and Reyner Banham, who gave him the latest issue of the little magazine *Archigram*.

The early 1960s were the first years of Quebec's Quiet Revolution and marked the beginning of profound changes in Quebec society. The creation of a Ministry of Education and the conclusions of the *Rapport Parent* on education led to great reforms and fostered a building boom in educational facilities. In 1964, Charney was one of the winners of a competition aiming at building prototypical primary schools in the province of Quebec. In 1966, he designed with Oscar Newman[2] a "Cité des jeunes" for the City of Hull, which consisted of a campus housing buildings for 2,000 students and reinvented the traditional concept of a secondary school. In parallel, he received a grant from Schokbeton to study and promulgate the use of concrete in Quebec architecture. He wrote several essays on concrete and edited an issue of *The Canadian Architect* on the subject. His innovative primary school project, the école Curé-Grenier (now, école du Boisé 2), was built in Notre-Dame-des-Laurentides (now Beauport) in 1965, but problems with the building's windows occurred a few years later and a lawsuit ensued. This difficult experience may explain why he shied away from traditional architectural practice.

Charney got tenure in 1966. In 1968, he founded the graduate program in aménagement, which he directed until 1972. From 1968 onwards, he also taught as visiting faculty at several universities including the University of Toronto (1968–70), Harvard (1971), and Université du Québec à Montréal (1972). He was also invited speaker at meetings such as the International Design Conference, held in Aspen, Colorado (1968), and the symposium "Form and Use in Architecture" at MIT (1969). In 1967, he submitted a self-erecting kit rather than a traditional building to the competition for the Canadian pavilion at the 1970 Osaka international exhibition. With his project for Osaka published in several international magazines in 1969 and 1970, Charney was recognized as a significant, radical architect and was invited to the International Futures Research Conference in Kyoto (1970) to present his work along with Cedric Price, Archigram, and Yona Friedman.

Political Affirmation

In October 1970, Montreal was the stage for Canada's biggest political crisis of the postwar period. The deployment of the Canadian Army in the streets of the city after the kidnapping of a British diplomat and Quebec's Minister of Justice by the Front de Libération du Québec was followed by mass arrests of innocent people who were considered suspects because of their separatist sympathies. Many of them were Charney's artist friends and university colleagues. This violation of civil rights led him to denounce what he termed the "self-colonizing" of Quebec by its political elite in architecture, housing, urban planning, and the development of northern Quebec. Published in the spring of 1971, the first of these texts was a manifesto arguing for the existence of an authentic modern architecture in the *quartiers populaires* – the working-class neighbourhoods – of Montreal and in the villages of Quebec. From 1970 to 1972, he was, with Colin Davidson and Serge Carreau, co-director of a Canadian federal government task force on postwar, low-income housing in Canada. The resulting report led to some alarming conclusions that Charney wrote about in a series of essays published during the 1970s.

Charney's public involvement in Montreal's art world started in 1972 with his organization at the MMFA of the collective exhibition called Montréal plus ou moins/Montreal Plus or Minus? The exhibition celebrated Montreal's urban culture and is still remembered as one of the most popular ever presented at that institution. Concurrently, his original reflections on the liberating potential of technology and the repressive use of architecture crystallized in two original works, the *Memo Series* and the *Dictionnaire d'architecture*, which were shown at the Milan Triennale and at the Musée d'art moderne de la Ville de Paris in 1973. Then his work shifted with the production of a series of installations, which were intended as alternate monuments to those of official architecture. The first one of these was *The Treasure of Trois-Rivières*, presented at the Musée d'art contemporain de Montréal (MACM) in 1975. On the occasion of the 1976 Olympic games in Montreal, he created Corridart, an outdoor exhibition of art installed along a corridor starting in the city centre and proceeding eastwards along Sherbrooke Street to the Olympic stadium. Charney invited sixty young artists from Quebec and Canada to create sixteen installations, which included his own *Les maisons de la rue Sherbrooke* situated at the south-west corner of Saint-Urbain and Sherbrooke. One week after the opening and two days before the Olympics, city workers, acting on the orders of Mayor Jean Drapeau, took the exhibition down overnight.

In the aftermath of the Olympics, Charney's first solo exhibition, entitled Other Monuments, was presented at the Graduate School of Design, Harvard University, in March 1977. Other solo exhibitions succeeded rapidly, at the Art Gallery of Ontario in Toronto (1978), P.S.1 in New York and the Musée d'art contemporain in Montreal (1979), the Canadian Cultural Centres in Paris and Brussels (1980), and the Museum of Contemporary Art in Chicago (1982). For each major show, he designed a site-specific installation. His work was also presented in a large number of collective exhibitions and discussed in related catalogues and in the international art press. In parallel, he was invited to lecture on his work in museums, art galleries, and universities in Canada, the U.S., England, France, Holland, and Australia.

A Charismatic Mentor

When, in 1975, the École d'architecture modelled the structure of its studio teaching on the Architectural Association thematic units, Charney founded and directed "L'unité d'architecture urbaine" (AU), the Urban Architecture Unit. During two consecutive semesters and sometimes more, AU introduced a mixed group of students in their second, third, or fourth year to the study of Montreal's urban fabric. Among the students, AU quickly acquired the reputation of being extremely demanding and challenging, yet intellectually satisfying. In the first five years of its existence, AU concentrated on political and social issues: critical analysis of urban facts often constituted the "project" itself. In 1980, year of the first referendum about the independence of Quebec, the publication of "The Montrealness of Montreal" acted as a manifesto for a symbolic refoundation of Montreal based on the reappraisal of the figurative content of its urban architecture. Concurrently, a major shift occurred in the Unit as drawing became a fundamental tool in the collective analysis of the city. By the mid-1980s and until the dissolution of AU in 1990, analytic obsession and critical figuration gave way to more metaphorical visions in which drawing gave Montreal's urban architecture a degree of poetic autonomy. Throughout the years, Charney invited a number of sharp critics to review students' work and used the ritual of the reviews as a pedagogical instrument to expose the students to a variety of perspectives. In the fifteen years of its existence, AU welcomed approximately 300 students, all of whom were deeply affected by Charney's teaching and charismatic personality. As a mentor, he was active in the organization of exhibitions of his students' work in art galleries in Montreal and in Toronto. He also invited a number of them to work in his studio on the production of his artwork and installations.

If AU was a laboratory in which one learned by doing, Charney's course entitled "Built Environment" was the most stimulating intellectual experience offered by the École. In a series of captivating lectures, Charney developed, within a network of architectural and extra-architectural references, a personal interpretation of contemporary architecture in Quebec and abroad, from Team X to the Postmodern. His teaching stimulated many students to pursue graduate studies in leading institutions in the U.S., England, and France. He also maintained close and long-term relationships with his students and the curators with whom he worked.

An International Career

Charney represented Canada at the exhibition Documenta Urbana in Kassel, West Germany, in 1982, and created an installation for Stuttgart in 1983. In that same year, he was asked to stage the exhibition Les villas de Pline, co-organized by MMFA and the Canadian Centre for Architecture (CCA), which had recently been created in Montreal by Phyllis Lambert. Charney first met Ms Lambert during his studies at Yale in 1959–60. Their friendship developed during the 1970s, when both became public actors in the political debate surrounding the destruction of Montreal's popular neighborhoods. When Lambert decided to build a new building to house the CCA collections, she also launched a competition for the design of a garden on the site facing the institution. Charney won that competition with a site-specific garden of sculptures. Widely acclaimed, the CCA garden was the first of a series of permanent public installations Charney realized in the 1990s. Other salient examples of permanent installation work from this period are *The Canadian Tribute to Human Rights*, completed in Ottawa in 1990, and the *Gratte-ciel, cascades d'eau/rues, ruisseaux... une construction* for the new Place Émilie-Gamelin, inaugurated in 1992.

The 1990s was a decade of accolades for Charney, with major retrospective exhibitions at the CCA, 1991–92; the Israel Museum, 1994–95; the Fondation pour l'Architecture, Brussels, 1994; and FRAC Basse-Normandie, Caen, France, 1998. He was finalist in several competitions

and continued to produce portable works of art, which were shown in important collective exhibitions including La Ville: Art et Architecture en Europe 1870–1993, Musée National d'Art Moderne, Centre Pompidou, Paris, 1993; After Auschwitz – Responses to the Holocaust in Contemporary Art, 1995–96, presented in museums in Great Britain; Déclics, Art et Société, le Québec des années 1960 et 1970, Musée d'art Contemporain de Montréal, 1999; Utopia: The Search for the Ideal Society in the Western World, Bibliothèque nationale de France, 2001; Sans commune mesure: Image et texte dans l'art actuel, Centre national de la photographie, Paris; and Against Architecture: The Urgency to (Re)Think the City at Espai d'Arte Contemporani de Castello, Valencia, 2002. He represented Canada at two Venice Biennales, the 42nd Venice Biennale Internation Exhibition of Art, 1986, and the 7th Venice Biennale International Exhibition of Architecture, 2000.

In 2002, the Musée d'Art Contemporain de Montréal organized a retrospective exhibition focusing on relationships between his photography, photo-based paintings, and installations. Another exhibition of his photo-based paintings, entitled From Observation to Intervention: The Painted Photographs of Melvin Charney, was presented at The Americas Society, New York, in 2008.

Charney received numerous awards and honours throughout his career, including the Berliner Künstler Programme, Deutscher Akademischer Austauschdienst (DAAD) Award, 1982; senior arts awards from the Canada Arts Council; the Prix du Québec Paul-Émile Borduas in the visual arts, 1996; and the Canada Arts Council Lynch-Stanton Award to distinguished artists, 1997. In 2003, he was named Chevalier of the Ordre national du Québec for his outstanding contributions to Quebec culture. In March, 2006, he was named Commandeur of the Ordre des Arts et des Lettres by the French government, the highest honour bestowed by the

French government for individual contributions to culture. In 2009, McGill University granted him the degree of Doctor of Letters *honoris causa*.

Melvin Charney died in his studio on 17 September 2012. He was seventy-seven years old.

NOTES

1 While Melvin wanted to become an artist early on, his younger brothers also developed an interest in the visual arts: Israel made a career as a graphic designer and Morris became an architect.
2 Newman had worked for Aldo van Eyck in Holland. Van Eyck put him in charge of editing the proceedings of the last CIAM meeting held in Otterlo in 1959. Oscar Newman, ed., *CIAM '59 in Otterlo* (London: Tiranti, 1961).

ILLUSTRATIONS

Every effort was made to contact the copyright holder for every illustration appearing in this book. Authors and publisher apologize for any image used without accurate accreditation and, once informed, will emend in any future edition.

Figures

18.7   Mobile Launcher for the Saturn V rocket. Photographer unknown, n.d. Reproduced from *Architectural Forum* (Jan.–Feb. 1967)   175

18.8   Grain Elevator No. 1, Montreal, ca. 1967. Photograph: Pierre Beaupré. Collection of the artist   176

18.9   Grain Elevator No. 1, Montreal, ca. 1967. Photograph: Melvin Charney. Collection of the artist   176

18.10   Spout loading ship, Montreal, n.d. Photographer unknown. Collection of the artist   177

18.11   Shipping side of Grain Elevator No. 4, Montreal, n.d. Photograph: A. Sima. Collection of the artist   178

18.12   Baie-Comeau, Quebec, n.d. Photograph: J.J. Lavoie. Collection of the artist   178

19.1   Marie-Joseph Bernard, "Concours pour deux groupes scolaires à Levallois-Perret" (Seine) ca. 1880. Reproduced from *Croquis d'architecture Intime-Club* (André G.-J. Bourmancé editor), 15e année, 2nd series, 5th volume, no. 12 (Paris: Imprimerie Monroq Ducher, 1881): sheet 1. Collection of the artist   180

19.2   School Construction Systems Development Project (SCSD) planning system, author and date unknown. Reproduced from Educational Facilities Laboratories, *SCSD, the Project and the Schools: A Report from Educational Facilities Laboratories* (New York: Educational Facilities Laboratories, 1967), 74   183

19.3   El Dorado High School (First increment). Plancentia, California, Architects William E. Blurock and Associates. Photographer unknown. Educational Facilities Laboratories, *SCSD, the Project and the Schools: A Report from Educational Facilities Laboratories* (New York: Educational Facilities Laboratories, 1967), 42   184

19.4   Interior, Connecticut General Insurance Building, Hartford, Connecticut, ca. 1960. Skidmore, Owings, and Merrill Architects. Source and photographer unknown. Collection of the artist   185

20.1   Concrete mixer. Reproduced from *The Cement Age, A magazine devoted to the uses of Cement* (Robert W. Lesley ed.), New York: Bruce and Johnston, vol. 1 no. 12 (May 1905)   189

20.2   Concrete mixer, 1871. Author unknown. Reproduced from *Architecture Canada* 45, no. 6 (June 1968): 42   189

20.3   Lifting jack, n.d., author unknown. Reproduced from Milo Smith Ketchum, *The Design of Walls, Bins and Grain Elevators*, 3rd ed. (New York: McGraw Hill, 1919), 391   190

20.4   On-site field factory of Hochtief AG on Campus Lahnberge. © Hochtief AG, from "Universitätsbau in Marburg a. d. Lahn," *Hochtief Nachrichten* 37 (December 1964). Reproduced with the permission of Silke Langenberg   191

20.5   Slip-forming of the San Luis Canal, 1967. Photographer unknown. Reproduced from *Architecture Canada* 45, no. 6 (June 1968): 43   192

20.6   Factory casting of "architectural" concrete. Reproduced from *Architecture Canada* 45, no. 6 (June 1968): 43   192

20.7   On-site mechanization. Reproduced from *Architecture Canada* 45, no. 6 (June 1968): 43. Reproduced from *Cement and Concrete Reference Book, 1956–1957* (Chicago: Portland Cement Association, 1956), 75   192

21.1   Walker Evans, *Birmingham Steel Mill and Worker's Houses*, Birmingham, Alabama, 1936, Gelatin silver print, 19.1 × 24.1 cm. Yale University Art Gallery, gift of the Ethne and Clive Gray Family Collection. Courtesy Yale University Art Gallery   204

21.2   Hans Hollein, *Air Carrier City in the Landscape*, 1964, photomontage (cut-and-pasted reproduction on four-part photograph mounted on board), 21.6 × 100 cm. © 2011 Hans Hollein. Philip Johnson Fund (434.1967). Digital image © The Museum of Modern Art. Licensed by SCALA / Art Ressource, NY   204–5

21.3   Delage "Grand-Sport" 1921. Photographer unknown. Reproduced from Le Corbusier, *Vers une architecture* (Paris: Crès et Cie, 1923), 107   206

21.4   Hydraulic press, 1927. Source unknown. Collection of the artist   206

21.5   Grand Trunk Pacific Elevator, 1910. Photographer unknown. Reproduced from Le Corbusier, *Vers une architecture* (Paris: Crès et Cie, 1923), 17   207

Photograph: MMFA / Henry Koro. Collection of the artist 274

27.3 Opening of Montreal Plus or Minus? 11 June 1972, at the Montreal Museum of Fine Arts. Photograph: MMFA / Henry Koro. Collection of the artist 274

27.4 Opening of Montreal Plus or Minus? 11 June 1972, at the Montreal Museum of Fine Arts. Photograph: MMFA / Henry Koro. Collection of the artist 274

28.1 Melvin Charney, *Monument 30: Monument to the Dormitory Barracks*, 1973, collage. Photograph Melvin Charney. Collection of the artist 277

28.2 Melvin Charney, Plate from *Un dictionnaire …*, executed between 1970 and 1996, acrylic on gelatin silver print, mounted on archival board, 28 × 35.6 cm. Collection of the Canadian Centre for Architecture, Montreal, DR1999:0003:010:005 © Melvin Charney / SODRAC (2012) 278

28.3 Melvin Charney, Plate from *Un dictionnaire …*, executed between 1970 and 1996, acrylic on gelatin silver print, mounted on archival board, 28 × 35.7 cm. Collection of the Canadian Centre for Architecture, Montreal, DR1999:0003:012:001 © Melvin Charney / SODRAC (2012) 278

28.4 Melvin Charney, Plate from *Un dictionnaire …*, executed between 1973 and 1996, acrylic on gelatin silver print, mounted on archival board, 28.1 × 35.8 cm. Collection of the Canadian Centre for Architecture, Montreal, DR1999:0003:011:006 © Melvin Charney / SODRAC (2012) 278

28.5 Melvin Charney, Plate from *Un dictionnaire …*, executed between 1971 and 1996, acrylic on gelatin silver print, mounted on archival board, 28.1 × 35.2 cm. Collection of the Canadian Centre for Architecture, Montreal, DR1999:0003:032:001 © Melvin Charney / SODRAC (2012) 279

28.6 Melvin Charney, Plate from *Un dictionnaire …*, executed between 1970 and 1996, acrylic on gelatin silver print, mounted on archival board, 28.1 × 35.2 cm. Collection of the Canadian Centre for Architecture, Montreal, DR1999:0003:033:002 © Melvin Charney / SODRAC (2012) 279

28.7 Melvin Charney, Plate from *Un dictionnaire …*, executed between 1970 and 1996, acrylic on gelatin silver print, mounted on archival board, 28.1 × 35.6 cm. Collection of the Canadian Centre for Architecture, Montreal, DR1999:0003:016:007 © Melvin Charney / SODRAC (2012) 279

28.8 Melvin Charney, Plate from *Un dictionnaire …*, executed between 1970 and 1996, acrylic on gelatin silver print, mounted on archival board, 28.1 × 35.7 cm. Collection of the Canadian Centre for Architecture, Montreal, DR1999:0003:016:004 © Melvin Charney / SODRAC (2012) 280

28.9 Melvin Charney, Plate from *Un dictionnaire …*, executed between 1970 and 1996, acrylic on gelatin silver print, mounted on archival board, 28.1 × 35.6 cm. Collection of the Canadian Centre for Architecture, Montreal, DR1999:0003:025:002 © Melvin Charney / SODRAC (2012) 280

28.10 Melvin Charney, Plate from *Un dictionnaire …*, executed between 1979 and 2001, acrylic on gelatin silver print, mounted on archival board, 28 × 35.6 cm. Collection of the Canadian Centre for Architecture, Montreal, DR2004:0001:031:004, Gift of Dr Dara Alexandra Charney © Melvin Charney / SODRAC (2012) 280

29.1 Dismantled housing, Montreal, ca. 1975. Photograph: Melvin Charney. Collection of the artist 282

29.2 Advertisement for single-family homes. Source unknown. Collection of the artist 283

29.3 Fabre Street, Montreal, ca. 1975. Photographer unknown. Collection of the artist 284

29.4 Newspaper clipping: *Le Jour*, no. 111, Montreal, 1975. Photograph: Pierre Boisclair 285

29.5 Newspaper clipping: *La Presse*, Montreal, 28 October 1975. Photograph: J.-Y. Létourneau 285

29.6 Newspaper clipping: *La Presse*, Montreal, 30 December 1975. Photograph: Michel Gravel 285

29.7 Mass-produced housing modules, ca. 1975. Source unknown. Collection of the artist 287

29.8 Mass-produced housing modules, ca. 1975. Source unknown. Collection of the artist 287

36.10   Melvin Charney, *A Chicago Construction No. 4*, 1982, graphite on paper, 15.0 × 22.0 cm. Collection of the Canadian Centre for Architecture, Montreal, DR1984:0050 © Melvin Charney / SODRAC (2012)   377

36.11   Ruins of the Tribune Building after the Chicago fire, 1873   377

36.12   Melvin Charney, *A Chicago Construction No. 6*, 1982, coloured ink on paper, 76.3 × 57.2 cm. Collection of the Canadian Centre for Architecture, Montreal, DR1984:1577 © Melvin Charney / SODRAC (2012)   378

36.13   Melvin Charney, *A Chicago Construction*, Installation at the Museum of Contemporary Art, Chicago, 1982. Photographer unknown. Collection of the artist   379

37.1   Photo of Polish WWII photographer, ca. 1947. Photograph: Wideworld. Reproduced from Boris Shur and Bernard Quint, *Since Stalin: A Photo History of Our Time* (New York: Swen Publications, 1951), 125   381

37.2   Vitruvius, *Description of The Invention of the Corinthian Capital*, 1st century B.C. Reproduced from Dieussart, Charles, *Theatrum architecturae civilis*, 3 vols., Dintzenhofer, Leonard, editor, 1697. Courtesy of Saxon State – University Library Dresden (SLUB Etching no. 47, df_tg_000105), Deutsche Fotothek, 01054 Dresden   382

37.3   House by the river (fragment of Quattro paesaggi fluviali), Fourth style (45 A.D.–79 A.D.), encaustic painting, Museo Archeologico Nazionale, Napoli. Photograph: Luciano Pedicini / Archivio del'Arte no. 9409   382

37.4   Pliny, *Laurentian Villa Facing the Sea*, 1st century A.D. Reproduced from Robert Castell, *The Villas of the Ancients Illustrated* (1728). Collection of the Canadian Centre for Architecture, CAGE MW249   383

37.5   Pliny, *Plan of the Laurentian Villa*, 1st century A.D. Reproduced from Robert Castell, *Villas of the Ancients Illustrated* (London: Pierre Foudrinier printer, 1728), 78. Collection of the Canadian Centre for Architecture, CAGE MW249   383

37.6   *Temple rustique, Ermenonville.* Reproduced from *Promenade, ou, Itinéraire des jardins d'Ermenonville: auquel on a joint vingt-cinq de leurs principales vues* (Paris: Chez Mérigot, 1788). Collection of the Canadian Centre for Architecture, ID: 86-B22032 pl. 12   384

37.7   Temple Grove, Residence of David Ross McCord, Côte-des-Neiges, Montreal, 1872. Photographer: Alexander Henderson, MP-0000.33.1 © Musée McCord   384

37.8   Karl Friedrich Schinkel, Reconstruction of Pliny the Younger's villa Laurentinum, 1841, coloured engraving, 34 × 49.8 cm. Collection of the Canadian Centre for Architecture, Montreal, DR1984:0568:024   385

37.9   Karl Friedrich Schinkel, Project for the Castle Orianda, Yalta (Crimea, Ukraine). (1845). Side elevation, Druck, lithography, colour on cardboard, 61.5 × 108.8 cm, Inv.-Nr. 18784, TU Berlin Architekturmuseum   385

38.1   George Grosz, *The Diabolo Player*, 1920, watercolour on paper, 42.5 × 46 cm. XIR 234409, Private Collection / Giraudon / The Bridgeman Art Library. © Estate of George Grosz / SODRAC (2012)   389

38.2   House, St Hubert Street, Montreal, ca. 1981. Photograph: Claude Lamoureux. Courtesy Luce Lafontaine   390

38.3   *House VI*, Cornwall, Connecticut, 1974. Peter Eisenman, architect. Photograph Dick Frank. Reproduced from *Progressive Architecture* (June 1977): 59   391

38.4   Crematorium ovens, Auschwitz (Poland), n.d. Photographer unknown. Courtesy of Memorial and Museum Auschwitz-Birkenau Archives   393

38.5   John Hejduk, Detail of *Berlin Masque*, 1983. Reproduced from John Hejduk, *Mask of Medusa: Works 1947–1983* (New York: Rizzoli, 1985) with permission of the John Hejduk estate   393

38.6   Melvin Charney, *Better if they think they are going to a farm ... No. 2*, 1982, coloured pencil, conté, pastel, 106.7 × 152.4 cm. Collection of the Canadian Centre for Architecture, Montreal, DR1997:0003 © Melvin Charney / SODRAC (2012)   394

Pl. 20   Melvin Charney, Detail of *Lower Level Plan and Section for a Competition ENTRY for the Canadian Government Pavilion*, Japan World Exposition, Osaka, 1967, black ink over graphite on illustration board, 76.5 × 101.8 cm. Detail showing main elevation. Collection of the Canadian Centre for Architecture, Montreal, DR1997:0004:003 © Melvin Charney / SODRAC (2012)   200

Pl. 21   Melvin Charney, Detail of *Lower Level Plan and Section for a Competition ENTRY for the Canadian Government Pavilion*, Japan World Exposition, Osaka, 1967, black ink over graphite on illustration board, 76.5 × 101.8 cm. Detail showing left side elevation. Collection of the Canadian Centre for Architecture, Montreal, DR1997:0004:003 © Melvin Charney / SODRAC (2012)   200

Pl. 22   Melvin Charney, Detail of *Upper Plan and Section for a Competition Entry for the Canadian Government Pavilion, Japan World Exposition*, Osaka, 1967, black ink over graphite, 76.4 × 101.8 cm. Detail section. Collection of the Canadian Centre for Architecture, Montreal, DR1997:0004:004 © Melvin Charney / SODRAC (2012)   200

Pl. 23   Melvin Charney, architect, Harry Parnass, architect, Janos Baracs, engineer, Marcel Pageau, engineer. View of the model for a competition entry for the Canadian Government Pavilion, Japan, World Exposition, Osaka, 1967, gelatin silver print, 50 × 66.5 cm, Collection of the Canadian Centre for Architecture, Montreal, Purchased with support of the Canada Council's Acquisition Assistance program DR1997:0004:008 © Melvin Charney / SODRAC (2012)   201

Pl. 24   Melvin Charney, *Les éléments de la rue*, 1976, gelatin silver prints, chromogenic colour print, and typewritten text, 71 × 60.8 cm. Collection of the Canadian Centre for Architecture, Montreal, DR1984:1568:001-002 © Melvin Charney / SODRAC (2012)   307

Pl. 25   Melvin Charney, *The Site ... Les maisons de la rue*, 1976, gelatin silver print, 40.4 × 50.5 cm. Collection of the Canadian Centre for Architecture, Montreal DR1984:1570 © Melvin Charney / SODRAC (2012)   308

Pl. 26   Melvin Charney, *The Site Altered ... Les maisons de la rue*, 1976, photomontage, gelatin silver prints, 40.5 × 50.5 cm. Collection of the Canadian Centre for Architecture, Montreal, DR1984:1569 © Melvin Charney / SODRAC (2012)   308

Pl. 27   Melvin Charney, *Les maisons de la rue Sherbrooke*, 1976, coloured pencil and wax crayon on a photostat copy from a photomontage, 43.2 × 57 cm. Collection of the Canadian Centre for Architecture, Montreal, DR1984:1571 © Melvin Charney / SODRAC (2012)   309

Pl. 28   Melvin Charney, *Les maisons de la rue Sherbrooke (corr. 26.3)*, 1976, graphite on vellum (paper), 65.0 × 91.0 cm. Collection of the Canadian Centre for Architecture, Montreal, DR1987:0337 © Melvin Charney / SODRAC (2012)   310

Pl. 29   Melvin Charney, *Les maisons de la rue Sherbrooke*, Corridart Montreal, Quebec: view of the installation, 1976. Photographer unknown. Collection of the artist   311

Pl. 30   Melvin Charney, *Les maisons de la rue Sherbrooke*, 1976. Photograph by Gabor Szilasi   312

Pl. 31   *Les Maisons Demolished*. Photograph: Yvan Boulerice, 14 July 1976. Collection of the artist   313

Pl. 32   Cover of the course catalogue for the Université du Québec à Montréal's Arts Studies Masters Program, ca. 1980. Collection of the artist   313

Pl. 33   Melvin Charney, *Panorama of the City from the CCA Garden*, Montreal, July 1987, gelatin silver prints and graphite, 40.7 × 153.5 cm. Collection of the Canadian Centre for Architecture, Montreal, DR1990:0005 © Melvin Charney / SODRAC (2012)   406–7

Pl. 34   Future site of the CCA garden, Montreal, 1986. Photograph: Michel Boulet. Courtesy of the Canadian Centre for Architecture, Montreal. Collection of the artist   407

Pl. 35   Montreal in 1761. Paul Labrosse, cartographer (with additions by E.Z. Massicotte, archivist), Montreal, 1761. Centre d'archives de Montréal, Édouard-Zotique Massicotte Collection, No. 105734. Bibliothèque et Archives nationales du Québec   408

Pl. 36   Detail of *Topographical and Pictorial Map of the City of Montreal*, James Cane, 1846, ink on paper, lithography, 129 × 101 cm. Archives de la Ville de Montréal, VM66-S4019   408

Pl. 37   Melvin Charney, *The Canadian Centre for Architecture Garden: Urban Axes*, July 1987, coloured pencil and ink on vellum (paper), 118.7 × 90.2 cm. Collection of the Canadian Centre for Architecture, Montreal, DR1990:0001 © Melvin Charney / SODRAC (2012)   409

Pl. 38   Melvin Charney, *The Historical Layers of the CCA Garden Site between 1800 and 1950*, Montreal, July 1987, coloured pencil over photocopy, 91.6 × 122.4 cm. Collection of the Canadian Centre for Architecture, Montreal, DR1990:0003 © Melvin Charney / SODRAC (2012)   410

Pl. 39   Melvin Charney, *The Canadian Centre for Architecture Garden: Plan,* graphite, black ink, and coloured pencil over photocopy, 119.0 × 90.6 cm, Collection of the Canadian Centre for Architecture, Montreal, DR1990:0006 © Melvin Charney / SODRAC (2012)   410

Pl. 40   Melvin Charney, *The Canadian Centre for Architecture Garden: Model*, Montreal, 1987, cardboard, balsa wood, dyed foam rubber, plastic tubing, adhered with glue and nails, 93.8 × 160 × 16.3 cm. Collection of the Canadian Centre for Architecture, Montreal, DR1990:0008 © Melvin Charney / SODRAC (2012)   411

Pl. 41   North axis view of du Fort Street from the position of column number 11 on the esplanade of the CCA garden, 1987. Photograph courtesy of Melvin Charney   412

Pl. 42   Jean Antoine Watteau, *La perspective A View through the Trees in the Park of Pierre Crozat*, ca. 1715, oil on canvas, 46.7 × 55.3 cm (18 3/8 × 21 3/4 in.) Marie Antoinette Evans Fund, Museum of Fine Arts, Boston. Photograph: Erich Lessing / Art Resource, NY   412

Pl. 43   Canefori, giardino segreto del Palazzo Farnese, Caprarola, ca. 1978. Photograph: Christopher Thacker. Reproduced with permission from Christopher Thacker, *The History of Gardens* (London: London Editions, 1979), 106   413

Pl. 44   William Andrews Nesfield, The Emperor's Walk, Grimston Yorkshire, n.d. Reproduced from *Country Life*, 12 October 1901   413

Pl. 45   Melvin Charney, *The Canadian Centre for Architecture Garden: Allegorical Columns*, January 1989, coloured pencil and ink on vellum (paper),

87.8 × 210.6 cm. Collection of the Canadian Centre for Architecture, Montreal, DR1990:0007 © Melvin Charney / SODRAC (2012)   414–15

Pl. 46   Melvin Charney, *The Canadian Centre for Architecture Garden, Column No. 5, Dancing De Stijl Study*, 17 June 1987, graphite on paper, 27.9 × 21.7 cm. Collection of the Canadian Centre for Architecture, Montreal, DR1993:0005 © Melvin Charney / SODRAC (2012)   415

Pl. 47   Sainte-Cunégonde church from the west end of the esplanade, 1987. Photograph: Melvin Charney. Reproduced from Larry Richards, ed., *Canadian Centre for Architecture: Building and Gardens* (Montreal: Canadian Centre for Architecture, 1989), 98   416

Pl. 48   Melvin Charney, *The Canadian Centre for Architecture Garden, Column No. 8, The Sacred Column, Study*, 31 October 1987. Collection of the artist   416

FURTHER READINGS

Melvin Charney: œuvres, 1970–1979. Foreword: Denis Chartrand. Introduction: Alexandre Tzonis. Works and commentaries: Melvin Charney. Montreal: Ministère des Affaires culturelles, Musée d'art contemporain, 1979. French and English. 64 pp.

Melvin Charney, 1981–1983. Foreword: Robert Swain. Introduction: Louise Dompierre. Works and commentaries: Melvin Charney. Kingston, Ontario: Agnes Etherington Art Centre, Queen's University, 1983.

Parables and Other Allegories: The Work of Melvin Charney, 1975–1990. Preface: Phyllis Lambert. Texts: Alessandra Latour, Patricia C. Phillips, Robert-Jan van Pelt. Interview by Phyllis Lambert and studio notes by Melvin Charney. Montreal: Canadian Centre for Architecture, 1991. 214 pp.

Chevrier, Jean-François, Johanne Lamoureux, and Jun Teshigawara. *Melvin Charney: parcours de la réinvention = about reinvention.* Cæn: FRAC Basse-Normandie, 1998. French and English. 255 pp.

Charney, Melvin, et al. *Tracking Images: Melvin Charney, Un Dictionnaire …* Montreal: Canadian Centre for Architecture, 2000. English, French, and Italian. 95 pp.

Landry, Pierre. *Melvin Charney.* With the collaboration of David Harris, Melvin Charney, and Gilles A. Tiberghien. Montreal: Musée d'art contemporain de Montréal, 2002. French and English. 183 pp.

The Painted Photographs of Melvin Charney: Between Observation and Intervention. Edited by Gabriela Angel and Gwendolyn Owens. New York: Americas Society; Quebec: Musée national des Beaux-Arts du Québec, 2009, 80 pp.

INDEX

participation: in competition for Canadian Pavilion at Osaka,10; of the spectator, 22, 86, 141, 195; definition of, 22; choice and, 128; audience, 140; environment keyed to human, 141, 182; of children in learning, 163, 180, 182, 186, 195, 215; of people, 224, 329; of Anglo-Canadian banking, 338

Pei, I.M., 59, 118, 146, 248, 327, 338

Pevsner, Nikolaus, 34, 47

Phalanstère, 261, 390

Piaget, Jean, 183,

Picard, Michèle, 47

Picasso, Pablo, 82

Pinon, Pierre, 387

Place Alexis-Nihon, 31, 327, 338

Place Bonaventure: as urban megastructure, 10; usurping the notion of place, 31; better than the other Montreal Places, 146; ARCOP, 148; as multifunctional block, 149, 327; caught in the ambiguity of its own architectural rhetoric, 262; as extension of the city, 263; trapped in an obsolete formalism, 263, destroying the city, 338

Place de la Paix, 44

Place des Arts, 126, 139, 140, 398

Place du Canada, 166, 258, 263

Place Victoria: systemic design features of, 10; as dynamic system, 30; semi-successful insertion in the city, 58; as extension of the city, 59; sense of process in, 59; integration of technology in the form, 59; analysis of, 117–19; as individual building, 146; usurping the notion of place, 148; as superblock, 338

Place Ville-Marie: as urban megastructure, 10; overt formalism, 30, 58; usurping the notion of place, 31; as extension of the public city, 58–9, 119, 263; as urban centre, 89, 139, 146; glass surface, 91; identical details, 91; as building cluster, 117; in Montreal's skyline, 118; typical of U.S. corporate architecture, 119; as first-generation cluster, 126; as assembly of prefabricated elements, 133; as individual super-block, 327, 338; as focus of the centre of Montreal, 328, 338; and pedestrian network, 335–6

plastic: pointing hand, 14, 303, 317; use dominating expression in contemporary architecture, 57, 75; as building material, 61; space, 75; environment, 80; bag in Rosenquist's painting, 84; and concrete, 123, 145, 166, 188, 256, 443; as environmental system, 126; inevitable, 127; version of suburban bungalow, 127; analysis of, 133–6; mobile home, 137, 154; impersonal intestines, 138, 153; folded homes, 151; flowers, 153, 212; Arthur Quarmby's capsule, 154; fiberglass-reinforced, 155, 156; as formless material,

165; plug-in tenements, 203; as spin-off from aerospace industry, 211; laminated tables, 211; fabrication techniques, 211; skin, 212; suburban shopping centre, 272

Plasticiens, 327, 344

Pliny the Younger, 364, 461

plug-in: Place Victoria's base, 118; predicted cities, 127, 149, 152–5, 160; architecture in Urbland, 138; Arthur Quarmby's capsule, 153; polemic, 154; hospital pod in Vietnam, 158; Warren Chalk, 160; plastic tenements, 203

pluralistic: design of artifacts, 131, 215; environment, 145; 212, environmental conditions, 210; Montreal's downtown buildings as extension of the city, 263

Polanyi, Michael, 126, 132, 264, 370, 434

Police Headquarters building, Philadelphia, 166

Polieri, Jacques, 141

politics, 10, 11, 283

pop art, 51, 59, 60, 81-87, 130, 369, 443

popular architecture: Quebec's, 34, 229, 234; and Quebec's avant-garde, 150; as embodiment of people's struggle for a place, 221; elite and, 224–5, 229, 233, 257; authentic, 225; as source of contemporary Quebec architecture, 225, 250, 258; as natural sign, 233; and tradition, 250, 257; and history, 258; pastiche of, 259; anonymous, 297; and specialized context of, 366; as reified memory, 370

Portoghesi, Paolo, 235

postmodern: original critique 5; anticipation of, 18; game of language, 19; moment, 232, 361, 365, 446; return to history, 232, 365, 384; genre; 342; discourse, 344; insignificant drawings, 364; Léon Krier, 365; sensibility, 380

postmodernism, 361, 384, 443

postmodernist, 342, 364–5, 423

Pothier, Jean-Paul, 150–1, 258, 452

Potteries Thinkbelt, 129, 157, 218, 452

prediction: and flexibility, 126; dialectics of extrapolation and demonstration, 127; evocation of technology, 127; of the unknown, 152; apocalyptic and parascientific, 152; formalized role, 153; pessimistic, 153; social and behavioural, 156; post-industrial and post-capitalist, 160; in school design, 161; as excursion into the shapes of things to come, 162; and use of computers, 167; architectural project as anticipation and, 227; in environmental design, 443

prescription, 37, 40, 42, 46, 48

preservation, 9–10, 30–2, 44, 45, 90–1, 330, 340

Price, Cedric: interest in the work of, 10; action architecture, 18; technological optimism, 123;

system-to-live-in, 126; Fun Palace, 127, 134, 140, 153, 155, 157; citizen architect, 127; Potteries Thinkbelt, 129, 142, 157; Rice University design fete, 129, 217–19; change, 156, 157; acknowledgement of human action, 157; 1970 Future Research Conference, Kyoto, 444

process: systems and, 10; construction of the city, 28; and conventions of photography, 29, 426; technical and social, 30, 32; in Place Victoria, 30; of defining *Québécois* identity, 34; and customs, 34; and innate knowledge, 34; of reading and reinventing, 38; conceptual, 40; imagination, 40; precedent and analogy in design, 42; and grammar of urban forms, 43; and forms, 44; vs formalism, 51, 60; vs preconceived vision, 56; of inquiry into the nature of things, 57; a building's sense of, 57, 59, 109, 118, 188; of excavation, 58; in Turkish architecture, 71; in contemporary architecture, 71; of weathering, 73; of erosion, 79; in making a place, 80; Pop art's mechanical, 83–4; of preservation, 90; technological, 123, 130; environmental, 123, 128, 155–6, 163–4, 165; and grain elevators, 125, 174–5, 177; and visionary projects, 127, 160; building, 128, 144, 166, 189–90; flexibility and, 128; education as a, 128; concrete as the result of a, 128, 129, 162, 167, 188; of human organisation, 130, 160; design, 131, 190, 202, 205, 212, 237; industrialization, 133, 219, 249; plastic filaments winding, 135, 155; of megalopolization, 138; drawing the spectator into art's active, 141; pupils as part of the learning, 142, 158, 162,183, 186; weapons development, 153; change in education, 157, 162, 163, 186, 187; new synthesis of building and learning, 163, 180, 182; on-site concrete factory, 190, 191; in exhibit buildings, 194; and prediction, 204; complex fabrication, 212; cognitive, 220; communication, 220; of selecting a suppress range of experience, 224, 237, 433; of proliferation and dissemination, 224; image over, 225, 234; of improvement, 228; of destruction, 232; information and energy, 262; of housing, 266, 267; of the city, 275; Canadian institutions and cultural, 320; great man's conception of historical, 321; of evolution in *Quartiers populaires*, 336; of restitution, 364, 381, 384; of emulation, 364; of layering, 367; of decomposition, 368; of allegorical narratives, 368; of transformation of CCA garden's site, 369, 405; in Charney's itinerary, 369; Lacanian, 370; and habitus, 381

Prochazka, Alena, 45, 50

Progressive Architecture, 193, 246

Prus, Victor, 443

psychoanalysis, 37, 38, 230

psychoanalytic, 5, 38, 370

Quarmby, Arthur, 153, 216

quartiers populaires: built forms of, 34; appropriation of inhabitants of, 226; vs single-family house, 226–7; rehabilitation of, 227; as collective ecology of settlement, 228, 290; as authentic city, 233; as working-class tenement neighbourhoods, 282, 336; collective tradition and conflicts, 283–6; housing in, 290; heroic trust, 322; destruction of, 328; views of, 337; and the *habitus* of city building, 365; anonymous architecture of, 365; authentic modern architecture of, 444

Québécois: election of Parti Québécois, 11; definition of identity, 34; building, 34; French-speaking, 230, 299; architecture distanced from the lives of, 257–8; nationalist expression, 258; workers, 283; architecture, 298; art, 301; specific history, 301; traditional themes, 331; Montreal as *Québécois* city, 338; idealized visions of existence, 340

Québec Pavilion (Expo 67), 249, 327

radical: transformations of architectural thinking since the 1960s, 3; anti-architectural trend, 18; change in Urban Architecture Unit, 40; interventions of the postwar period, 46; Brutalist trend, 54; mobile homes, 127, 154; future environment, 138; technological implication, 153; quasi-revolutionary political position, 225; political base of the *quartiers populaires*, 283; history, 319; contextualism, 330; use of existing codes, 331; changes in the value-systems which relate personal creations with death, 385; Milan's left, 421; architect, 444

Ramsay, Sir William, 77

rangs, 35, 47, 254, 321–3, 333–4, 336–7, 386, 401–2

Rauschenberg, Robert, 82, 159

realism, 59, 82, 84, 202, 274, 342, 421

realization: of an urban architecture, 17; of a series of public works, 24; Louis I. Kahn's concept of realization, 55–6; of Place Victoria, 119; of urbland, 128; of École Curé-Grenier, 131; metropolitan transformation of Montreal, 149; technically feasible, 203; that the transfer of technology does not transform old buildings, 216; of memorial network, 224; of Adam's House in Paradise, 230, 300; that society makes every use a sign of itself, 232; painful rediscovery of figuration, 367; of the CCA garden, 368

Régimbald, Manon, 234

reinvention, 27, 38, 44, 48, 50, 234, 465